THE JERUSALEM ACADEMY

The
JERUSALEM ACADEMY

Loren R. Fisher

WIPF & STOCK · Eugene, Oregon

THE JERUSALEM ACADEMY
Second edition

Copyright © 2012 Loren R. Fisher. All rights reserved. Except for brief quotations in critical publications or reviews, no part of this book may be reproduced in any manner without prior written permission from the publisher. Write: Permissions, Wipf & Stock, 199 W. 8th Ave., Eugene, OR 97401.

Wipf & Stock
An Imprint of Wipf and Stock Publishers
199 W. 8th Ave., Suite 3
Eugene, OR 97401
www.wipfandstock.com

ISBN 13: 978-1-61097-284-0

Cataloging-in-Publication data:

Fisher, Loren R.
    The Jerusalem academy / Loren R. Fisher.

    Second edition.

    x + 382 p. ; 23 cm.

    ISBN 13: 978-1-61097-284-0

    Note: First edition 2002.

    1. Bible. O.T. Genesis—Authorship—Fiction. 2. David, King of Israel—Fiction. I. Title.

PS3606 F57 2012

Manufactured in the U.S.A.

For Daniel, John, Susan, Deborah, and Rachel

Acknowledgments

THIS IS A NOVEL. I have prepared new translations for all of the Ancient Mediterranean Texts (which includes the Hebrew Bible) that are used in my story of the scribes of Jerusalem. In these translations, my editorial additions are always put in brackets. Sometimes these additions are for clarity, for referring to an older form of the text, and sometimes they help the poetic structure; they are important for the translations, but they are not a part of the text.

Some good friends have read this story and have made helpful suggestions or have helped in other ways. I want to mention their names and extend my thanks: Judy Fisher, Dan Fisher, Norman Schockley, Stan Rummel, Warren Johnson, Charlie Baron, and Anne Funkhauser. I want to thank Suzanne Byerley for reading my first draft and for her writing seminars.

The picture on the cover is of an Ugaritic tablet before it was cleaned. This tablet (RS 1957.702 in *The Claremont Ras Shamra Tablets*, ed. Loren R. Fisher, [AnOr 48; Rome: PIB, 1972]) is usually referred to as the Marzeah text. It was written before the twelfth century BCE, and it deals with establishing an association for celebrating special occasions including funerals. In this novel Jonathan belongs to such an association.

Prologue

My name is Keziah. I am the daughter of Gad, one of David's prophets, and Jael, who was my loving mother. My husband, Jonathan, is a scribe in The Jerusalem Academy. He did a wonderful thing for me when he taught me to read and write, a gift that has opened my life to many worlds. It has turned existence into adventure. In the following story you will see that I have taken on several writing projects, and I do not need another one. However, I would like to write our story before I forget the details, and since we live here at the academy. I have access to material that makes my task possible. My father and Jonathan have helped, but in places I have had to imagine the connections between events and the conversations between people. In other places I will just have to say that I do not know how and why certain things happened. This story does not always agree with our official documents, but it needs to be told.

1

Ziklag

OUR HOUSE IN ZIKLAG was on a natural bit of high ground some distance from the main gate. In the late spring we spent time on the roof; we could catch a breeze up there. We were there on that disastrous day. We saw the Amalekites attack the guards at the gate and enter the town.

"Keep calm," mother said. Nevertheless terror seized our bodies, and our hearts pounded. Mother and I kept low, huddled on the roof of our house.

Mother said, "We will have to hide. If they find us we will be raped, taken captive, or even killed."

We crawled over to the ladder and climbed down. We hid in the bedroom under a pile of goatskins. For us this worked. We could hear others screaming as they were thrown out of their houses and gathered in the street. Mother whispered, "David should have left more troops to guard us."

Then our luck turned for the worse. As the Amalekites left with their captives and all of the livestock, they began to set fires. We were not prepared for this. We could not leave our house before they set it on fire, but we would have to leave soon after in order to survive. Obviously, the mud brick walls of our house did not catch fire, but there was plenty of material, such as the ceiling and ceiling beams, that burned fast. We tried to time it just right; in this we failed. We moved out of our hiding place, and we crawled on the floor under the smoke. We were almost to the door when the ceiling began to fall. A large beam hit mother. I could not move it, and I could not pull her out from under it. She was unconscious. I was crying and choking. I could not leave her, but I had to leave her. The heat and the smoke were unbearable. I managed to crawl out the doorway, but could not get up. My chest was full of smoke, and I had to roll in the dirt to extinguish the flames on my skirt. I crawled around to the back of the house. I had to get away, and I was able to make it to a pile of rocks. I got behind them before all went dark.

When I regained consciousness I was in terrible pain from my burns; I was thirsty, but I could only think about mother. She died, and I could not help her. I had a difficult time crawling, but I was able to move to the shade of a wall. Later, just after dark, I went into a house that was not burned. I found some water and waited, but the waiting was not easy. I slept some, but my dreams were full of night terrors. My father found me there when he returned.

He kissed me, and said, "Keziah, where is your mother?"

I told him our story. He held me, and we both wept for mother. I thought father would not stop. Finally he said through his tears, "As soon as we got back to Ziklag, while David was deciding what to do, I looked for you and your mother, but I did not see you anywhere. I hoped I would find you both when we caught up with the raiders. But when we defeated the Amalekites and rescued the captives, you were not among them. Then I thought that you both might be in one of those burned out buildings, and I hurried back ahead of the others."

Father left me for a short time. Soon he was back with ointment for my burns, food, and clothing, though I wouldn't feel better until the next day. At that time, I asked my father how they had caught the Amelekites so fast.

He said, "We knew that Ziklag was burning. The smoke climbed high and then flattened out into a horizontal stream. It could be seen against the clear sky from a great distance. We caught sight of it while still at least two hours from Ziklag. We did not need to express our fears; fear engulfed us like a flash flood in a barren wadi. As you know, we were returning from Aphek, which is about three days north of Ziklag, and we were exhausted. But our fear energized us, and we began to march faster and faster. We were all thinking, 'Our town is burning. What has happened to our women and children?'

"When we arrived here, we were overcome with grief. There were only a few buildings that were not burned. Most were still smoldering, and the stench of burning flesh was in the air. All of us wept for our wives and for our children. After an examination of the ruins, it was clear that most of the people and the livestock had been taken captive. Some of the men threatened to stone David, because he should have guarded against such a possibility."

"Mother mentioned the same thing when we were hiding under the goat skins," I said. "But I didn't mean to interrupt you."

"That's all right. I hate to say it, but the trip was a waste. I know David had no choice in the matter; he had to go to Aphek. From David's point of view, Saul had driven him from his friends, from his family, and from Judah, his country; he was exiled."

Then father explained to me that as a vassal of Achish, the Philistine king of Gath, and having been granted the town of Ziklag, David owed Achish military service. We sometimes forget that David defected; he joined the ranks of the Philistines! When Achish said that the Philistines would be mustering their troops at Aphek in order to go up against Saul and the forces of Israel, David left at once. The other Philistine lords did not trust David. They thought that he would turn against them in the heat of battle. Achish could not convince them that David could be trusted, and David was sent back to Ziklag.

Father said, "Yes, the trip was a wasted effort. Since David's men were making threats, David had to act with speed. He knew he should pursue the raiders, but at this point it would help to do so with his God's, that is Yahweh's blessing. He called on Abiathar, the priest, to help him get some word from Yahweh. Yahweh's word came immediately. David should pursue and rescue."

I said, "I must have been unconscious during the time David was deciding what to do and while you were looking for mother and me. You must have left to follow the raiders at once?"

"Yes, and their trail was not hard to follow. When we arrived at the Wadi Basor, some of David's men were too weak to continue. So David left those men to rest and to guard the baggage of the entire group, and David continued the march. Soon we came upon a young man who had collapsed along the trail. This young man was brought to David, and David gave him some fig and raisin cakes and water to drink. Then David asked who he was. 'I'm an Egyptian soldier,' he said. 'But an Amalekite captured me and made me his slave. About three days ago I became ill, and later my master left me here. He and the other Amalekites had plenty of new slaves from recent raids. He left me here to die, just after the raid and the burning of Ziklag.'

"Then David asked, 'Can you lead us down to these Amalekites?' The soldier answered, 'If you will protect me, I will lead you down.'

The Jerusalem Academy

"When we reached the camp of the Amalekites, the raiders were eating, drinking, and singing. David attacked them just at dawn. Only a few of the Amalekites escaped. The rest were killed, and David rescued his people and recovered his property plus the spoil that the Amalekites had taken from other places in the Negeb. It took some time to get things organized. We had to gather the livestock and load the booty. The first goal was to get back to the men whom we had left at Wadi Besor. When we reached those men, there were many happy faces. However, some of the men thought that only the men who had gone into battle should share the spoil. But David made a rule that those who guard the baggage shall receive a share of the spoil equal to those who go into battle. David was once more in control."

"I'm glad you came back before the others and found me. It was horrible when I was by myself. I kept weeping for mother and my burns were painful"

The next few days were filled with work. When David got back to Ziklag, he sent some of his booty to the elders in several cities in Judah including Hebron. He still had his eye on his homeland. Also work crews had to set up a camp; others cleaned buildings and streets. For some the experience was more painful, because the dead had to be buried. My father was in his sixties (I was almost twenty). He was an astute man, a keen observer. He was different from many of the men in David's camp. My parents were in love and were married for twenty-five years. I wondered how he would get along without mother, without his Jael. But my constant thought was that I had managed to get out of the building, which had claimed my mother, and I was unable to rescue her. This fact was branded into my flesh. Now father and I had each other, but the loss of mother was overwhelming. We buried her without much ritual. We stood by her grave with a few friends and father called forth her name:

> We call forth your name, "Jael."
> Jael, as wife and mother,
> There shall not be another.
> Thus, we shall remember you,
> And we shall give you your due.
> So, we shall call forth your name;
> Jael, we seek your blessing.

It was on the third day after returning to Ziklag that David found out about the Philistine victory and the death of Saul. A young man came

Ziklag

to David from the camp of Saul. He brought with him Saul's crown and the news of the death of Saul and of Jonathan. In fact, this young man said that Saul, who was defeated and wounded on Mt. Gilboa, had said to him, "Please stand over me and kill me." At this point in time David knew nothing about another report that Saul had killed himself, so David took it as a fact when the young man said, "I killed Saul."

David said to the young man, "Just who are you?"

"I am an Amalekite."

"After the events of the past few days around here that is hardly a recommendation. How could you lift your hand against Yahweh's anointed? Weren't you afraid?"

"No! I wasn't afraid, and I'm not afraid now. I, your humble servant, have given you Saul's crown!"

"I'll be damned if I'll take his crown or his kingdom from the likes of you. You deserve to die."

The young man's last words were: "You, David Ben-Jesse, must punish my crime against Yahweh's anointed, even though you gain by my crime. Why punish me? There is only one reason. You were also anointed by Samuel to be the next king. You are safe if I and others like me die."

David ordered his execution: "Your blood shall be upon your head, for your mouth has testified against you: 'I have killed the anointed of Yahweh.'"

David ordered his men to take the body of the Amalekite to the desert for the birds. There would be no burial for such a one.

My father told me that David mourned the death of Saul and his son, Jonathan. But he did so with mixed emotions. He certainly loved Jonathan, but he did not love Saul. David had convinced himself over the years that he should respect Saul as Yahweh's anointed, as king of Israel, but this was not easy for David when that same king's main interest was in killing him. Samuel, Yahweh's prophet, priest, and judge, who had anointed Saul as king, only added fuel to Saul's flames of jealousy when he anointed David as the next king of Israel. It did not help that David was young and powerful. He was good looking, and the women in the streets and markets sang:

> Saul has slain his thousands,
> David, his tens of thousands!"

David not only mourned with mixed emotions, he mourned with mixed motives. If he wanted to succeed Saul, it was politically important for him to mourn. But there were also some genuine reasons for David's

5

mourning, at least for Jonathan. His love for Jonathan was true, and in our world death is real and final. Burial is most important.

My father says that many Egyptians deny death. They believe in and hope for immortality, but this belief is the exception in our world. In Egyptian thought, the "West" or the "other world" gives one a place for a better life. But for us, the dead languish in Sheol or the netherworld; this does not equal life, and one who mourns, remembers, and cares for the dead receives blessings from the departed. So David was plagued with questions. Who buried Saul and Jonathan? Where? Or were they buried? Their bones should not be picked clean by the birds.

David ordered that the threshing floor should be cleaned and made ready for a public day of mourning and fasting. Everyone would first mourn the death of those who died by the hand of the Amalekites, and then they would mourn the death of Saul and Jonathan. David went to the threshing floor; he rent his clothes. When all of us had finished lamenting the death of our loved ones, David lamented, and he wept. During the ritual of mourning, he sang a dirge for Saul and Jonathan, which he had written, accompanied by two musicians who came forward with flute and lyre.

> How the heroes have fallen,
> In the midst of the battle.
> O mountains of Gilboa,
> Let there be no dew on you,
> Let there be no rain on you,
> Nor overflow from the depths.
> How the heroes have fallen.
>
> Saul and Jonathan, they were:
> Beloved and so delightful.
> In their life and in their death,
> These two were never parted.
> They were swifter than eagles;
> They were stronger than lions.
> How the heroes have fallen.
> (Parts of 2 Samuel 1:19–27)

Several days after the mourning and the burials, David summoned my father, who was his prophet, and Abiathar, his priest.

Ziklag

They came before David, and he said to them: "I want you to find out from Yahweh what I should do next. Ask him, 'Should David, our leader, go up to one of the cities of Judah?' If the answer is 'Yes,' then ask, 'Which city?' It is essential that we get back to Judah. If I'm ever going to take over Saul's kingdom, we should start at home; we should start with our southern state of Judah. Go now, and report back just as soon as possible."

When they got back to what was left of our quarters, my father said, "Abiathar, you should go to the altar and do your daily sacrifices and then come back and start packing. I don't really think there is any question what Yahweh will say. He will say, 'Yes.' In any case, I'll find out."

"You're right, because Samuel anointed David to be the next king. It's clear what Yahweh wants."

"Yes Abiathar, it's clear what Yahweh wants, but how will Yahweh get what he wants? The followers of Saul and his line may have plans of their own."

"Right! But that's why we must go up to Judah. David is from Judah. The elders of Judah have never really liked being part of Saul's kingdom. They like David."

"And it hasn't hurt David at all to send those gifts to them," my father said. "But Abiathar, you need to think politics. One of the main reasons for going back to Judah is that the Philistines will support us. For them David's presence in Judah will be the opening wedge. David could create a lasting split between the House of Saul and Judah."

"So we agree on Yahweh's 'Yes,' but David wants to know where?"

"Right," answered father. "David knows that there is really only one place in Judah for us to go. We will go to Hebron, because there David can be blessed by his ancestors at their tombs. But enough of this. Hurry on to the altar."

After Abiathar left, father spoke to Yahweh:

> O Yahweh, god of my lord David,
> Please make this my very lucky day.
> Maintain kindness with my lord David.
> If when Abiathar returns he says,
> "Today things went well at the altar,"
> Then I will know that you have said, "yes";
> Then I will know to Hebron we'll go.

Father finished this prayer, and I was rescuing a few things that were not burned in the fire. It wasn't long until Abiathar returned. He brought with him a few lamb chops from the sacrifices, and he put them on the table. Then he said, "Today things went well at the altar."

"That's it!" shouted father. "Yahweh has answered. We are going to Hebron."

Abiathar was puzzled. "Was it the meat? Did I say something special?"

Father said, "You said something special. When I spoke with Yahweh, I said that if you came back and said, 'Today things went well at the altar,' then I would understand that we were suppose to go back to Judah, to the city of Hebron. You said those words. We must tell David."

"But first we should eat our lunch," I said.

Father agreed, and we ate the chops with a little bread. However I did not enjoy the meal, because I was sickened by the thought of leaving the grave of my mother. Also father was sad, but he knew that we had to move on. He said, "We will return each year to call forth her name and receive her blessing. As for now, I must speak to David, but I will not be long."

"Hurry back."

With a bit of lamb grease still on their lips, father and Abiathar made their way back to David's hall. Father told me that David and those who ate at his table looked like they were ready for a nap when he and Abiathar entered. David saw them, and said, "What did you find out?"

Father said, "Yahweh wants you to go up to Judah; he wants you to go to Hebron!"

"Yahweh has spoken, and we will obey."

2

The Move to Hebron

I WAS SITTING BY mother's grave when father came back. He joined me, and we were just silent for a time. Then he said, "We will have some time during the next few days to sit here like this."

I nodded, "There was not much to pack. The fire destroyed most my clothes; there were a few of mother's clothes that did not burn."

Father said, "I only have the clothes on my back and those in my pack. We'll have to get some when we get to Hebron. It is going to take several days for the first group to be ready to start out for Hebron, and we'll leave with them."

Even though Ziklag was only about two days south of Hebron, the road was uphill all the way. Hebron was one of the highest cities in Judah. They had cold winters, but the cool summers were delightful. The amount of work that had to be done was tremendous in order for David, his men, and all the families to move to Hebron. Of the six hundred men at Ziklag, David decided to leave two hundred to rebuild the city and to protect it from raiders. Also David had to set up some form of government to rule in his absence and to show the Philistines that he was still a vassal in name if not in fact. So he took with him four hundred men and their families plus his two wives, Ahinoam and Abigail, and their children; there was much packing and loading of donkeys and wagons. My father and I did not participate in all this work, and we were able to remember mother and help each other. As it turned out everyone soon knew that they would have to make many trips to Ziklag during the next few months in order to move all their belongings and their livestock.

Finally we were on our way. The trip was slow, but the view was terrific as we climbed higher and higher. We were going north along a high ridge. To the west of us we could see the coastal plain, and to the east there was the terrifying terrain of the Judean desert with its deep ravines and layers of earth and rock all twisted and diving down to the Salt Sea. Beyond the Salt Sea were the mountains of Moab. The difficulties of the trip were nothing compared to the problems that we encountered when we arrived in Hebron. There was not enough room for all of David's men, and he instructed them to settle just outside of town. But this meant that they had to camp. I felt sorry for the women who had to prepare meals and wash clothes in that situation. They could not begin to keep their children clean or anything in order.

Father and I went on with David and his guards and found a small place in the city. I say small, but it did have two stories. There was room on the ground floor for animals and food storage. An oven and a fire pit were located near the front opening. The second floor was adequate for eating and sleeping, and we also had access to the roof for the evening breeze. David's men brought us some supplies, but it would still take time to turn this house into a home.

Soon after we entered the city, David was visited by the elders of Judah and was not surprised at their request. Since they wanted to break away from the House of Saul, they asked David if he would be their king— king of the House of Judah. This was, of course exactly what he wanted. "I will be your king," he said, "and Hebron shall be my royal city. Just give me a little time to prepare, and you may anoint me."

There was much to do. David called his officers, and they made plans and assignments for ruling the city and the state. My father pointed out, in one of their planning sessions, that there had to be a coronation.

David said, "I look forward to a coronation here in Hebron. In fact, this is the only place that a real coronation is possible; it is here that my ancestors are buried. The coronation shall be at the tombs, so that the departed may bless my kingdom and my house. Gad, you get my scribes together. It may be difficult to find all the documents that you will need. If you can't find them, then the scribes will have to get busy and write up some new material or at least listen to the minstrels at the tombs and copy their songs. This has to be done with taste and tradition."

I should insert at this point that the minstrels at the tombs sang songs daily concerning our ancestors. They had kept our early traditions alive for many years, and they had memorized these traditions.

My father hurried out to find the scribes. They had set up shop not far from David's headquarters in a building, which was far from adequate.

The Move to Hebron

They still did not have their files arranged, and many documents were not even unpacked; they were still rolled up in large jars. Sheva, the chief scribe, was not a happy man. He could not find anything. He looked at father and said, "I've been looking for a document all morning, and now I've just been told that it is still with some material that has not arrived from Ziklag. One can create order out of material chaos, but it is impossible to arrange things if they are not here! Now what the hell do you want?"

"It really makes no difference what I want. Your question should be, 'What does David want now?' He wants a coronation done with 'taste and tradition.'"

Sheva responded with not a little sarcasm, "A coronation with 'taste and tradition!' You know that we have little tradition concerning kings, and just whose 'taste' are we talking about?"

"Come now Sheva! You know whose 'taste' we're talking about. We may not have much of a tradition concerning royal matters, but we must plan for what is to come. If David ever becomes king of Israel as well as Judah, every step has to be right. We have lived among the Philistines, and we know that they will be watching. The scribes of Tyre are the real experts at such things; they can probably help us. David wants to impress the city-states with his coronation, and he wants to lay a foundation for future."

Father told me that Sheva was not usually so cranky even though he often looked that way. He was thin with narrow set eyes, but those eyes could light up, and sometimes he even smiled.

"So, what will we need?" Sheva asked, with a much more cooperative tone. "If the coronation is here in Hebron at the tombs, we will have to remember the ancestors with our usual funeral ritual and gather up *The Stories of the Fathers* to be recited just before the ritual. After the ancestors join us in blessing the new king, we should have a psalm or two."

"Sounds good, but since David will only be king of Judah, I would only recite the *Story of Judah* and not the stories of all the fathers."

"I will have to think about that. It is difficult to start in the middle."

"Sheva, you are always in the middle! Just don't look back so far. We can save that for another day. Someday when David becomes king of both Judah and Israel we will have to do as others have done; we will have to begin before there were any fathers at all in order to really tell his story. But for now start gathering up some materials, and I will come back this evening with a skin of wine. We'll burn a bit of your midnight oil."

The Jerusalem Academy

Father left Sheva to his confusion and hurried back to David, who was standing at the entrance to his quarters and talking to the last of his luncheon guests. The others had left. When David saw father, he motioned for him to come over, "I want you to meet my uncle Jonathan. He is a scribe from Bethlehem."

Father told me that he was almost speechless. Jonathan looked younger than David. He was certainly as tall as David, and they both looked like they had come out of the same mold. It was a striking experience to see them standing together. And yet there was a difference. When you looked in David's eyes, he was on guard. With Jonathan, it was somehow different. His eyes revealed an openness that was thoughtful, sincere and friendly.

Father said, "I can't believe this! I was going to ask permission to go to Bethlehem for some family documents. I must say that I am glad to meet you. A scribe from Bethlehem is just what we need. How long will you be here?"

"I really don't know." Jonathan replied with open hands.

David added, "We were just about to discuss that when you arrived. How do you think Jonathan can help us?"

Father answered, "Well, I know that you don't have time to dictate to Sheva or one of his scribes some of your family history. I can't see how you can go to Bethlehem to get the things that we might need. Sheva could go, but he is trying to create some order in his office. We really need Jonathan if he can stay, and if we do not need documents from Bethlehem, he can work on texts that we have and will be using. In fact, he could go with me tonight when I go back to work with Sheva. Also on another subject, I need to ask you, David, if you will write the main coronation psalm?"

"I will write the psalm, and I want you to keep the coronation simple. There will be another day for something bigger and better. Whatever you do, clear it with Sheva. Tell Sheva to give Jonathan a place to stay in his building, but he will take his evening meals at my table. I want him to know what is going on in my administration."

As they were leaving, father said to Jonathan, "Have you spent much time in Hebron?"

"I have been here with David's family to honor our ancestors at their tombs. So, that's once a year, but I do not know much about Hebron. Whenever I wanted to get away from Bethlehem, I would usually end up

The Move to Hebron

in Jerusalem. As you know, the Jebusites control Jerusalem and none of us were really welcomed, but I had a friend, Zadok, who went to the old scribal school there. It has been turning out scribes ever since the time of their king Adonizedek. My training in Bethlehem could not match the education that Zadok was receiving. So, he would take me to his school from time to time, and he even allowed me to use their library. I met some of their teachers; they didn't really care if I was from Judah. In fact, they had a teacher from Judah. At least a few of the scribes from that school were open to the world around them even if their Jebusite rulers were narrow-minded."

As father and Jonathan continued walking through the narrow streets of the main part of Hebron, father said, "I can see that we will have a great deal to talk about. Sheva knows quite a bit about the schools in the Philistine cities. When David served Achish, king of Gath, and was in Ziklag, Sheva spent time in Gath at the scribal school. By the way, Jonathan, David said that you were his uncle, but you must be about the same age as David?"

"I'm actually younger than David. David's father Jesse is my brother. I came along when our father, Obed, was old; I was his youngest. In fact, Jesse was like my father and David my brother. I never knew anything about my mother. David and I were trained at an early age, and we tended the family's sheep. We spent a great deal of time in the Judean wilderness in dangerous situations. After David left to serve Saul, I also quit tending sheep; I wanted to become a scribe."

" If I can ask, what kind of 'dangerous situations' did you experience?"

"We always had to be on the lookout for predators, both bear and lion. Also eagles were eager to catch a lamb. But it was not just the other animals who were hungry. Humans would steal a lamb by night, and the terrain itself was dangerous.

"One evening two wild dogs ran into the flock just before dark at the time of gathering the flock for the night watch. The sheep scattered like quail. Now it would be difficult to bring them into the fold. One dog had already killed a lamb with one quick bite in the throat. He was about to rip open the lamb's belly to drink the milk in it, when David hit the dog with a large rock and ran his knife into its heart. Even so the dog managed to slash David's arm. David yelled for me to get the other dog. However I saw the other dog was running away, and it was more important to gather up the flock. So I said, 'Take care of your arm. I'll gather the flock before it gets dark.'

"I ran around the flock and started them back toward the fold. But one ewe and her lamb did not follow; she, with lamb following, bolted down a narrow trail that led to a deep ravine. I had to climb above them in order to get out in front of them and turn them. I did get past them, but I slipped and was sliding down to the trail. I knew that I had to stop at the trail or fall a hundred cubits into the wadi. When I hit the trail, I grabbed a bush. I was hanging over the edge, but I managed to climb back. I pushed the ewe and her lamb back to the flock, and all of them were put into the fold. That evening as we sat at our fire, David complained that I did not get the other dog. I said, 'I didn't get him, but the flock is safe. We lost one lamb. We'll get the dog on another day. When time is short, I have to decide for the many, and even so, I was led astray.'"

"That is an interesting story. Dangerous situations do call for quick decisions. Well we haven't seen much, but we have had a good walk and here are the famous tombs of the ancestors. It was good to have a chance to talk with you. Perhaps, I should get you back to David's quarters, and we'll continue this at another time. It's beginning to get cool. Of course in Hebron, we are closer to the stars than any other city in this country."

"Yes, and I have always loved the area between Hebron and Jerusalem."

When they arrived at David's quarters, father said, "It was good to meet you, and I know that you can help us a great deal. I'll be here about the time you finish your meal, and we can walk to Sheva's office."

Sometime after David's coronation Jonathan told me about that first evening meal at David's table. It was not relaxing.

Jonathan hurried on into the building, and before he could make his way to the dinning area, he saw David in the hall walking toward him. David said, "You're back. I hope all went well. Gad asked me to write a psalm, so I just wrote it while you were gone. I'm going to spend more time on another coronation psalm, but this will do for now. Let me read it to you, and you can make a copy."

David led Jonathan into a small room where there was a desk, some parchment, ink and brushes. He began to read:

> O Yahweh, my god, and my rock.
> I called on you by name, Yahweh.
> Now I'm free from my enemies,

Delivered from a certain death.
You have anointed me with oil;
You have chosen me to be king.
You said to me, "You are my son;
Yes! This day, I have fathered you."
Therefore, grant to me your justice,
And give to me your righteousness,
That I may care for the needy,
And help the widow and orphan.
Blessed be Yahweh and his name.
(Lines from Psalms 2, 18, 72, plus)

"Now Jonathan, take that copy with you tonight, and see how it all fits together. But, we must eat, so come on, just follow me."

As they were walking to the dinning room, Jonathan thought that things were busy around here. "I just came in and David put me to work, and here we go again. I wonder if I can ever be alone? There isn't even time to spit. On this schedule, you just swallow and say, 'Yes sir.' I wonder if David ever has time alone? The answer may be 'yes,' but as soon as we entered the dinning room, I knew that if he had time alone it wasn't at the dinner hour."

There were a lot of people in the room and the table was huge. It appeared as if there was plenty of food, even though nothing was fancy. The entire arrangement had been set up just a few weeks ago, and it was only a temporary situation.

David introduced Jonathan to those of his staff who had not met him at lunch, and David said to Jonathan, "Now you just get to eating, because you will need to get out of here. Gad is usually on time."

There was plenty of good bread and lamb. What with a little wine, Jonathan was feeling fine in just a few moments. But the noise was too much. It did not take him long to excuse himself and head for the street. As he left the building, my father stepped out of the shadows and said, "You're right on time. I hope that you got enough to eat."

"I got plenty to eat. Did you have a chance to rest and eat?"

"Yes, my daughter had something ready for me when I got home."

"Your daughter does the cooking?"

"Yes, because Jael, my wife, died in the fire when the Amalekites raided and burned Ziklag. My daughter, Keziah, has been a real help for me."

Just then they reached the scribal quarters.

3

An Evening with Sheva

AT THIS POINT I should interrupt my story to say I think events happened the way I am relaying them to you, but I am relying on accounts from Jonathan and father. But I must say that my father had a lot of wine during the meeting. The next morning there were some things he could not remember.

Father and Jonathan entered the building and found Sheva still working at his desk. Things really had to be pushed along these days. Sheva's desk did not look as bad as it did earlier in the day, but the office was still more like a storeroom than an office.

Father said, "Sheva, I want you to meet Jonathan, who is David's uncle. Perhaps you have heard of him; he is a scribe from Bethlehem, and David has arranged for Jonathan to help us."

Sheva got up to greet Jonathan saying, "*Shalom!* You look a lot like David. I must say that we can certainly use your help. I am short on help, and the people in David's administration keep asking us to do more."

"It will be a great experience for me to be able to work with you; I hope I can give you the help you need. David wants me to stay here with you. He thought you could find a place for me, but I will be eating my evening meals at David's table."

"That should work," Sheva answered with just a bit of doubt in the tone of his voice. "If you're at David's table, it is some times hard to know why. In some cases, he likes you, and in others he wants to watch you."

"But in this case, it is probably because Jonathan is his uncle."

"No Gad. That is not the reason. David sees it as a way to keep in touch with what we are doing. Well, it could be helpful, but Jonathan, you will have to be careful not to tell David everything we are doing in this place. Some things must be made public at just the right time. In order for

An Evening with Sheva

you to really help us, you must know what we are doing and when you can talk about it. This puts you in a difficult situation, but we'll work with it."

"I can handle it. Also, it could work the other way around, because we might need to know what David is thinking."

"No question," said Sheva.

Then he turned back to view the things on his desk, and he said, "I found some of the things for this coronation this afternoon, but we still have a lot to do."

Father interrupted, saying, "David reminded us today to keep this one simple, and that you are the boss. Have you decided where we should start?"

"Yes. We should just start with *The Stories of Judah*. After all, David will be king of Judah, and this is one way of keeping everything focused. And, if David wants it simple, we will just list the names of the fathers from Perez to Jesse."

When father was telling about this he remarked that Sheva had just come around to the position that father had suggested earlier. Now it was his position to defend.

But then Sheva added a rather strange note that they should begin now to work on *The Stories of Perez*, because one of these days we'll want all of this material. He said, "I'm going to suggest that you, Jonathan, collect all you can on your family's history. After we get this coronation finished, you'll have to get some of the minstrels to sing of your ancestors and then write it all down. Which reminds me, Jonathan can you line up some minstrels for the coronation?"

"I can do it, but I'll want you to listen to them and make the final decision. By the way, David wrote a coronation psalm this afternoon. He said that he was going to work on another one, but this one would work for this occasion. He read it, and I copied it just before dinner. Here is the copy."

Sheva took it. He did not read it, but he said to Jonathan, "You have a nice hand. So Gad, where is that skin of wine you promised?"

"Damn! I forgot it. I'll go get it."

"You'll do nothing of the kind. I have some here, but we can't drink much until we have an outline of the coronation."

Sheva got three old cups from a shelf behind him and took down a skin from the same shelf. He poured the wine, and they sat down. Sheva continued, "My other scribes are asleep by now. Jonathan you can take some notes. So first, we will have *The Story of Judah*, and . . ."

Father interrupted again, "Sorry, but the first thing is the processional. David should leave from his quarters, riding his mule, and the rest of his entourage should walk behind him. We should send word to Benaiah to be in charge of the processional and have his Cherethite and Pelethite guards bring up the rear."

"I agree," said Sheva. "Put that first on the program. Now we have everyone at the tombs of the ancestors and our part starts. I would like to have at least three minstrels to sing *These are the Stories of Judah*. Next, we will present the 'names' from Perez to Jesse. Then comes the funeral ritual. Now for this ritual, I still have some work to do. I will work on it tomorrow, and Gad, you must find Abiathar and send him here to help me on the sacrificial part of it."

"Right."

Sheva continued, "After the funeral ritual and the blessing of the king by his departed ancestors, someone will sing the coronation psalm. Then Gad, you, Abiathar, and the elders of Judah will anoint the king; the horn will sound, and the people will shout, 'Long live King David!' Have I left anything out? If not let's have another cup of wine."

As Sheva was pouring, he said, "Tomorrow, I will work on the ritual and Jonathan you should work on *These are the Stories of Judah* and *These are the Names*. Before we have a third cup of wine, allow me to grab a bit of bread. You fellows ate an evening meal; I did not."

While Sheva was getting his bread, father said to Jonathan, "Sheva gave this a lot of thought today. We should do this in about two weeks."

Just then Sheva returned, so father said to him, "Can we do this in two weeks?"

"I don't know. But on second thought, the answer is yes, because we will not be sending out invitations to other kings. This will be a rather low profile occasion. However, we will send many letters after the event. Yes. We can do it. So, I will send word to David and get his approval. Now, Jonathan, we have to find a place for you for the night."

But father said, "Sheva, you get a place ready for Jonathan tomorrow. Tonight, he can stay at my place. Besides, we have almost emptied one skin, and Jonathan can take my hand on the way home. Thanks for everything and *laylah tov*."

"Good night!" said Sheva with a yawn.

Jonathan joined father, and as they were leaving, they said again, "*laylah tov!*"

An Evening with Sheva

The darkness and the cool night air soon swallowed them up. Father said to Jonathan, "I hope you do not mind staying at my place tonight. I just thought the project of getting you settled could wait until tomorrow. I'm sure I could have made it home by myself, but it is nice to have you along. Besides, you should know where I live."

Jonathan agreed. Later he said to me that father had told him about me earlier in the evening, and he was interested in meeting me. At the evening meal, father had also told me about Jonathan, and I was hoping that I could meet him soon. I think that father must have had a plan. After a bit, father stopped at a door in a courtyard wall. He opened the door, and they entered. The house was not far from where they entered the courtyard and all was dark. Father said, "It's very late, and it will be best if we just find a place to sleep down here on ground level. There is some straw here in the manger we can use."

"That's fine with me," answered Jonathan.

The hour, the wine, and a long day conspired against them; they were both asleep almost immediately.

4

Breakfast with Jonathan

THE NEXT MORNING I got up, and I wondered where father was sleeping. I started down the ladder, and then I saw father and someone else sleeping on some straw. I retreated up to the second floor and began to prepare breakfast. I thought that the other person must be Jonathan. I guess my preparations woke him up, because when I looked down again only father was asleep on the straw. Just then Jonathan came back to the stable area, and I decided that I should say something. I climbed down the ladder and said, "*Boqer tov!*"

"And a good morning to you!"

"I'm Keziah, Gad's daughter. It appears that the two of you had a late night. Sorry about the noise from the kitchen, but I see that it did not do much for father."

"No. He's still in a deep sleep. He mentioned you last night; I must say that I'm glad to meet you. I'm Jonathan."

"Yes, I know. Come on up to the table. We'll not wait for him," I said with a glance toward father.

Jonathan followed me up the ladder. He sat down at the table, and I finished preparing the food. I had already put on the table a large bowl of yogurt and a plate of bread and some cheese as well. I was still chopping some cucumbers, and then I brought them to the table and sat down across from Jonathan. Father had neglected to tell me that Jonathan's good looks would send chills down my spine.

"Go ahead. We'll not wait for father. You may need to get at your work."

"That is the situation, and before I forget, remind him that he needs to find Abiathar and send him to see Sheva. He needs some help with a ritual."

"I'll remind him. Now here is a small bowl for the yogurt, and if you want, feel free to put the cucumbers right on top. Just help yourself."

"This is wonderful! I'm reminded of that line in *The Song of Deborah*: 'He asked for water; milk she offered. In a royal bowl, she brought him curds.' I quote things when I don't know what to say. Am I babbling?"

"Just a bit. Why don't you eat?"

"I'll eat if you will tell me more about yourself and Gad."

Just then father came up the ladder, and I did not answer Jonathan's question.

I said to father, "*Boqer tov*! How are you feeling?"

"I'm fine, but I'm still tired. Also, my back aches, but it appears that the two of you are having a nice breakfast. What's with the cucumbers? You don't usually fix those for me," he said with a wink to Jonathan.

"Father, please sit down, and you don't have to tease me about such things."

"Who's teasing? So, Jonathan, are you ready to go to work this morning?"

"I suppose so, but it will take some time just to get set up over there. Maybe, I'll be ready by noon. If Keziah doesn't mind, I'll take a bit of her wonderful bread with me when I leave here, and then, I won't even stop for lunch. Is that all right?"

"That will be fine, and take some cheese as well."

Then Jonathan said to father, "Don't forget to tell Abiathar to see Sheva today. Sheva wanted some help on that ritual."

"Right"

Jonathan was not quite finished eating. I knew that he wanted to talk with me some more, but that would have to wait. Father was still eating and enjoying the cucumbers. Jonathan asked father what he, as David's prophet, did. He knew that father was helping on this coronation business, but what else does a prophet or seer do? So, he just said, "Gad what do you do for David as his prophet?"

Father said, "That's a big question? Actually, I spend a lot of time with the scribes, because they are the ones who are writing letters and receiving letters. They read a lot of literature from other countries in their studies. In other words, they know what's going on in this world. A prophet must know what's going on. For that same reason, I spend time with the people of the land; I have to know what they're thinking. If you know what's going on and have some common sense, it is not too difficult to understand what options are available for the near future. Of course the king also has his counselors from among the scribes who are sometimes critical of both prophets and priests: the priests for not thinking and the prophets for being so damn certain that they have a word from God. But I must say that the words from God have been few and far between for us. According to our traditions, he did a lot of talking in the past but no more. So, if David wants the direction of Yahweh, I have to find out what Yahweh wants, even if Yahweh is not talking! It's difficult to be a royal prophet. You want to please the king but not too much. If you please him too much, you'll be wrong, and then you'll really be in trouble. It would be much easier to be a prophet on the fringe of things; it is much easier to point out the problems than to help a king work through them. I hope I continue to be of some help to David, but there are others who are waiting to take my place. Some of them could do a fine job. Which reminds me, Sheva may waiting for you."

"You're right. But thanks for telling me about your work, and thanks for everything. I'll see you later today. And Keziah, thanks for the breakfast and my lunch."

"Not a word! You come back again."

After Jonathan left, father said, "I'll invite Jonathan to join us at our table again unless you have any objections?"

"I have no objections, and you knew that before you asked the question."

"You're right again. Now I have to go and find Abiathar."

After father left I thought, "I have no objections at all. Jonathan is good-looking, and he thinks—no objections at all."

5

These Are the Stories of Judah

For the next three parts of my story, I had to ask Jonathan what happened, and he also supplied the texts, on which he was working, and I was able to copy them for my story.

When Jonathan reached the office, Sheva was already at work at his desk. Sheva looked up and said, "*Boqer tov!* I trust that you had a good night's rest. I have fixed your desk in the next room, and I put on your desk some of the things you will need concerning the Judah material. Take a look at the material and review it even though you are probably familiar with it. You may need some help in copying what you decide to use. I haven't arranged your sleeping quarters. I'll do that a bit later when the rest of the staff arrives."

Jonathan went to his desk and found the documents. One of them was a large scroll. He opened it and began to read:

> [*These are the Stories of Judah*]
>
> It was at that time that Judah parted from his brothers;
> he camped near an Adullamite, and his name was Hirah.
> There, Judah saw the daughter of a Canaanite, and his name was Shua.
> He took her; he went in to her.
> She conceived; she bore a son.
> He called forth his name, "Er."
> She conceived again; she bore a son.
> She called forth his name, "Onan."
> She repeated again; she bore a son.
> She called forth his name, "Shelah."
> He was in Chezib, when she bore him.
> Judah took a woman for Er, his firstborn;

The Jerusalem Academy

Her name was Tamar.

Er, the first-born of Judah, was evil in the eyes of Yahweh;
Yahweh killed him.
Judah said to Onan:
> "Go in to the wife of your brother;
> be a brother-in-law to her;
> raise up a descendant for your brother."

Onan knew that the descendant would not be his,
and whenever he went in to the wife of his brother,
he wasted [his semen] on the ground so as not to give a descendant to his brother.
What he did was evil in the eyes of Yahweh;
he killed him as well.
Judah said to Tamar, his daughter-in-law:
> "Dwell as a widow in the house of your father,
> until Shelah, my son, grows up."

(He said that, for he too might die like his brothers.)
Tamar left, and she lived in the house of her father.

After many days, the daughter of Shua, the wife of Judah, died.
Judah was comforted; he went up to the shearers of his flocks at Timnah
—he and Hirah, his friend, the Adullamite.
It was made known to Tamar:
> "Now, your father-in-law is going up to Timnah
> to shear his flocks."

She removed her widow's garments;
she covered herself with a double wrap.
She was disguised.
She sat down in the gate of Enaim, which is on the road to Timnah,
for she realized that Shelah had grown up,
yet she had not been given to him for a wife.
Judah saw her;
he took her for a harlot,
for she had covered her face.
He turned to her by the road.
He said:
> "Give, please, I will go in to you"

(For he did not know that she was his daughter-in-law).

She said:
"What will you pay me for coming in to me?"
He said:
"Surely I will send a kid from the flock."
She said:
"Only if you give a pledge until you send it."
He said:
"What is the pledge that I shall give you?"
She said:
"Your seal, your belt, and your staff that is in your hand."
He gave [them] to her;
he went in to her;
she conceived by him.
She got up;
she left.
She removed her wrap;
she put on her widow's garments.
Judah sent the kid in the possession of his friend, the Adullamite,
to redeem the pledge from the possession of the woman.
But he did not find her.
He asked the men of her sanctuary:
"Where is the cult-prostitute?
She was in Enaim by the road.
They said:
"No cult-prostitute has been here."
He returned to Judah.
He said:
"I did not find her. Moreover, the men of the sanctuary said,
'No cult-prostitute has been here.'"
Judah said:
"Let her keep [the pledge] for herself,
for we might become involved in a scandal.
Note that I did send this kid,
but you did not find her."
It was about three months later when it was made known to Judah:
"Tamar, your daughter-in-law, has become a harlot!
Moreover, now she is pregnant from harlotry."
Judah said:

"Bring her out! She will be burnt."
As she was being brought out, she sent to her father-in-law the following:
"By the man to whom these belong I am pregnant!"
She said:
"Please observe! To whom do these belong,
the seal, the belt, and the staff?"
Judah knew.
He said:
"She is more in the right than I,
inasmuch as I did not give her to Shelah, my son."
(He never again knew her.)

When the time of her delivery came,
there were twins in her womb.
During her delivery, one presented a hand;
the midwife took;
she bound scarlet upon his hand saying:
"This one came out first."
But just as he was drawing back his hand,
his brother came out.
She said:
"What a break you have made for yourself!"
[Judah] called forth his name, "Perez."
Afterward his brother came out,
on whose hand was the scarlet.
[Judah] called forth his name, "Zerah." (Genesis 38:1–30)

When Jonathan reached this point in the story, he thought, "This story goes on and on. I had forgotten how long it is. It goes through the life of Perez, his marriage, and the birth of his children. Then let's see. Yes, it ends as all these stories end: a death and burial, a word about descendants, and another death scene. In this case, the death and burial of Tamar, some material on Hezron and Hamul, the sons of Perez, and the death and burial of Judah. It may be important to use all of this material at our annual ritual for our departed ancestors, but for the coronation, I'll suggest we just use this story through the birth of Perez and Zerah. Then I can list the names from Perez to Jesse. I saw some genealogical lists here on my desk. Yes, here they are. So, I need to make a list and give it a title."

These Are the Stories of Judah

I agree with Jonathan's suggestion, because, in part, I don't want to copy any more. His thinking was correct. The coronation did not need the entire document. I have also copied the following list, which he made. It is not interesting, but it does bring us right down to David's father (and Jonathan's brother).

These are the Names from Perez to Jesse
Perez
Hezron
Ram
Amminadab
Nahshon
Salmon
Boaz (and Ruth)
Obed
Jesse

For Jonathan this list was interesting, because there were nine names. He told me about his thoughts concerning the nine: "This will work out just right. Abraham, Isaac, and Jacob will be summoned at the beginning of the ritual. Then, the minstrels will sing about Judah down through the birth of Perez and Zerah. Next we will summon the list of nine. This will work out well. The three plus Judah, plus the nine is thirteen plus David makes the ideal number, fourteen generations. Since we do everything in terms of seven, this is great and twice seven is even better! I didn't even have to leave out anybody to come up with this number."

Jonathan got up and went into Sheva's room. He said, "I need to talk with you concerning the Judah material."

Sheva was at his desk working on the tomb ritual when Jonathan came in to talk with him. Sheva said, "Since it's time for some lunch let's go out under the old olive tree behind this building. I have a little food I can share with you."

"That won't be necessary. I brought some lunch with me; Gad's daughter makes good bread (Please note that he likes my bread!)."

"Good. We'll eat some lunch, talk about your questions, and I want to introduce you to the other scribes. Then we must arrange a place for you to sleep."

They picked up their food and went out the back door. There was a bench and a couple of chairs under the tree, and it looked as if this old tree had provided the shade for more than one conversation. Sheva sat down, and began eating a bit of bread and cheese. He said, "We might be feeding you too much. If I know Gad and his daughter, they probably fed you this morning, and as you said, they provided you with a lunch. This will be my first meal of the day. As the Egyptians say to their scribes, 'Beware of rushing to the table.'"

Jonathan saw a smile on Sheva's face, and he started eating his lunch with no apologies. Then he said, "I just read through the first part of *These are the Stories of Judah*, and I think the entire document will be too long for the coronation. My suggestion is that we first call Abraham, Isaac, and Jacob to the ritual. Then the minstrels can sing, *These are the Stories of Judah* down through the birth of Perez and Zerah. I have made up the list of names from Perez to Jesse. When these names are called to the ritual, thirteen fathers will be present with us. This turns out just right, because David will be number fourteen in this line. What do you think?"

"You have made some good points. I accept the limit you are suggesting on the Judah material, but if we do this again, for Israel, our northern kin who have been ruled by the house of Saul, our coronation should last for seven days. At that point, we will be able to do a lot more with all of our stories. However, I don't want to follow your suggestion about calling Abraham, Isaac, and Jacob first and then the others after the story of Judah. First we need to deal with the Judah story, and then start the ritual and summon all thirteen at the same time. It would really upset the priests if we interrupt their ritual in any way."

Jonathan said, "That's fine with me. I can see that this is all going to be interesting. How is the ritual coming along? Did Abiathar come by to look at the ritual?"

"Yes. He had a look at my first draft, and it seems that all is well. That's another reason I don't want many changes to the program as it was presented to him. Also, he will be responsible for the sacrifices. We are closing in on this job. I will ask David this afternoon when we can have the coronation. I think you should look for those minstrels after lunch."

"I will. But, first I need to meet the others who work here, and we were going to see about my quarters."

"That's right. I forgot. There's just too much to do. Let's go in the office now and find the others."

There were three main rooms in the building, which needed a lot of repair: Sheva's office, the office where Jonathan was working, and a larger room (about twenty cubits square), which was the library. They went into the library, and there they saw three young men. Sheva said, after getting their attention, "Come on over here and meet Jonathan, a scribe from Bethlehem, who will be helping us. Jonathan, here we have Elimelech, Danel, and Noah."

Jonathan greeted them, and Sheva continued, "These three were with us in Ziklag, and they went to a school for scribes in Gath. They learned a great deal there. Of course it is a Philistine school, but they also have two teachers from Tyre and a fair library. The three of them work in this room, and they are setting up our library in here as well. After they were in school for about six weeks, they all changed their names which explains why there are three people in this office with only the best in scribal names."

Jonathan said, "I was wondering about that. I thought they had just stepped out of the classics. It is wonderful; you all had the courage to change your names and look to the future. I will enjoy working with you."

As Jonathan and Sheva left for Sheva's office Jonathan said, "So, Sheva, where will I spend the night?"

"I usually go to my house, though I didn't last night, and Elimelech, Danel, and Noah sleep in the library. I have been trying to think of a good answer for you, but I can't. For now you will just have to bed down in your office. I hope we have better arrangements soon."

"I don't mind sleeping in my office, but I have one more question. Can one of these fellows go with me this afternoon to find out about some minstrels?"

Sheva was quick to respond. "Elimelech can go with you. He has been here longer than any of us, and he should know his way around."

6

The Tomb Ritual for the Coronation

Elimelech and Jonathan set out at once, and Sheva went to his office.

I should say that what follows concerning what Sheva did is Jonathan's best guess based on what Sheva later told them about his work.

Sheva decided to try a final draft of the ritual following the main points of his first draft. He had worked on it during the morning, but most of his time was spent collecting materials. He had copies of the annual funeral rituals held in Hebron at the tombs of the Machpelah. But he needed something a little different for a coronation. Then he was also looking at some texts that he had from Gath. He used to go there to the school and get things that he thought would be useful. Two of these texts were texts from Tyre. Actually, the more he looked at these texts, the more certain he became that they were all structured in the same way.

They all began with a section called "the summons." Here the departed fathers/rulers were summoned or called from the netherworld by name. In this way, the fathers were present during the ritual. They were present for the purpose of receiving the gifts and sacrifices and for giving their support and blessings to the living, who called or summoned them. In the case of a coronation, they gave their blessings to the new king.

After the summons, there was a section on mourning. Here the most recent ones to depart from this world were mourned and there was a lot of weeping. Next, there was a search for the ones who had been summoned, and when they were found, they were guided to where the gifts were being offered. Therefore the next section dealt with the sacrifices, and the last part had to do with the blessings. In the case of a coronation, the new king took charge as the legitimate king, and he expected an heir and the continuation of his line.

After reviewing his thoughts, notes, and with his first draft before him, Sheva began to write:

The Tomb Ritual for the Coronation

A Document of Celebration of Ancestors

You have been summoned, O ancient fathers
Abraham has been summoned.
Isaac has been summoned.
Jacob has been summoned.
Judah has been summoned.
Perez has been summoned.
Hezron has been summoned.
Ram has been summoned.
Amminadab has been summoned.
Nahshon has been summoned.
Salmon has been summoned.
Boaz has been summoned.
Obed has been summoned.
Jesse, the father of David, has been summoned.
You have been summoned, O ancient fathers.

O House of Jesse, weep!
Let all the descendants of Judah shed tears.
Bereft, bereft, and bereft!

O Yahweh! Send your angel,
That he might help our ancient fathers.
Let him descend to the netherworld;
Let him guide them to this place.
Below are the ancient fathers!
Below is Jesse, as well.

Offer generous gifts to our fathers:
Gifts of food and drink for all of them.
Present a dove for Jesse.
As Noah's dove returned to her land,
So Jesse's son has returned to his land.

A blessing from our fathers:
Shalom!
Shalom David!
Shalom to his house, as well!

The Jerusalem Academy

> Shalom to David's wives!
> Shalom Hebron!
> Shalom to her gates!
> Shalom!

For me, this ritual is not interesting just to read, but in a ritual setting the priests make it livelier. After completing this text, Sheva was anxious to show it to the others as soon as Jonathan and Elimelech returned.

Sheva started cleaning up. He returned some of the documents to their jars. These jars were at least a cubit tall, and they all had tight fitting lids. There were certainly many advantages in using parchment instead of clay tablets for writing, but parchment did demand a lot more care.

Just then Sheva heard Jonathan and Elimelech's voices. "How did you do?" Sheva asked.

"We went to the tombs," said Elimelech, "and we found out who usually sang the stories of the fathers. Everyone, with whom we talked, agreed that a singer by the name of Heman, a Levite of the line of Kohath, was probably the best of the minstrels. He is coming here to see us tomorrow morning. If he decides to take part in the coronation, he will bring another singer or two in order to divide up the parts. So, Sheva, you can interview him in the morning."

"I will be here. Now I want you to hear the ritual, which I just finished. Elimelech, please get Noah and Danel."

Soon everyone was gathered in Sheva's office, and he said, "This morning, I looked at some local funeral texts and even some texts from Tyre, which I had collected from my days in Gath. Even though these texts are quite different in terms of general background, names, gods, and sacrifices, they are the same in terms of their structure and intent. In the case of texts used at the time of coronation, the main purpose was for the fathers to bless the new king."

With that introduction, Sheva began to read. They all listened with interest.

After Sheva finished, Jonathan was the first to speak. "The ritual is good. I like it. I note that the list of thirteen fathers has been put into the first section as you had suggested. That works out well. By the way, does this angel of Yahweh, who looks for those who are called, have a name?"

"If he does, I don't know it," Sheva replied. I was actually thinking of the angel in the story of the birth of Samson. His name is never given. It may be the best way to handle such things. The texts from Tyre have an ancient tradition where the task of guiding the fathers belongs to the sun goddess. But that will not work for us. Any other questions?"

Elimelech had a question. "In this tomb ritual, we call or summon the fathers from the netherworld, from Sheol. This is done by families, clans, and states for annual events or special occasions like this coronation. What I would like to know is how does this relate to King Saul's ban on calling up the dead?"

Jonathan, as he was telling me about all of this, stressed that Sheva was pleased with Elimelech's question. Sheva loved to explain things. He said, "The two things are really not related. Yes, in both cases you are dealing with the dead, but that is the only common element. What Saul banned was the use of magic or necromancy. In other words, mediums or wizards, who by their knowledge and magical powers, bring up the dead in order to find out about the future. Here, the medium takes the credit and collects the fees. In the tomb rituals, Yahweh is asked to help find those who are summoned. No one asks for a look into the future. Here we ask for a blessing; here we hope for *Shalom*. By the way, there is a rumor that shortly before the death of Saul when he had no word from Yahweh in any shape or form, he consulted a medium! Perhaps we will find out about that one day."

At this point, Sheva remembered that he had to see David concerning the date of the coronation, so he left. Jonathan returned to his office in order to do a few things before he left for dinner at David's table. The other three went back to the library. They probably did not work anymore, but it is likely that they talked a long time about Saul's ban and tomb rituals.

What I don't understand is in what way Sheva's final draft was different from his first draft, which he discussed with Abiathar. It doesn't really matter, but he told Jonathan that he didn't want to change what Abiathar had approved. I suppose that he made a few corrections.

7

The New Time Frame

JONATHAN RETURNED TO HIS office after an uneventful dinner. He was preparing a place to sleep when Sheva arrived. Jonathan said, "I did not expect to see you again today."

"I did not expect to come back here, but I couldn't see David until after dinner. He told me that he didn't talk to you this evening, and when I asked him about a date, he said, 'Make it in three days.' Well that means that we have to really get on with it. I stopped by Gad's place on the way back. He is coming here any moment now to have a look at the ritual. Also, he will have to notify the elders of Judah, who will help with the anointing."

"Did David say why he was in such a hurry?"

"No. He didn't say, but we can ask Gad about that."

Just then my father arrived. Sheva said to him, "We were just discussing David's decision to hurry this up. Do you know why he is in such a hurry?"

"Yes. It is quite clear. David is already beginning his campaign to win over to his side the House of Saul. Abner, Saul's army commander, has set up Ish-baal, Saul's son, as king over all Israel. So, we must act at once. In addition, the elders of Judah told David a different story from the one we heard in Ziklag about the death of Saul and his sons. The new account says that Saul's sons were killed, but Saul and his arms-bearer committed suicide. Then, the Philistines hung their bodies on the wall of Beth-shan. Later, the men of Jabesh-gilead took the bodies, burned them, gathered the bones, buried them, and fasted for seven days. David wants these people on his side; he wants to thank them at once for what they did, but he wants to thank them as king of Judah. In fact, he wants us to write the letter tonight and get it on its way tomorrow. Don't look so worried

Sheva. It will take a messenger three days to get there, and in three days David will be king."

"I'm not worried, but I wasn't planning on working tonight. Let's do the letter, and then, Gad, you must look at the ritual. Jonathan, you and I will both make copies as Gad dictates to us. In this way, we can send one and keep the other. But Gad, wait a moment until we write the opening address. You start with the salutation."

Both Sheva and Jonathan started in the standard manner:

> Thus says David, the king of Judah,
> to the men of Jabesh-gilead.

> *Shalom* to you, *shalom* to your houses,
> and *shalom* to all that is yours!
> You are blessed by Yahweh,
> because you did this kindness
> to your Lord, to Saul; you buried him.

> And now, Yahweh will show you
> kindness and truth. Also, I, yes I,
> will continue this goodness for you,
> because you performed this act.

> And now, you shall strengthen your
> hands and become an honor guard,
> because your Lord, Saul, is dead.
> But even so, the house of Judah
> has anointed me king over them.
> (Most of this from 2 Samuel 2:5–7)

When they were finished Jonathan remembers saying, "That is some letter. It is alluring and captivating. I'm willing to bet that with this letter the 'men of Jabesh' will be on David's side."

"It may be all of those things, but it's just plain politics," said Sheva. "If David does this sort of thing with other groups, it won't be long until there is another coronation to think about."

My father nodded and said, "Sheva! You are supposed to worry about the past and present; the future is my territory! See, Jonathan. I told you this morning that everyone wants my job."

"Never!" said Sheva. "I don't want to be closer than I am to the king; it is my dream to be distant from him."

I have to stop my story again. I must say that I wish Sheva had maintained this attitude in the coming years. But he changed, I'm sorry to say.

Then Sheva said, "Gad, let's get on with it. I'll read the ritual for you."

After reading the ritual, Sheva looked at Gad, "Will that work, Sir Prophet?"

"Yes, it will, and I like the part about David's return to 'his land.' Now I should head for home."

"Don't forget to notify the elders of Judah of the date. That should be done tomorrow."

Jonathan said to father, as he was about to leave, "It's not late tonight, and we haven't had any wine, but let me walk with you for a ways. I need to get some fresh air."

8

An Enjoyable Evening

I WANT TO THANK Jonathan for giving me all of that material, and I will call on him again. I will always remember this next section, because on this evening father and I had our first fun and laughter since mother died.

As father and Jonathan walked along the street, they both enjoyed the cool evening air. Father said, "It is nice to be in Hebron. When you go down to the coast it gets hot and the air is so thick. I hope we stay up here for a long time."

"We will be here for a long time; David has a lot to do. However, he is not going to waste any time doing it, which means that five scribes will not be able to keep up with David. We will have to keep some chronicles, write a lot of letters, record all sorts of traditions and rituals, and start up a school. This list doesn't even deal with the task of working on our library and our own writing."

Father was not expecting such a flood of words. He agreed with Jonathan, but said, "Just slow down a bit and don't try to do everything. If things don't get done, you will get some more help."

"I hope so. You're probably right. Also we are getting close to your house; I'll turn back and go to the office."

"You should not turn back and go to the office! You should take it easy. Come on to the house with me. You won't have to stay long. I know Keziah is up and wondering if you will be with me. I told her I might bring you home for some of her raisin and fig cakes."

"Gad, you are persuasive."

"Not at all. You are interested and perhaps a bit lonely."

As they came up the ladder, I greeted them; I was obviously pleased to see them and especially Jonathan. There were things to eat on the table, and Jonathan seemed glad to be here.

"So, what have you been doing?" I asked.

"We were trying to get everything ready for the big coronation. David wants to have it in three days! And as your father, I suggest that you put it in your plans. You will want to observe it and shout, 'Long live King David!'"

"Well, I doubt if I'll be shouting anything, but I do want to see the coronation. Please sit down here at the table."

Jonathan said to me, "Since Gad will be participating in the ritual of anointing, perhaps you and I could get a good place to watch, and we can rescue Gad from the crowd when it is all finished."

"Sounds good to me. Where will I find you?"

"You can stop by my office, and we'll go from there."

Father broke in on our planning session with, "I'm glad that's all arranged. Can we eat something now? And by the way, Jonathan, are you certain that I will need rescued from the crowd?"

"I'm not certain at all, but I thought that we should offer our help."

"I can help myself and so should you."

Jonathan took some of the raisin cakes, and he said, "I will be glad when this hurried-up coronation is out of the way. I have already thought of several things that should be added to the ceremony, but those things will have to wait until the next one."

"What do you mean 'the next one?'" I asked.

Father answered, "Perhaps we are mistaken, but it is beginning to look like David will someday be king of Israel as well as Judah. If so, we will have to do this again. This could be the dress rehearsal."

"Now, I would like to change the subject, since the two of you could talk about this for the rest of the evening. Today, Joab, the commander of the army, so he said, came by. He said, 'Where is Gad?' I told him that I did not know. However, I did not like him, and I did not like the way he looked at me. He was in a hurry and left at once."

Father was quick to respond. "This man is treacherous; he has noticed you, and that is a worry. With a dog like him one has to answer every question with a 'yes' or a 'no'. In other words, a conversation should not get started. Perhaps I'm too cautious, but I worry about you. Jonathan, I don't like Joab even if he is related to you."

"He has always been a problem. David's half-sister, Zeruiah, raised three boys, Joab, Abishai, and Asahel; they were hard to handle, and Joab was their leader. I really don't understand why David made him the commander of the army. I have always wondered what Joab has on David?

An Enjoyable Evening

You can trust him to do the wrong thing, if he has the chance. If Joab ever bothers you in any way, let me know. I will try to help."

"I did not intend to start such a vigorous conversation. I will heed your suggestions, but it sounds like Joab is not worth any more of our time. Jonathan, what do you do when you are not working?"

"Lately, I'm always working, but I like to do other things. When I am at home, there is always something that needs fixed, and I like to have contact with things that are completely different from my work. But, some of the things I like to do are related to my work. I like to read material from other countries, and I like to write poetry."

"What do you write about?" asked father.

"Many things, but up until a few days ago, I was spending all of my spare time on an old story that I heard many times as I was growing up. You have probably heard it as well. It is the story of Job."

"We used to hear it," said father. "In fact, Job had three daughters, and he named one of them Keziah! I always liked that name, and when my daughter came along, I knew what to name her from the beginning."

Jonathan responded with a smile. "This old prophet is really good. He knew when you were a baby, Keziah, exactly what your name should be, even though it would take years for you to grow into your name."

"What do you mean by that," I asked.

"Gad, should I tell her?"

"Go ahead."

"The name Keziah means 'a bow,' and the shapeliness of a bow with its flowing curves has always made it a fitting name for a beautiful girl."

By this time, I was blushing, but I did not lose my composure. Instead, I spoke calmly and said, "Perhaps, I should stress the primary meaning of my name and say that this 'bow' has two arrows, one for each of you, if this conversation is repeated outside of this room."

By then my color was back to normal, and I began to laugh and soon we were all three making additional comments.

After that bit of fun, Jonathan said, "I should be going. I do want to thank you for the food and for the laughs. As I leave, I will run to avoid an arrow."

Father said to me with not a hint of fear, "Jonathan is apparently unaware that he has already been shot!"

With that, I threatened father and said, *"Laylah tov"* to Jonathan.

As Jonathan was leaving, he could hear father and me; we were chasing about and laughing, and he thought, "That was fun."

9

The Coronation

LATER JONATHAN TOLD ME that when he arrived at the scribes' quarters the moon gave enough light for him to see without a lamp that something was on his chair. It was a bag of wool. Now that was a wonderful gift. He put the bag near his desk, and it made a perfect bed. "I will sleep well tonight," he thought, but he didn't go to sleep at once. He said that he couldn't turn off the sound of my voice or erase the picture of me taking aim at the two of them, and to be honest I could not get to sleep. I was thinking about him.

In the morning, Jonathan got up, and then he remembered that Heman was coming to the office. "I hope Sheva remembers the interview," he thought to himself. Sheva remembered and was at work before Jonathan got up from his sack.

The interview with Heman went well. Sheva was pleased, and Heman was happy to help. However, he was not pleased that he would only be doing the first part of *These are the Stories of Judah*. But, when Sheva told him that there would be more to do in the future, he was willing to go with the plan.

The next two days were full of details. Everyone had to be notified of the event. Copies of the program were made, and the priests delivered their supplies. Finally, the day of the coronation was a reality. Everyone was up early and getting ready. Even David's mule got cleaned up. The guards were in their finest clothes, and the people began arriving from near-by towns and drifting in from the hills.

Jonathan was ready. In fact he told me that he felt odd, because he had been so busy, and now he could only wait with the others. He knew that in a short time, I would be there, and we would go to the tombs just ahead of the procession. The tombs were in a cave in a field on the east side of Hebron. Abraham had purchased this field, called "the Machpelah," from Ephron. Nobody seems to know why it was called "the Machpelah" which means "the double." But it became an important place, because there they buried Abraham and Sarah, Isaac and Rebekah, and Jacob and Leah.

Just then two things happened. Jonathan heard a long blast of a horn; David was on his way. Also, I arrived at his door. It was clear that Jonathan was glad to see me, and he said, "We should walk on to the tombs; we can find a good place to sit, so that we can see and hear. Most of the people will wait along the streets, and follow the procession."

In a few minutes we arrived at the tombs, and we found a good place to sit. A large area had been cleared at the entrance to the tombs where the ceremony would take place. Workmen had constructed a public threshing floor that could be used for such ceremonies. I noticed that my father was talking to other participants. Heman and the musicians were ready to start. When David arrived, everyone became quiet. He was escorted near the tombs and seated in a chair, and all was ready.

Heman stepped to center of the threshing floor. He was a very handsome man with a bass voice. He began to sing:

> It was at that time that Judah parted from his brothers;
> he camped near an Adullamite, and his name was Hirah.
> There, Judah saw the daughter of a Canaanite, and his name was Shua.
> He took her; he went in to her.
> She conceived; she bore a son.
>   He called forth his name, "Er." . . .

As Heman sang, Jonathan and I both noticed that the people were really interested in this story. Of course, most of them were hard working people, and they have never had a chance to see or hear things like this. Heman was a skilled minstrel. When the story reached the point where Judah meets Tamar by the road to Timnah, a woman stood beside Heman to sing the lines of Tamar:

> He turned to her by the road.
> He said:
>   "Give, please, I will go in to you"
> (For he did not know that she was his daughter -in-law).
> She said:
>   "What will you pay me for coming in to me?"
> He said:
>   "Surely I will send a kid from the flock."
> She said:

"Only if you give a pledge until you send it."

He said:

"What is the pledge that I shall give you?"

She said:

"Your seal, your belt, and your staff that is in your hand."

He gave [them] to her;

he went in to her;

she conceived by him.

The woman remained with Heman as he continued singing the story. Later in the story, after Judah was told about of Tamar's condition and after she was accused of being a harlot, the two of them sang again:

Judah said:

"Bring her out! She will be burnt."

As she was being brought out, she sent to her father-in-law the following:

"By the man to whom these belong I am pregnant!"

She said:

"Please observe! To whom do these belong,
the seal, the belt, and the staff?"

Judah knew.
He said:

"She is more in the right than I,
inasmuch as I did not give her to Shelah, my son."

This was the high point in the story for the people. When the woman sang, "By the man to whom these belong, I am pregnant," the crowd cried out, "Yes! Yes! Tamar is in the right!" After this point, the birth of Perez and Zerah was anticlimactic.

When Heman finished, the people cheered. I spoke in Jonathan's ear, "His singing and the people's response has given me chills."

Next, Abiathar began the ritual. He gave the title: *A Celebration of Ancestors*, and then another priest summoned the fathers. He went through all of the names. When he said, "O House of Jesse, weep!" there were a lot of people weeping. Then Abiathar asked Yahweh to send his angel to guide the fathers to this place. Abiathar with the help of three others, offered up the gifts of food and drink and then the special gift of

The Coronation

the dove for Jesse. Finally, there was the blessing of the fathers for David, his house, his wives, and for Hebron.

We were glad to see Heman come forward again. Heman said, "I have the pleasure of singing for the first time a coronation psalm written by the one whom we have come to honor."

Everyone appreciated the fact that Heman sang once more, but the people were not really caught up by psalm.

At this point, father and Abiathar brought David to the center of the threshing floor. The elders of Judah joined them, and together they anointed David with these words: "David Ben-Jesse, you have been anointed, and now you are King David of Judah!"

The horn sounded, and all of the people shouted, "Long live King David!"

"Well, it is over," said Jonathan. "I did not think I would like it, but I did. What made it a good experience for me was the participation of the audience. Now a scribe would be interested in the birth of Perez and Zerah, because in that way the line is continued which leads to David. But the people were not interested in such a thing. I'm going to remember that the people want drama."

I said, "I liked it too, and I'm glad we enjoyed it together."

"Yes and that goes for me as well."

"But I said it first."

"That you did."

We remained in the same place after the ceremony, and father spotted us. As he approached, he said, " 'O yes, we can rescue Gad from the crowd.' You two were in another world; I hope I don't need any help soon. I should tell you I'm going over to Sheva's place for a while. Jonathan, I take it you can get 'my-little-bow' home."

"That I will, my brave friend."

Father turned away before I could respond, but I said to Jonathan, "This day is getting better all the time. But perhaps you want to see some of your family and friends from Bethlehem? If so, I can find my way home."

"I don't want to see anyone from Bethlehem."

"Perhaps there is some pretty girl who would like to see you?"

"Now, you're teasing. But, let me say it, there is no pretty girl from Bethlehem; the only pretty girl I know is one who is called Keziah. Say, have I told you about the meaning of Keziah?"

I made no comment, but I did take his hand as he helped me to my feet, and we left the tombs and the people, hand in hand.

10

An Afternoon Alone

AT FIRST, WE WALKED in silence. I was the one to break that silence. "Since the coronation is over, does that mean things will slack off just a bit for you?"

"I'm afraid it will be worse. There are so many things we need to catch up; but tomorrow, we have to start writing letters to all of the major city-states. David wants them all to know about his coronation. But, this afternoon is not for such business. The other morning at breakfast, you were just about to tell me some things about yourself, and then Gad walked into the room. I would like to hear some of those things."

"I'm not so sure I was going to tell you anything. In fact, it was good that my father did arrive. At that point, I did not know enough about you to say much. But now, I can tell you a few things. I'm an only child who misses her mother more than I can tell. I'm trying to make my father happy, but our life isn't easy without mother. You, Jonathan, have helped us both. The other night was the first time we have laughed together, since her death."

"It must be difficult for both of you, and I can wait to find out more about you. I'm certain the waiting will be worth it. However, I hope I can ask you questions from time to time."

"Of course you can, but for now let's go back to your office. I would like to see where you work."

"We'll do it." Jonathan responded with a big smile.

As we were walking towards the office, we passed Joab and several of his men. Joab said to me, "You're that pretty girl of Gad's. I saw you just the other day; I like what I see. Also, I can give you some advice. You may not know it, but you are walking with a scribe not a man. Jonathan may be my mother's uncle, but even that does not make him a man."

An Afternoon Alone

I did not respond, but Jonathan said, "Joab, your bad side is showing. You have always pushed people around. Perhaps, that's why you are the commander of the army, because I can't think of another good reason."

With that we walked on, and Joab seemed content with some well-chosen curses thrown at Jonathan. I said nothing until we were in Jonathan's office. Then I said, "I don't like that man. Now I understand why my father was upset the other night. I take it he doesn't like you?"

"He never has liked me, but he has never just come out and said so. He wanted to put me down in front of you. You're the one he likes. We'll have to find a way to keep him from bothering you. I expect a person like Joab to make fun of anyone who is a scribe. For him all scribes are the same; they are weaklings who fear God and man. The truth is that there are many scribes who fit such a description. I should tell you that I have real problems with such scribes, and among the scribes, I am usually classed with the minority; I seem to always take the unpopular opinion. Someday, I'll write a long poem or book on this. I will call it *The Minority Report*."

"Well, thanks for taking over back there, and let's forget Joab. This is our afternoon, and I want to see what you do."

Jonathan showed me his office; we went to the library, and we looked at some documents. It was at that point I asked him how and when he had decided to become a scribe. Father had told me some about this, but I wanted to hear about it in Jonathan's own words.

"David and I were taught at an early age to read and to write. In addition we were both poets and musicians, but we could not pursue such things all the time. We had to learn how to take care of ourselves and how to care for our family's flocks. So we spent a lot of time in the Judean desert. Eventually, others would be brought in to take over. This happened when David left to serve Saul, and I also made a change.

"I told Gad I had a friend in Jerusalem whom I visited at least once a month. On one such visit, my friend, Zadok, introduced me to Ahban, a fine teacher and a sage. In the evening Ahban gave a lecture on scribal schools in Egypt. He read from a document that we refer to as *The Satire of the Trades*. The author had something bad to say about every occupation, and he concluded that 'there is no profession without a boss, except for the scribe; he is the boss.' Everyone enjoyed the satire. I was well on my way to becoming a scribe at this time, but I credit Ahban's lecture as being the pivotal moment when I became certain of what I wanted to do. It was not just the satire that did it. For me the most important consideration was my interest in the big scene. That such satire existed was new to me. I liked the cosmopolitan atmosphere of the schools. Scribes were able to read literature from around the Mediterranean world, and it was all interesting. I was curious about what others thought and how past and present thought helps to determine the future. It was like living on the edge; not the edge of a ravine but the edge between the present and the future."

"Living on the edge could be dangerous."

"Yes."

Then I asked, "Could you teach me to read? I'm not interested in becoming a scribe, even if that were possible, but I would like to read and perhaps be able to write."

"I would like to teach you to read. Let's sit down at my desk, and we'll have the first lesson."

"I didn't mean that we had to start right now."

"The first lesson will be very short, and after that we'll still have time to do some other things. The first thing for you to do is to learn the alphabet. So, I will write it out on this shard. Which reminds me, if you break a pot, save the pieces for writing, because you will want to practice writing the alphabet. Here is some ink and a brush, and here we go. The first letter is *'aleph*. As you know this means 'an ox.' The form of this first letter actually looks like an ox, if you just turn it upright. The next letter is *bet*. This of course means 'house.'"

Jonathan went through the twenty-two letters of the alphabet with me, and as a result I had my own copy. I said, "Now, if I can just remember their names and sounds."

"You'll remember, because we'll start using them. Since you know the language, it will not be difficult. So, what else do you need?"

"I need to thank you. You're so willing to help me. I too am a bit different, at least from the other girls I know. Perhaps you can put me in your *Minority Report*. Most of the other girls already have babies. But, I have memories, and I have my father. For me, life is interesting, because I am very curious. Thanks."

With that I gave Jonathan a fleeting kiss on the cheek. He wanted more, but said, "You've helped me in this lonely place. I hope that as your teacher I'll help your curiosity, but I would like to be more than your teacher."

An Afternoon Alone

"You are more than my teacher. I just need some time, and you will have to figure out how to string this 'bow' with your string."

"So, the fun continues. I'll go along with that; I'll practice my archery."

"By the way, Jonathan, what does your name mean?"

"I really hate to tell you."

"Please!"

"Well *Jo-* is a short form of Yahweh, and you know that *nathan* means 'to give.' So, this really means that I am Yahweh's gift to the likes of you." Jonathan pretended to duck as if I was going to throw the shard at him, but instead I gave him another fleeting kiss on the other cheek. This time I wanted more.

"So now, Mr. Scribe, please take me home, and we'll have something to eat."

"That's a good idea, because I forgot about eating at David's table. I should have gone there about an hour ago. I hope he doesn't care, but with all of the extra people, he probably won't notice that I'm not there. Also, even if I had remembered about David's table, I would not have missed this last hour for anything on his table or anyone around his table."

We left the office hand in hand, and we enjoyed our walk. When we arrived at the house, I prepared some food. We didn't know when father would be coming home, so we started our meal. Both of us were hungry. It had been a long day.

Jonathan said, "How old are you? I'm twenty-seven."

"You're not only a scribe, but you're an old man! I'm only twenty."

Jonathan shook his head, "Twenty years old and no babies."

Just then father came home. I started to set a place for him, but he said, "Thanks, but I can't eat anything. At Sheva's we ate all afternoon not to mention the wine. Did you have a good time?"

"Yes. Jonathan is going to teach me to read and write. I now have a copy of the alphabet."

"Jonathan that may be a dangerous move, not only for you but for Keziah. It is well known that the gift of writing destroys the memory, but you probably don't remember that."

"Remember what?"

I said, "Father, don't give him a bad time, because he's been helpful. He even told me that his name meant, 'God's gift to women' or something like that."

"And I was just beginning to trust him," said father.

"You can trust me," said Jonathan. "You are Gad; you are fortunate."

Father just had to say it. "The question is, am I fortunate or are the two of you fortunate?"

And we said in one voice, "We are the fortunate ones."

"Allow me to change the subject," said Jonathan. "Did Sheva like the coronation?"

"Yes. He liked it, and he said that David liked it as well. But, Sheva thinks we can do better. He was interested in the way the people took to Heman, and said we need to use him a lot more."

"I agree."

"Also, Sheva said that his scribes had to start writing letters in the morning. Sheva will get a list from David."

"That's right, and I should get some sleep. I will say thanks to Keziah for a wonderful afternoon and for this good food, and to you Sir for helping me to remember that I've work to do in the morning. *Laylah tov*!"

I followed Jonathan out of the house. I said, "*Todah*, thanks so much."

Then we kissed, and he said, "*Laylah tov*," and departed. That was our first real kiss. It was wonderful, and I'll never forget it.

11

Civil War

WE HAVE A SONG that goes, "*Hinneh mah-tov umah-na'im shevet 'ahiym gam yahad* (Oh how good and how pleasant [it is when] brothers dwell in unity" [Psalm 133:1]). But this was far from our situation. What was the cause of this horrible war between the house of Saul and the house of David? As I have said earlier in my story, Saul forced David to go into exile. That was one cause of our problem. Of course it did not help when David, as a Philistine vassal, became king of Judah. This was a real break; Judah, the South, seceded from Israel, the North. To Philistines ears, this was good news, because it meant that the House of Saul and the House of David would be at war for a long time. This allowed the Philistines to have a free hand in the area; they would certainly not be bothered along the coastal plain in any way.

Abner, son of Ner, Saul's army commander, had set up Ish-baal, son of Saul, as King over Israel. So, when war broke out, it was Abner against Joab, David's commander. In one of the battles between these two and their armies, Abner killed Asahel, the brother of Joab. He tried to avoid this killing, but he could not. Joab would never forget this.

David was engaged in this war with Israel, but he was also busy on the political front. I believe he wanted to end the war and unite the country. As I have told you earlier, David wrote a letter to the men of Jabesh-gilead shortly before his coronation to win them to his side; but he wrote to many other groups in the north in an attempt to win their support. Also, David added more wives to his harem, and at least one of these marriages was important politically. The woman was Maacah, the mother of Absalom, and she was the daughter of King Talmai of Geshur. All of these efforts were important, but it was Abner, who ended up helping David to win Israel.

The Jerusalem Academy

During all of this turmoil Jonathan and the other scribes had been working hard. They were still writing letters to the neighboring city-states and telling them that David was now the king of Judah. Sheva asked my father to talk with the scribes concerning this civil war. We all went to Sheva's house one evening for dinner, and I helped Sarah, Sheva's wife, with the preparations. I must say that the three younger scribes enjoyed that dinner. It was as if they hadn't had a good meal for some time. After dinner, we all listened with interest to father's talk. He expressed his own sorrow concerning our civil war, but he went into more detail than I have given you; he explained how and why Abner helped David.

Father said, "Abner took a liking to one of Saul's concubines by the name of Rizpah. As you know, if a person takes a wife or a concubine of a king, this act is more than adultery. It is an act of rebellion. Such a person by this act takes the place of the king. Abner took Rizpah, and he went in to her. Ish-baal accused Abner of rebellion. He said to Abner, 'You want to rule on my father's throne.' This made Abner angry, and he said, 'Am I a dog's head from Judah? I have been loyal to you and the house of your father; I have not given you over into the hands of David. Yet you reproach me over a woman. I swear to God that I will do for David what Yahweh promised David; I will help to move the kingship from the House of Saul and to establish the throne of David over Israel and Judah from Dan to Beer-sheba.'

"It is possible that Abner flew off the handle when Ish-baal got after him, but Abner could have taken Saul's concubine so that Ish-baal would get mad. In other words, Abner might have wanted out. In any case, Abner immediately approached David, and he told him that he would help him bring all of Israel over to his side. David was glad to hear this, but he asked Abner to bring Michal, Saul's daughter, whom Saul had given to David for his wife, to Hebron. David wanted her back, and Abner agreed to get her. Then Abner proceeded to win over Israel to David, and he may have expected to be put in command of David's army. Abner convinced Israel to follow David, and he brought the good news to David in Hebron. In fact, David had a big party for Abner and his men.

"When Joab heard about this he was angry. In fact, he lost his temper with David. He said, 'David what have you done? Don't you know that Abner just came here to spy on you? Why did you let him go?' Joab left at once to catch Abner. His men found Abner, and they brought him to Joab. Joab took Abner aside to talk with him, and promptly put a knife in his belly. Joab claimed that he killed Abner for the murder of Asahel, his brother. But that was only an excuse. Joab was worried about his job as commander of David's army.

"When David heard about the death of Abner, he was upset. Abner had arranged the transfer of the kingdom of Israel to him, and now this could be reversed if Israel thought that David had arranged the murder of Abner. David claimed before Yahweh that he was innocent in this matter. Then David forced Joab and all of his troops to participate in the funeral of Abner who was buried in Hebron, as you all know. All of you were at Abner's funeral, and you saw David weeping before Abner's grave. What you might not know is that Jonathan, your new colleague, wrote the dirge that David lifted up before Abner:

> Did Abner die a felon's death?
> Your hands were not bound with cords;
> your feet were not locked in bronze.
> You fell as one who falls down
> when facing treacherous men. (2 Samuel 3:33–34)

"After this, most of the troops believed that David was innocent, and again he came down hard on Joab. He said that the sons of Zeruiah, Joab and Abishai, were too savage. David admitted that they made him weak. When Ish-baal heard of Abner's death, he was afraid. How could he hold on to his father's kingdom? What should he do? As it turns out he did not have to answer these questions. Not long after the death of Abner, Rechab and Baanah murdered Ish-baal. They brought Ish-baal's head to David, and David rewarded them in the same way that he rewarded the man in Ziklag who told him about the death of Saul. They were killed and hung up for the birds. The head of Ish-baal was buried in Abner's grave.

"David wondered what would happen now that both Abner and Ish-baal were dead, but he did not have to wait long. All the elders of Israel came to David in Hebron. They said to him, 'We are your bone and your flesh, and long ago, Yahweh said to you, "You shall shepherd my people Israel, and you shall be a leader over Israel." We want you to be our king.' David said, 'I will be your king and we will make a covenant together. But we need to plan and write up the pact and have a coronation. We will have it here in Hebron in just a few weeks.'"

Then father said by way of conclusion, "All of this means that you will soon be preparing for another coronation. Also, this situation may cause you some problems as you copy documents and write your letters. We must all be sensitive to our terminology. At the present time David is King of Judah. We know that Judah broke away from Israel, which was ruled by the House of Saul. During this next coronation when we speak of Israel, we will not be just talking about the north. True, that Israel will be making a covenant with David, but as a result of David's dual kingship a united Israel will be born. After the coronation when we say Israel it will refer to a united kingdom—the north and the south.

"Now I want to add a personal note. David has asked me to spend the next week traveling in the north. He wants to know how the people feel about a Davidic administration up there. My daughter Keziah will be going with me. Our visit will be less than official. We hope to enjoy ourselves and listen to the people."

After father's talk there were questions and more wine. Jonathan came over to me and said, "I did not know that you would be gone. I'm going to miss you."

Jonathan walked with father and me back to the house. Jonathan thanked father for the talk, and father went inside. Jonathan and I had a long good-bye.

12

Gad and Keziah Return

According to what Jonathan told me when I got home, Sheva called a meeting of his staff the next day after we left. He said, "It was good to have you at the house last evening. In light of what Gad told us, we have a lot to do in the near future. We are fortunate that we have just been through a coronation, and many things will be the same. But we have to make some changes, and there are several things that have to be added to the program. This means that we will have to do the following:

1) Stop all work we are doing on other projects.
2) Start sending out invitations for this second coronation.
3) Write up a new coronation program.
4) Write a covenant, which will be made between David and the present Israel.

"This will change and delay our work. Jonathan will not be able to collect *These are the Stories of Perez*, and the library work will have to stop. I'll try to keep some notes for our chronicles, but everything else will have to stop. Perhaps we'll get some more help out of all this. One of the biggest jobs for us will be writing a covenant. We will not start on this today, but I want you here early tomorrow morning, and we will make the assignments."

After Sheva's talk, Jonathan sat in Sheva's office waiting for the others to leave. Then he said, "We must have more help."

"That's right, Jonathan, and we will have it. We will have to get some scribes from Shechem who know our northern traditions. But, we are going to have a rough time at first, because David keeps talking like we'll not be in Hebron much longer. What does that mean? Do we pack or unpack? We have to get some information on his plans. Anything that you can find out would be appreciated."

"That reminds me. I should get over to David's table right now. See you in the morning."

Jonathan hurried over to David's quarters. In the dinning area, things were confused. There were more people than usual, and the news of another coronation was the main topic of conversation. There were so many questions. What does all this mean for the administration? Everyone who worked for David could multiply the questions of Jonathan and Sheva. A small kingdom was about to become much greater and more complex. There would be new people and new ways of doing things.

Jonathan said that David was in a good mood. Just before they were ready to eat, David came over to Jonathan and said, "I hear you have been busy. We will try to get more help for you. I was talking with Sheva yesterday, and we discussed some of the changes that will be necessary in this second coronation. I gave Sheva a new coronation psalm or in part a rewrite, and I told him to let you have a look at it."

"I'll be glad to look at it, and we do need more help. Also, we are cramped in our quarters, and that will become even more of a problem when we get our needed help."

"We'll have to think about moving in the near future."

Just then the meal got underway, so David turned to other matters. Jonathan did not have a chance to ask what David meant by the word "moving." Soon, Jonathan was finished. As Jonathan was leaving David's quarters, he thought, "Moving in the near future is a thought that is too vague to be of much help. Sheva has heard things like that before. I'll have to try again to get some information about this moving business."

Jonathan had only walked a few minutes, and he heard a familiar voice calling his name from the other side of the street. It was father. Jonathan ran toward him, and they embraced.

Jonathan said, "You're back. I'm so glad to see you."

"Naturally, you're glad to see me, because that means you can see Keziah. Right?"

"Half-right. I need to talk to you as well."

"I came here to find you, so let's go to the house. Keziah will be pleased."

They were soon here, and I ran and threw my arms around Jonathan. I kissed him, and said, "I missed you."

"I missed you too."

Gad and Keziah Return

Father said, "Come on now. We were only gone a few days. That's nothing between friends."

"That's right, my friend, and that's why I didn't kiss you back there on the street. But Keziah, she's something else!"

Father smiled, "Isn't she. Jonathan, we know you have just had a big meal, but sit down here at the table, and we can catch up on a few things."

I poured three cups of wine, and we all sat down. But things were different; this time I sat next to Jonathan.

Jonathan said, "Where did you go, and what did you do?"

Father answered, "We went to several northern cities, including Shechem. It was a good experience. David sent us to find out how the people were feeling about all the recent developments. They remember David, and they see him as their only hope. Actually, Abner did a remarkable job of bringing the northern people over to David. I'm glad that he did, and by the way, no one really thinks that David was behind the murder of Abner. David had too much to lose. Only Joab stood to gain with Abner out of the way."

"Since you have mentioned Joab, is there anything that can be done to get him out of our lives?"

"Well, Jonathan, I heard that you told him a thing or two. That was good, but I hope this will take care of itself. When the Philistines find out that David will become king of both the present Israel and Judah, they will wage war against this united Israel. It would be nice if some Philistine arrow found Joab's heart, but on second thought, he probably doesn't have one. At any rate, he may be too busy to bother us."

"I hope so. Now, back to your story. How did you find out what you wanted to know?"

"We did not announce ourselves in any way; we just listened without asking many questions. Also, we went to places where the conversation would naturally be about the things that we were interested in. It was interesting for us to see the grave of Joseph in Shechem. It was clear from talking to some of the minstrels that their funeral rituals were like the one we used here for David's coronation. Also, they used *These are the Stories of Joseph* in much the same way as we used *These are the Stories of Judah*. We had a good time, and the information which we have will please David."

"I wish I knew just what David was planning to do, because when we complain about our quarters, he brings up the subject of moving. This makes us a bit uneasy. But what did your helper do on the trip?"

"I enjoyed the trip as well. I had never seen the northern cities, and Shechem was best. I also enjoyed the food, and I didn't have to cook."

Father said, "Keziah was helpful. People talked with me, because she was there."

"I'm not sure about that, but when we were not busy, I always had my alphabet in my pocket. I think I know it. I'm ready for lesson number two."

"You'll get lesson number two before I leave tonight, if you will give me one or two of those olives."

"Here, take the bowl."

"*Todah.*"

Then father said, "I am going to get some sleep in my own bed. The two of you can eat your olives and recite the alphabet, but I'm tired."

I hugged father and Jonathan said, "*Laylah tov.*"

After father left, Jonathan watched me write the alphabet. He said that I did it well. Then, he asked me to recite it. He corrected my pronunciation on a couple of the letters, and said, "That's good. Now, we will see if you can read. We usually call our language 'Judean,' but we may have to change that term in light of our new united Israel. The languages of our neighbors are also written with the alphabet that you have learned, but the reader must add vowel sounds in order to pronounce the words. This method saves on ink. Let's write Gad's name. We only write 'g' and 'd.' You have to supply the 'a' sound when you read the name, so, we write 'Gd,' and we read or pronounce 'Gad.' I'll write David's name. I write 'Dvd,' and you read 'David.' This means that you must know how to pronounce the words that are written, and the context will usually make it clear for anyone who knows the language."

"I think I understand, but it doesn't seem easy."

"I'm going to write two short lines for you. You work on them, and next time, I will give you something more difficult."

Jonathan started writing:

"Kzh mns 'bw' nd Jnthn mns 'th gft f Yhwh.'
Jnthn s n lv wth Kzh, nd h nds nthr kss."

But, when he finished the second line, I stopped him and said, "I think I understand the system. Tomorrow evening, bring me one of your

Gad and Keziah Return

poems to read; I can tell you now what you have written, and you made one mistake. The last phrase should be written: 'nd h wnts nthr kss.' Correct?"

With that, I was in his arms, and I said, "I can't believe that I have found someone to love; I did not think it would ever be."

He said between kisses, "I missed you so much."

13

Another Coronation and the Mystery of Zion

WHEN YOU GET BACK from a trip there is a mountain of work to do. Unpacking and getting the household to function again was as difficult as packing and leaving. Where to begin? The yogurt had to be started, and I needed to bake bread before the day got too hot. After that I went to the market for more olives and cheese.

When father got up, we ate a quick breakfast, and he said, "I think David will be pleased with my report."

"He should be. While you are at David's quarters please order olive oil, flour, wine, and salt. We are getting low on most everything."

"I'll do it."

By the evening meal, things in the house were almost back to normal. Father and I were just finishing our meal when I heard Jonathan arrive. I hurried down the ladder, and he picked me up and swung me around. "Last night, when I went back to the office, I could not stop thinking of how you cut short our reading lesson."

"Umm. Just kiss me, and we'll go up to the table. Father is still there, and you can have some of my fresh bread."

"Greetings," father said. "You'll be happy to know David was pleased with our efforts on the trip, and of course he was glad the people in the northern cities seem to welcome his rule."

I added, "And I'm pleased with my efforts; I worked hard all day on this house."

"Yes she did," father said. "Even though you have just eaten, I must say that Keziah's fresh bread is really good."

"I wouldn't miss it."

He took a bite and thanked God for bread makers, and said, "This is so good."

Another Coronation and the Mystery of Zion

Then I said, "Jonathan, what did Sheva have his scribes doing today?"

"Sheva asked Elimelech, Danel, and Noah to start writing invitations to our next coronation but not to bother with the Philistines, because they will find out soon enough that David is no longer their loyal servant. He asked me to design a new program. Sheva is still interested in a seven-day ritual, and he wants to know if it is possible. I listed the events in the program for a one-day ceremony and for a seven-day ceremony. But I did not like the longer one. So instead of working on it any more, I read David's psalm. It is better than his first one, which was awful. I want to read it for you."

"Before you do, let me say that I do not want a seven-day coronation," father said. "Go for one. We have enough of those seven-day rituals."

"I'll turn in your vote to Sheva. What do you think Keziah? One or seven? With seven you get more stories of the fathers and remember, Heman knows how to make them come alive."

"I vote for one day. Seven would be too much of Heman and not enough time around this table."

"I'll give Sheva your votes in the morning. He is the only one who wants seven days.

"But don't tell him our votes are only two," I said.

Then Jonathan read the psalm:

> Why do, the city-states join forces,
> and the peoples number their troops,
> [the] kings of [the] earth take their stand,
> and rulers unite together
> against Yahweh and against his anointed?
> "Let us break their bonds,
> and let us throw off their shackles!"
>
> From the heavens, he who is enthroned laughs.
> Yahweh ridicules them.
> Then he threatens them in his anger,
> and in his burning anger he terrifies them.
>
> But I, yes I, have been anointed his king,
> on Zion, his holy mountain.
> Let me recite the decree of Yahweh.
> He said to me: "You are my son.

The Jerusalem Academy

> This day, I have fathered you.
> Ask of me, and I will give
> the city-states as your inheritance,
> your estate, [to the] ends of [the] earth.
> You will smash them with an iron mace;
> like a potter's pot, you will shatter them."
>
> And now O kings be prudent;
> be disciplined O rulers of [the] earth.
> Serve Yahweh with fear;
> rejoice with trembling,
> O men of the grave,
> lest he grow angry; and [then]
> you will perish en route,
> for his anger flashes over the smallest thing.
> Happy are all who trust in him. (Psalm 2)

"David has given this psalm some thought, and he knows that the Philistines are going to be angry," Jonathan said. "But what is the meaning of 'But I, yes I, have been anointed his king, / on Zion, his holy mountain?' That's strange. I only know of one hill or fortified area called 'Zion,' and it isn't much of a hill, certainly not a mountain. It is the fortified area of Jerusalem. Perhaps, it could be a symbolic mountain? But even though David will become king of Israel in Hebron, he wants to say it is happening on Zion. Why? Because David intends to make Jerusalem, or Zion, his royal city! How is that for a theory?"

"It makes sense," father answered. "If you're right, it means that you and the scribes will have to struggle along in your cramped quarters until such a move is made. I can't see moving now to a larger place in Hebron and then moving later as well. You could be right about Jerusalem, a neutral city as the center of the new Israel. I am certain that the elders of Israel do not particularly like to come here at the center of Judah for this coronation of David."

"If Jerusalem does become the royal city what does that means for us?" I asked. "I mean the three of us."

Father said, "It means that we would all three end up in Jerusalem."

"Which means," I said, "that I am not going to spend a lot of time trying to fix up this house. I can understand how the scribes feel about their place."

Another Coronation and the Mystery of Zion

"But if I am wrong," Jonathan said, "you will end up a little behind."

"Perhaps, but if that happens, you will just have to help me catch up. Would Jerusalem be a good place for you to work?"

Jonathan nodded, "I was telling Gad there is a good school there. It will be interesting to see if the scribal school in Jerusalem could become a part of our operation. The city is old and interesting, and the climate is as good as Hebron. Yes, it would be a good place for us."

Father added, "I would like it. I could work anywhere, but Jerusalem would make things better. Foreign diplomats know Jerusalem; they have no knowledge of Hebron."

He got up and patted my head. "Well I'm going to bed. *Laylah tov!*"

We put the food away, and I brought out a large pillow for us to sit on and poured a little more wine. "I'm sorry I didn't bring a poem for you to read," Jonathan said, "but I will leave this psalm for you."

We both took a sip of wine, and he put his arm around me. "I think about you all the time," he said. "I'm in love, and I feel like I am going out of my mind."

"I know, Jonathan. I know how you feel, because I feel the same way."

"Keziah, I want you to be my wife. For some, that does not mean too much. David takes wife after wife, but for me it means everything. The scribes have a proverb that goes something like this: 'Find joy in the wife of your youth; let her breasts satisfy you at all times.' This is the way I feel about you."

"I will be 'the wife of your youth.' I like what you said, but there is father. You know that I could not think of leaving him, which is the custom among our people."

"I wouldn't want you to leave him. The three of us have had a lot of fun together, and that's the way it will always be. If we get married soon, and if Gad approves, I could move in here, or if we wait until we move to Jerusalem, assuming that I'm right, we can all three find a place there. But I must say that I can't wait long."

"Neither can I. Father will be happy. You'll see. Yes, we can be married in Hebron, but we really know that Hebron is Zion!" I smiled.

"I love you, because you make me smile. We should talk to Gad about this tomorrow."

"Yes. I'll talk to him in the morning.

The Jerusalem Academy

I asked Jonathan if I could have the last word of the evening, and he agreed. "Remember, you can't say a thing after I say that I loved you first, and father was right, that arrow went right to your heart."

He did not say another word, but I know he could feel my heart beating next to his.

14

The Making of the Covenant

AGAIN JONATHAN AND MY father had to help me with this section, and I obtained a copy of the covenant from the library at the school.

The next day Jonathan read the one-day program to Sheva and the other scribes:

1) The Procession
2) *These are the Stories of Jacob* Sung by?
   These are the Stories of Judah Sung by Heman
3) The Funeral Ritual (with several changes, Joseph and sons should be included)
4) The Crown and the Decree (another addition)
5) Anointing (Gad, Abiathar, and the Elders of Israel)
6) The Blowing of the Horn and the Shout of the People. ("Long live the King!")
7) The Covenant (another addition)
8) The Coronation Psalm

"Do you have anyone in mind to sing *These are the Stories of Jacob*?" asked Danel.

"I would like Heman to do it, because the people like him. However, we want to involve the north in this, which means they should provide one of their minstrels. Gad was in Shechem recently, and he heard some of their singers. We might ask him about this."

Sheva said, "Ask him, and we should line up the best."

"What is the new part that you called 'The Crown and the Decree'?" asked Elimelech

"I thought we needed a time to place the royal crown on David. At that point the decree, which says that David is Yahweh's son and in which David talks about in his new coronation psalm, should be given to David by Abiathar."

The Jerusalem Academy

Sheva said, "It sounds good, but what about the seven day plan?"

"I have it here, and I can read it. But first, I would like to make a few comments. I have discussed this plan with friends, and they don't like it. 'It's just too long' is the main comment."

"But you have to remember that we are not doing this just for friends," said Sheva.

"I am aware of that. I wanted to add that what you gain is all the *Stories of the Fathers*, and each day the funeral ritual is repeated (if that is a gain?). Finally, on the last day we have:

These are the Stories of Judah (about Perez)
The Funeral Ritual
Plus: The Crown and The Decree
The Anointing
The Horn and the Shout of the People
The Covenant
The Coronation Psalm
A Seventh Day

We have in our traditions a lot of seven-day rituals, and it may be the proper thing to do, but there are too many problems connected with it."

"What kind of problems?" Sheva asked.

"Where will all these people stay for seven days?" It might work if the main guests came for the last day."

"Damn," Sheva said.

It was clear that Sheva was still interested in the seven-day plan, and he would have pushed it, if they had a better royal center and if they could house at least some of the guests. The rest went for the one-day plan.

Sheva said, "I am not happy about this, but I had better go along with the rest of you on the one-day plan. So, I must tell you that I had a difficult time coming up with this covenant. In part, neither David nor the elders of Israel seem willing to put into the covenant any exact stipulations that would make everything in the relationship clear-cut. So, on the basis of traditional covenants and of our history together, I came up with the following:

The Covenant

Proclaimed and Enacted by Abiathar, the Priest

Years ago Samuel anointed David. Yahweh has said that David should shepherd his people and rule his people. In addition, Israel has said to

The Making of the Covenant

David, "We are your own bone and your own flesh. You have led us in time of war, and Saul's son, Jonathan, gave you his royal robe, thus giving you his place as heir apparent." Therefore, the elders of Israel have come to Hebron to anoint David to be their king and to enact this covenant.

This day, Yahweh has issued his decree concerning David. In that decree, Yahweh has announced that David is his son. This decree and testimony is in fact a covenant between Yahweh and David. Yahweh has sworn that the House of David will continue. Yahweh has said to David, "If your sons keep my covenant and my stipulations, they will sit upon your throne."

Also on this day, we establish a covenant before Yahweh between David and the people of Israel. From this day, David is to be your shepherd, your leader, and your king, and you the people will help to establish this state and secure its borders.

In addition, Yahweh renews his ancient covenant with this union of David and the people. Yahweh says, "I hereby renew the second covenant that I made with Moses and the people, and I will drive out before you the Amorites, the Canaanites, the Hittites, the Perizzites, and the Jebusites. Your friends will be my friends, and your enemies will be my enemies. Do not make covenants with the inhabitants of the land, and do not worship their gods. You are to keep the major feasts and the Sabbath. Write down these stipulations upon which this covenant, between me and the union of David and the people, is based."

And now, may Heaven and Earth witness these covenants, and may Yahweh watch between David and Israel.

"This is the best that I can do without more input from David or the elders."

Jonathan said, "It works well with the new section in the program on 'the Crown and the Decree,' about which you just asked me. I would like to ask another question, but I will need to look at your text in order to ask it. I can do that later."

"Right. So, I will see all of you tomorrow morning, if not before, and we will see what's left to do. Try to get the invitations out, and Jonathan you need to talk with Gad about those minstrels from Shechem."

As Jonathan was leaving, he asked Sheva to see the text of the covenant. Then he said to Sheva, "Perhaps you have noticed that in his new psalm David refers to Zion as the place of his anointing. I think David is planning a move to Zion, which is in Jerusalem. This old tradition concerning how Yahweh will drive out the inhabitants of the land, including the Jebusites, is great. If Yahweh would take care of the Jebusites, Zion would be ours!"

"I didn't make up that part of the promise, but if you are right about Jerusalem, and I hope you are, it is important to include it. I'm going to work on the expanded funeral ritual. See you later."

Jonathan went back to his office. He had only been there for a moment or two when father appeared at the door.

"Come on in and have a seat. Sheva just told me to check with you on a matter. But, we have other things that we need to discuss."

"Yes, we have other things. Keziah talked to me about your conversation last night. It was obvious to me that the two of you were in love. It was obvious, because it happened around our table. I'm glad that you were both open with your feelings for each other. It had to happen, because you have both resisted previous involvements for good reasons. You both had things to do when you were younger. Keziah wanted someone who could think, and there are not many who even know what that means. So, I want both of you to know that I'm happy. She also said you were both in a hurry, so I suppose we had better do something about this in the near future."

"Your words are helpful. Keziah said you would understand. Did she tell you that we wanted to live with you?"

"She told me. Right or wrong, it would have to be like that if it happens soon. As we discussed last night, we just might be moving to Jerusalem, so there is no need to make changes right now while things are still up in the air. I should tell you that as David's prophet, I sense he is about to put me out to pasture. I don't think such a thing would cause you any problems in terms of your relationship with David."

"I don't think so, and I really don't care."

Father put his hand on Jonathan's shoulder and said, "But you should care, because you want to continue your work. I know you want to have a school and a good place to work."

"You're right. I want those things, but I will not pay the price for them if the price is too high."

"There is a problem in all of this we need to address. I do not have a wife and Keziah does not have many female friends. Who are the women who will have a party for Keziah? They should have their party when the men are having their party. Keziah will want something small, but it still

The Making of the Covenant

has to be something. So, you should come over this evening, and we will make some plans."

"I knew there must be some reason for me to come over tonight."

"Also, come for dinner. You can explain to David there are some changes taking place. Now, what did Sheva want you to ask me?"

"He wanted some information on the minstrels whom you heard in Shechem when you were on your trip."

"Well, I'll just go to his office and tell him about that."

Father discussed his trip with Sheva and told him about the singers at Shechem. He was getting ready to leave, and he thought, "Perhaps Sheva's wife, Sarah, could help with the women's party?"

Then father said to Sheva, "As you know, I just talked with Jonathan, but we talked about more than singers. We also talked about his wedding plans."

"Wedding plans! I didn't know."

"Well, I didn't know until this morning, and my daughter, Keziah, and Jonathan did not know before last night. Things have been moving at a fast pace. But they have a lot of fun; they were meant for each other. Sheva, we have a problem in that Keziah's mother is gone, and we really don't have a place for a women's party. In fact, we don't have any women for the party."

"That is no problem," said Sheva. "My wife can have the party. You can ask them what they want, but the men could meet here at the office, and the women could meet at our house. As for the women, Elimelech, Danel, and Noah have girl friends; they would probably come to a wedding."

"Well, it should be a small group, and that might just do it. I'll talk to Keziah and Jonathan tonight, and you had better talk to Sarah. We will want to do this soon. I'll see you tomorrow."

After father left, Sheva went to Jonathan's office and said, "I just heard that you don't like sleeping in this office, and I thought perhaps you might sell that bag of wool. Some days I really need to take a nap."

"I guess I had better not sell the bag of wool. As you no doubt know, it was a gift," Jonathan said with a big smile.

"Gad told me about your plans. It was clear that he was happy, and it sounds like you and Keziah will be a good for each other. I understand that you will be making some wedding plans tonight. I told Gad my wife could help out with the women, and I would get the men together here at the office. Just let me know tomorrow morning."

"Yes, we will. I really thank you for your offer, and I'll let you know."

Jonathan tried to get back to work. He even thought of dividing the one-day program into seven sections, which could be called "days." He was trying to make Sheva feel better about the one-day program. But, nothing was really working, and he decided to quit early. He needed to go by David's quarters and tell him there would be some changes in the near future.

15

Wedding Plans

It was another busy day for me. I wanted to make our wedding plans over a good meal. I went to the market and got some nice lamb chops; the butcher always gives me the best he has. I came back to the house, and I started a fire in the pit on the ground floor near our main entrance. I was there when Jonathan arrived; once again he picked me up and was acting a bit silly. I said, "Did father see you today?"

"Yes he did, and he seemed happy about our plans. When he gets home, he will have some good news for you."

"What's the good news?"

"You'll have to wait for Gad. He'll want to tell you."

"That's not fair."

"Nothing is fair. Should I let you down now or after I kiss you?"

"After."

After he put me down, he said, "I was able to see David on my way over here. I reached David's quarters and went in the front door. I asked a guard if David was around. The guard just pointed me to the little office where I had earlier made a copy of David's first coronation psalm. David was there, and he was alone. We had a good conversation, and I'll repeat it. David said, 'You are here a bit early. Is there a problem?'

'There's no problem. But, I did want to tell you that Gad's daughter, Keziah, and I are getting married, and I will be moving in with them. This means I will want to take my evening meals with them.'

'I'm glad to hear that you have found a wife. When will you have the wedding?'

'I don't know when it will be, but it will be soon. I'm going over to Gad's place now, and we will try to work out the time.'

'Well, just let me know. I probably can't come to your wedding, because of this next coronation and about twenty other things. However,

I will want to send a gift for the procession, and I will send the wine for the men's party and the women's party. Also, I will have Gad's supplies increased, because you will be eating there.'

'*Todah*. Your help is important.'

'Jonathan, I will want to see you at least once a week, because I want you to do a few things for me after this coronation. So keep in touch and have a great wedding night.'"

"I left David wondering what David wanted me to do. I came directly here. You were already preparing the meal, and when I saw you I thought, 'She is beautiful tonight.'"

"So will you carry the meat up the ladder for you beautiful lady?"

"Yes."

When we got upstairs, I told Jonathan to sit down and I would join him in just a moment.

Just then father came home, and he was in a good mood. He said, "This is the perfect night to make some important plans, and I have some good news."

"I need your good news," I said.

"Well, you will be happy to know that Sheva is certain Sarah will be glad to be in charge of the women's party for your wedding. It can take place at their house while the men are meeting at the office. Jonathan works with three young men, Elimelech, Danel, and Noah, at the office, and Sheva thinks their girl friends would like to attend. So, it looks like there will be a party. Sheva will have the final word tomorrow, and we need to be able to say yes or no."

"It sounds like it just might work," I said. "I really don't want a lot of people. I just hope those girls really want to come."

"They will want to come," said Jonathan. "It's a good idea, because I would like for us to know the other scribes and their friends. In fact, I am sorry that I haven't spent more time with them. I can invite them tomorrow, if we agree on this."

"We agree, but I want both of you to sit down at this table."

We started eating, and Jonathan said to father, "I just told Keziah that I stopped by to see David, and I was lucky he was there. He was glad to hear of the wedding, and he said he would increase your rations, if I were going to move in here. Then David told me I should make certain that you gave me a marriage contract. He said the amount of the dowry should be specified in the contract. Also, Gad, you will need to list the woman who will bear children for us if Keziah is barren. The surrogate must be named in the contract."

"This man has gone mad," I said.

"Not at all," said Jonathan. "This is according to the traditions of our fathers. The surrogates were named in Jacob's marriage contracts."

With fire in my eyes, I said, "You had better be joking, because I'm not living in the past. As members of the minority, we will be living in the future. I come without dowry, and I'll have the babies, if there are babies."

"Gad, this daughter of yours just got you off the hook. No dowry! Also, it sounds like she is serious about this 'no surrogate' business."

"Jonathan, you should know by now that she is difficult at times."

"I'm not difficult. I'm starting new traditions."

"So much for David's advice," said Jonathan. "Guess I'll have to forget the contract."

"Good idea, but I will accept a love song for our wedding."

"I'll do it."

Then father laughed and said, "I'm glad that is all settled. Seriously, it's good to know that David will do something to make this work."

"Plus wine for the parties and a gift for the procession," said Jonathan.

Father said, "We need to plan this wedding procession. After the men have finished their party, Jonathan will come back here to the house. The rest of us will go to Sheva and Sarah's house, and the procession will start from there with the bride and her gifts. We can come directly to our house, or we can take a long route. Do you want it long or short?"

I said, "Short!"

"When we get to the house, we will leave the gifts and the bride at the door, and the two of you will have to figure out the rest."

"We can," we answered as one. "So, when can we do it? Tomorrow?"

"Not that soon."

Then I said, "It doesn't have to be tomorrow, but it should be within five days or the 'way of women' will be mine."

Father said, "I'll talk to Sheva tomorrow, and I'll tell him that you want it as soon as possible. It could happen in two or three days. It has to be before the coronation."

Jonathan said, "What time of the day will we start?"

Father replied, "We should start in the late afternoon. This means that we can bring your bride to you at dusk. Don't worry; you will have your wedding night to yourselves. I know a fellow who has an office and a woolsack. I can stay there for one night."

"It pays to have friends."

"Here, have some wine," I said.

The next morning father got up early. He called on Sheva at his home before he left for the office. Father greeted Sheva and Sarah, and he said, "Well, Sarah, did Sheva shock you with our news and our request?"

"Yes, but I like to do such things, and I am happy for Keziah."

Sheva added, "We have two requests. First, our daughter and her husband would like to attend, and if that is acceptable, we really have to do this tomorrow afternoon. Our daughter will be too busy the following day, and this coronation is coming fast."

"The answer is yes to both requests. Jonathan and Keziah will be happy to know that it will be tomorrow. I want to thank you both. I'm going back to the house to tell Keziah, and Sheva, can you tell Jonathan?"

"I'll tell him as soon as I get to the office."

With that, father was gone, and he came home and reported this to me. Needless to say, I was pleased, and I danced around father singing, "My wedding day is tomorrow."

When Sheva arrived for work he said to Jonathan, "I just talked with Gad, and we have set the time for the wedding; it will be tomorrow afternoon."

"That's great, but it means I will have to spend some time today getting ready, and I need to invite the others."

"Yes. In fact, you had better do that right now so that the girls can be told as well."

Jonathan went at once to the library, and everyone was there and working. He said to them, "Before the meeting this morning, I want to tell you that tomorrow afternoon I'm getting married. I would like for you and your girl friends to join us. The men will meet here and the women will go to Sheva and Sarah's house. If you want to come, one of you should inform the girls this morning, after our meeting. Will they want to come?"

Noah said, "There is no doubt in my mind; they will want to come. But, Jonathan, you will just put ideas in their heads by inviting them."

Danel said, "They'll enjoy the wedding, but you didn't even tell us about your bride."

"I'm sorry. My bride is Keziah. She is the daughter of Gad, the prophet. You have heard him speak, and he participated in the anointing of David in the last coronation."

"And she was with you at the last coronation," said Elimelech.

"That's right."

"She is a beautiful woman, and you are a lucky man."

"I'm lucky."

After the morning meeting, Jonathan thought, "I was going to work some more on the program, but I don't have time for that today. I have to work on Keziah's love song. If I finish it this afternoon, I can work on the program tomorrow morning."

He began to work on the song, but things just didn't come together. He read some wedding psalms, but they were all too traditional and usually for a king and his queen. Then he recalled some Egyptian love songs, and he thought, "They used the terms brother and sister for the lovers, but we do that as well in our love songs. These terms seem to be important. They indicate that lovers can be as bothers and sisters; they can be of the same bone and flesh. They can become one flesh, because they are of the same substance. These reflections are interesting, but I'm not getting anything written."

Finally, Jonathan started writing:

> For Keziah on Her Wedding Night
> Your heart has encompassed me,
> O my sister and my bride . . .

Jonathan worked on this until quite late. He decided that he would have to finish it in the morning. He left his office and walked by David's quarters in order to leave a message for David, which informed him that the wedding was being held tomorrow afternoon. Then he hurried to the house. Father and I were waiting for him when he arrived.

"Sorry. I'm late. I won't make a habit of this."

I gave him a kiss. Then father said, "Now get your wine, and I'll propose a toast:

> 'Eat, friends, drink,
> and become drunk with love.'" (Song of Songs 5:1b)

"We'll drink to that," we said.

Jonathan said, "It appears that Gad got a lot done today and even read a few love songs. Also, I had a good day and wrote a love song. What did you do Keziah?"

"Well, father came home in the morning to let me know about the plans for tomorrow, and I've been trying to get ready. But, I had to quit and get dinner. So where's the love song?"

"That you will get tomorrow night."

"Why is everything always tomorrow?"

"I don't know, but I do know tomorrow is an important day."

Father said to Jonathan, "Did your three friends want to come to the wedding?"

"Yes, and they said their girl friends would want to come. But to change the subject, I am so happy I am eating this meal with the two of you on this night. It is good for us to be together, and I was getting so disgusted with 'David's table.' The noise, the people, the clamoring for David's ear, the pretense, should I go on? It was everything that I dislike. This is where I need to be."

"But you probably had better food there," I said.

Without a moments thought, Jonathan said, "We have a few good proverbs and here is one:

> Better a meal of vegetables where there is love
> than a well-fed steer where there is hate. (Proverbs 15:17)

By the way, please pass the vegetables."

Father said, "Jonathan, what are you doing in the morning?"

"I'll put some finishing touches on my love song for Keziah, and I suppose I should help Sheva get things ready for the wedding."

"That's fine. I will help here at the house in the morning, so that Keziah has plenty of time to get ready. So, I will see you at the party. Right now, I'm going over to Sheva's place to see if I can help them."

"You may also see me when you get back from Sheva's. I don't want to leave my bride until you get back."

"Then I will try to get back soon."

After father had gone, Jonathan and I sat a while longer at the table.

Then we cleaned up the kitchen. While we were working at that, Jonathan asked me if I was still working on my reading. I said that I got better everyday. Then I said, "My reading is going to make my life worth living. I know we will have a wonderful life together, and I will be able to read what you write."

Wedding Plans

"And, you will be able to write. Someday, I want to teach you another alphabet. Then we can write to each other in our own language, and others will not be able to read what we write."

"That sounds mysterious."

"I don't mean to be mysterious, but it just may be useful sometime in the future."

Then I said, "Do you still want to get married tomorrow?"

"Of course. Are you having second thoughts?"

"No."

"In fact, I wish the wedding had been today, because I want to take you into your room and stay all night."

"You can if you want."

"I know, but everyone is going to a lot of trouble so that we can have this wedding. We have to wait until tomorrow at about this time."

After we finished the work, we sat down on some cushions. He held me close to him, and he said, "Tonight is the first time that I have seen your beautiful breasts. Your low-cut blouse frames a wonderful view when you're pouring the wine. Are you going to wear that tomorrow?"

"No. That view is only for you. Besides, I'm not pouring wine tomorrow."

"But you knew that you were pouring wine tonight, so you did plan to make it difficult for me on this last night before our wedding?"

"Of course I did, because I intend for you 'To find joy in the wife of your youth.'"

"I have found joy mixed with difficulty."

"Let's take a walk," I said. "Father will be here soon, and then you can go back to your office and dream."

"Good idea."

We went outside and started for the courtyard door. When we reached it, it opened from the outside. Father was back.

"I'm glad I went over there," said father. "They didn't really need me, but I was able to see all they were doing and thank them. I'll see both of you tomorrow. *Laylah tov!*"

We held each other and kissed. Jonathan said, "I must go. Tomorrow night, I'll string my bow; tomorrow night will be the best night of my life."

16

The Morning of the Wedding

It has been a long time since the morning of our wedding, but I can remember what I was doing. Jonathan has helped me with what he did on that morning, but he does not remember everything. Nevertheless the following is close to the facts.

Jonathan was able to work on the love song before the morning office meeting. He made a second copy for his office files, and he put the first copy in a small jar for me. After doing these things, he went to Sheva's office for the meeting. When Jonathan arrived, everyone was there, and the meeting started at once.

Sheva said, "We need to talk about several things. We will not get much done today, because we are all taking part in a wedding this afternoon. However, we need to make some plans for tomorrow. This means that we will not have a meeting tomorrow morning. We'll do tomorrow what we plan today. So this is what we need to do. Jonathan, if you are able to work in the morning (Sheva tried to keep a straight face), I would like for you to divide the one-day program into seven sections and label these sections as if they were each a ritual day. This means that *The Stories of the Fathers* will have to be limited. Tomorrow I want you to write up this new program, and Elimelech and Danel can help you come up with the limited parts of each story for the minstrels to sing. I will be working on a new form of the funeral ritual, because even though I started to do this several days ago, I was not able to finish it. Jonathan, I want you to remind me of some the changes that you think I should make. Noah, you can help me tomorrow, because we will need several copies of the new ritual.

"So, Jonathan, what were some of those changes that you were thinking about?"

"Since at this coronation, David will become the king of Israel, we will have to make certain that Israel's fathers are summoned. In addition, our purpose is to unite both Judah and Israel under King David, and we

The Morning of the Wedding

do not want to offend Israel in any way. This means that after Jacob is summoned, we will summon Jacob's twelve sons (of the twelve we only summoned Judah at our last coronation). Also, we will have to summon the sons of Joseph, Ephraim and Manasseh. In the second section of the ritual that begins 'O House of Jesse, weep,' we should include at least two lines for the House of Joseph. I think we had better mention Joseph in section three and four as well. But the real difficulty is the last section or the blessing. The fifth blessing reads: 'Shalom Hebron!' I know Israel is coming here to make David king, but we should not expect them to like Hebron. This should be changed to 'Shalom to David's royal city.' I don't remember anything else that we were going to change, but we should check all of this out with the minstrel from Shechem, who works with this kind of ritual at Joseph's grave. Gad told you about him, and then you wrote to him."

"Yes I did, and he'll be here in a couple of days. That is a good idea to have him check this out. I did not tell you, but he is also bringing a scribe with him who will have some texts about the fathers that you may want to use in your program. We are too busy. I forgot to tell you about that."

"This is good news," said Jonathan, "but we will still want to make most of our changes before these two see our program and ritual."

"That's right," responded Sheva, "and we also want to make certain our own attitudes are correct in all respects. We must not appear to them as narrow-minded pro-Judah scribes. From our first contacts with these colleagues, we want to start thinking as cosmopolitan scribes and speaking of Judah and Israel as two parts of the 'greater Israel.'

"One other thing should be mentioned in light of everything that has just been said. A few people in the north might think that Saul and Ish-baal, as recently departed kings, should be summoned in the funeral ritual. But, this would never work, and we need a tactful answer if we are asked about this. Our answer to this should contain at least two elements: first, king lists that are used in funeral rituals at coronations in most city-states do not include all the kings. There are many reasons for this, and most of them are political reasons. Second, in this case, Yahweh took the kingdom from Saul, and in this coronation Yahweh proclaims David as his son. Here we have the beginning of something new. It would not be appropriate for us to re-install Saul as a departed 'king' from a defunct line. This question may not come up, but if so I have just stated my position. So, do what you can today before the wedding, and then let's try to get these things finished by tomorrow."

As they were leaving Sheva's office, Jonathan said to Sheva, "I know that my wedding is slowing things down. I want to thank you once more, and I should help you get things ready for this afternoon if you need some help?"

"You can do one thing for me, and then you are free to do whatever will speed things up for tomorrow. Early this morning, David sent some men to my house with gifts and wine. At least half of the wine needs to be brought over here. Take Noah with you and get the wine."

It took Jonathan and Noah several trips to bring the wine to the library. While Jonathan was in the library he spoke to Elimelech and Danel. "I wanted to tell you that I will be here in the morning, but I will not be here early. I'm going to do some work now on the new program of seven ritual days, and the two of you could try to find some of the texts that we will need."

"I wondered if you would or could get here in the morning," Elimelech said with a big smile.

"I'll be here but not early," repeated Jonathan with a groan. "When Sheva said we were working that was bad news to me. At least we don't have a meeting."

"So, what texts are we talking about?" questioned Danel.

"*These are the Stories of Terah, Abraham, Isaac, Jacob and Joseph*. I already have on my desk *These are the Stories of Judah*, and we may not have anything on *These are the Stories of Joseph*, but I hope that the scribe from Shechem brings that text. Just see what we have, because we have to select passages from such texts."

Jonathan returned to his office. He got out the one-day program and the seven-day program. He had to study them to figure out the best way of having a one-day program with seven sections or days. He said to himself, "I remember that I thought of doing this seven-day ritual in one day, but I never followed through on it. This will not be too difficult, but it is going to be longer than the last coronation."

So, he began to put it together:

The Procession
These are the Stories of Terah (about Abraham)
These are the Stories of Abraham (about Isaac)
Day One

These are the Stories of Isaac (about Jacob)
A Second Day

These are the Stories of Jacob (about Joseph)
A Third Day

These are the Stories of Jacob (about Joseph)
A Fourth Day

These are the Stories of Judah (about Perez)
A Fifth Day

The Funeral Ritual
A Sixth Day

The Crown and the Decree
The Anointing
The Horn and the Shout of the People
The Covenant
The Coronation Psalm
A Seventh Day

It was not difficult to divide the one day into seven sections, but it was difficult to select only a small section from each of the stories for the minstrels to sing. Jonathan made selections from the things that he could remember, but he knew that he would have to look at the texts tomorrow if Elimelech and Danel could find them. If not, he would have to wait until the scribe from Shechem arrived. For his selections, Jonathan made the following list for the first five sections or ritual days:

Day One—The Testing of Abraham
Isaac's Marriage and His Sons
A Second Day—Jacob's Return to Bethel
A Third Day—Joseph, His Beginnings (?)
A Fourth Day—Joseph, His Final Days (?)
A Fifth Day—Judah and His Sons
(Genesis 22:1–19; 24:59–67; 25:19–34; 35:1–15;?; ?; 38:1–30)

Jonathan decided that he really needed the texts for the above list, and he went down the hall to the library to find Elimelech or Danel. They were both there. Jonathan said, "Have you found *These are the 'Stories of Abraham*? I really need to see in that text the part about Isaac's marriage."

"Marriage is what you're thinking today! Right?" said Danel. "But, I did see that text today."

They all started to look for it. In a moment they found it, and Jonathan was pleased to have it. He thanked them and said, "Are you finding any more of the texts that we will need?"

"We have found about half of them," said Elimelech. "If the scribe from Shechem doesn't have the ones that we are missing, we had better get some minstrels in here to sing some of these stories, and we'll make copies."

"Yes, we must do that," answered Jonathan.

He took the text back to his office, and he read until he had finished the story of Isaac's marriage. After reading about Isaac's marriage he thought, "This story about the marriage of Isaac is told in the form of a marriage. I would like to read this to the others at our party."

Meanwhile back at the house, father and I were busy. I wanted to have the house cleaned up for our wedding night, and I wanted some food to be ready for us. Father helped me with all of this. Then I needed to think about what I should wear.

I said to father, "I need to get my clothes ready. We were lucky that some of mother's clothes were not burned; they were in a sealed jar. I want to wear mother's linen shift and also the embroidered robe. I'll use another piece of linen I found for my headdress and veil. I do have a new pair of sandals."

Father and I got out the shift and the robe, and as we touched them we both began to weep. Father said, "If your mother were here she would be giving these to you. I wish she could be here. Also, I want to give you your mother's bracelets and earrings. She wore them for our wedding, and I know she would want you to have them."

"*Todah*," I said and gave him a kiss.

Back at the office, Jonathan decided that he would quit for the day. He was getting excited, and he couldn't really think well. He went to the library, and there he helped Sheva move some things around. They put the wine on a table as well as the food that Sheva had brought from home.

17

The Wedding

SHEVA AND JONATHAN WERE still busy when Elimelech, Danel, and Noah arrived. They had just taken their girl friends to Sheva and Sarah's house.

They were in a good mood, and they told Sheva that his son-in-law would be along in a few moments with Gad. He was waiting for father and me.

Before long, father and Sheva's son-in-law arrived at the office.

"I want all of you to meet Samuel, my son-in-law," said Sheva to the assembled friends in the library. "He married my daughter, Naomi, two years ago, and they still live in Ziklag."

"Where life is good," Samuel said with a laugh.

Sheva smiled and held up his hands. "Today we take time for the wedding of Jonathan and Keziah. Jonathan asked me if he could share something he found today. Why don't you do that now, Jonathan, before we eat and drink."

Jonathan stood before his friends. "Today I was reading from *These are the Stories of Abraham*. Perhaps you remember how Abraham sent his servant to Aram-naharaim, to the city of Nahor, in order to get a wife for Isaac. With God's help the servant selected Rebekah, who was born to Bethuel, son of Milcah, the wife of Nahor, the brother of Abraham. Rebekah's family hated to see her go to Canaan, but they sent her with Abraham's servant.

> They sent away their sister Rebekah, her nurse,
> the servant of Abraham, and his men.
> They blessed Rebekah; they said to her:
>> "Our sister, surely you are.
>> Be thousands and myriads.
>> Your descendants shall conquer,
>> [Conquer] the gates of their foes."

>
> Rebekah and her maids got ready; they rode on the camels.
> They followed after the man.
> The servant took Rebekah; he departed.
>
> Isaac had come to the entrance of Beer-lahai-roi;
> he was living in the land of the Negeb.
> Isaac went out to walk in the field toward evening;
> he lifted his eyes; he saw: there were camels coming.
> Rebekah lifted up her eyes; she saw Isaac.
> She jumped from the camel.
> She said to the servant:
> > "Who is the man out there,
> > who is walking in the field to meet us?"
> The servant said:
> > "He is my lord."
> She took the veil; she covered herself.
> The servant recounted to Isaac everything that he had done.
> Isaac brought her to the tent of Sarah, his mother.
> He took Rebekah; she became his wife.
> He loved her.
> Isaac was comforted after his mother's [death]. (Genesis 24:59–67)

"You may have noticed this before, but this story is told in the form of a wedding and is a wedding. At the beginning we have the blessing of the bride, which we do at the women's party. Then there is the procession, which was a real journey for Rebekah. Finally she puts on her veil, and Isaac receives her at the tent; the marriage is consummated within the tent. We are doing everything as they did, except we don't have a camel for Keziah, and I do not have a tent!"

"Somehow I don't see Keziah following after a servant to marry a man she'd never seen," said Sheva.

Father laughed, "Indeed not." He helped himself to wine. "Jonathan came for her himself. The food is good, the wine is excellent (thanks to King David), and this company of seven is tops."

"Jonathan can be thankful that he didn't have to work for seven years to earn Keziah like old Jacob when he worked for Rachel," said Noah. "However, Jonathan, I have heard that Gad is pretty sly. If I were you, I would check under the veil when your bride is delivered to you tonight.

The Wedding

Gad may be giving you Keziah's older sister. I'll bet they didn't tell you that there was an older sister."

"That's right. They didn't tell me, so I'll look under the veil for Gad's Leah. You'll all be at the house, and if you see me look under the veil and kiss her, you will know that indeed it is Keziah. Then I'll pick her up and carry her over the threshold, the place where the demons live, but she will be safe in my arms."

"And then what will you do?" asked Danel.

"I'll disappear from your view, and you will just have to guess."

The teasing and good wishes went on for some time with not a little wine. Finally, Sheva said, "We must give Jonathan our blessing and send him on his way."

With that, Jonathan left for our house, and the others followed Sheva to join our women's party.

When the men arrived, we were still partying. They all said I looked lovely in my wedding garments. I talked at length with Sarah's daughter, Naomi. I knew that she could be a real friend.

Sheva spoke up, "We had better get this procession underway. Poor Jonathan is probably wondering if we'll ever get there. Gad, you should lead your daughter."

"It will be my pleasure."

"The rest of us will follow, and each one of us will carry one wedding gift. Jonathan can pick up the rest of the gifts later. Because Jonathan just read for the men the story of Rebekah's wedding, I will repeat the blessing for Keziah that was used years ago for Rebekah.

> Our sister, surely you are.
> Be thousands and myriads.
> Your descendants shall conquer,
> [conquer] the gates of their foes.

"Sarah, you veil the bride, and we can leave."

With that, we left. Everyone was carrying gifts, and we were singing songs. It did not take too long, because we used the short route as I had requested. Jonathan came out to meet us. Each person put a gift at the door; then father, with tears in his eyes, brought me to Jonathan. Jonathan lifted my veil and kissed me.

Everyone else cheered, and shouted, "We have a new tradition!"

Then Jonathan picked me up and carried me over the threshold, and the friends departed.

From this point on, I remember every detail.

"This is the night we have been waiting for. You are so beautiful," said Jonathan.

"These clothes are nice for a wedding, but they are just too much for a wedding night. Right?"

"That's right."

"I'll go to the bedroom and get out of them. You come in when I call your name."

"You are making me wait again."

"Yes, but not for long."

I was just a little nervous, but mostly I was happy and eager.

Jonathan went to the table and poured just a bit of wine. It was only a few moments before I called his name. When he entered the room he saw my clothes folded neatly on a table. I was sitting on the other side of the bed with my back to him. He said, "Without clothes, you live up to your name, even from the back."

Jonathan quickly removed his robe and shirt. He did not fold them. He moved across the bed and gently held my shoulders. He kissed my neck and the side of my face. Only then did I turn slightly so that he could see my breasts. His hands could not resist. As he held them, he kissed my parted lips and my breasts. We said nothing. I was under him, and we were one. Jonathan had never expected such a moment, and I could not believe our passion. When we were finished, we lay in each other's arms, still together as one. Only then, did we speak words not well chosen or ordered, but full of love and pleasure.

After the second time, I said, "Where is my love song?"

"You wait right here."

Soon Jonathan was back. He held me and began to read:

For Keziah on Her Wedding Night
Your heart has encompassed me,
O my sister and my bride.
Your heart has encompassed me,
with one [flutter] of your eyes,
with one strand of your necklace

([one that lies on your left breast]).

How beautiful is your love,
O my sister [and] my bride.
Your love is better than wine,
And the fragrance of your oils
[Is better] than any spice.
Your lips drip honey, my bride.
Honey and milk are under your tongue,
and the fragrance of your robes
is like the scent of Lebanon.

A garden, which is locked up
is my sister [and] my bride.
A spring locked, a fountain sealed,
a garden spring [is my bride],
a well of living water.

I have come to my garden,
O my sister [and] my bride.
I've gathered my myrrh and spice;
I ate my honeycomb and honey;
I drank my wine and my milk;
[we were together as one.
Your heart has encompassed me,
O my sister and my bride.] (Song of Songs 4:9–12,15; 5:1a plus a few additions)

Jonathan put the small scroll with its ornate lettering back in the little jar and gave it to me. On the lid was inscribed, "For Keziah."

"That is a wonderful song, and it will give us the words to express our love for years to come," I said. "But before you visit your garden again, we should go to the table. As you may have noticed, there are some good things there, and I didn't eat much at the party; I was waiting to be with you."

"I'm willing to go to the table with you and taste the 'good things,' but I am certain the taste will be dull compared to the delicacies of my garden."

We slipped on our robes and ate and drank.

Jonathan said, "I can't take my eyes off the woman who is now my wife." After some time, Jonathan carried me back to the bed.

It was light when we woke up. Yes, we made love again before we got up. I got up first. When Jonathan came out to the kitchen, I was cutting the cucumbers.

He said, "Just like my first breakfast with you."

I said, "No! Not at all like our first breakfast. Same food, but more love. Then, I felt it was much too soon to think about you the way I did. Now I think, we can make more love any time. We could even interrupt our breakfast for love, or we might wait until just after we eat."

"I had some of those same thoughts, and you are right. This breakfast is different. Only one thing is the same. I have to go to work."

"But even that is not the same, because this time I will miss you more. Perhaps, you can come home for lunch?"

"Come home for what?"

"For whatever!"

"I will have the 'whatever.'"

18

The Guests from Shechem

As I cleaned up the house, I was happy; I was a married woman. I read the love song again and smiled.

When Jonathan arrived at his office, he found father still asleep on the woolsack. He quietly went out of the office and down the hall to the library. There he found Elimelech and Danel. Noah had already gone to help Sheva.

"Well look who is here," said Elimelech.

Danel added, "We didn't expect to see you until after lunch. Jonathan, did everything go as expected? Were you able to complete your marriage? He looks married."

Jonathan smiled and said, "I'm glad that I look married, because you'll understand when I tell you that I'll be going home for lunch today."

"Lunch? Sure, Jonathan, you're going home for lunch," laughed Danel as he ducked his head for fear of some missile coming his way.

"So, we had better get started. It will soon be time for lunch. Have you found all the texts that we will need?"

"We've found most of the texts, but we don't have *These are the Stories of Joseph*," said Elimelech.

"Well, I hope the scribe and the minstrel from the north bring something on Joseph, but we can copy the passages we'll use from the texts we have here. So, let's get started," Jonathan said as he looked for his list.

"Here is my list. I haven't cleared this with Sheva yet, but since we are almost out of time, we must proceed as if it were approved. I'll copy the passages for 'Day One' about the testing of Abraham and Isaac's marriage. Elimelech, you can copy what we have on Jacob's Return to Bethel. We'll skip the 'Third Day' and the 'Fourth Day' until our guests arrive with some Joseph stories, and Danel, you can do another copy of *Judah and His*

Sons to give to our guests. You know what to do. We'll meet later today to see how it is working out."

Jonathan returned to his office, but father had already left. There was a note on the woolsack, which said, "*Todah* for the sack-time. I'll see you this evening around the table."

Jonathan smiled and got to work. He had always liked this story of Abraham in the land of the Moriah. The disastrous request on the part of God was a favorite story of the people. Of course the people knew that since human sacrifice was not allowed, the life of Isaac would somehow be spared. He was writing with his favorite brush and using a nice piece of parchment. When he got to the line "He grasped the knife to kill his son," he decided to quit for lunch.

When he arrived at the house, he looked for me in the kitchen. I was not there. He looked in the bedroom; I was there waiting for him. After we had made love, Jonathan said, "Why did I wait so long to find you?"

"I don't know why, but when you found me, you didn't waste any time. Did you get anything done this morning?"

"Not very much. I kept remembering last night and anticipating my lunch. I also had to endure a lot of teasing."

"About what?"

"About what you and I love to do."

"Well we have done that, so you should have something to eat."

"But, I don't need to eat."

"Come on. Let's at least have some bread and cheese. Then I'll walk back with you, and we can be together a little longer."

When we got there, Sheva called us to his office. Sheva said, "Keziah I'm glad you came back with Jonathan, and I want you both to meet Joshua and Elishama from Shechem. Joshua is the minstrel whom Gad heard sing at the tomb of Joseph, and Elishama is a scribe who has copied a lot of the material that Joshua sings."

I said, "Gad is my father, and I was with him at the tomb of Joseph. We did enjoy our time in Shechem."

Joshua said, "We're glad for that."

Jonathan greeted them both with a hearty welcome, and he said, "We're glad you are here. You have come just at the right moment. We need some help, and we want to know more about what scribes and singers are doing in Israel."

The Guests from Schechem

Sheva added, "Later this afternoon, Noah will take you, Joshua, to see Heman, our local singer, and you and Heman can compare notes. But first, I want to show you the ritual that we have prepared."

While Sheva was speaking with Joshua, Jonathan asked Elishama, "Did you bring with you any texts that deal with the 'Stories of Joseph?'"

"Yes, we brought several; we use them at Joseph's tomb when we call forth his name and seek his blessing."

"We really need such materials to make this work," responded Jonathan. "We do not have many texts on Joseph. What we have are stories in the *Stories of Jacob*."

Sheva was ready to work, so he got out his text of the ritual for the coronation. He said, "Forgive me for rushing, but we only have two days to get ready; we might as well get started."

Elishama re-joined Sheva and Joshua to look at the ritual text. Jonathan and I slipped out of the room. I went on home, and it was not long before Sarah came by and asked me to help with a dinner for the guests from Shechem. I dropped what I was doing, and we went to her house.

Jonathan found Elimelech and Danel, and told them to come to his office with all their materials. He wanted to have everything ready to check as soon as Sheva was finished.

It was not long before Sheva and the guests came to Jonathan's office. Sheva said, "Joshua and Elishama think the ritual will work. Also, they will show the elders of Israel the covenant that I drew up. So now, maybe they can help you with your selections. I'll be in my office if you need me."

Jonathan said, "Come on in, and I want you to meet Elimelech and Danel; they are also working on this project." After the introductions were taken care of, Jonathan got out his list of selections and continued, "We are dividing the ritual moments of the coronation into seven sections; we are calling these sections 'days.' In days one through five, the singers will sing a few selections on each of the fathers. For 'Day One' we want to use the story of the testing of Abraham and a piece about Isaac's marriage and the birth of his sons. For the 'Second Day,' we will use the story of Jacob's return to Bethel. The third and fourth days are reserved for the Joseph material, which we hope to get from you, and on the 'Fifth Day,' we will deal with Judah and his Sons. We would like to have something from the beginning of the story of Joseph and something from the end. Do you have any suggestions for us and do you have the texts?"

89

The Jerusalem Academy

Elishama answered, "We brought a text of the story of Joseph. It is a new edition that puts together some older and newer texts. Many years ago, we had some texts written in the first person as if Joseph was telling his story from the tomb. That is the way the Egyptians wrote such stories. But, we found out that it works better for us, if we want to praise our father Joseph, to speak for him and about him. This text is the one that Joshua uses at the tomb of Joseph."

Jonathan said, "Joshua, do you have some favorite parts of this story that would fit this occasion?"

"Yes. Since you want something from the beginning and the end, I would like to sing the part in the beginning where it shows that Joseph will become a great ruler (Genesis 37:2–36) and from the end of the story I want to do a scene where Joseph and his sons are blessed by Jacob" (Genesis 48:1–22)."

Jonathan said, "I'm sure those passages will be fine. I know you are to go with Noah to meet Heman, but it would be helpful for me if Elishama could stay here; he could help us copy those two selections. When you get back, we'll probably still be here."

Just then Sheva stepped into the room and asked for everyone's attention. He said, "I want all of you to come to my house this evening. Sarah and I will provide the dinner, and we will all have a chance to talk with our guests. They will be staying at our house. Sarah has already talked with Keziah and Gad. In fact, Keziah is helping Sarah as we speak. I say this for Jonathan's benefit. Jonathan, you won't have to go home to let Keziah know about these plans."

Jonathan said through the laughter, "Thanks, Sheva! That's just what I needed."

Sheva left and everyone got to work. Elishama showed the new texts to Jonathan and they began to work. Soon Jonathan said, "I like this new material. The second passage is important for us in many ways. Elimelech and Danel, I want you to hear this blessing of Jacob in which he blesses Joseph by blessing Joseph's two sons:

> He blessed Joseph.
> He said:
>> "The God before whom my fathers, Abraham and Isaac, walked,
>> The God who has been my shepherd from my birth until this day,
>> The Messenger who has delivered me from all harm,
>> May he bless these young men.

The Guests from Schechem

My name and the names of my fathers, Abraham and Isaac,
Shall be called forth by them.
They will become a multitude in the land." (Genesis 48:15-16)

This is perfect for our coronation, because this shows clearly how Joseph's sons were to call forth the names of the fathers or summon them at the tomb. Then, the sons would be blessed; they would become a 'multitude in the land.' In our coronation, we are clearly following the regular practice at the tomb in order that King David will be blessed. This passage is a gem."

After this, they all went back to work. They finished all their work in a few hours. About then Noah and Joshua returned from their visit with Heman. Sheva called everyone together and said, "This has been a productive day. Tomorrow we'll meet and put all of our work together, and then we can see how it looks as a completed work. We are going to be ready for the coronation on the following day. Since Sarah and Keziah will be expecting us soon, we should be on our way."

When the seven of them arrived at the house, Sarah, father, and I were ready. Sheva introduced the guests.

"I recently heard you at Joseph's tomb in Shechem," said father. "I was impressed."

Joshua said, "Keziah mentioned this earlier. We have not had many guests from Judah, but perhaps we will have more from now on. We hope so."

Jonathan and I had moved to a corner of the room. Father said to Joshua and Elishama, "Keziah and Jonathan were just married yesterday. I guess they still have a few things to talk about."

Elishama said, "I can understand. I was married just a few weeks ago."

"Elishama, where did you take your scribal training?" Sheva asked.

"We have some good teachers at Shechem, but I also went to the school in Jerusalem for a short time."

When father heard that, he called to Jonathan, "Jonathan, bring your wife over here and join this conversation, because Elishama has just mentioned that he went to the school in Jerusalem. Perhaps he knew your friend who, went there."

Jonathan was interested in father's comment and said, "My friend's name was Zadok. Did you know him?"

The Jerusalem Academy

Elishama said, "There were at least two fellows called Zadok. One of them was tall."

"That's my friend, and his best teacher was a man from Judah. His name was Ahban; he was from the town of Giloh."

"Yes, I knew them both, and they are still there at the school. Ahban is one of the best teachers in the school."

"That's interesting," said Jonathan. "I would really like to visit them. Do you still go back there?"

"Once in a while, but I would like to go more often."

At that point, Sarah called everyone to the table and they all began to eat. Both Sarah and I brought out the food and wine. We worked well together. There were ten of us, but the table was large. We could not have put the table in our eating area. When Sarah was serving Jonathan, she said to him, "You are a lucky man. Your wife is a wonderful person."

Jonathan replied, "I agree to both statements, and I should add that Sheva is also a lucky man."

About then Noah spilled a jug of wine, and I ran over to clean it up. He said, "I'm sorry to cause this mess and to waste the wine."

I said, "There is plenty of wine left over from the wedding."

As the evening progressed, it was clear that everyone had a good time. It was a great party and a good idea. When father, Jonathan, and I were leaving, we all thanked Sheva and Sarah. Also, Elimelech and Danel, said, "Jonathan, we hope that you're on time tomorrow."

On the way home, Jonathan and father talked about the importance of the connections with the school in Jerusalem. This could be important if we move to Jerusalem. When we got home father went to his room with some words about his bed being better than that woolsack. At last, Jonathan and I were alone. There was not much talking but a lot of loving. Just before we went to sleep, Jonathan said, "Sarah told me that I was a lucky man. She also said that you were a wonderful person. I told her that she was correct, but that you were the really lucky one."

"Jonathan, I don't believe you."

"You're just too smart."

We held each other, and soon we were asleep.

19

The Second Coronation

THE NEXT DAY THE finishing touches were put on the program. By evening guests were arriving, and the streets were full of people walking and talking. From our roof we could see the street in front of our house was like a moving stream. The noise was unbelievable. The next morning, there was also a great deal of hustle and bustle. This time, Jonathan and I got to the threshing floor at the tombs earlier than last time, because we wanted our same seats. It was not long before we heard the trumpet, and we knew that the procession had started from David's quarters. It took longer, this time, for the procession to arrive at the tombs, but when David got there he was seated, as before, near the entrance to the tombs. Also, the elders of Israel were seated at the front, just on the edge of the threshing floor.

When everyone was seated, Sheva announced that each section of the program was to be considered a ritual day. He said, "We will celebrate the lives of the fathers in days one through five. Musicians and singers from Judah and from Israel will participate in this part of the coronation."

Then Heman stepped forward and said, "First we will sing about how Abraham was tested by God. I will sing all the parts at first, but when we come to Isaac's part, my son, Hanani will sing for Isaac." He began to sing:

> . . . God tested Abraham.
> He said to him:
> > "Abraham!"
> He answered:
> > "Here am I."
> He said:

"Take your son, your only one, whom you love, Isaac,
   and go, yes you, to the land of the moriah.
   There offer him as a burnt offering upon one of the hills
   that I shall make known to you."
In the morning when Abraham got up, he saddled his ass;
he took two of his attendants and Isaac, his son, with him. He split the wood for the burnt offering;
he got ready; he left for the sanctuary
that this God had made known to him.
On the third day, Abraham lifted up his eyes;
he saw the sanctuary from afar.
Abraham said to his attendants:
   "You stay here with the ass, and I and the boy will go yonder.
   We will worship, and we will return to you."
Abraham took the wood for the burnt offering.
He placed [it] upon Isaac, his son.
He took in his hand the fire and the knife.
The two of them walked off together.

(At this point, Heman's son joined him to sing Isaac's part.)

Isaac spoke to Abraham, his father; he said:
   "My father!"
He said:
   "Yes, my son."
He said:
   "Here is the fire and the wood,
   but where is the sheep for the burnt offering?"
Abraham said:
   "Elohim will see to it (that is, the sheep for the burnt offering) my son."
   The two of them walked off together.

They arrived at the sanctuary
that this God had made known to him.
Abraham built the altar there;
he arranged the wood;
he bound Isaac, his son;
he placed him upon the altar on top of the wood.

The Second Coronation

Abraham reached out his hand.
He grasped the knife to kill his son.

(Here the crowd was very silent. They were worried. Someone gasped and said, "Oh no.")

The messenger of Yahweh called to him from the heavens.
He said:
"Abraham! Abraham!"
He said:
"Yes."
He said:
"Do not move your hand to the boy!
Do not do anything to him!
For now I know that you are a god-fearer;
You did not withhold your son, your only one, from me."
Abraham lifted up his eyes and saw there a substitute ram,
who was caught in the thicket by his horns.
Abraham went; he took the ram;
he offered him up to be a burnt offering in place of his son.
Abraham called forth the name of that sanctuary, "Yahweh-yireh,"
which is expressed today as "On the mountain of Yahweh, he appears."

The messenger of Yahweh called to Abraham a second time from the heavens.
He said:
"By myself I have sworn ([this is] an oracle of Yahweh)
that since you have done this,
and you have not withheld your son, your only one,
so I will indeed bless you, and surely I will make
your descendants as numerous as the stars of the heavens
and as the sands that are on the seashore.
Your descendants shall take possession of the gates of their enemies.
Through your descendants all the states of the earth
shall bless themselves, because you listened to my voice."[1]
Abraham returned to his attendants.

---

1. Here the translation "listened to my voice" is given, because the general meaning "voice" is all that is intended. Many would translate this "obeyed my command," but when the Hebrew text wants to be explicit, it can tell you in no uncertain terms what is contained within the word "voice" (for an example see Genesis 26:5).

The Jerusalem Academy

> They got ready; they left together for Beersheba.
> Abraham settled in Beersheba. (Genesis 22:1–19)

(Heman continued this remembrance of the fathers with selections about Isaac's marriage and his sons. Jonathan and I listened for the blessing.)

> They blessed Rebekah; they said to her:
> > "Our sister, surely you are.
> > Be thousands and myriads.
> > Your descendants shall conquer,
> > [Conquer] the gates of their foes." (Genesis 24:60)

(Jonathan looked at me and said, "There it is; it was your blessing as well." Actually, we both got lost in thoughts about our wedding and Rebekah's wedding was lost on us. When, Heman started the part about the birth of Jacob and Esau, once again he captured our attention.)

> *These are the stories of Isaac*, the son of Abraham.
> Abraham fathered Isaac.
> Isaac was forty years old when he took for his wife Rebekah,
> the daughter of Bethuel the Aramean from Paddan-aram,
> the sister of Laban the Aramean.
> Isaac made a petition to Yahweh on behalf of his wife for she was barren.
> Yahweh responded to him; Rebekah, his wife, conceived.
> The children were being crushed inside her; she said:
> > "If this is the case, why me?"
> She went to seek Yahweh.
> Yahweh said to her:
> > "Two states are [now] within your womb;
> > two peoples shall come from your body.
> > one shall be stronger than the other,
> > and the older shall serve the younger."
> Her days were fulfilled to give birth;
> there were twins in her womb.
> The first one came out red, all of him like a hairy mantle.
> They called forth his name, "Esau."
> Next his brother came out with his hand grasping the heel of Esau.
> He called forth his name, "Jacob."
> Isaac was sixty years old when they were born.
> The boys grew up.

Esau became a hunter, a man of the wild.
Jacob was a complete man, one who dwelt in tents.
Isaac loved Esau, because [Esau's] game was in his mouth,
and Rebekah loved Jacob. (Genesis 25:19-28)

Day One

(After each ritual day was complete a priest shouted the day and number.

The crowd liked Heman very much and at the end of Day One they cheered. Heman thanked them and continued.)

Elohim said to Jacob:
"Arise, go up to Bethel; settle there,
and make there an altar for the God
who appeared to you when you were fleeing
from the face of Esau, your brother."
. . .
Jacob came to Luz (that is, Bethel) in the land of Canaan,
he and all the people who were with him.
He built there an altar; he called the sanctuary El-Bethel,
for there the gods were revealed to him
when he was fleeing away from his brother.

Deborah, the nurse of Rebekah, died;
she was buried below Bethel, under the oak;
he called forth its name, "Allon-bacuth."

Again, Elohim appeared to Jacob
upon his arrival from Paddan-Aram; he blessed him.
Elohim said to him:
"Your name is Jacob;
Not again will your name be called forth, 'Jacob;'
But Israel shall be your name."
He called forth his name, "Israel."
Elohim said to him:
"I am El Shaddai.
Be fruitful and multiply;
a people, [yeah], a community of peoples,
shall come from you;

> kings shall come forth from your loins
> the land that I gave to Abraham and to Isaac,
> to you, I give it;
> To your descendants, [the ones who] follow you,
> I will give the land."
>
> Elohim went up from him,
> from the sanctuary in which he had spoken with him.
> Jacob set up a sacred pillar in the sanctuary
> in which he had spoken with him (a sacred pillar of stone);
> he offered a libation on it; he poured oil on it.
> Jacob called forth the name of the sanctuary,
> where Elohim had spoken with him, "Bethel." (Genesis 35:1–15)

A Second Day

(During this song, Jonathan and I noticed that the people from Israel cheered when Jacob was told, "Israel shall be your name." Also everyone stood and shouted when Heman sang: "Kings shall come forth from your loins." I heard some people singing, "and David is his name!")

(Heman stepped back and Joshua of Shechem came to the center of the threshing floor. The people from Israel cheered before he started his song.)

He sang:

> *These are the stories of Jacob.*
>
> Joseph was seventeen years old, he was shepherding with his brothers among the flocks. He was an assistant to the sons of Bilhah and to the sons of Zilpah, the wives of his father. Joseph brought their bad record to their father. Israel loved Joseph more than any of his sons, for he was the child of his old age. He made him a royal robe. His brothers saw that their father loved him more than any of his brothers; they hated him; and they could not overcome his perfect speech. Joseph had a dream. He told [it] to his brothers; they hated him even more.
>
> He said to them: "Please listen to this dream that I dreamed: There we were binding sheaves in the field; There my sheaf stood up and presided; There your sheaves surrounded and bowed down to my sheaf."
>
> His brothers said to him, "Indeed! Are you going to be king over us, or shall you really have dominion over us?" They hated him even more for his dreams and for his words.

The Second Coronation

He had another dream. He recounted it to his brothers; he said, "Yes, I had another dream. In it, the sun, the moon, and eleven stars bowed down to me." He had narrated it to his father and to his brothers.

His father scolded him; he said to him, "What is this dream that you had? Indeed, shall we really come, I, your mother, and your brothers, to bow down to the earth before you?"

His brothers were jealous of him; his father observed the situation. His brothers had gone to pasture their father's flocks in Shechem.

Israel said to Joseph, "Are not your brothers shepherding in Shechem? Come, I will send you to them."

He said, "I'm willing."

He said to him, "Please go! Note the health of your brothers and the well-being of the flocks and bring back word to me."

He sent him from the valley of Hebron. When he arrived in Shechem, a man found him wandering about there in the fields.

The man asked him, "What are you looking for?"

"I'm looking for my brothers," he said. "Please tell me where they are shepherding."

The man said, "They have moved from here; they were the ones that I heard saying, 'Let's go to Dothan.'"

Joseph went after his brothers. He found them in Dothan. They saw him from a distance, and before he reached them, they plotted [against] him to kill him.

They said to one another, "There comes that master-dreamer. Now come on! We will kill him and throw him into one of the pits. We will say, 'An evil beast devoured him.' We shall see how his dreams turn out."

Reuben overheard; he [wanted] to rescue him from their hands. He said, "We must not destroy [this] person!" Reuben said to them, "You shall not shed blood! Throw him into this pit which is in the desert, but do not lay a hand on him." ([This he said] in order to deliver him from their hands and to restore him to his father).

So when Joseph reached his brothers, they stripped Joseph of his robe, the royal robe that was his. They took him; they threw him into the pit. The pit was empty; there was no water in it.

[Meanwhile], some Midianite traders passed by. They pulled; they brought up Joseph from the pit. They sold Joseph to the Ishmaelites for twenty [shekels] of silver; they brought Joseph to Egypt. Reuben returned to the pit, and there was no Joseph in the pit! He tore his clothes.

He went back to his brothers; he said, "The boy, he is not there! And I, where will I go?"

They took the robe of Joseph; they slaughtered a billy goat; they dipped the robe in the blood. They sent the royal robe [ahead]. They came to their father.

They said, "We found this. Please observe. Is it the robe of your son or not?"

He recognized it. He said, "My son's robe! An evil beast has devoured him; yes, Joseph has been torn up!"

Jacob tore his clothes; he put sackcloth on his loins; he mourned his son many days. All his sons and all his daughters tried to comfort him; he refused to be comforted.

He said, "In mourning, I will go down to my son in Sheol." His father wept for him.

The Medanites sold [Joseph] in Egypt to Potiphar, an officer of Pharaoh (the head of his stewards). (Genesis 37:2–24, 28–36)

A Third Day

(Before Joshua continued his singing he told the people that the signs of Joseph's greatness were many. He was not to stay in the prison. Instead, he rose to power in Egypt. He saved Egypt, and he saved his family. Then he said, "I want to sing about how Jacob blessed Joseph by giving him Shechem and by blessing Joseph's two sons.")

Joshua sang:

It was after these events that [a messenger] said to Joseph, "Your father is ill."

He took with him his two sons, Manasseh and Ephraim.

[A messenger] informed Jacob and said, "Here he is! Your son Joseph has come to you."

Israel strengthened himself and sat up in bed.

Jacob said to Joseph:

"El Shaddai appeared to me at Luz, in the land of Canaan.
He blessed me. He said to me:

'Yes, I am the one Who will make you fruitful.

I will make you many;

I will make you a community of peoples.

I will grant this land to your descendants,

[The ones who] follow you,

[as] an everlasting possession.'

Now your two sons, the ones who were born to you in the land of Egypt before the time of my coming to you in Egypt, they are mine; Ephraim and Manasseh just as Reuben and Simeon, they are mine.

The Second Coronation

Your children whom you fathered after them, they are yours; instead of the names of their brothers, they will be called in their inheritance.

And I, when I was returning from Paddan, Rachel died on me in the land of Canaan, on the road to Ephrath, with still some distance to go. I buried her there on the road to Ephrath (that is, Bethlehem)."

Israel saw Joseph's sons; he said: "Who are these?"

Joseph said to his father: "They are my sons whom Elohim has given me here."

He said: "Please bring them to me. I will bless them." Israel's eyes were dim from old age; he was not able to see. Joseph brought them close to him. He kissed them and embraced them.

Israel said to Joseph: "I never expected to see your face again, and here Elohim has allowed me to see your descendants as well."

Joseph took them from his knees. He bowed low before him to the earth. Joseph took the two of them, Ephraim in his right [hand] opposite Israel's left and Manasseh in his left [hand] opposite Israel's right. He brought [them] close to him. Israel put forth his right [hand] and laid it on the head Ephraim, who was the younger, and his left [hand] on the head of Manasseh, although Manasseh was the first-born (he crossed his hands). He blessed Joseph.

He said: "The God before whom my fathers, Abraham and Isaac, walked, the God who has been my shepherd from my birth until this day, the Messenger who has delivered me from all harm, may he bless these young men. My name and the names of my fathers, Abraham and Isaac, shall be called forth by them. They will become a multitude in the land."

Joseph saw that his father was laying his right hand on the head of Ephraim. This was wrong in his eyes. He took hold of his father's hand to move it from the head of Ephraim to the head of Manasseh.

Joseph said to his father: "Not so, my father, for this one is the first-born. Lay your right [hand] on his head."

His father refused. He said: "I know, my son, I know. He too shall become a people; He too shall become great, but his younger brother shall be greater than he, and his descendants shall become the masses of the peoples."

He blessed them on that day as follows: "By you shall Israel bless itself saying, 'May Elohim make you like Ephraim and like Manasseh.'"

He put Ephraim before Manasseh.

Israel said to Joseph: "I am about to die. Elohim will be with you and return you to the land of your fathers. And I, I grant to you, as

The Jerusalem Academy

one above your brothers, Shechem, which I captured from the power of the Amorites with my sword and with my bow." (Genesis 48:1–22)

A Fourth Day

(When Joshua sang about the gift of Shechem, those from Israel once again cheered for a long time.) Now it was time for Heman to return to sing from *These are the Stories of Judah* about Judah and his sons (Genesis 38:1–30). He did it as he did at the first coronation along with the female vocalist. The people from Judah were very excited with his performance.

A Fifth Day

(Now Abiathar came forward to summon the fathers just as Joseph's sons had been requested to summon or call forth the names of the fathers.)
Abiathar said:

> You have been summoned, O ancient fathers,
> Abraham has been summoned.
> Isaac has been summoned.
> Jacob has been summoned.
> Reuben has been summoned
> Simeon has been summoned.
> Levi has been summoned.
> Judah has been summoned.
> Zebulun has been summoned.
> Issachar has been summoned.
> Dan has been summoned.
> Gad has been summoned.
> Asher has been summoned.
> Naphtali has been summoned.
> Joseph has been summoned.
> Benjamin has been summoned.
> Ephraim has been summoned.
> Manasseh has been summoned.
> Perez has been summoned.
> Hezron has been summoned.
> Ram has been summoned.
> Amminadab has been summoned.
> Nahshon has been summoned.
> Salmon has been summoned.
> Boaz has been summoned.

The Second Coronation

Obed has been summoned.
Jesse, the father of David, has been summoned.
You have been summoned, O ancient fathers.

O House of Joseph, weep!
Let all the descendants of Joseph shed tears.
O House of Judah, weep!
Let all the descendants of Judah shed tears.
Bereft, bereft, and bereft!

O Yahweh! Send your angel,
that he might help our ancient fathers.
Let him descend to the netherworld;
let him guide them to this place.
Below are the ancient fathers!
Below are the recently departed, as well.

Offer generous gifts to our fathers,
gifts of food and drink for all of them,
gifts for each of these seven days.

A blessing from our fathers:
Shalom!
Shalom David!
Shalom to his house, as well!
Shalom to David's wives!
Shalom to David's royal city!
Shalom to her gates!
Shalom!

A Sixth Day

After this ritual, Abiathar brought David to the center of the threshing floor.

Abiathar took the crown and put it upon David's head. Also, he handed David the Decree of Yahweh.

Then father, Abiathar, and the elders of Israel anointed David with these words: "David Ben-Jesse, you have been anointed, and now you are also King David of Israel."

The Jerusalem Academy

The horn sounded, and all the people shouted and clapped their hands, "Long live King David!"

Next Abiathar came forward with a scroll; it was the covenant. Abiathar read it slowly for all to hear.

(Jonathan made a few comments to me about the covenant, and again our minds were elsewhere.)

To everyone's surprise both Heman and Joshua came to the center of the floor to sing the coronation psalm. Heman said, "Both of us, for Judah and Israel, will sing the Coronation Psalm, written by King David."

As they were singing, Jonathan and I looked at each other. This psalm contained a word, which was our hope. That word was Zion. We hoped that David could quell the opposition and that we could move to Jerusalem.

When they finished singing the coronation psalm everyone stood and shouted: "A Seventh Day!"

After this long program, there was so much noise that we could not hear each other when we tried to speak. So Jonathan took my hand, and we made our way through the crowd at a slow pace. We finally reached Jonathan's office. We were too tired and thirsty to make it home.

"That crowd is huge. They were certainly interested in the coronation, but you could see that they had their special loyalties. However, that was a nice touch at the end; Heman and Joshua doing the psalm together."

"I thought the singing of that psalm really helped to break down a lot of walls. The two of them must have thought that one up. I don't think anyone of us ever suggested such a thing. Here, Keziah have a drink." Jonathan had a jug of water in his office.

I drank and thought of the first time that I had been here. Then I said, "The first time I was here with you is one of the best memories of my life."

"Why was it one of the best?"

"It was fun, and you were wonderful. You were willing to teach me, and you wanted to be more than my teacher. I think you got your wish."

"I did get my wish, and if the others were not going to come in here at any moment, you can bet that we would just try out my woolsack."

"That would be fun, but it will be better at home. I remember something else from that day. You said, 'I expect people like Joab to make fun of anyone who is a scribe. But, I also have some problems with other scribes. I seem to always take the unpopular opinion. Someday, I'll write a long poem or book on this. I will call it *The Minority Report.* Then I said, 'That's a terrific idea.' I hope we can make that an on-going project, and I hope I can contribute something."

"Keziah, you have already contributed a great deal. You don't follow tradition. We'll start to work on our project, realizing that anything that goes into it will probably not come to pass in our lifetime."

"Perhaps not, but I'm not so sure."

20

The Jerusalem School

When Jonathan and I got home father was already there. He was having some grapes, and he said, "Come in here and sit down. You both need to rest a bit. That coronation was good, much better than the first one. It was long, but I heard some people say they could have listened to more from the singers. As we have discussed before, our people spend most of their lives just working and trying to stay alive. They really like and need such entertainment."

"I agree," said Jonathan. "They do need entertainment, and it is important to hear about the past. I just hope that they don't expect too much from the 'fathers' in the way of blessings right away. When the Philistines hear about what happened today, there may be more bloodshed than blessing. David could still be useful to the Philistines as King of Judah, but to become king of Israel brings about the kind of union that the Philistines wanted to destroy."

"You're right," said father. "We are in for some trouble. The first question in the coronation psalm was a good one: 'Why do the city-states join forces?' It is clear. David has become too powerful."

Jonathan said, "I'll go see David tomorrow. I want to talk with him about Jerusalem and the school. He should know about Zadok and Ahban. I need to talk with him before he gets too involved in fighting the Philistines."

"That sounds good."

"I'll check it out with Sheva before talking with David, but he will go along with the idea."

I said, "There's no doubt about the fact that we need to eat. You can talk while you eat. Help me get things set out."

The Jerusalem School

"Gad, your daughter is living in the future. Someday men will help with the dinner, but for her, tomorrow is today. If you want to tell David what will be, just check what Keziah is doing now."

"I always do that, and it usually helps me. To live in the future in the present is fun."

"I'm glad you like it, because that's where we are."

Jonathan said, "We're having fun, and you, my dear Keziah, inspire us. This conversation may be silly, but there is a more serious side to it. In part, I was wrong today when I said that our book, *The Minority Report* would contain ideas that would not be realized in our lifetime. Keziah, your doubts at the time were correct. We can practice some of those things now, even though few people will want to participate in our activities."

"Then participate! Here is the knife, and here is the bread."

Father began to cut some cheese, and we were soon ready for our meal.

The next morning, Jonathan left early. I knew he would leave early, because he wanted to see David. Now I will have to wait to see what he finds out. When he arrived at his office, Sheva was already working. Sheva said, "I was hoping that you would be here, because I have some good news. Joshua and Elishama are going to stay here for a few days. They want to read some of our material, and they will share some more of their texts. In fact, Joshua will sing some things for us to copy."

"Perhaps we can all help on that project. However, I would like to do something else this morning. If you will agree to it, I would like to ask David about Jerusalem. My plan is to come right out and ask him. Also, I want him to know what we know about the school and our connections with it. After all the hints he has given us, he would think we were stupid if we did not know he is getting serious about Jerusalem."

"If you want to talk with David, it is fine with me. This morning would be a good time, because, as I said, Joshua and Elishama want to look at some of our things. Yes, you should talk to David. We may not be able to help him, but he should know from the beginning what we want if he does end up in Jerusalem."

"This will be good. The last time I talked with David, he told me to keep in touch. In fact, he said that he wanted me to do some things for him after the coronation. I need to find out what he has in mind."

Sheva looked concerned. He said, "You need to see him, but don't let him get you involved in other projects, because we need you here."

The Jerusalem Academy

"I will avoid all other projects."

As it turned out, Jonathan had to wait for about an hour before he could see David. He talked with several people about the coronation and about the increase in the general workload, now that the concerns and needs of Israel had to be added to everyone's responsibilities. Most people thought it would take a long time to get things under control, and if David had to spend much time securing the borders, the time would be increased. Jonathan walked down the hall closer to David's office. The door flew open, and Joab rushed out. He looked at Jonathan and said, "Out of my way, scribe!"

David appeared at the doorway and invited Jonathan to come in.

"What's Joab's problem?"

"That's just Joab. He always has a problem. We have heard that the Philistines are already mustering their troops. Joab wants to jump in and hit them hard. I told him we have to wait and find out exactly where they are going to start their attack before we make our plan. Also, we must make certain we protect our people still at Ziklag. Joab never wants to wait for anything. Enough of that. "I want you and Sheva to know that I thought the coronation was well done. What do you need today?"

"The last time we talked, you told me that you wanted me to do a few things for you. Second, we noticed that in your coronation psalm, you were, at least symbolically, anointed as king 'on Zion,' Yahweh's mountain. In fact, in the ritual, we changed the blessing from 'Shalom Hebron' to 'Shalom to David's royal city.' We thought this change would work for the future. Was the mention of 'Zion' in the psalm an important sign? Were we correct in doing so?"

"I'll deal with the second question first. I'm pleased that my scribes are smart enough to see things and to catch on. Yes, Zion is very important to my plans and to the health of this kingdom. You were right to change the blessing. But you want to know more. Right?"

"Right."

"I thought so. Well, I can't tell you as to when, but we will move to Jerusalem. A lot depends on how much time it takes to settle things with the Philistines. I do want to move as soon as possible."

Jonathan told David that this was good news, and he wanted him to know about some friends in the scribal school in Jerusalem. Then he said to David, "The Hebron scribes could join forces with the Jerusalem school. If that happened, we would have a good school, right from the

The Jerusalem School

start. We would still need to import a teacher or two from other countries but not at once. This would also help to bring together the scribes from Israel and Judah. Elishama, the scribe from Shechem, who helped us with the coronation, went to school there, and he knows some of the people whom I know in the school."

David said, "I'm glad you spoke to me about this. It sounds like we should do it just as soon as we get there. I do not want you or your friends to contact the school before we take the city. The scribes should remain neutral in all such matters. We are in the process of making a plan to take the city without a lot of fighting or destruction, so the school in Jerusalem will be safe. I'll let you know as soon as we secure the place."

"That will be fine."

Then there was silence. David walked to the window and thought for a moment. Then he said, "Now, as to your first question, what I want you to do for me is simple. About two weeks before we take Jerusalem, I want you to carry some letters and drawings to King Hiram of Tyre. He has already offered to send carpenters and stonemasons to build a palace for me. He will also send the cedar logs. I'll go over the plans with you, and you will discuss the details with Hiram and his men. This will give them a better idea of what to bring and how much to bring. In Jerusalem, we will have a great palace. Now, in light of what you told me about the Jerusalem school, I'll give you another task while you are in Tyre. You should try to fine a teacher from there for the Jerusalem school."

"This is getting better all the time. In the meantime, I'll talk this over with Sheva, I'll get his ideas on the teacher."

"That will be fine, but I don't want you to talk about these things to anyone else in your office; they will know soon enough."

"That's fine."

"It was good talking with you. I'll let you know when I want you to go to Tyre."

With that, Jonathan left.

Jonathan got back to the office and found Sheva. Sheva said, "Did you get to talk with David?"

"Yes, I did."

Jonathan told Sheva every detail of his conversation and warned him not to tell the others. Jonathan said, "You will need to tell me what you would like to have if we can get a new teacher from Tyre."

The Jerusalem Academy

"A new teacher is important, and I am pleased that you asked for one. We need a teacher who is able to teach two or three languages in addition to his own. So, his education is important, but I also think we need someone who can understand our problems and can help us bring the scribes from two states together."

"That's asking a lot to have a well educated scribe who is also a real human being with common sense."

"That's what I want!"

"Well, I hope I can get you what you want. If I can find such a person, the next problem will be convincing that person to come to Jerusalem."

"You can do that, but we should both give it some thought. We can even offer such a person the good summer climate of Jerusalem, which has to be better than any place on the coast."

"We will have a few days to talk about this. I would like to go home now. I need to prepare Keziah for my trip. For me that will be the bad part; I really do not like to leave Keziah. Tomorrow, I'll be in to help copy some of the material from Joshua and Elishama."

Jonathan arrived home to find me fixing the evening meal. He remembered he had never had any lunch. I was glad to see him, and I said, "You're home early. You missed me I'll bet."

"I did miss you. What have you been doing?"

"Just working around this house and wishing that we could fix it up."

"You don't need to fix it up, because we'll soon be leaving here."

"Do you mean that?"

"Yes."

Then Jonathan told me all the details. When he finished he said, "There I have told my story again, but this time I have a tear in my eye. I don't want to leave you."

"And I don't want you to go, but when will you go?"

"I don't know for sure, but it will be soon. He wants me to go about two weeks before he takes Jerusalem."

"How long will this trip take?"

"It will probably take about ten days round-trip travel time, and I will need to be there for two or three days. That's about two weeks."

"That's about two weeks too long," I said as I held Jonathan close to me. "What are we going to do? I don't like it."

"I don't like being away from you. Also, I don't like to take the chance of being gone when David takes over Jerusalem. I want to be here when

The Jerusalem School

that happens, because I want to talk with my friend Zadok who is at the Jerusalem school. I guess that Sheva could deal with all of that, but I hope I will be back in time to do it."

Just then father came home, and he said, "Keziah, why do you look so sad when you are holding your man?"

"Because he is going to take a trip and be gone for about two weeks."

Father said, "Yes, I know. David told me about the plan. It is an important trip, but that does not make it any easier."

"Gad, I would not go if you were not here; I would not leave Keziah alone."

"I'll be here, and in fact, we'll start packing our things during that time. We'll be ready to move when you get back."

I said, "How will we find a place in Jerusalem? This all sounds like a busy and a complicated time."

Later we found out that David took care of the Philistine threat in record time, and he turned his attention to Jerusalem without ever speaking to Jonathan.

The Philistines did consider David's act of becoming king of Israel an act of treason. As a vassal of the Philistines it was fitting that he took Judah from Israel, but by becoming king of both parts he was now king of a united Israel. He was no longer a vassal but a threat. The people of Israel were afraid. The Philistines could defeat David, and if so there would be no united Israel. The Philistines did march up in search of David, and they spread out over the Valley of Rephaim. David went to Baal-perazim and defeated them there. This was just a few miles west of Jerusalem. But, once again they came up to the Valley of Rephaim. This time David chased the Philistines from Geba (north of Jerusalem) all the way to Gezer (a bit north but mostly west of Jerusalem). It seems that this second defeat was more lasting. Everyone was pleased and happy; David was able to deal with the Philistine threat in a matter of a few days. No one thought that this was possible.

I got the following information with father's help on the taking of Jerusalem. We do not know if it is accurate, but it was sent to our library to be put in the Annals of the Kings.

Now David could think seriously about Jerusalem. Just outside the wall surrounding Jerusalem, there were two large towers. There were always guards in these towers, and they protected the spring Gihon and the pool near the spring. Water carriers could come from the city through a tunnel, which went under the city wall. This tunnel led to the pool where they could draw their water. David's plan was to have a small force distract the guards, so that a few men could get beyond the towers and reach the tunnel. From there they could use the tunnel to enter the city. Once they were inside, they would open the gates for David and his troops. However, David waited for two things: 1) a dark night and 2) a night when the ruler of Jerusalem, who had taken the old name of Adonizedek, was absent.

Later David was informed that his two conditions would be met on the following night. So, David and his troops left Hebron. They went to Bethlehem, and the next night was indeed a dark and moon-less night. During the early hours of the night they moved near to Jerusalem. David and his men remained there. Joab had two men who knew their way around Jerusalem and were well acquainted with the tunnel leading to the pool outside the city wall. These two, Joab, and twenty men went on to the spring. Joab sent fifteen men to distract the tower guards. One of the fifteen was shot during the attack. Joab and the other seven soon reached the tunnel just above the pool.

After Joab and his men got into the city, they made their way to one of the gates. Here they were almost caught by a guard, but Joab put a knife between the poor devil's ribs, and he sank to the ground. They soon had the gates opened. Joab sent two runners to get David and his troops. After David arrived, his men surrounded the guardhouse at the main gate of the city, and Jerusalem belonged to David. The ruler of Jerusalem never returned to his city. The people, who had heard of David's victories over the Philistines, were not really too upset by this turn of events. They probably felt more secure with David as their ruler.

The next day was a busy one. Messages had to be sent to a lot of people. A runner was sent to inform Sheva and Jonathan about the capture of Jerusalem. When they heard the news, Jonathan said, "David said he was sending me to Tyre about two weeks before he went up against Jerusalem. I guess he wanted to confuse us with such talk."

Sheva said, "It also shows that he does not trust us."

"He even told Gad the same thing."

The runners also told them that David wanted them to come to Jerusalem, and they should be prepared to talk with the people at the school.

The Jerusalem School

Sheva said, "We both need to go home and tell our wives, and I'll tell Elimelech and the others to work as much as they can. Meet me back here in one hour, and we will start for Jerusalem.

Jonathan walked home at a fast pace. I was surprised to see him. He told me the news, and he said, "Sheva and I will be gone for about four days. Obviously, the trip to Tyre will have to wait. David even used your father to misinform all of us. David has reached a new low; I don't like working for David."

"Try to forget about David, and if you have time, find us a house. I will help father pack some of our things. You be careful."

I threw my arms around Jonathan, and we had another long good-bye.

Jonathan told me that they made it to Bethlehem that day. Early the next morning, they set off for Jerusalem. When they got to Jerusalem, they asked a guard at the gate where they could find David. They found him, and he was busy dealing with the people who would manage the city.

"I'm sorry about the misinformation," David said, "but I had to do this on the spur of the moment. To take Jerusalem by surprise, I had to surprise myself. Jonathan, I'll still want you to go to Tyre, but that will have to be later. Both of you should go to the school. See if your friends are there, and tell them that we would like to join forces with them. Also see what they want and find out what they need. We want to help them, and if they are willing, they can help us. If they are not willing, let them die on the vine."

Sheva said, "I hope they will join with us. They will have a lot to gain."

As they were leaving, Jonathan said to Sheva, "I'm glad that you spoke up back there. I didn't want to say anything. I'm still mad. David did not have to treat us like that. He expected us to spread his misinformation after telling us not to tell anyone."

They were soon at the school. The building was old but in good repair. It was a stone building with two floors. It was certainly better than our building in Hebron. There were some trees and shade, which made it cool and inviting. It was just as Jonathan had remembered it. There were not many people around. After going inside, they found an office, and they asked a young man, who seemed to be in charge, where they could find Ahban and Zadok. The young man directed them to another office, and Zadok was there.

"Zadok, it's good to see you!"

Zadok was shocked. He could hardly believe his eyes. "Jonathan, I have not seen you for two or three years. What are you doing?"

"I have been trying to be a scribe. I want you to meet Sheva who is in charge of the scribes where I have been working in Hebron. We have been collecting materials and writing coronation programs just lately."

"*Shalom* Sheva. I have heard about the coronations. My teacher, Ahban, who is not here today, went to the last coronation, and he was impressed with your work."

Sheva said, "Zadok, it is a bit awkward for us to be here so soon after David has invaded and taken your city. We hope there was no harm done to the school, the students, or the teachers."

"We did not suffer any harm. Some of the people here may not like the idea of David taking over, but most of us see it as a good thing. He will not allow the Philistines to take us, and we have had students from both Judah and Israel in our school."

Sheva said, "We met a student from here just before our last coronation, and he is still with us in Hebron working on some texts for us. His name is Elishama, and he is from Shechem."

"I remember him well."

Jonathan asked, "Who is in charge here?"

"Ahban is in charge at the present. It is not normal for this school to pick some one from Judah for our leader, but Ahban is a wise man. Also, he has been here a long time. We have two good scribes who could have taken charge when our last leader died, but neither one of them is in good health. Ahban has been doing a good job."

Sheva said, "If he is not here today, could we see him tomorrow?"

"I know you could see him tomorrow, because we have a meeting scheduled for the purpose of discussing what our relationship will be with the new government."

Sheva said, "Your relationship with the new government and with its scribes is just what we would like to talk about."

Jonathan added, "Those of us who are working with David at the present really need your help. It will take a lot of work to bring the scribes of Judah and Israel together. Your school can help us do it. Also, David will provide a great deal of support for this school."

Sheva asked, "What time should we come here tomorrow?"

"Be here early. Ahban will come back this evening, and he will want to start the day when it is cool."

The Jerusalem School

"We'll be here."

When Sheva and Jonathan got back to David's quarters, it was time for the evening meal. They went in to the dining area. After they finished eating, David came over to them and asked how things went at the school.

Sheva said, "Things went well. We are going back tomorrow morning, because they are having a meeting on how to relate to the new government. We want to be there and help them sort things out."

Jonathan added, "We have heard great things about Ahban, a Judean, who is now the director of the school. He will be there in the morning."

David seemed interested. He said, "If he is from Judah, this just may work out well. I want both of you to listen carefully to everything that Ahban says."

The next morning Sheva and Jonathan got on their way early. Even so, when they got to the school, there was a lot of activity inside and outside the building. It looked like the students were cleaning the building and doing some yard work. Jonathan said, "It must be difficult to keep this school going. Everyone has to work, and the students are also expected to pay for classes and food. We should try to point out to Ahban and the others that David could make things a lot easier for the school."

"He could do just that, but they could counter with some argument about freedom. If David pays, what will they owe David?"

"They would owe him a certain loyalty, but we could say that if David wants a great school with a cosmopolitan flavor and stance, he can not dictate their every thought. That is why it will be important to mention that David is willing to bring in some outside help."

With those thoughts, Sheva and Jonathan entered the school. Zadok was on the lookout for them, and he took them to the room where the meeting would be. There were already a few people there. When Ahban arrived in the room, things got quiet. He was an elderly man. He had white hair with a white beard. He was probably about seventy. Zadok introduced Sheva and Jonathan to him. Ahban did not remember Jonathan, but he did congratulate them both on the way in which they had arranged the coronation of David as king of Israel. He also said that when he heard the coronation psalm, he knew that David would soon come to Jerusalem. Ahban introduced Sheva and Jonathan to the rest of the teachers and scribes who were there. Then he asked Sheva to make an opening statement concerning the entire situation.

The Jerusalem Academy

Sheva stood up and thanked Ahban for this opportunity to speak. He said, "Jonathan and I have been working in a very small scribal center in Hebron for King David. We have had to write a lot of letters, collect many texts and traditions, plan coronations, and now we will be moving to Jerusalem. The number of our scribes will be increased in the near future, because some scribes from Israel will join us in our work. Some of those scribes were educated in this school. Also, our school will be adding some teachers from other countries. In fact, Jonathan is scheduled to go to Tyre to look for another teacher to help us. We can try to build up our school, and you can continue your school as you have been doing. That is certainly one way of dealing with this situation. However, we think that it would make a lot more sense to join forces at this time. I am not sure what that would mean. It could mean we would have one Jerusalem Academy. Or, we could have two schools working together and sharing the workload.

"We would like to work with you. Together, we could build something exciting. With your history and reputation and with David's support, this school could realize some of your hopes and our expectations."

Ahban thanked Sheva for his comments and asked Jonathan if he wanted to add anything. Jonathan said that he would perhaps add something later. So Ahban said, "I liked the tone of what I heard. At this school, we have fallen on hard times. We spend too much time just writing letters for hire, and it is difficult to find time to study and discuss important issues. In fact, if we do not have a connection with the government, it is almost impossible to fulfill one of our responsibilities, which is to educate royal scribes for Foreign Service. On the other hand, if we join with Sheva and the Hebron School, or should we just say the New School, we will give up some things, such as, neutrality and freedom. If David helps us, he will expect help from us. We should think this through with care, and I call on some of the rest of you to speak."

One elderly man said, "You mentioned that we might have to give up our neutrality and freedom. That would be difficult, but it would not be difficult to give up our poverty. Also, we have two ill teachers who just had to worry too much over the problem of how to keep this school from dying."

At this point, Jonathan asked to speak. He said, "You have mentioned your neutrality. I want to say that it is your neutrality that is appealing to us, and it can be your gift to us. We need your help in bringing together not only the scribes of Israel and Judah but also the traditions of those two states. Also, I know that you would have to give up some things, but in the cosmopolitan school of our dreams, what you will gain in the long run will protect your freedom."

Ahban responded, "I like that thought. It may be possible for us to work together in some way. My suggestion is the following: I will talk to everyone in this room today. You could come back here this evening and eat with us. After dinner, I will be able to discuss with you, at least, the direction that we want to move."

Sheva thanked Ahban and said that he and Jonathan would be back.

As they were leaving the school, Jonathan said to Sheva, "We are going to be able to work this out."

"Right. It will be good to get this settled, because we need to get back to Hebron. We not only have to move ourselves to this city, but we have to move all of our documents and supplies. I'm glad we did not unpack all of it."

"Since you have brought up this business of moving, I propose that we look around in this area for any housing possibilities. It may be a waste of time, because we don't know what will happen. But, it could give us some ideas."

"We need ideas. So where do we start?"

"I don't know. I wish that I had asked Zadok about housing."

"We could ask David to take over some buildings for us, but that is not the way to make friends for our new school."

"There is another possibility. If there are any government buildings in this area, David could use them without displacing anyone."

They had not walked far from the school, and Jonathan heard someone call his name. It was Zadok, and he said, "I was sent out for some food and supplies. What are the two of you doing?"

"I'm glad you saw us. We were just discussing the possibilities for housing, for ourselves and for the school. Do you know if there are any government buildings in this area that David will be using? We don't want to displace anyone."

"There is a government complex just down the street from our school. It was used by former governments to house foreign traders and diplomats. In recent years, we have not had many visitors, and the last ruler, Adonizedek, only used the buildings for storage. It would take a lot of work to fix it up, but it would be a great place to live and work. You wait for me right here, and I will do the shopping. Then I can show you these buildings on my way back to the school."

Zadok left, and Jonathan said, "This sounds good. I'm sure that David will provide us with some workmen to fix up a place."

"He'll do that, but if we like it, we must get him to let us have it before he or his men see it."

Soon, Zadok returned, and they followed him. As they were walking, Sheva said, "We want to thank you for arranging our participation in your meeting this morning. We were pleased with the meeting, and we hope all is going well."

Zadok said, "We can work out something. It would be an interesting situation, but you should know that even if we can work it out, you will always find some opposition in a school like ours, opposition to ideas and plans. Now we are approaching the complex. This wall surrounds the area. We will enter here to get a better look at the grounds and buildings. The large building in the center was used for meetings, and there are four smaller units that were used as living quarters. You can see things really need to be fixed up."

Jonathan said, "That it does. Fixed up and cleaned up. Thanks again for showing us this place. You need to get back with your supplies. We'll see you this evening."

Zadok left, and Sheva and Jonathan stayed there to have a better look at the place. Finally, Sheva said, "This place is just what we want. We'll need it regardless of the exact relationship that is worked out with the Jerusalem School. We should speak with David about this place this afternoon. Let's go to David's quarters now, and we can come back after we see David."

"That's fine with me."

They were able to see David, and he was interested in their report. He agreed that the old Bet-Hanokrim ("The House of the Foreigners") should become the Bet-Hasophrim ("The House of the Scribes"). In addition, he agreed to get it fixed up. He said that they would start cleaning the place, and that Sheva should get some plans to him as soon as possible for the repairs. It seemed that things were going well. It is a good thing they acted fast on this because in the following days David had several requests for the old foreign quarter.

Sheva and Jonathan had to hurry back to the school to be there for dinner. They arrived on time, and Ahban and Zadok greeted them. No

The Jerusalem School

one said anything about the outcome of the afternoon discussions. In fact, most of the teachers were not present for the evening meal, but there were some students. They had a good time with their food, drink, and conversation. After the meal, the students took care of the clean up, and the others moved to a more comfortable room.

Ahban said, "I should begin this conversation with a report. I was able to talk with everyone today. Some of those people could not be here this evening, but they have trusted me with their views. I was even able to talk with some of our teachers who are ill. The outcome of all of these conversations is that we want to work out a plan where we can join together with you as The Jerusalem Academy and at the same time our Old School and your New School could retain their separate identities. This makes sense to us at least for the present. We think this will work as long as the two schools have separate responsibilities. We think of ourselves as doing the basic education for the scribes, and we thought your school would probably spend most of its time, at least at first, dealing with the traditions of Judah and Israel. We also noted that both schools could work together on creating the cosmopolitan setting for both of these tasks. In other words we can support you when you make your requests for teachers from other centers. How does that sound?"

Jonathan leaned over and said to Sheva, "The plan sounds good."

So, Sheva said to the group, "You have come up with a plan that will work. It allows us to get to know each other as we work together in The Jerusalem Academy. We are bound to have some problems when we begin working together, but we can probably solve most of them. This does not mean we will all think the same thoughts. Since scribes are those who keep records and in some sense conserve the past, they can become conservative. But, there are always those who want to reconsider and to think new thoughts. We need such new thinking more than we need agreement on every issue."

Ahban responded by saying, "It will take a long time to work out all the details, but the first problem I see for you is what will you do about housing and buildings?"

Sheva smiled and said, "We have good news on that point. This afternoon, David gave us the go-ahead on using the old foreign quarter just down the street from this school. We hope that it will be adequate, and David said we could start the clean-up at once."

"That sounds good," said Ahban. "This is the first example of how it pays to work together. We have wanted that place to be cleaned up, but we were always afraid it would be used for something incompatible with our school."

Sheva and Jonathan and the others talked about many things that evening. After the two of them left, they felt tired. When they got back to David's quarters, they went to sleep at once. Morning came too soon for both of them. But, since they wanted to get home, they got up early. They left a full report with David, and they told him they would be back in a few days with the plans for the repair work.

21

The Move to Jerusalem

It was late when I heard Jonathan coming up the ladder. "I'm home," he said.

I had not been in bed long, so I was up in a flash. Jonathan and I were still holding each other when father came from his room. He wondered what all the fuss was about. Jonathan said, "I'm starved. We left Jerusalem early this morning. We had something to eat in Bethlehem, but that was a long time ago."

"We had better feed him," I said.

Father said, "Yes, we had better feed him but not too much at once. So, did you have a good experience in Jerusalem?"

"Yes, I did."

I brought Jonathan some bread, cheese, and wine. As he ate, he told us about his trip. He said that things went so well he wondered what would go wrong.

I said, "It sounds like The Jerusalem Academy will become a reality, and the government building complex is ideal. I can't wait to see it."

"It will look good when it is cleaned up."

"Father and I did a lot of packing while you were gone. When will we leave?"

"We will leave just as soon as it is possible. Sheva and I talked about that on the way home. He wants me to go soon and look after the clean up and fix-up. He will stay here and work with the others on packing all the things in our offices. These government buildings used to be for foreigners who had business in the city. There is a large building for the school and four houses. The largest of the houses will be used for students and single scribes. Sheva and Sarah will have one house; we will have another one, and it has an extra room for Gad; and the fourth house will be used for guests."

Father said, "This sounds like an ideal place, and I think I have seen it. When will David send a wagon for our things?"

"Just as soon as I order it."

"Do you still have to go to Tyre?" I asked.

"I don't know. If I go, it will not be soon. There is too much to do, and we also need to involve the old Jerusalem School in the selection of any new teacher who would like to come to Jerusalem."

Father said, "We could be ready to leave in about two days."

"That would be great. It will take me about that long to get my office in order."

"Which reminds me, let's get to bed," I said as I took Jonathan in hand.

In the morning, everyone was in a big hurry. Jonathan got to his office and began to pack some things. Elishama stopped by to ask Jonathan about the trip. He was pleased to hear about it, and he said that he hoped he could work with them in Jerusalem. Jonathan told him that such a thing was a real possibility. Jonathan also talked with Sheva concerning some of the details of the move, and they went over a list of needed repairs on the buildings in Jerusalem. He requested a wagon be sent to father's house, and he came home. He helped father and me with our packing. We also worked most of the next day. The morning of our move, we had a difficult time getting everything on the wagon, but we did manage, and soon, we were on our way.

When we reached our new home in Jerusalem, father and I were both impressed. Even Jonathan was surprised to see so much had been accomplished. We could not move into our house yet, because of the needed repairs, but that would not take too long. So, we unloaded our things next to the house and set up our camping spot. In the evening, Zadok and Ahban came by. They met father and me, and they told Jonathan that the students and teachers at the old school were excited about what was going on.

The next day, Jonathan talked with David concerning the repairs, and David said to Jonathan, "It is a good thing you asked for that place when you did. I went by there the other day, and now I know why almost everyone who works for me wants those buildings. By the way, I had a message from Hiram, king of Tyre, and he is sending some men to plan my palace. They will bring two scribes with them to work on the plans and

The Move to Jerusalem

the lists of materials. You will not have to go up there just now, and you can talk to the scribes about a teacher."

"Good. I didn't want to make that trip just now. There is too much to do."

Then David said, "I want you to know that you are not living in Jerusalem. I have renamed it. You are now living in the 'City of David.'"

As Jonathan was walking back to the school, he thought, "David may have renamed Jerusalem, but I will use the old name. The 'City of David' may be a descriptive phrase, but it does not qualify as a name for this great place. Jerusalem is David's royal city, but that does not call for a new name."

The rest of the day, Jonathan worked with the workmen. I had already told them some things I wanted done to the house, but the men did not want to do those things until Jonathan gave the order. He told them in the future, they should follow my orders. This was hard for them to understand, and Jonathan did not try to explain that we were living in the future. In the afternoon, father went to check in with David, so Jonathan and I both worked on the house with the workmen. The workmen were still uneasy around me. It is not easy to live in the future. Everything and everyone pulls you back into your old paths. Also the necessities of life create a wall, which is difficult to scale, but I will not give up.

After a few weeks, the house was ready, and we moved from the yard to the house.

Our small house was made of stone. We had one floor, four rooms, and the roof. It faced east, and the morning sun warmed it. For the winter this was good, but in the summer and fall, we had to put up shades so that the house could retain the cool of the night. In the evening we were in the shade of the higher ground to the west, and the roof was a cool spot. One day we had a few clouds, and the view from the roof at twilight was beyond belief. Though we were in the shade, rays of light played upon the high ridge to the east just beyond the Kidron valley. Our house was situated just right for this view. Jonathan and I were sitting there watching as shadows moved across the hill. That night Jonathan and I wrote this poem:

The Jerusalem Academy

> It was cool all day.
> Shadows on the hills,
> They're moving, not still;
> They follow their clouds.

Now we could turn our attention to the other houses. We had to get at least two more houses repaired, and then the workmen could start on the large building for the school. Jonathan wanted to have Sheva and Sarah's house ready for them, so everyone worked hard on that project. It took longer to fix up Sheva and Sarah's house. But, it all worked out well, because they got here about two days after their house was ready. Sheva said the workmen should at least get one room done in the school building. He wanted to be able to unload all of the documents and other things, which they brought with them from Hebron.

It took about seven months to get everyone settled in their quarters, and the school building was still not finished. Sheva and Jonathan began to think they must get back to their scribal activities. In fact David was asking them to do a lot of things. Elimelech, Danel, and Noah were busy writing letters. Sheva said to Jonathan, "Let's invite Ahban over here tonight. We should talk to him about getting some of their students to help with some of the letters. Ahban said they wanted to deal with the basic education of the scribe, and this would give their students some practical experience."

Jonathan said, "We should do it. Also we need to talk with Ahban about a teacher. Those workmen and scribes from Tyre should be here in the next few days. I'll talk with the scribes concerning a teacher, and we need to know what Ahban thinks on that subject."

Sheva said, "I'll go over to the Old School right now, and I'll invite Ahban over here for this evening. Let's get together after our evening meal at my place."

Jonathan came home to tell me about these plans. He thought he could help me, and then we could eat a little early. When he got here, I was glad to get the help. I was depressed, because father was not happy just now. It seems that David has not said much to father since the move to Jerusalem, and father feels like David does not want him around anymore. But, father does not know if this is really the case. It did not take long to get the meal ready. Jonathan called father, and soon we were at the table. Jonathan said, "It is great to be around this table. Here is where we have

The Move to Jerusalem

always had our best moments. Keziah tells me that she would not have married me if I had not found a place at your table."

"That's right Mr. Scribe."

Then Jonathan told father, "Ahban is coming over here tonight for some planning. I would like for you to go over to Sheva and Sarah's house with Keziah and me, because I want to know your evaluation of this man. He is really quite impressive."

"I'll go with you. I'm not really in demand these days."

Jonathan said, "Well, perhaps we have kept you working too much for us. I hope we have not been too demanding, but we could not have made this move without your help."

Father wanting to change the subject said, "Perhaps you have told me before, but why are you so interested in Ahban? Keziah and I did meet him once. He came by one evening when we were still camping, but there was really not any conversation."

"Well, he is the head of the Old School, and we need to work with him on many things. His students may help us on some letter writing jobs, and I want to know what kind of a teacher he would like from Tyre. Also, he is just an interesting person in that he is from Judah, and he has become a leader in this school."

I said, "Let's finish this meal. I would like to hear this discussion myself."

Father and Jonathan helped me pick things up, and then we walked over to Sheva and Sarah's house. We got there just after Ahban had arrived. Jonathan reintroduced me to Ahban, and he said, "The other evening when we first met, I thought to myself, 'I finally have the pleasure of meeting one of Job's daughters,' but then I met your father, Gad, and I thought, Keziah is more 'fortunate' than Job's daughter."

"I am fortunate."

Ahban said, "Gad, it's good to see you again."

Sarah brought out some fruit and raisin cakes, and I helped her with the wine. Ahban told the group that he was pleased with the way things looked since the big clean-up project. After a short time, Sheva said to Ahban, "We wanted to talk with you about several things. The first thing has to do with writing letters. David has us writing lots of letters these days. We were wondering if some of your students could help with a project such as this?"

The Jerusalem Academy

"Of course. This is exactly what they need. Send one of your scribes to my office tomorrow with the letters and lists of those to whom the letters will be sent."

Sheva said, "I'll send Elimelech the first thing in the morning. The next thing we need to talk about can best be explained by Jonathan."

Jonathan said, "Sometime in the near future, we will have some guests from Tyre. King Hiram of Tyre is sending some people to plan a palace for David. Among those people will be two scribes. Sometime ago, David asked me to go to Tyre to look for a teacher. Now he thinks that I should talk to these two scribes concerning a teacher and wait until later for the trip. What I need from both of you, Sheva and Ahban, are comments concerning the qualifications that such a teacher should have. Sheva has already mentioned to me that such a teacher should know at least two languages other than his own. He also said that a teacher should be a sensitive human being. Ahban, can you add anything to these comments?"

"The comments are good. I would like to make them in a more concrete fashion. The two-language suggestion is a good one, but one of those languages should be Babylonian. Babylonian has been the language of diplomacy for a long time (even though this is beginning to change), and most of the great literature of our area can be found in Babylonian. I also think we will need a second teacher who is good at Egyptian. Egyptian is important for us. Now, if you are going to get a teacher from Tyre, he will know their traditions, but I think this person should also know the traditions and the language of his ancestors from places like Ugarit. Most of the scribes from Tyre know a little bit about their past but not much. They might know about the great Danel and his son Aqhat, but that is about it."

Jonathan said, "You will be glad to hear that one of our scribes has taken the name Danel. He heard about Danel from one of his teachers who was from Tyre. What you have said is important. I will keep in mind the points you have made."

Ahban added, "It may be difficult to find a teacher who is really sensitive. It is important to have someone with whom you can work, but I would not demand an understanding of our problems on the part of a teacher from Tyre. In fact, it may be important to learn from such a teacher everything he knows and to try to understand his situation and his problems. It is always difficult for another person to help us. I have usually not found answers to my problems when I set out to find answers; I have uncovered answers when I was not looking for answers. But, it is

The Move to Jerusalem

important to keep looking at this world and watching others deal with problems. We must remain curious, and that is another thing that a good teacher must have; he must have curiosity."

Sheva said, "I have learned from what you have said, because when I first talked with Jonathan about getting a well educated and sensitive person, I must say that I was thinking of a person who could help us bring together the scribes of Judah and Israel. In light of what you have said, we should not expect such a teacher to solve that problem for us. You are correct."

Ahban was quick to add, "But a good teacher can interest students in greater things than their problems. This does not solve such problems, but it may shrink them."

Jonathan said, "This conversation is helpful, and I hope we can have this sort of exchange on a regular basis. I will, of course, report to all of you what I find out from the scribes, who are coming from Tyre."

Sheva said, "I want to thank Ahban for this discussion, and I'm sure if anyone has more questions they should feel free to carry on. But, right now my cup is empty, and I am going to fill it."

Father wanted to talk with Ahban; he said, "I have enjoyed this evening, and I liked what you said about being curious. Curiosity and observation are so important if one wants to really be alive."

With a smile, Ahban said, "Here, I have found a prophet with the heart of a sage."

I was standing next to father, and it was good to hear Ahban's words, and father seemed to come alive.

When we got back to our house, Jonathan asked father what he thought of Ahban. "Ahban is obviously a able person. He knows what's going on; he knows what to look for and where to look for it. He will help The Jerusalem Academy in many ways."

Jonathan replied, "I agree with you, and I guess I need some more help from you. The other day, David told Sheva and me to listen carefully to Ahban. I'm afraid that David will want Ahban for a counselor, but we need him. Of course, if he became a counselor to the king that does not mean he would not help The Jerusalem Academy, but, I just don't want this to happen too soon. I will discuss this with Sheva, and I will try to convince him we should not even mention Ahban's name when we are talking to David. Perhaps you can help to keep Ahban for the school?"

Father said, "It is hard to hide a bright star in the sky, but perhaps we can keep David so busy that he will have no time for the stars."

"I don't think either of you can stop such a thing. You might slow things down, but in the end only Ahban can say, 'No.'"

Jonathan said, "You're probably right. In any case, we need to be ready to deal with such an eventuality. If it happens, we will need a new leader for the Old School."

Father said, "As usual, I'm going to bed. I'll leave the problems with you. *Laylah tov.*"

I said, "We should go to bed. I really feel at home here, and I want you to be able to enjoy the wife of your youth before you get too old. The problems father left with us can wait until tomorrow."

"You're so right."

Jonathan carried me to our bed, and said, "You must be the wife of my youth."

Enjoy they did. It was late when they went to sleep.

22

The Census and the Threshing Floor

IN THE MORNING FATHER was a little more cheerful, and he got an early start. He wanted to see if David needed him for anything. He arrived at David's quarters and was able to see David at that early hour. David said, "You are just the one I wanted to see. I've got a real problem."

"You had better tell me about it."

"You should sit down, because this will take a while. Shortly after we settled in Jerusalem, Yahweh became angry at our new united Israel. I don't know why he was so angry, but I think it was a continuation of his anger at the northern part of the kingdom, or really Saul's kingdom, for allowing the ark to be captured by the Philistines. After all, the ark was the cultic symbol of Yahweh's presence. So, the ark was in exile, which meant that in some way Yahweh was in exile. At any rate, Yahweh was angry, and he incited me against Israel and said, 'Go number Israel and Judah.' I called Joab to my office, and I told him to go to all the tribes from Dan to Beer-sheba and to take a census. This census was necessary for our new administration, for taxes, and of course for the military draft. Joab did not want to do this, because he knew the people would not like it. However, I insisted it was the thing to do. It took Joab and his men a long time to complete this census, but finally Joab gave me the numbers. There were 800,000 fighting men in Israel and 500,000 in Judah. Now we knew what we could count on when it was time to expand and secure our borders."

David continued, "Since then I have had second thoughts. In fact, I'm certain that I've done wrong; I should not have counted the people. The people did not like this at all, and I'm now certain that Yahweh is also displeased. Gad, can you find out for me what this is all about? Is Yahweh still angry?"

"I'll try to find out about this. Perhaps there will be some way that you can now make things better. All of this is far from clear. There are two clear things: 1) You wanted to muster the troops, and 2) the people did not like what you did. You have said that Yahweh 'incited you to number (*manah*) Israel and Judah.' But you did much more in your so-called census; you 'mustered (*paqad*)' the troops. Then later you say that you regret that you 'counted (*saphar*)' the people. Do you regret that you mustered the troops? You are using too many terms. Is your sin that you counted the people or does your real sin have to do with the fact that you have mustered the troops, and you have blamed Yahweh for inciting you to do just that?"

"Gad, you are a hard man."

"No. I just know we must try to understand what you have done and what we can do about it. I will try to find out. As soon as I have any word from Yahweh, I will bring it to you."

With that, father left, and he headed for Ahban's office. He had to talk with someone about this problem. When he got there, Ahban was gone, and father decided to wait for a while. This was really what he needed. It gave him time to sort things out. It was not long until Ahban returned. Father asked him if he had time to talk, and Ahban said he did. Father explained the problem that David was having and also what David wanted from him. "David wants me to tell him if Yahweh is still angry. This makes me wonder how David found out Yahweh was angry at Israel and how Yahweh incited David. I told him I would get back to him when I had some word from Yahweh. I did not tell him a word from Yahweh is a scarce item in these days."

Ahban said, "You were right when you put it to David in a clear manner. But, now we have to try and help him. It will not change things even if we found out Yahweh was never angry. It is possible something bad happened to someone, and David took it as a sign that Yahweh was angry. In any case, David wanted an excuse to do what he did, and now he is afraid. I wonder if David is really sorry?"

"I doubt it, because he thinks he had to do what he did."

"Then we should try to make him sorry. It will do him good. Now, I agree with you a word from Yahweh is rare, but Yahweh gave us minds to use. We can figure this out."

"I agree, but I must say I'm getting tired of passing off my best thinking as a word of Yahweh."

The Census and the Threshing Floor

"I understand, but you may have to make such a claim to get David's attention. Even if you avoid such a claim, others will credit you with delivering a word from Yahweh if what you say has an important impact on future events. I have heard that in the far north near Dan they are having a serious plague. Lots of people are dying. This plague will spread. Let it be David's punishment. We can even let him choose it as his punishment. As you know the three stereotypes of divine punishment are usually covered in our traditions by the sword, famine, and plague/pestilence. All we have to do is let David choose the lesser of the three evils."

Father said, "You are on to something. I will say to David that Yahweh will let him choose his punishment from three things: 1) a seven year famine, 2) three months of being pursued by enemies, or 3) three days of pestilence."

"Good. David will choose number three, and there is a pestilence or plague."

Father said, "I should just present him with the choice and then wait a few days until he hears about the plague. Then I can return and offer some suggestions as to what he should do about it. He should offer some sacrifice or something."

Ahban said, "You told me that David thought that Yahweh was still angry, because Israel lost the ark. You could suggest to David that he should bring the ark to Jerusalem. We need an important cultic center here in Jerusalem. You could help bring this about in your instruction to David as to what he should do to stop the plague. The threshing floor of Araunah is already an important cultic center. Tell David to buy it and set up an altar. Then he should offer sacrifices and stop the plague."

"I can do that, but how will it help to get the ark back?"

"It will create a place for the ark; this threshing floor will be its sanctuary. I'm so glad you came here today to talk about this. Together we came up with ideas that would have never surfaced if we had been working by ourselves."

Father said, "I have tried to work alone and nothing happens. I did not even know about your interest in a cultic center for Jerusalem. Now I know, and it makes sense. Perhaps we have helped each other, but you have helped me more than I have helped you. I will present the options to David tomorrow. If all goes according to the plan, we will only have one worry. Can the plague be stopped, and will it be stopped before it reaches Jerusalem?"

The Jerusalem Academy

"The plague will be stopped before it gets here," Ahban answered. "We are too high in the mountains for this sickness to come to our city."

In the evening father had a good time with Jonathan and me, but he did not feel like talking about his day. That night a strange thing happened. He actually did dream that Yahweh had given David three choices as to his punishment. The next morning, father went to see David, and David dropped everything else to talk with father.

Father said, "Yahweh has indicated you can choose your punishment from the following three things: 1) a seven year famine, 2) three months of fleeing from your enemies, or 3) three days of pestilence in your land. He wants you to consider this carefully, and I will take your answer to him."

David said, "I'll take number three."

Father left at once. He did not want to discuss anything with David. It was not long before David was told that there was a serious plague in the land. It was reported that many had died. When David heard this he said to Yahweh:

> "I, I have sinned.
> I have done wrong.
> These of the flock,
> what have they done?
> Let your hand fall,
> please, upon me
> and my father's house." (2 Samuel 24:17b)

Then David sent for father again. When father arrived David said, "The plague is bad, and it is my fault. What can be done?"

Father said, "You must go and set up an altar to Yahweh on the threshing floor of Araunah the Jebusite. Purchase the threshing floor without delay."

David left at once and headed for the threshing floor. Araunah saw David coming, and he greeted him and asked him what he wanted. David said, "I want to buy your threshing floor and build an altar. The plague against Israel must be stopped."

Araunah tried to give the threshing floor to David, but David insisted it must be purchased. So, David bought the threshing floor and some oxen, and he sacrificed the oxen to Yahweh. The plague against Israel was stopped.

The Census and the Threshing Floor

A few days later, father saw Ahban, and they had another long talk. They were glad the plan had worked, and Ahban reported he had already suggested to David that he should bring the ark to Jerusalem and the threshing floor of Araunah should be used to house the ark. Then he said to father, "Some day this threshing floor will be the site of a temple for Yahweh. It will be Yahweh's mountain."

In the evening, father told Jonathan and me about his recent activities, and he said some things about his plans for the future. He said, "A few days ago, I felt useless. I was not doing anything, and then during the past few days there was too much to do. I want to be busy, but I have decided I do not want to claim I have a word from Yahweh. I like to solve problems with the mind Yahweh gave me, and if the answers are correct and helpful that is enough. I will not give my words extra authority by claiming that they are from Yahweh. This is a farce! I should gradually withdraw from being one of the loyal-royals. I want to begin my book entitled *The Acts of David*."

Jonathan said, "This is good news. We can find an office for you at the school."

"I would like that."

23

The Growth and Agenda of the Jerusalem Academy

THE GUESTS FROM TYRE arrived one month later than the time that Jonathan had expected them. The delay was helpful in some ways. Even though the school building was still not ready, the guesthouse was finished by then, and the two scribes were able to stay there. They had to work with the builders, who were planning the palace, during the day, but in the evenings, Jonathan and Sheva were able to talk with them. On at least one occasion, Ahban talked with them. These two scribes were helpful, but nothing was really settled from these talks. They thought someone would be available in either Tyre, Sidon, or Byblos, but they did not know for certain. They promised to spread the word that Jerusalem needed a teacher when they got back to Tyre. Jonathan was disappointed in the talks, because he had hoped to come up with some names. It seemed not many of the available teachers could handle Babylonian. One encouraging factor was that several of the scribes at Tyre could handle their ancient traditions from places like Ugarit. Jonathan asked the scribes to write to him when they had some names.

Sheva, Jonathan, and Ahban were now meeting at least twice a week in order to plan the work. Ahban was busy in the Old School, and Sheva was trying to get some of the chronicles of both Judah and Israel caught up. Danel and Noah were helping him. Many things needed recorded following the coronations and the move to Jerusalem. Elishama from Shechem, who had helped on the second coronation, was now with the New School in Jerusalem. He, Jonathan and Elimelech were organizing a lot of traditions from Israel and from Judah. Elishama and his wife were living in the guesthouse, and in a real sense, there was no longer a guesthouse. Elimelech, Danel, and Noah were in the house they would share with students in the near future.

The Growth and Agenda of the Jerusalem Academy

At one of their meetings, Ahban suggested that Jonathan and his associates should start to think about bringing some of the traditions together in a work that could be used for an occasion like the dedication of David's palace. Ahban claimed any great king who brought together two states such as Judah and Israel should publish such a work. This would be a royal epic, which would unify the people in a kingdom, which had been planned from the beginning. In such works, there is usually a God who brings order out of chaos, and who rules the world as its king. This divine king blesses certain fathers. and their descendants finally produce a king such as David.

This work would show the world that David's kingship is not only legitimate, but it is also according to the will of Yahweh, who is the divine ruler of this world.

Then Ahban said, "The Babylonians have published such a work. They call it *Enuma elish*. In this work they show how Marduk brought order out of chaos and became king of the world. It was then that Babylon and Marduk ruled a united Babylonian kingdom. This is what we need to say concerning Jerusalem and Yahweh. Here we have Jerusalem and Yahweh, or if you want Zion and Yahweh, ruling a united and greater Israel. David as the king of this Israel serves a greater king, namely Yahweh. You could bring together enough materials to do such a thing and make it interesting."

Jonathan said, "We could give it a try. I'm not sure we could finish it in time for the dedication, but if we're lucky, it will take a long time to build the palace. In any case, we need to do such a work."

Sheva said, "I agree! You should start on it at once. This does not mean you can spend all of your time on it; you will have to do other things as well, when they come along, but you should start now and have as much time as possible. A project like a royal epic will be demanding."

Jonathan said, "If Elimelech and Elishama can help me and if the two of you will help us as critics, I would like to do it. I will let you know next week how we are doing."

That evening during the evening meal, Jonathan told father and me about the project. It was easy to see that Jonathan was excited about it. Gad asked him if he could find enough materials. Jonathan said, "I don't know, but we will try. Also, we may have to write up some new material. I will have Elimelech and Elishama start on the second half of our work, that is, on the stories of the fathers. We have worked with such texts for our coronations, and we know more about such things. I will try to come up with something on the time before the fathers. Also, I'll have to bring together all that I can find on how God formed our world and how he became king of the world."

Father said, "You will find many different stories about such things. It will be important to find the stories that both Judah and Israel will be able to see as their stories. This is interesting, because I remember telling Sheva, when we were working on the first coronation, before you came to Hebron, that someday when David becomes king of both Judah and Israel, we will have to do as others have done; we will have to begin before there were any 'fathers' at all in order to really tell David's story."

"Are you going to let me read some of these stories about the beginning of the world?" I asked. "I want to if possible."

"Of course, you can read them. Also you should come to work with me and listen to some of our discussions."

"I want to do that whenever I can. You have a new project, and it is interesting. However, I have a new project; it will interest you. We are going to have a baby!"

Jonathan put his arms around me; he kissed me and said, "You should have stopped me from talking about my work. It is not important compared to what you are doing. Gad, you'll be a grandfather!"

"This is wonderful; I'm going to be a happy grandfather."

Jonathan found it difficult to speak. He was happy, and he just held me. Finally I said, "Let's finish eating. Both of you will have time to get ready for our child so don't try to say everything tonight. I know I'm happy, and I want to enjoy every moment as we anticipate the birth of our first child. Today, I talked with Elishama's wife, Deborah; she is also expecting. There are going to be babies around this New School and in our new home."

The next morning when Jonathan saw Elishama at work, he greeted him with a big smile and said, "I heard last night that we are both going to be fathers."

Elishama was obviously happy and noted that the women had planned to tell the fathers on the same evening.

They talked about all of this until Elimelech arrived. They informed him of the news, and then Jonathan attempted to explain their new project. Then he asked, "How can we start this project? We must begin by collecting materials. We already have many texts dealing with the fathers. The two of you can start your work by putting them in order. But, we need everything we can find on the creation. I will begin to collect creation materials. There are psalms that deal with creation, but we must look everywhere. For example, I know the priests have a text on creation, because I remember seeing a ritual that praises God as the creator. I will have to ask Abiathar about that text. In addition, I need to see some creation materials from some of the other countries; I want us to produce materials that will be better than those. Now I wish we had our new teacher. He could help us understand the foreign stories."

Elimelech said, "A new teacher might be helpful, but it seems to me if we start now, we can always correct and change our work at a later time."

"True. We can change it, unless we get too attached to what we have done," said Jonathan.

Elishama said, "We had a teacher when I was at the Old School who taught us about Babylonian creation stories. They even deal with stories about the birth of the gods. Where would we start?"

Jonathan said, "We would not start at the beginning in that sense. Judah and Israel are not interested in where the gods came from; they are not interested in where matter came from. They are interested in their claim that Yahweh defeated the sea or the power of chaos; they are interested in how Yahweh shaped the matter, and how he established our world. We start with Yahweh as the king of our world. We do not know about anything before that moment. Perhaps, we should not even refer to our stories as 'creation stories,' because others may think that we are talking about 'the beginning' in the Babylonian sense. But what can we call such stories? On the one hand, they are really 'enthronement stories;' God reigns. On the other hand, they deal with how God orders and establishes our world. We could just call them *These are the Stories of the Heavens and the Earth*, or in other words, the stories of everything in our world as we know it."

After this discussion, Elimelech and Elishama started working on the stories of the fathers. Jonathan decided to go see Abiathar and ask him about a priestly creation ritual. He ran into Abiathar at David's quarters. They talked about some of the recent developments. What Jonathan found interesting was that Abiathar was conferring with David concerning the advantages of using some of the Jerusalem priests in cultic rituals.

The Jerusalem Academy

Abiathar was also interested in re-establishing a priestly center at Nob, northeast of Jerusalem. This is the place where Saul massacred a group of priests. Abiathar, who had been at Nob, escaped that fate. One of the priests Abiathar was working with in Jerusalem was named Zadok. So, the priests were uniting with the priests of Jerusalem just as the scribes were bringing together the Old School and the New School. Interestingly there was a Zadok among the priests and a Zadok among the scribes.

Jonathan said to Abiathar, "All of this is interesting. You are joining with the Jerusalem priests, and we have joined with the Jerusalem scribes."

Abiathar said, "It is going to be helpful in our case, and I suppose in yours as well. It may be more difficult in our situation, because priests are not usually noted for a willingness to change. But, with priests from Israel and Judah coming together, there is a lot of change in the air, and we hope the priests of Jerusalem will help us."

"We are finding our work is much easier with the two schools working together. Abiathar, I'm glad that I found you, because I need your help. We are preparing a document for the dedication of David's palace. We need some material on how God established the heavens and the earth. I remember a seven-day ritual that went through such material. Do you have that ritual among your things?"

"I do, but I will have to look for it. We observed that ritual at our spring New Year celebration. At that time, we were reminded that Yahweh defeated chaos; he established order; he was our king, ruler of our world. Also, some of the priests from Israel may have a slightly different text of that ritual, because they always combined establishing the world with establishing the people of Israel at the time of the exodus from Egypt. At the exodus, God as the man of war defeated the sea; this time he created for himself a people. I'll look for such a text, and I'll send it to you soon."

"*Todah*! I can't thank you enough. This will help us. Keep in touch. We will be interested in how things work out with you and the Jerusalem priests. *Shalom.*"

About a week later, a messenger from Abiathar brought Jonathan the text he had asked about. The messenger also said Abiathar would send other such texts if he found them, but he wanted these texts returned as soon as Jonathan could copy them. Jonathan was excited when he unrolled the text. The first thing he noticed was God was called Elohim (the plural form). The personal name, "Yahweh" was not used. This seemed to make

God more distant, but the one who controlled the waters of chaos was in fact more distant. But Jonathan was surprised; there were few details in this ritual text. On each of the seven ritual days, there was the implication that God should be praised for what he had made, but there were not any instructions as to how to praise God on each day. It was a hymnic reminder of the value of an established order. After looking it over, he began to read:

> When Elohim first began to form the heavens and the earth,
> The earth was devastation and desolation,
> Darkness was over [the] deep,
> The wind of Elohim was storming over the waters,
>
> Elohim said:
> "Let there be light."
> There was light.
> Elohim saw that the light was good.
> Elohim divided between the light and between the darkness.
> Elohim called the light day.
> The darkness he called night.
> There was evening.
> There was morning:
> Day one.
>
> Elohim said:
> "Let there be a vault in the midst of the waters.
> Let there be a division between waters and waters."
> Elohim made the vault.
> He divided between the waters that were under the vault,
> and between the waters that were above the vault.
> So it was.
> Elohim called the vault heaven.
> There was evening.
> There was morning:
> A second day.
>
> Elohim said:
> "Let the waters under the heavens be pooled into one place.
> Let the dry land appear."

So it was.
Elohim called the dry land earth.
The pools of waters he called seas.
Elohim saw that it was good.
Elohim said:
> "Let the earth produce vegetation
> (plants that scatter seed, [and] fruit trees that bear fruit
> of their kind in which is their seed) upon the earth."

So it was.
The earth brought forth vegetation
(plants that scatter seed of their kind, and trees
that bear fruit in which is their seed of their kind).
Elohim saw that it was good.
There was evening.
There was morning:
A third day.

Elohim said:
> "Let there be lights in the vault of the heavens
> to divide between the day and between the night;
> they will be for signs and seasons and for days and years;
> they will be for lights in the vault of the heavens to give
> light upon the earth."

So it was.
Elohim made the two great lights,
the greater light to rule the day
and the lesser light to rule the night,
and the stars.
Elohim placed them in the vault of the heavens,
to give light upon the earth,
to rule in the day and in the night,
and to divide between the light and between the darkness.
Elohim saw that it was good.
There was evening.
There was morning:
A fourth day.

Elohim said:

"Let the waters swarm with swarms of living beings.
Let birds fly about—above the earth
and under the vault of the heavens."
Elohim formed the great sea monsters,
and all the living beings—
the moving ones who swarmed in the waters—with their kind,
and all the birds of wing with their kind.
Elohim saw that it was good.
Elohim blessed them saying:
"Be fruitful, multiply, and fill the waters in the seas,
and let the birds multiply on the earth."
There was evening.
There was morning:
A fifth day.

Elohim said:
"Let the earth bring forth living beings with their kind:
domestic animals, moving ones, and wild animals with their kind."
So it was.
Elohim made the wild animals with their kind,
the domestic animals with their kind,
and all the moving ones of the ground with their kind.
Elohim saw that it was good.
[There was evening.
There was morning:
A sixth day].

Elohim said:
"Let us make human beings in our image—after our likeness;
they will supervise the fish of the sea,
the birds of the heavens, the domestic animals,
all of the earth, and all the ones who move upon the earth."
Elohim formed the human beings in his image;
in the image of Elohim he formed them;
male and female he formed them.
Elohim blessed them;
Elohim said to them:
"Be fruitful and multiply; fill the earth;
make it a servant; and supervise the fish of the sea,

> the birds of the heavens, and all the living ones
> who move upon the earth."
>
> Elohim said:
>> "See, I give you every plant that scatters
>> seed that is upon all the earth and every tree that scatters
>> seed (that is in the fruit of the tree); it will be yours for food.
>> To all the wild animals, to all the birds of the heavens,
>> and to all the ones who move upon the earth
>> (that are living beings), [I give] all the green plants for food."
>
> So it was.
> Elohim saw all that he had made, and behold, it was very good.
> There was evening.
> There was morning:
> [A seventh] day
> (Genesis 1:1–31, plus two additions in brackets = an older form)

After reading the entire text, Jonathan thought that it was interesting, and he wondered why this ritual was not used anymore either at the spring New Year or the Passover. Perhaps people got tired of seven-day rituals, but since the Passover is for seven days, a ritual like this could be used in connection with it as Abiathar had said they did in the north. Jonathan was giving this some thought when Sheva and Ahban dropped by his office.

Sheva said, "Jonathan, how is the new project coming along?"

"It is coming along just fine. Elimelech and Elishama are working on the stories of the fathers, and I have been collecting material concerning the formation of our world. Abiathar just sent me this seven-day ritual dealing with these matters. It is interesting. He said this was used a long time ago at the spring New Year celebration and at times for the Passover."

Ahban said, "I remember using such a ritual, but we have been too disorganized for too long. We can hardly find time to continue the Passover. Also, this ritual seemed a bit dull to some of the people. At the new year celebration, they always wanted some of the more dramatic enthronement psalms celebrating the reign of God."

Jonathan said, "I have seen some psalms of that type, but I would like to collect all of them."

Ahban said, "Come by my office after lunch, and I will have one for you. But, right now we want to talk with you about a couple of things.

The Growth and Agenda of the Jerusalem Academy

David wants me to join his staff as a counselor. David says that I can still work with all of you in the academy, but I know it will not be the same."

"I knew this would happen. Your leadership is important in the academy. What will we do?"

Sheva said, "That's the reason we came here to see you. We thought you could take over the leadership of the Old School."

"I do not want to. You need someone from the Old School, and I would suggest Zadok."

Sheva said, "Zadok was going to be our second choice, but you have made him our first."

"I'm glad," said Jonathan. "I really do not want such a job. I know it is important, and both of you are good at such work, but it is not for me. I want to continue my writing."

"I can understand that," said Ahban. "Now there is a second matter. The scribes, who were here from Tyre, have put out the news of our need for a teacher. Tomorrow, a teacher from Tyre will be here for an interview. We want to spend most of the day on this meeting."

"So, you bring me bad news and good news. Tomorrow will be an interesting day."

Jonathan continued working on his texts and then came home for lunch. On his way back, he went by Ahban's office to get the psalm. Ahban had the psalm ready, and Jonathan thanked him. Then Jonathan said, "I hope you will be here at the school, whenever there is any time David does not need you. I'll miss you around here."

"I'll try to be here often. You will also be able to see me at David's quarters now and at the palace later. I can do some good for the academy, so you will have to keep me informed as to what you need. I want to see your work from time to time. You should try to finish this work for the dedication as soon as possible. We need a royal epic."

Jonathan worked all afternoon, but he did not look at the new text he had from Ahban. He wanted to look at it later with me.

24

Yahweh, the Warrior

THAT NIGHT AT THE dinner table we talked about Ahban's departure. Jonathan said, "David or those around him will not appreciate Ahban's wisdom. It was so important for us to have him here. In our discussions, Ahban always had a contribution to make that usually set the course for any subsequent discussion on the matter at hand. I hope he can help David, but most politicians do not understand wisdom."

"Can Zadok handle the task of leading the Old School?" I said.

"I think he can."

Father said, "You will miss Ahban, but my work will be made easier with Ahban in the picture. As you know, he has already helped me once before."

"That's right, and I must say my remarks were self centered. I am certain he will help you in various ways."

I said, "I heard some one mention Ahban's son, Eliam, but I have never heard anything about his wife."

Jonathan said, "His wife died many years ago. He does have a son named Eliam, and he has been a member of one of David's best military units. Eliam has a daughter, and her name is Bathsheba. She is married to Uriah the Hittite, who is a remarkable fellow and a military man. At times, Ahban mentions Bathsheba, and you can tell that he really loves his granddaughter."

Father said, "I hope this move works out for everybody."

After dinner, Jonathan unrolled the text Ahban had given to him. He wanted me to read it, and he hoped father might have some comments on it. I read:

> Yahweh reigns;
> [In] majesty he is robed;

> Robed is Yahweh;
> [With] victory he girds himself.
>
> Thus, established is the world;
> Never again shall it collapse.
> Your throne was established from old;
> You are from antiquity.
>
> The oceans have lifted high, O Yahweh;
> The oceans have lifted their thunderous voice;
> The oceans lift their crashing [waves].
>
> Mightier than the thunders of the waters,
> Mightier than the breakers of the sea,
> Mightier than the heights is Yahweh.
>
> Your coronation testimonies are very firm;
> Your temple is made beautiful with holiness,
> O Yahweh, for all times. (Psalm 93)

Jonathan said, "I like this psalm. Gad, have you heard it before?"

"I probably have heard it, but there are several psalms, which deal with this theme, so I can't be certain."

"I'm not certain that I know what the theme is," I said.

Father said, "The main point is Yahweh is king; he rules. He is mightier than the sea or chaos, and as king he rules the world he has established."

"I can understand that, but what about the testimonies and the temple? Our God has never had a temple."

Father continued, "When God becomes king it is like when David became king. At the coronation, a decree or testimony was given. David in the decree was declared to be God's son and the legitimate king. Here God becomes king and gives his promise and firm testimony he will order all things and make life possible. As to the temple, our God will have a temple on Zion some day, but our God, and the gods of others, has always had a temple on his own mountain in the north. The king rules the earth from such a temple."

Jonathan added, "I like these enthronement psalms, because they take us back as far as we can go; we can not push things back before God becomes king. Also, these psalms are full of life and drama. I would be willing to just use some of these psalms in our royal epic when we deal with the formation of the earth. I get the feeling some people, like Ahban, would agree. But, I read a ritual text today that I received from Abiathar, and it gives a lot more detail concerning how everything was formed but almost nothing on how God defeated the sea or chaos and became king. It just assumes you know he is king when it says, 'The wind of Elohim was storming over the waters.' It was used at celebrations of the spring New Year and also at Passover. For seven days, God was praised for the things he had made. It was all put into an ordered progression starting with the plants and ending with the human beings. We may use it, but it is not as dramatic as this psalm we have here."

Father said, "I remember that celebration. It did not really catch on. It was too formal. The people would always rather have a song."

"True, but if this royal epic is for the dedication of the palace, and if it is to be used for diplomatic propaganda, the ritual text might work better."

"It might."

I said, "Can you bring a copy of the ritual text home with you? I would like to read it."

"I'll do it."

"The sooner the better, but what I want to know is do you, my dear father and my dear husband, really believe that God was victorious over the sea and became king of our world?"

"Gad, your daughter is going to get us into trouble asking questions like that?"

"I know it. I thought you might tame her just a bit, but I see it is not happening."

"You're just stalling for time. I was serious with that question."

Jonathan said, "I took your question as a serious question, and I don't know how to answer it. If we want to communicate with others about the formation of our world, we have to speak in this way. We cannot invent a new language or new symbols in order to talk about these things. We will have to talk about God defeating the sea, the sea monster, the serpent, and Rahab. I guess I don't believe God fought the sea, but that is the way I'm bound to deal with this subject. I don't even know much about God, but I talk about him as if I did. However, I do think it is important to use this language in a new way. For one thing, we can say that God's kingship is our beginning. Others have dealt with questions like where did God come from? Or where did matter come from, but we can rule such questions 'out of order.' We start with God's ordering of chaos. This to me is an advance."

Yahweh, the Warrior

"I accept that as an honest answer, and it was long enough to give father time to think up a good answer."

"Thanks for the time, Jonathan. I knew that I could count on you. I told Jonathan when we first knew him that I had to speak for a silent God. That was my way of saying I don't know much about God, but I try to imagine what he would say in any given situation. The priests seem to always know what God wants, but I have never really believed they knew. If we are trying to be honest, we can say there are natural events such as storms, with their thunder and lightning, or the crashing of the powerful breakers on the shore of the sea, which amaze most people. It was natural for ancient poets to say the one who brings order to our world would have to have more power than the raw power of such natural events. Hence, God must be 'Mightier than the breakers of the sea.' But that does not mean we know much about him."

I said, "Tonight, I am learning some important things not only about God as king, but about my prophet and my scribe. But Jonathan you want another word?"

"Yes. After Gad's statement your scribe wants to recite for you the last seven lines of his poem on Job:

> By his power he stilled the Sea;
> By his cunning he smashed Rahab.
> By his wind the heavens were cleared;
> [By] his hand he pierced the fleeing Serpent.
> Lo, these are just traces of his rule;
> What a whisper of a word we hear from him;
> Who can understand the thunder of his might?
> (Job 26:12–14)

We really don't know much; 'What a whisper of a word we hear from him.'"

"I also want to read all of the poem on Job. That ending is powerful."

"First I have to finish it."

I looked at father and his head was nodding. Then I said, "It is time for all of us to go to bed."

Father said, "What?"

Before Jonathan and I went to sleep, Jonathan remembered they would interview the new teacher from Tyre tomorrow. "I forgot to tell you and Gad that tomorrow we will interview a new teacher from Tyre. I was too excited about that psalm. Sorry. By the way, how are you feeling?"

"I'm fine, but I'm glad you asked."

25

Magon of Tyre

JONATHAN GOT TO WORK early. He wanted to get something done before their guest arrived. But, he didn't get started before Ahban, Zadok, and Sheva came by. They came by to take him to Sheva's house where the teacher from Tyre was staying. When they arrived Sarah was ready with food and drink. Sheva introduced Ahban, Zadok, and Jonathan to Magon of Tyre.

Magon was a man of about forty. He was a small man with black hair and a dark complexion. He spoke with a heavy accent, but he did quite well with the language of Judah and Israel. After all, the language of Tyre was not so different. Ahban asked him why he wanted to come to Jerusalem.

"In Tyre, we were informed that you needed someone who could teach Babylonian. I can do that for you. Also, we were told that you were interested in a teacher who knew something of our ancient traditions that came to us from Ugarit. Actually, your two requests go hand in hand. About three hundred years ago, the best center for Babylonian studies was north of Tyre in the city of Ugarit, which was destroyed about two hundred years ago. Also, in Ugarit, they had a great library of works and traditions that later became important in the development of our coastal culture. So, any of our teachers in the past, who came out of the school at Ugarit, came with Babylonian plus ancient Ugaritic traditions. The scribes from the school at Ugarit were employed by the city-states along the coast. Most of the letters in those days were written in Babylonian, and these scribes performed a useful service. But I should add, that students at Ugarit knew several languages. They worked with the two local languages: Ugaritic and Hurrian. Then, they studied Sumerian, Babylonian, Hittite, and Egyptian. Our schools do not do as much today. However that is another reason for wanting to come to Jerusalem. King Hiram of Tyre thinks this will be a great center of learning in the near future. If he is correct, then I would like to work in such a center. I guess it depends on the success of King David. King Hiram wants to help, and so do I."

Ahban said, "You have given an interesting answer. Do you work with any of the languages that you have mentioned other than Babylonian and of course the language of Tyre?"

"Yes, I work with Egyptian and Ugaritic. We do not have many things in Ugaritic; we only have what was around at the time of the destruction of Ugarit plus a few things that were written by scribes who fled from Ugarit."

Sheva said, "You seem to have a good background in languages. Do you like to teach?"

"Yes, I like to teach. It is rewarding to be able to open up new worlds for students. Some of them do not take advantage of such new worlds, but a few do. Those few are the voices of the future."

Jonathan said, "But why are there so few? We expect the politicians and the priests to be conservative in religious matters and policies, but the educated know something of the mistakes of the past. They know the 'good old days' were not so good, and they are willing to seek new answers to most questions."

"Why are there so few? Not many of us are able to be free. Our past, our families, our associates, our homeland, our religion, our health, or something has a hold on us. It is not realistic to seek complete freedom, but there has to be a certain degree of freedom in order to bring new solutions to old problems and to be a voice for the future."

Ahban said, "I like this conversation, but we should share it with the rest of the school. Let's go to the school and eat a bite with them during their lunch. After lunch, if students and teachers have the time, they can listen and add to our conversation."

On the way over to the school, Jonathan thought, "This Magon is interesting. We need him."

The rest of the day went well. In the late afternoon, Danel and Noah took Magon for a tour of the schools. This was a needed break, and Ahban, Sheva, Zadok, and Jonathan had a chance to discuss the interview. All of them were impressed with Magon, and they decided to invite him to teach. He would be appointed to The Jerusalem Academy and both schools could send students to his classes.

That evening there was a large group that met at Sheva and Sarah's home, and more people were able to meet the new teacher. Jonathan and I did not stay long, because things were just too crowded. On our way back to our house, I said, "We must have Magon over for a meal; we need to talk with him in a better setting."

Jonathan agreed and said, "I'll try to set up a visit soon. I'll see him in the morning, because I'm supposed to help him get set up in an office. You'll be interested in some of his thinking. He is interested in the future in almost the same way as we are."

During the next few days, Jonathan helped Magon with his office. Magon brought a lot of things with him, but since he was going to teach in Jerusalem, more of his things would be sent when the supplies for David's palace were brought to Jerusalem.

One day, while taking a break from their work, Jonathan told Magon about his project. He also explained how it was difficult to get started, because he would like to use enthronement psalms, but some other descriptive texts might be better suited to the entire work.

Magon said, "I'll be glad to discuss some of the Babylonian stories with you, but I can show you an enthronement psalm right now that is a good one. This copy was written for Baal, as it would have been in Ugarit. In Tyre, we substitute Melqart or Baal-Melqart for Baal in this psalm. It would work for you if you would just put in the name Yahweh instead of Baal. Here it is:

> Grant to Baal, O gods,
> Grant to Baal glory and victory;
> Grant to Baal the glory of his name.
>
> Bow down to Baal,
> When [his] holiness appears.
>
> The voice of Baal is on the waters;
> The God of glory thunders;
> Baal is upon the mighty waters.
>
> The voice of Baal is powerful;
> The voice of Baal is majestic.
> The voice of Baal shatters the cedars;
> Baal shatters the cedars of Lebanon.
> He makes Lebanon skip like a calf,
> And Sirion like a young wild ox.

The voice of Baal hews out bolts of lightning;
The voice of Baal makes anguish in [the] wilderness.
Baal brings anguish in the wilderness of Kadesh.
The voice of Baal puts the hinds in labor
And strips the forests bare.

But, throughout his temple [his] glory appears!
Baal has been enthroned on the Flood.
Baal has been enthroned king from ancient times.

Baal will give his people victory;
Baal will bless his people with [his] Shalom.
>   (Psalm 29 with the name Baal instead of Yahweh.
>   This was probably an early form.)

Jonathan said, "You're right; this would work for us. I like that line 'Baal has been enthroned on the Flood.' In our enthronement psalms we make the same point, because Yahweh is 'mightier than the breakers of the sea.' May I copy this psalm?"

Magon said, "Of course. The point that 'Baal has been enthroned on the flood' is important, and it is also referred to in a text I have seen where it seems that Baal's throne is the Flood or Sea. This is not unusual. In Babylon, the same thought is expressed concerning Marduk and Tiamat. The goddess Tiamat or Sea is defeated by Marduk, and she becomes his seat or throne."

"So all of these people in the past and the present use almost identical words and pictures to talk about God's kingship."

Their discussion could have gone on for a long time, but they returned to their work. Jonathan did invite Magon for dinner, so he left a little early for lunch. He wanted to tell me that Magon would be here for dinner.

While Jonathan was at work I went to the market. I needed some cheese and olives. I was getting the cheese, and Joab came up and stood beside me. He said, "I didn't know that a scribe could get a woman pregnant. I have always liked the swollen breasts of a pregnant woman. When are you going to enjoy the pleasure of a real man?"

I turned away from him. When I turned I hit a basket of cucumbers, and they rolled all over the ground. Then I ran home, and just as I got home I saw Jonathan arriving for lunch. I was crying as I ran to meet him.

"What's the matter?" he asked.

"Joab frightened me."

Then Jonathan held me, and I told him all the details.

"That dog! I'll see David about this today. We don't have to live in fear of that bastard. I invited Magon for dinner tonight, but perhaps you don't feel like doing it."

"I'll be fine by tonight. Let him come, and we will be able to think of other things."

"We cannot live here if we have to worry about Joab's lust and anger," Jonathan said to David after lunch. "I'm sure you remember how we dealt with wild animals when they got after our lambs years ago. If Joab does anything like this again, his bones will be picked clean by the vultures, and I will not give him the chance to murder me. You can count on it."

"I will speak to Joab about this," David said. "I will send him to Ziklag for duty and that will keep him out of the way for now. After that we will be busy expanding our border areas. I'll find a way to deal with him. I really don't care about his threats anymore."

"What do you mean when you say, 'his threats?' "

"I told you I would tell you some day, and I guess this is the day. Joab has always threatened to make it known that I did not kill Goliath of Gath. I took the credit, but it was really Elhanan, son of Jair, who killed Goliath. You remember him from Bethlehem. I'm sorry about this, but I really don't care who knows the truth. I'm not going to let Joab push me around anymore."

Jonathan came back to the house to check on me and then on to his office. He found out Magon could still use his help, and they worked the rest of the afternoon.

In the evening, Magon came to the house for dinner. We had a good time at the table. Father was there, and the four of us enjoyed a leg of lamb. At first, the conversation was all about Tyre and the other cities on the northern coast. It became clear that Magon would miss the coast but not the heat along the coast in the summer. Jonathan suggested that if we took a vacation, we should visit Tyre in the winter when it was cold in Jerusalem. At one point, Magon said, "When I live on the coast, the world seems so much bigger. It opens up to the west, and out there is another world of trade and adventure. Also today, Jonathan and I were talking about God ruling the sea and being enthroned upon the sea. After our conversation, I thought for us who live on the coast that is a more powerful picture and a bigger scene than others could ever imagine."

Father said, "I'm sure that you are right."

Jonathan said, "Perhaps that means we should not only study texts from other countries, but we should go to those countries if we ever hope to really understand their literature."

Magon replied, "That is exactly the situation. You even have to know the 'lay of the land' to understand such simple things as the words people use to indicate directions. Here, 'to go down' means 'to go south' because the Jordan runs south. But, in Egypt, 'to go down' means 'to go north' because the Nile runs north."

I said, "Magon, tell us something about your family."

"My father was a scribe, as was my grandfather. My mother was related to a brother of King Hiram. There were three children. We had a good life. I was able to travel and get a good education. But, shortly after my father died, my wife died, and I really wanted to move from the place that gave birth to most of my memories. My sister and brother live close to my mother, and they see her often. This does not mean that my answer to Ahban's question about why I wanted to come to Jerusalem was not a true answer; it was another answer, and I still want to belong to the great center this school can become. Most of our good decisions are based upon several reasons."

I said, "I hope that someday we can meet your mother, brother and sister."

"I am sure you will meet them. Jonathan told me that you could read, and it would be a wonderful experience for my sister and for you if you would write to her. We will have messengers going to Tyre on a regular basis."

"I'll do it. Will she understand the language of Judah and Israel?"

"She will understand most of it, but at first, you could send your letter, and I could send her a translation of your letter in the language of Tyre. Since our languages are very much alike, it will not take long to solve that problem, and I can help Jonathan and you to translate her letters."

"What is her name?"

"Elissa"

"I'll start my letter tomorrow."

26

The Royal Epic Begins to Take Shape

A FEW WEEKS LATER, when Jonathan left the house, he made a promise: today he would make some decisions to get things moving on the royal epic. When he got to his office, he called Elimelech and Elishama in for a meeting. Jonathan asked, "How is it going with the stories of the fathers?"

Elimelech said, "We are doing fine, but it is a big job. It is a good thing we have worked on these texts recently for the coronations. We have decided we need to emphasize the traditions of Abraham, Isaac, Jacob, Joseph and Judah as we did in the coronations. But we can not give much space to Ishmael or Esau; they do not lead to David in any way."

Jonathan said, "I agree. It seems to me that you are making a lot of progress. I wish I were as far as you seem to be on some basic decisions. Let me share some of my findings with you. I have collected several enthronement psalms. You will recall from our previous discussions that I suggested the formation of our world begins with God's kingship. That's where we start. So, I was thinking of starting with the enthronement psalms, because in them God defeats the Sea, Chaos, the Flood, or the Deep and establishes our world. He rules from his temple situated upon his mountain. However, I'm beginning to realize there are some people who will not understand these psalms in this way. It is becoming clear we need to start with a description of how God ordered our world. Therefore, I have decided we should start with the seven-day ritual text that Abiathar gave to me. It gives little detail on how to worship God and praise him for his role as the one who ordered our world, but it does show an orderly development of the things that make up our world. This text begins by describing the situation, which existed, when God began his activity:

> When Elohim first began to form the heavens and the earth,
> The earth was devastation and desolation,
> Darkness was over [the] deep,

The Royal Epic Begins to Take Shape

The wind of Elohim was storming over the waters, . . .
(Gen 1:1–2)

"It also shows God as ruling chaos, and this fact explains the circumstance at the time of God's action. I don't think any reader will suggest we are trying to talk about the origin of God or matter, but they can clearly see the subsequent material describes the building of our world. But, you need to see the entire text."

Jonathan showed them the text, and they read it together. Elishama was the first to speak. He said, "In Israel we have a text almost identical to this one, and we have used it in connection with our Passover ritual."

"Abiathar told me about your use of this material, but I'm glad you have remembered it."

Elimelech said, "On each ritual day God is praised for some act. Will you leave the ritual days at the end of each paragraph?"

"I don't know, but I see where you are going with the question."

"Well, for people who don't know this is a seven-day ritual, the seven days will soon be understood as the time it took to order the world."

Jonathan said, "You may be right, but I would have to ask, does it make any difference? Magon informs me that at Ugarit, Baal builds his temple on his mountain in seven days. His temple is a miniature world from which he rules the world at large. If the miniature is built in seven days why not the world?"

Elishama said, "I'm glad you want to use this text. I know the people of Israel will only see the seven days as the ritual days they know. If others see the days as Elimelech suggests, I really don't care, and as you say that also fits in with the way some have thought concerning the ordering of the world."

Elimelech said, "It does not matters too much to me either, but I just wanted to point out some people will take it that way."

Jonathan said, "I guess I'm like Sheva with the coronations. I like the seven-day pattern, and it is another way of emphasizing that God is king. His coronation is filled with order and promise."

Elimelech said, "Is it possible to use another such story as well? This one does not have much in it about the humans. Among the traditions of Judah there is another story everyone loves, and it is centered more on the formation of the humans. The human being is formed from the clay and his mate is made from the human's rib."

The Jerusalem Academy

Jonathan said, "I know the story you are thinking about, and I have completely neglected it. Now, we are seeing the value of talking about these things. Yes, that is a good story, and I was thinking about it shortly before my marriage; I was thinking about the human and his wife and how the two became one flesh. Let's take a break, and I will find the text somewhere in this school."

During the break, Ahban found a copy of the story Jonathan needed. Ahban had taken it to his new office only a few days ago. Jonathan also stopped by Magon's office, and they discussed Jonathan's work. As Jonathan was leaving to go back to his meeting, Magon said, "The individual stories you use can be different in many ways from the stories used by others, but the general outline should be the same for all of us. For that reason, I have written down an outline for you to use if you want it. All who start such an epic should deal with: 1) how the world was ordered, 2) how the humans gained all knowledge, 3) how civilization developed or the building of the cities, 4) the pre-flood kings or sages, and 5) the flood. You will have to deal with those items and in that order if you want the scribes from other countries to be interested in this work."

Jonathan thanked Magon for the outline and hurried back to his office. Elimelech and Elishama were there and waiting. Jonathan said, "Sorry, I'm late. However, I received a lot of help from both Ahban and Magon. Magon gave me an outline. Take a look at it. He indicated that people would read our work if we dealt with the items in the outline. Also, I got the text of the story that we were talking about. Let's read it together."

Before Jonathan could start, I walked in and said, "I wanted to see what you were doing this afternoon, and I think I got here just in time. I would like to hear this next story if no one objects."

Jonathan said, "Keziah you are welcome; there are no objections. In fact your observations on the role of Eve may be helpful for us."

> When Yahweh-Elohim was about to make earth and heaven,
> there was as yet no wild shrub on the earth,
> as yet no wild grass had sprouted,
> because Yahweh-Elohim had not sent rain upon the earth,
> and there was no human (*'adam*) to till the ground (*'adamah*),
> but a flood began flowing from the netherworld,
> and watered the entire surface of the ground,
>
> Yahweh-Elohim formed the human [from] the clay of the ground;
> he blew into his nostrils the breath of life;

the human became a living being.

Yahweh-Elohim planted a garden in Eden, in the east;
he placed there the human whom he had formed.

Yahweh-Elohim caused to sprout from the ground
every tree desirable in appearance and good for food,
and the tree of life was in the middle of the garden
and also the tree of the knowledge of good and evil.
. . .
Yahweh-Elohim took the human;
he settled him in the garden of Eden to till it and guard it.
Yahweh-Elohim commanded the human, saying:
> "From every tree of the garden you may certainly eat,
> except from the tree of the knowledge of good and evil,
> you shall not eat of it,
> because when you eat of it, you shall certainly die."

Yahweh-Elohim said:
> "It is not good for the human to be alone;
> I will make for him a helper just like him."
Yahweh-Elohim formed from the ground all the wild animals
and all the birds of the heavens.
He brought [them] to the human to see what he called them,
and whatever the human called each of the living beings,
that was its name.
The human gave names to all the domestic animals,
to the birds of the heavens, and to all the wild animals,
but as for the human, he did not find a helper just like him.

Yahweh-Elohim cast a deep sleep upon the human;
while he slept, he took one of his ribs;
and he closed the flesh there.
Yahweh-Elohim built up the rib,
which he had taken from the human, into a woman;
he brought her to the human.
The human said:
> "This one, at last, is bone of my bones
> And flesh of my flesh.

> This one shall be called woman (*'ishshah*),
> For from man (*'ish*) this one was taken."
Therefore a man leaves his father and his mother;
he is joined with his wife;
they become one flesh.

The two of them were naked (*'arummim*)—
the human and his wife,
and they were not ashamed.

Now the serpent was the wisest (*'arum*) of all
the wild animals that Yahweh-Elohim had made;
he said to the woman:
> "Indeed, did Elohim really say,
> 'From every tree of the garden,
> you shall not eat?'"
The woman said to the serpent:
> "From the fruit of the trees of the garden we may eat,
> but from the fruit of the tree that is in the midst of the garden,
> Elohim said, 'You shall not eat from it,
> and you shall not touch it,
> or you shall die.'"
The serpent said to the woman:
> "Surely, you shall not die;
> Elohim knows that when you eat from it,
> your eyes will be opened;
> you will be like gods—ones who know good and evil."
The woman saw that the tree was good for food,
that it was a delight to the eyes,
and that the tree was desired to make one wise.
She took from its fruit; she ate.
Also when she gave [some] to her husband,
who was with her, he ate.
The eyes of both of them were opened;
they knew that they were naked (*'erummim*).
They sewed together fig leaves;
they made for themselves loincloths.

. . .

The human called forth the name of his wife, "Eve,"

because she was the mother of all living.
Yahweh-Elohim made for the human and his wife garments of skins;
he clothed them.

Yahweh-Elohim said:
>"Yes, the human has become like one of us,
>knowing good and evil, so now,
>he must not reach out his hand,
>taking also from the tree of life,
>he would eat and live forever!"

Yahweh-Elohim sent him from the garden of Eden,
to till the ground from which he was taken;
he drove out the human;
he stationed, east of the garden of Eden,
the cherubim and the flaming sword,
which turned every way to guard the way to the tree of life.
(Genesis 2:4b—3: 24)

Jonathan said, "This is a favorite story. Our first story deals with human beings, but this story deals with them and their importance in this world. Many interesting points are made. The human being and all the other animals are not only from the ground, but they are all called 'living beings.' Yet, you can distinguish between all these animals. Now it turns out the human could not find a mate just like him! So, God made a mate just like him. The man and the woman can become one, because they are exactly the same; they are of the same substance. The main thrust of this story satisfies one need in our outline. We need to deal with how the humans gained all knowledge. Here, they gain all knowledge (the knowledge of all things from good to evil), but they give up immortality and their close relationship with God. This was a trade off, acceptable to both of them. They had access to the tree of life, but in the end they must leave the garden and the tree of life. Why? Because they have gained all knowledge and if they still had immortality, they would be as the gods. The fact that humans must die is not necessarily bad, and the fact that they have all knowledge is a real plus. This allows for the next step in our outline, that is, the development of civilization. Here we have a story that deals with what it really means to be human. It has to do with the rise of civilization."

I said, "This story gives me a better understanding of what you have told me about the two becoming one flesh. But I don't understand why no one in our literature or in our society is aware that the human and his mate are equal?"

"I don't know why, but this is probably the only place where equality is mentioned, and I suppose that it is convenient to forget it."

Elimelech said, "Keziah's question is important, and it shows that there are some things which scribes tend to forget, because they have never been asked to account for such things.

"I was always interested in an observation that my father made concerning this story. The human names the animals and even names his wife; he calls her 'Eve.' However, this human in this story has no name! My father put it this way:

> He gave names:
> To his wife,
> To all life,
> But for him,
> The human,
> There's no name.

"Of course, later minstrels and writers of the lists of pre-flood sages name this first human, but it is an odd name. They name him *Adam*, which means 'human.' I like this story because the human is not named. It can become my story; it shows me it is knowledge, which is helpful, and it helps me to understand that humans are mortal."

"I like your father's poem," I said.

Elishama said, "The Babylonian story of Adapa does almost the same thing for the Babylonians as this story does for us. Humans have all knowledge but they are mortal. The Adapa story is a good one, and our story is also good, and it is best for us."

Jonathan said, "It sounds like we all want to use this story. That being the case, I will ask the question, how do we put the story of the formation of world and this story of the human and his wife together? Do we just set them side by side? Or, do we relate them in some way? It's time to quit for the day, but think about this, and tomorrow we will try to deal with it."

Jonathan and I took the two texts home with us. He wanted me to read the first one and compare them. He helped with the evening meal so I could read. Later we were still discussing what to do. The epic needed the two stories, but using them both made one think the second one was

The Royal Epic Begins to Take Shape

starting all over. Jonathan said, "Some people are going to be confused by our use of both stories, but the epic needs them both."

I said, "The confusion may be good for the readers. We want to make certain points, but we don't want to give the impression we were there; we don't know much. Didn't you say so the other night?"

"I did, and you may be right about the confusion. There are so many ways to talk about our beginnings, and none of them is really adequate. But, we can make certain the message is clear. For example, God is king, human beings have all knowledge, and humans are mortal. Also we need to remember one part of our task has to do with accounting for the human condition."

With that, we decided to go to bed. Jonathan asked me if I had been thinking of names for our baby. " I have been thinking about it, but I have not thought of the right one yet."

"What about Adam?"

"Or we could just call him 'the human,' but what makes you think we will have a boy?"

"If not, name her Eve."

"It's not that easy."

"The name can wait, but I can't. Let's prove once again that one plus one can equal one."

We did, and we fell asleep, after Jonathan said, "I'm glad you came by this afternoon."

The next morning at the office, Jonathan opened the discussion by asking if anyone had come up with a good answer.

Elimelech said, "Last night I got into a conversation with Magon after dinner, and he said it was important to deal with the outline regardless of how many stories we used. The stories may contradict each other in some details, but use them. People should not expect some kind of perfect chronology when dealing with the time before time."

Jonathan remarked, "That sounds like the discussion that Keziah and I were involved in."

Elishama said, "I do not disagree with what has been said, but I do have a suggestion, which might be helpful, though it shows a slight change in my position of yesterday. At the end of the first story it says:

> Elohim saw all that he had made,
> and behold, it was very good.

> There was evening.
> There was morning:
> [A seventh] day.

"I have added after that the following:

> The heavens and the earth were finished and all their entourage.
> Elohim finished on the seventh day his work that he had been doing.

"What I have added will change the ritual days into the time it took to establish the world. I have also used the word 'finished' for a very important reason. This word can have two meanings. If you don't worry about the two stories of our beginnings standing side by side, then you can just take the first meaning which is 'to complete,' but if you have an ordered mind, take the second meaning of 'finished' which is 'to come to an end.' In other words, God didn't like his first attempt, and it was destroyed. Then the opening words of the next story could be understood, without any changes, in this way: 'On another day when Yahweh-Elohim was about to make earth and heaven, ...' This seems a bit drastic, but just remember that in a few days we will be talking about the flood, destruction, and a new beginning.

"Next we should put in a title for the following story:

These are the stories of the heavens and the earth
since their formation. (Genesis 2:4a)

This title works in the same way that our titles are working in the stories of the fathers. For example, *These are the stories of Terah* is the title that heads the material about Abraham. You use the person or thing that has already been introduced in the title and then give the subsequent developments."

Jonathan said, "You just may have the best approach yet. I would understand 'finished' as meaning 'completed,' and I would not worry about the next story's inconsistencies with the first story. Rather, I would try to get the point of the second story. But if my neighbor wanted to make the reading of the two stories chronologically pleasing, he could see the first world as being destroyed, and then, there becomes a real need for the second story in the sequence of things. What do you think Elimelech?"

"I would go along with the suggestion, and it is clear that we have material in the first two sections of our epic which both Israel and Judah will appreciate. So what do we do next?"

The Royal Epic Begins to Take Shape

Jonathan looked again at his outline and said, "It looks like we need to deal with the development of the cities and the rise of civilization. In our traditions Cain is the first builder of a city. I'll have to see what we have on Cain. In the meantime, you can get back to your work on the fathers. As soon as we get this early period finished, I will be anxious to look at what you have done."

27

The Ark of God

JONATHAN WENT TO SHEVA'S office to ask about the stories of Cain. However, when he arrived, Sheva, Ahban, Zadok, and Abiathar were discussing something. Sheva motioned for Jonathan to come in and join them. Abiathar wanted some help in planning a celebration. David, in an attempt to make Jerusalem the cultic center of the new Israel, was going to bring the ark of God to Jerusalem.

Abiathar was just giving some background on the ark when Jonathan came in, and he continued, "Years ago, the ark had been housed in the cultic center which was in Shiloh. It was the symbol of God's presence. During the time of Samuel, the Philistines were winning most of the battles with Israel. Israel decided to take the ark of God into battle with them. This would mean that God was in their midst. It was not difficult to take the ark, because this chest was transported on a cart pulled by two oxen. However, the Philistines captured the ark. After keeping the ark for about seven months, the Philistines wanted to get rid of it, because they all suffered from having it in their cities. Their cities were plagued, and Dagon, their God, was destroyed in his temple. The Philistines sent the ark back to Israel, and the men of Kiriath-jearim took the ark to the house of Abinadab. His son Eleazar was put in charge of it, and it stayed there for twenty years.

"After all this time, David wanted to bring the ark to Jerusalem, and he also planned to house it in a special tent. He had pitched this tent on the threshing floor of Araunah the Jebusite.

"Bringing the ark to Jerusalem was to be done with a great celebration. David and some of his best soldiers went to the house of Abinadab. There they loaded the ark of God on a new cart in order to bring it to Jerusalem or the City of David. Abinadab's sons, Eleazar and Uzzah, walked beside the ark and guided it. At the same time David and the people of Israel danced and sang before Yahweh or in other words before the ark. When the procession came to the threshing floor of Nacon, Uzzah reached out his hand to steady the ark. This made Yahweh angry, and he struck Uzzah on the spot and killed him. Uzzah fell beside the ark. David was afraid of Yahweh, and he did not bring the ark into the City of David and to the threshing floor of Araunah. Instead, he sent it to the house of Obed-edom, where it has been for three months. David has kept this aborted attempt to bring the ark to Jerusalem silent, but recently he has heard that Yahweh has blessed the house of Obed-edom. So, David is now in the mood to try again.

"This time David wants to do everything right. There will be dancing, music, sacrifices, psalms, and food for all. We want it to be a good time for the people of Jerusalem, and this needs to happens soon."

Sheva spoke up, "So, Abiathar, what do you want us to do for you?"

"I want you to find a psalm that will work for this occasion and to write up, from my notes, a formal program."

Ahban, who already knew about the need for such a psalm, informed the others that he had been looking for a psalm, but he could not find one that was just right. Therefore, he had been writing one. Then he said, "I will leave a copy of what I have done, but I would like for both Zadok and Jonathan to edit it."

Sheva said, "I'll write up the program, and Zadok and Jonathan can work on the psalm."

With that the meeting broke up, and Jonathan said to Zadok, "When can we do this? I'm very busy."

"Ahban's writing is difficult to read. Let me make a copy for you, and then we'll get together in a few days."

After everyone was gone, Jonathan asked Sheva about Cain. Sheva told him that Noah and Danel had been working in the libraries of the Old School and the New School and that they should be able to help him.

Jonathan found Noah and Danel in the New School library. The Cain material had been put with some genealogical lists, and Jonathan took it and all the lists as well. As he left he asked them to begin collecting anything on the story of the flood. Jonathan went back to his office, and found on his desk Zadok's copy of Ahban's psalm. He decided that he would take it home with him for an evening reading with me. Now, there was still a little time to look at the material on Cain.

The Jerusalem Academy

He unrolled the scroll, and he was interested from the start. There was some material on the birth of Cain, which was intriguing. The first three lines read:

> Now the human knew Eve, his wife.
> She conceived; she bore Cain.
> She said, "I have procreated a man with Yahweh."
> (Genesis 4:1)

Jonathan thought, "This poor devil, the human, does not have a name; he makes love with Eve; she conceives; she gives birth; she names her son; and Yahweh gets the credit. Considering what Cain became, perhaps the human was lucky to be disqualified as the real father. This is a bit strange, because in our stories God is usually given credit as the sire of the great heroes rather than the not-so-great."

Jonathan continued to read this text. It certainly had something about the building of cities and the rise of the arts and crafts. It should probably be used for that reason alone. He briefly looked at some of the other texts. One of them was probably important. It dealt with ten pre-flood sages or kings. They should try to decide on these texts tomorrow morning. With that, Jonathan left for home.

He came in the house and said to me, "How is my wife and a beautiful soon-to-be mother today?"

"I'm gaining weight, and I am tired."

"But, you are beautiful. I brought home a psalm for us to read tonight. Ahban wrote it for a celebration that we'll have when David brings the ark of God to Jerusalem."

"I suppose that will be important, but I want you to help me with a letter to Magon's sister. I wanted to do the letter several days ago."

"Good we'll do the letter, and I'll take it to Magon in the morning on my way to work. Is Gad home?"

"Yes, he's here. Today, David talked to him about doing something. It seems that in some areas of the country the crops are failing, and David wants father to find out about it."

We had a good supper. Jonathan told father and me about Abiathar's visit, and he asked father about David's first attempt to bring the ark to Jerusalem. "Abiathar told us that Yahweh killed Uzzah at the threshing floor of Nacon. Gad, did that really happen?"

The Ark of God

"There is no doubt that Uzzah died at the threshing floor, but the cause is not so clear. As you know, there are some other gods who are worshipped at that threshing floor, and some people think those gods were angry, because Yahweh was entering their space. Others say Yahweh was angry, because the procession should have gone directly to the threshing floor of Araunah the Jebusite. There is a great deal of mystery about threshing floors. In older times, during court sessions on the threshing floors, the judge, in order to determine the truth in a case with little evidence, would ask the accused to carry the gods as some kind of an ordeal. The accused would always refuse; he would rather be found guilty than carry the gods. In such a tradition, Uzzah would have been considered brave or foolish. I don't know if Yahweh killed him, but David thinks so."

Jonathan said, "For David, Yahweh must be an angry God. Of course, he is seen exactly like that in the story of Judah where Yahweh kills Judah's first two sons. I wonder if Yahweh is like that? If he is, then fear is the correct response to such a God. There is some Egyptian teaching that says you should not be too free with a God during his procession. The saying goes on with 'Do not approach him to carry him.' Uzzah should have been told about that."

Father said, "David wants to bring the ark to Jerusalem real soon. When will everyone be ready?"

"We'll be ready in about two days. I brought a copy of Ahban's psalm, which he wrote for the occasion. I thought we would read it tonight."

"Fine. I would like to hear it."

"Let's help Keziah clean up, and as usual, she can read it for us."

We were soon ready for the reading; I read:

> Remember Yahweh, O David,
> And all his triumphs.
>
> He who swore to Yahweh,
> He vowed to the Bull of Jacob:
> "I will not enter the tent of my house,
> Nor will I go up on the couch of my bed,
> I will not give sleep to my eyes,
> Or to my pupils slumber,
> Until I find a sanctuary for Yahweh,
> A tabernacle for the Bull of Jacob."

The Jerusalem Academy

> Look! We heard of it in Ephrathah;
> We found it in the fields of Jaar.
> Let us enter his tabernacle;
> Let us prostrate ourselves at his footstool.
> Advance, O Yahweh, to your resting-place,
> You and the ark of your strength.
> Your priests are clothed in righteousness,
> And your loyal ones sing for joy.
> For the sake of David, your servant.
> Turn not away from the presence of your anointed.
>
> Yahweh has sworn, O David,
> A true promise that he will not change:
> "From the fruit of your body,
> I will set [one] upon your throne.
> If your sons keep my covenant,
> And my stipulations that I will teach them,
> Then their sons also, until the end of time,
> Shall sit upon your throne."
>
> For Yahweh has chosen Zion;
> He has desired it for his dwelling.
> "This is my resting-place until the end of time.
> Here, I will dwell for I have desired it.
> Her provisions, I will abundantly bless,
> Her needy, I will satisfy [with] food,
> And her priests, I will clothe with salvation,
> And her loyal ones shall sing for joy.
> There, I will make a horn shine, O David;
> I have prepared a lamp, O my anointed.
> His enemies, I will clothe with disgrace,
> But upon him, his crown will sparkle."
>   (Psalm 132)

I said, "This psalm just flows."

Jonathan said, "Right. Ahban is a good poet, and he has something to say. He has picked up on some things from the covenant for David's second coronation with reference to the Davidic dynasty. He shows that

David is providing a resting-place for Yahweh before David's palace is finished, and he explains how David will provide for the needy."

Father said, "During the celebration, David will give each person some food. This gift of food is important, because there may be a food shortage in the near future."

"Keziah mentioned that you were trying to find out about a food shortage."

"Yes, I am, but I have not done much yet."

I said, "What were you suppose to do with this psalm?"

"Zadok and I were suppose to edit it, but I don't see the need. That's what I 'm going to tell Zadok."

I said, "I wonder how this sanctuary for the ark will compare with David's palace?"

Father said, "Jonathan, I'm repeating myself, but this girl and her questions will be our undoing. Her questions are more piercing since she became your wife."

"Then it must be my fault."

"It's not your fault. It's to your credit that you bound me and gave me freedom at the same time."

Father said, "When faults become virtues, it's time to go to bed."

After father left, Jonathan said, "I need to help you with the letter. Since it is late, I will just give you the form of the letter, and you can fill it in with what you want to say. Let's write it this way:

> To Elissa, my sister and friend:
> Thus says Keziah, your sister and friend:
>
> _____
>
> *Shalom* to you, *shalom* to your house,
> and *shalom* to all that is yours.
>
> _____
>
> And now, . . .
>
> And now, . . .
>
> _____
>
> And now, your brother, Magon, is fine,
> and may you know it.

"You should follow this form. You can add what you want to say in the two places after 'And now, . . .' Or, if you want to write about more than two subjects add another paragraph or two but begin each one with 'And now, . . .'"

"Does it have to be so formal?"

"I think so. At least the first few letters should be this way."

"I may have time in the morning to fill in the form. I have thought about what to say for some time. If so, you will be able to take it with you to work, but let's go to bed now."

"Jonathan, are you asleep?"

"Not now."

"Sorry, but I was just thinking. I like to write letters, but sometime I hope we can travel to Tyre. I want to see for myself."

"I know, and you will."

When Jonathan got up, the next morning, he found me at the table completing my letter. I said, "You read my letter, and I'll fix something to eat."

I handed it to Jonathan and he read:

> To Elissa, my sister and friend:
> Thus says Keziah, your sister and friend:
> _____
>
> *Shalom* to you, *shalom* to your house,
> and *shalom* to all that is yours.
> _____
>
> And now, Magon, your brother, said that
> we should write to each other. I wanted
> to write to you. Not many women can
> read or write. We are very fortunate.
> My husband, Jonathan, taught me, and this
> has lifted me and made me free.
>
> And now, Jonathan and Magon are working
> at the school. We live close to the school.
> I am expecting our first child in a few months.
> Do you have children?
>
> And now, this is my first letter.
> You can tell that. The next time,
> I would like to send a poem.
> _____

> And now, your brother, Magon, is fine,
> and may you know it.

Jonathan said, "That's good. I'll take it to Magon, and you can get busy on your poem."

"I will, but please help me."

"I'll help you, and tonight we may read some stories about Cain and Abel."

"Will I see you at noon?"

"I hope so."

28

The Development of Civilization and the Pre-flood Sages

JONATHAN LEFT A BIT early in order to stop by Magon's office before going to his own. He gave Magon my letter. Magon said, "The letter can be sent in a few days when we will have people going to Tyre. How is the epic coming along?"

"It is coming along but at a slow rate. We have covered the first points on the outline you gave to me. We have ordered the world, and we have accounted for the fact that humans have all knowledge and are mortal. This means we are just beginning to deal with the development of civilization and the pre-flood sages. The problem is that we have a lot of material in our libraries from which to select our texts, and we need to look at it all. There are two texts that we really need for this section, but if we use them both, there will be some differences that are glaring, for example the number of pre-flood sages."

Magon said, "I told Elimelech the other day I would not worry about the things that don't fit. The main question is to ask is this: are we making the point that needs to be made? Every minstrel and poet will vary things within the basic outline, but the people don't care about that. Also the people don't care if you repeat yourselves in a slightly different way."

"Elimelech mentioned you had talked with him about this. Your remarks are always helpful, and when we have a little more of this finished, I hope you will read it."

"I'll be glad to read it."

"The material we are discussing right now has to do with city building and the beginnings of certain occupations. I think your own traditions deal with some of these things. When you read our work, perhaps you could comment on this."

The Development of Civilization and the Pre-flood Sages

"I will. Also, I want to share with you, at that time, what our tradition has to say about human mortality."

"Great. I'll get our work to you as soon as possible."

When Jonathan went to his office, he found Elimelech and Elishama waiting for him. Jonathan said, "I'm sorry to be late, but I was talking with Magon about our work. He is helpful."

"Yes, he is," said Elimelech.

Elishama added, "We should let him help us in a more direct way. I am going to take his Babylonian reading course, which starts in a few days. Perhaps we could read the Babylonian story of the flood. That could really help us with our work, because I don't think many students will take it; we should have time to ask questions."

Jonathan said, "That's a good idea. Yesterday afternoon, I began to read some of the Cain material and I found it useful. It does two very important things for us. It gives us a nice story on Cain who is our first city builder, and it deals with other developments of civilization by discussing the beginnings of certain occupations. Let's look at it."

Jonathan read to them:

> Now the human knew Eve, his wife.
> She conceived; she bore Cain.
> She said:
> > "I have procreated a man with Yahweh."
> Next she gave birth to his brother Abel.
> Abel became a keeper of flocks,
> and Cain became a tiller of the ground.
> In the course of time,
> Cain brought from the fruit of the ground an offering to Yahweh,
> and Abel, he also brought from the first-born of his flock
> and from their choice portions.
> Yahweh paid attention to Abel and to his offering,
> but to Cain and to his offering he paid no attention.
> Cain became very angry; he became downcast.
> Yahweh said to Cain:
> > "Why are you angry?
> > Why are you so down?
> > Is it not true [that],
> > Either you do well

> [And you] are upbeat,
> Or you don't do well,
> [And so in this case,]
> Sin is the demon,
> [Who is] at the door?
> His desire is for you,
> But you will rule him."

Cain spoke against Abel, his brother,
and when they were in the field,
Cain rose up against Abel, his brother;
he killed him.
Yahweh said to Cain:
> "Where is Abel your brother?"

He said to him:
> "I do not know. Am I my brother's keeper?"

He said:
> "What have you done?
> The voice of the blood of your brother is crying to me
> from the ground,
> and now you are cursed from the ground
> that has opened its mouth
> to receive your brother's blood from your hand.

. . .

Cain knew his wife.
She conceived; she bore Enoch.
He was the builder of a city.
He called the name of the city after the name of his son, Enoch.
To Enoch was born Irad.
Irad fathered Mehujael.
Mehujael fathered Methushael.
Methushael fathered Lamech.
Lamech took for himself two wives.
The name of the one was Adah,
and the name of the other was Zillah.
Adah bore Jabal.
He was the "father" of those who dwell with tents and herds.

The Development of Civilization and the Pre-flood Sages

The name of his brother was Jubal.
He was the "father" of all who are skilled with lyre and pipe.
Also, Zillah bore Tubal-Cain,
the master craftsman of all who are workers with copper and iron
(and the sister of Tubal-Cain was Naamah).
(Genesis 4:1–22)

Jonathan said, "There are so many things about this story that are important for our work. Notice, that as civilization develops, we can see the age-old tension between the farmer, in the person of Cain, and the shepherd, in the person of Abel, manifesting itself. The first 'sin' in our epic is the result of what happened when the two brothers worshipped Yahweh. Cain became jealous, but Yahweh thinks Cain will rule over sin. Yahweh is wrong, because Cain does not rule. He murders his brother. Now, Cain leaves the land and builds a city. Next, we have a shortened form of a genealogy of the pre-flood sages, but it is important in that it contains some more details about the development of the occupations. It starts with the shepherds, but it goes on to deal with the musicians and smiths. "Father" in this context means "teacher" or "founder."

Elishama said, "What did you mean when you said that we have here a short form of the genealogy of the pre-flood sages?"

"Well, if you start with 'the human' and add the six names from Cain through Lamech, you end up with seven. There are old traditions in other countries that have seven pre-flood sages. But there is a Babylonian text, and one text of ours, that has ten names."

Elimelech said, "Do we need to use the one that has ten names?"

"We do, because that one also gives the age of each sage. In most traditions, it is important, especially for the priests and their rituals, to add up these ages and establish the time between the first human and the flood. Most groups, among our people and in other countries, vary this time span to suit their needs. We need to keep this one in order to say something about that time span."

Elimelech spoke again, "We will either have to not worry about the differences, as Magon has suggested, or we could make the list of seven longer. What names are lacking in the short form?"

Jonathan said, "You may be on to something. Let's list the ten names, and then we can put the list of seven beside it."

Jonathan made the list of ten and then the list of seven:

The Jerusalem Academy

The Ten	The Seven
Adam	The Human
Seth	
Enosh	
Kenan	Cain
Mahalalel	Enoch
Jared	Irad
Enoch	Mehujael
Methuselah	Methushael
Lamech	Lamech
Noah	
(Genesis 5)	(Genesis 4)

Jonathan said, "That is really helpful to be able to see the differences. Also there are some differences in spelling and order. However, that should not bother us. What we need to do is name 'the human' as in the longer list and then account for the next two names as well."

All three of them worked on this for a while, and this is what they added to the short list:

> Adam knew his wife again.
> She bore a son.
> She called forth his name, "Seth," because, [she continued,]
> > "Elohim set for me another offspring in the place of Abel,
> > for his killer was Cain."
> Also to Seth, a son was born.
> He called forth his name, "Enosh."
> (Genesis 4:25–26a)

Jonathan said, "With this addition, we have added the first three names of the long list to the short list. So now, we have nine names in the short list. We can keep it at nine, because we all know that the tenth name is the name of the flood hero, Noah. Lamech's sons who start the trades and guilds are important to us in the material of the short list, and we don't need to bring in the last and most obvious name of Noah. If the two of you agree, I will put this all together and follow it with the text, which gives all ten sages. The flood is our next big project."

Elishama said, "And, I am looking forward to dealing with our flood stories. There are so many things to consider, but for now, Elimelech and I should get back to the fathers. We are probably getting too much material on the fathers. One of these days, you will have to help us deal with it."

"I'll do it, but now I'm going home for lunch. I should start to look in on Keziah several times a day. It seems like she is getting closer to having the baby. Elishama, how is Deborah?"

"She's fine, but Jonathan don't get too anxious. You have a few months to go."

"These are going to be busy times."

As they were leaving the building, Zadok came by. He said to Jonathan, "What did you think of Ahban's psalm?"

"It was great, and we don't need to edit it."

"I agree, and it's a good thing, because I understand that they will have the procession and ceremony tomorrow."

"Is Sheva ready with the program?"

"Yes, he's ready. He's the one who told me it would be tomorrow."

"I hope all goes well tomorrow. We don't need any more dead men."

Jonathan got home, and I was not ready for lunch. "I thought you would get too busy to come home. Also, I have been working on my poem, which I'll send in my next letter, but I'm finding out that a poem can be difficult."

Jonathan held me in his arms, and he could feel the baby who was just then kicking. He said, "When do you think you will give birth?"

"I figure it will be in about two months, if my figuring is correct."

We started to eat some lunch, and father joined us.

Jonathan said to Gad, "I understand that you will all be busy tomorrow with the big celebration."

"Most of the people in the government will be busy, but I am too busy with this food shortage investigation. There is a prophet by the name of Nathan who will take over for me."

"What are you finding out?"

"I'm finding there are some sections of the country that are in bad shape. This is really a famine for them.

29

The Ark Is Brought to the City of David

THE NEXT DAY, JONATHAN went to work, Gad continued his investigation, and I was busy with my work. None of us found the time to attend the big celebration, but we could hear a lot of shouting and the blowing of horns. It started early in the day. David and his men brought the ark from the house of Obed-edom into the City of David with great rejoicing. David offered sacrifices at the beginning of the processional march. Also, there was music, dancing, and the blasts of horns. The city was really crowded with men, women, and children. When the ark entered the city, there was a group of minstrels singing at the main gate. They sang:

> Lift up your heads, O gates!
> Be lifted up, O doors of antiquity!
> The king of glory shall enter.
>
> Who is this king of glory?
> Yahweh strong and heroic,
> Yahweh, the hero of battle.
>
> Lift up your heads, O gates!
> Be lifted up O doors of antiquity!
> The king of glory shall enter.
>
> Who is this king of glory?
> Yahweh Sebaoth,
> He is the king of glory.
>   (Psalm 24:7–10)

After the minstrels finished their song, they kept repeating again and again: "Who is the king of glory? Yahweh Sebaoth." They did this all the

The Ark Is Brought to the City of David

way to the threshing floor. According to one report, "They brought in the ark of Yahweh. They set it up in its sanctuary inside the tent that David had pitched for it" (2 Samuel 6:17a). Next, the minstrels sang Ahban's psalm, but there was so much noise that the first part of it was never heard. The crowd did quiet down for part of it:

> For Yahweh has chosen Zion;
> He has desired it for his dwelling.
> "This is my resting-place until the end of time.
> Here, I will dwell for I have desired it.
> Her provisions, I will abundantly bless,
> Her needy, I will satisfy [with] food, ...
>   (Psalm 132:13–15)

Then David offered more sacrifices, and he blessed the people, giving them each a loaf of bread, plain cakes, and raisin cakes. Now it became clear why the people brought their children: the more children the more bread! The children had a great time running around and collecting as much as they could carry. After the blessing and the giving of food, there was more singing and dancing. Finally, the people went to their homes. The ark was finally in its place. This was an important occasion for David, and the priests were pleased; they had their cultic center.

30

Noah and the Flood

BACK AT THE SCHOOL, Jonathan had been working for some time before Elimelech and Elishama showed up for their morning meeting. They had observed the first part of the celebration. Jonathan greeted them, and he confessed he did not go to the big event. He said, "I should have gone, but there is just too much to do. It would be nice to finish our work before the dedication of David's palace. Now that he has a place for Yahweh, he will want to get the palace finished. Have you seen the building project lately?"

"Elishama and I walked by the site just a few minutes ago, but I didn't notice the progress."

Elishama said, "They have not made much progress, but Elimelech and I were talking about the singers at the gate, as we walked by the project. They sang 'Lift up your heads, O gates,' as the ark entered the city, and we liked it. Certainly the people in the gate lifted up their heads if not the gates."

Jonathan said, "I can understand that your conversation was probably more important than the progress of the building project. But we do need to get some word on the progress. That does not mean we will speed up just for the dedication. Why don't you both ask when they expect to be finished?"

"That will be easy," answered Elimelech. "I'll ask Magon. He keeps in touch with the builders."

"That will help. At the end of our last meeting, I said that I would put together the two texts we were working on (the short list and the long list of sages). I have done that. I also said the flood would be our next task. Well I have to go back on my word. I would like to add one or two more items before we come to the flood. The first item is from a text I found when I was looking for our texts on the pre-flood sages. It deals with pre-flood heroes and probably post-flood heroes as well. It goes this way:

Noah and the Flood

> When the human beings began to multiply,
> upon the face of the ground,
> and daughters were born to them,
> the sons of the gods saw that the daughters
> of the human beings were beautiful,
> they took for themselves wives from any of those they chose.
> Yahweh said:
> > "My spirit can not be bottled up in human beings forever,
> > In as much as they are flesh.
> > Their days will be a hundred and twenty years."
> The Nephilim were on earth in those days, and afterwards,
> for the sons of the gods did mate with the daughters of the human beings;
> they bore [children] to them—
> they were the heroes of old,
> the men of renown.
> > (Genesis 6:1–4)

"I would like to use this text before we start the flood story. We have already dealt with the ten pre-flood sages or kings. But we really need to account for other famous people. This text gives the popular explanation that the origin of special people is the result of their sires, namely, the sons of the gods. But, the real point is that these heroes are intelligent, and even though they have one divine parent, they are mortal. All humans are mortal, even the great humans who were sired by the gods."

Elimelech said, "I agree. We should use this story, but it should go somewhere after the flood story; it relates more to post-flood heroes."

Elishama said, "I agree with Elimelech. Gilgamesh was a post-flood Babylonian hero, and he had to find out that even though he was two-thirds divine, he was mortal."

Jonathan said, "Your points are well taken, but there are other problems. The story makes the point we want to emphasize, namely, even special humans are mortal. But, it also puts in a year limitation, which does not work in either position. The ten sages in the proceeding story live long lives, but the fathers after the flood also live long lives. Isaac, who seems to be sired by God, lives a hundred and eighty years. These problems are less noticeable if we refer to these heroes right after we have mention the famous ten sages."

Elishama said, "You mentioned that Isaac seemed to be sired by God. I don't remember seeing that."

Jonathan said, "Somewhere in the story it says,

> Yahweh visited Sarah as he had said;
> Yahweh did to Sarah as he had spoken.
> Sarah became pregnant;
> She bore a son to Abraham for his old age. . . .
> Abraham called forth the name of his son, . . . "Isaac."
>   (Genesis 21:1–3)

This passage makes Yahweh the real father. Of course, Abraham still carries on as the father."

"In any case, Isaac does live a long time," said Elishama.

"There is another reason to place the story before the flood," Jonathan quickly noted. "In this position, it serves as a reminder from the middle; it is a reminder from our own times to any reader or anyone who hears that the ages of the ten sages will never be repeated even if you have a divine father. It does all of this and still explains the existence of and the mortality of the great heroes."

Elishama said, "I thought it should be put in after the flood, when we began this discussion, but now you have changed my mind. Also, when you put it just after the notice about Noah, it makes one think of Gilgamesh who was a great hero, and as we just said, he was also two-thirds divine. I say this, because Gilgamesh sought out the Babylonian flood hero, Utanapishtim, who along with his wife had gained immortality, but they had to give up their humanity. They became like the gods. Gilgamesh sought out Utanapishtim so that he could ask him how to obtain immortality. Gilgamesh did not find immortality. He did not even extend his life. He was still human. We have kept our flood hero mortal whereas others have allowed their flood heroes to become immortal. But Noah did live a long time, so this story could say to any would-be-Gilgamesh, 'don't ask for immortality or even a long life. You have one hundred and twenty years. That's all.'"

Elimelech said, "Both of you are just trying to make this story work. Personally, I am about ready to change my mind. Let's throw the story out. We don't need it."

Jonathan said, "I'll keep what you say in mind. Also, I'll ask some others what they think. At this point, let's move on to talk about the flood. Our flood story begins like this:

Noah and the Flood

> Noah was a righteous man;
> He was perfect in his generation.
> With the gods, Noah walked.
> Noah fathered three sons:
> Shem, Ham, and Japheth.
> (Genesis 6:9b–10)

"Just before this beginning, we should put in one of our titles. In this case it would be *These are the Stories of Noah*. However, I would like to add a general introduction to the flood story just before this title. Among other things, the introduction will give a reason for the flood. In some of the other flood stories, either little is said concerning the reason for the flood or the reason given seems inadequate. Also if we put in the story about the heroes and an introduction between the list of ten sages and the flood story, the beginning of the flood story will not seem to be so repetitive. If we started the flood story just after the mention of the tenth sage which reads: 'When Noah was five hundred years old, Noah fathered Shem, Ham, and Japheth,' we would be repeating this information in the next few lines. The introduction, which I propose, would read like this:

> Yahweh saw how great was the evil of the human beings on the earth,
> and how every form of the thoughts of their minds was only evil, all of the day.
> Yahweh regretted that he had made the human beings on the earth.
> He was in labor with his thoughts.
> Yahweh said:
>> "I will blot out the human beings whom I formed,
>> from upon the face of the ground—
>> from human beings to domestic animals,
>> to moving ones, and to the birds of the heavens,
>> because I regret that I made them."
>
> But Noah found favor in the eyes of Yahweh."
> (Genesis 6:5–8)

Elimelech and Elishama both agreed that the introduction was needed. Then, Elishama said, "Our Babylonian class with Magon is now reading the flood story, and tomorrow, I'll be able to share some of the Babylonian parallels."

The Jerusalem Academy

Jonathan said, "I hope you can do that. Now I should get home. We talked right through lunch and into the late afternoon. I'll see you in the morning."

Jonathan came home after the meeting. I was working in the kitchen, and at the same time I was trying to write my next letter. Of course I had not received one from Elissa as yet, but I wanted to be ready. Jonathan held me and kissed me. He said, "How is that poem? Do you have any ideas yet on what you want to write?

"I have lots of ideas, but none of them seems just right."

"Then you are making some progress. You have to rule out many ideas in order to get to the right one. When you finally decide what you want to do, make it short. It will be easier that way, and often it is better. I can give you an example. We are working on the flood story now. After the flood, Yahweh says he will never again destroy all life. Then he says:

> Throughout all the days of the earth,
> Sowing and reaping,
> Cold and heat,
> Summer and winter,
> Day and night,
> They shall not cease.
> (Genesis 8:22)

"This is a meaningful way to say that things are going to be steady and sure. It is also brief and to the point."

"I like it as well, and I don't dislike being brief. But I just can't decide what point I want to make. Perhaps I will have to write about our baby. Right now, that is all I think about. Is it a girl or boy? The only thing I know is it will be our firstborn."

"Perhaps you should write about the baby. The baby is always with you and in your thoughts. You do need to select some experience you've had, and then consider it from every angle in the present. By doing this, you allow it to impact your future and the future of others. If all this happens, you probably have a poem which is a special creation."

"After what you have just said, I might write something about poetry. Since I am interested in our future, I would like to think about poems in the terms you've suggested. Poetry in this sense would not be just a word picture or copy of some aspect of nature like the pictures that sea animals and leaves have left in rocks. We should have a section on poetry in our 'Minority Report.'"

"You're probably right, and we should start a list of things to put in our book."

"I'll make the list and keep it handy."

"Fine, and now I would like to put some more seed in my garden."

"You don't need any more seed in your garden. There is no more room; your cup is overflowing. But, you do need to help me with dinner, and we can do some gardening later. Right?"

"Right."

As they were preparing the meal, they continued their discussion of poetry. At one point I said, "I should write up this conversation for the book. I have never heard a man having such a conversation with his wife. All men, including you, dear Jonathan, would rather plant seed than talk."

"Do I have to remind you that we were talking before I even thought of planting?"

"Do you mean to say that you were not thinking about me on the way home?"

"I'll have to admit I was thinking about you. You forced me to say that!"

"I know, but I want you to know that I love your talking and your planting."

"You're right. This conversation should be in our book. Put it on your list. I can't even imagine Sheva and Sarah having such a conversation."

When we were ready to eat, I said, "I forgot to tell you father will not be home tonight. He has gone somewhere to check on food supplies. So, we can eat now, and you can cultivate your garden later."

"I'm for that."

"I thought as much."

Jonathan said, "At work, we are also having some interesting conversations these days. Today we began our discussions of the flood. It will not be easy to tell this story. We have several texts that deal with the flood, and they all make important points. However, they also bring in some differences that can be confusing. In some texts, Noah takes seven pairs of each animal, but in others he takes just one pair into the ark. We will have to sort this out. Tomorrow, Elishama wants to talk about the Babylonians and their flood story."

The Jerusalem Academy

"Is Elishama getting excited about their baby?"
"I think so, but he is a calm fellow."
"Let's clean up here, and we can get to bed early."

Jonathan and I enjoyed each other for a long time. Several times Jonathan had to say as he caressed my full belly, "You are so beautiful. I cherish these moments."

And I was pleased with his touch and his words.

Jonathan left for the school early the next morning and this pattern continued for the next few days. One day, after Jonathan had left for his morning meeting, I began to work on my writing. I had learned so much from Jonathan during our nightly conversations, but I said to myself, "I'm not going to make this poem as short as Jonathan's example from the other evening. I need a few more words than those that God used. Also, I'm going to write about poetry and giving birth."

I worked most of the day, and I want to tell every reader of my story that I have never, to this day, really liked the poem I wrote. However, it did pull together some of my thinking. So with some hesitation, I put my poem by Jonathan's place at the table. Later, when he walked into the kitchen, he saw it at once. "What have we here?" he asked.

"I'm not certain what we have, but I worked on it all day. I decided to combine my obvious interest in giving birth with our interest in poetry, and I was in labor for about ten hours before this poem arrived. If we can call it that?"

Jonathan began to read:

A Poem is the Issue
First is the poet,
And if adventure,
A poem will come forth,
A gem of culture.

Adventure takes courage,
And life has its needs.
Yet, the issue is a poem;
Give her more than seed.

Noah and the Flood

> The real is dim,
> Appearance a must;
> Labor it needs,
> For clarity's thrust.
>
> Truth and beauty:
> They nourish this child,
> Who brings lively joy,
> For urban and wild.
>
> A poem takes from the past,
> Partakes of the present,
> Creates a new future;
> This is a novel event.

After reading these lines twice, Jonathan kissed me and said, "This poem must be placed in our book. I know we've been talking about such things, but there is much more than our conversations in this poem. 'This is a novel event.'"

31

Noah and the Flood Continued

JONATHAN WANTED TO FINISH the work on Noah and the flood, but it was confusing. As usual there were several texts and there were some major problems with some of these texts. When Elimelech and Elishama arrived for the morning meeting, Jonathan said to them, "We must get this flood story finished. We are taking too long."

Elimelech said, "We both agree with you, but it isn't easy. Sheva has been giving us some extra work to do which could be done by some of the students."

"I'll be glad to talk with Sheva about that. I need to report to him about several things. Did either of you find out anything about the building project?"

Elishama said, "I was talking with Magon about it shortly after you asked us, and he said that they are not making much progress. He thinks we still have a lot of time."

"Well, that's good news," said Jonathan. "We need all the time we can get for the stories of the ancestors. Let's try to finish this flood story today, even though we have twelve texts before us. Also, Elishama has told us about the parallels in the Babylonian traditions, and some of them are remarkable. These parallels may cause us to change a few things. The best thing is to look at a chart that I have made of these twelve texts. Here you can see how I have arranged these texts, and then we can discuss if it all fits together. So, here is the chart:

The Title   *These are the stories of Noah* (Genesis 6:9a)

Text 1   Noah was a righteous man;
            (Genesis 6:9b–12)

Text 2   Elohim said to Noah:
            "The end of all flesh was declared before me, . . .
            (Genesis 6:13–22)

Text 3	Yahweh said to Noah: "Enter, you and all your house, into the ark, . . . (Genesis 7:1–5)
Text 4	Noah was six hundred years old, and then the flood came— (Genesis 7:6–9)
Text 5	After seven days, the waters of the flood came upon the earth. (Genesis 7:10–16)
Text 6	The flood was upon the earth forty days. (Genesis 7:17–24)
Text 7	Elohim remembered Noah (Genesis 8:1–14)
Text 8	Elohim spoke to Noah, as follows: "Come out from the ark, . . . (Genesis 8:15–17)
Text 9	Noah came out, his sons, his wife, . . . (Genesis 8:18–22)
Text 10	Elohim blessed Noah and his sons; he said to them: . . . (Genesis 9:1–7)
Text 11	Elohim said to Noah and to his sons with him as follows: . . . (Genesis 9:8–11)
Text 12	Elohim said: "This is the sign of the covenant, . . . (Genesis 9:12–17)

Jonathan said, "In our general introduction that I presented a few days ago, we talked about 'the evil of the human beings on the earth,' and also about Yahweh's decision to blot out all life. However, 'Noah found favor in the eyes of Yahweh.' In text 1, we have the reverse. Here, there is a good word about Noah and then the poem about the corruption of the earth or 'all flesh.' Should we use this passage as well as the general introduction?"

Elimelech said, "We should use both of them. In the introduction there is more of a focus on the humans, and text 1 is more general. But, the thing that makes text 1 more dynamic is that 'the earth was found corrupt before the gods.' Here we have a decision that was made by the heavenly court. This passage has a stronger reason for the flood."

Jonathan said, "You have put your finger on an important point, and the beginning of the next section, as you will see, reinforces what you have said."

Elishama said, "And, both of them deal seriously with the reason for the flood. The Babylonian account of the flood in *The Gilgamesh Epic* does not even give a reason for the destruction, but you will recall that I reported the other day that Magon says some older traditions say that the god Enlil wanted the humans destroyed, because they were making too much noise. I agree with Elimelech; this court decision is important."

Jonathan said, "Let's continue. As I mentioned earlier, in text 2 the court's decision is repeated, and we have a set of detailed instructions on building the ark in this text."

Elishama said, "The detail is much greater than in *The Gilgamesh Epic*."

"Yes, and this ark is not just a square as in the Babylonian story," added Elimelech.

Jonathan said, "Text 2 is the first of seven where God speaks to Noah. In this one Elohim speaks and in the next one Yahweh speaks. I do not consider it to be an important point. We can let both sources and both gods speak. Of the texts that I have selected most of them end with a mention of the earth (as in text 1), but text 2, and the next three, end with a note about Noah's obedience. Shall we go on?"

"Text 3 may create some problems, because it mentions that Noah shall take seven pairs of the clean animals and one pair of the others. This is different from the above instructions, but it makes for a good addition. After all, Noah will need some additional pairs of the clean animals for his offerings. This text should make the priests happy. The next or fourth text just mentions pairs entering the ark. This could cause some more problems because it mentions the clean animals, but it does not mention anything about seven pairs. I guess that anyone who hears this would assume that it could refer to seven pairs or to one pair because of the earlier texts. In any case, here we have the story of the entering into the ark."

Elishama said, "It does not bother me that clean and unclean enter 'as pairs.' That's the way it would happen even with the seven pairs."

"Right. So, we won't worry about that."

Next Jonathan turned to the fifth text. "Here, we have a repeat of the entry into the ark, but I still would like to use this text. Here we have more than just rain. This is a return to the chaos before God structured our world. It is a return to 'devastation and desolation!' The 'fountains of the great deep' burst forth, and 'the windows of the heavens were opened.'

Noah and the Flood Continued

This calls for a new formation, a new order, and a new beginning. I like this text."

Elimelech said, "If you cut out the last half of this text, you would not have so much repetition. But, I suppose some singer would object."

"I'm certain some singer would."

Then Jonathan continued with the sixth text. "This is a sad part of the story. After this, things can only get better. We have said that in our story God takes a legal action against the type of violence that grew out of the actions of Cain and Lamech, but that does not help to reduce the violence of the punishment. Now there has to be a new creation."

"This is about the place in the Babylonian account where it says 'all of the humans had returned to clay,'" Elishama remarked.

Jonathan rushed on. "The seventh text is next. I want to point out to you that once again God must conquer the waters when he wants to bring about the new cosmos. He uses his winds for this purpose, and this is a common theme. 'The fountains of the deep and the windows of the heavens' were closed. The use of the birds at the end of these stories is perhaps the most interesting of the parallels. In the Gilgamesh tradition the flood hero uses a dove, a swallow, and a raven. In our story it is only two: the raven and the dove, but that is close enough.

"In Text 8 we have the instructions to exit from the ark, and Text 9 deals with the actual exit."

Elishama said, "Text 9 also has an important parallel in the Babylonian tradition. Both of the flood heroes offer sacrifices as soon as they exit the ark. In this case, the sacrifice is accepted, and there is the promise that from now on you can depend on the stability of this world."

Jonathan said, "That's correct, and I really like the final poem. In fact, I read it for Keziah a few days ago as an example of how one can make a powerful point with just a few words. But let's move on to the tenth section. Here we have God's blessing and the rules of the new order. All of this is put in the form of a covenant in the eleventh section. Here we have God's promise, and we should note that God's promise is made to 'all flesh.' This is not just a promise to humans; it is to 'all flesh.' The humans and the other animals are together in this covenant. Finally in section twelve, we are given the sign of the covenant. God says, 'My bow I have set in the clouds.'"

Then Jonathan added, "This flood story is important, because, there is an emphasis on the new order, on God's covenant and promise, and on the sign of that promise. There is also an emphasis upon the earth and upon all creatures. This is our home, and it is the best we have."

Elimelech said, "As we have mentioned, one big difference in our flood story and the Babylonian traditions is that in our Noah and his wife remain mortal and human. This we must hold up for all to see. What I miss in our story is something on how Noah brings to the post-flood world all of the pre-flood knowledge. We assume this, but it is never stated."

Jonathan said, "I will try to find something on this during the next few days. This has been a long session. I will leave these texts on my desk if you want to study them. I'll see you tomorrow."

32

Meribbaal and Gad

WHEN JONATHAN GOT HOME, father was helping me with the dinner. We had been talking about father's investigations of the food problems, but Jonathan's arrival stopped our conversation. Jonathan gave me a hug, and he asked Gad, "How did things go for you today. Is David still keeping you busy?"

"David is keeping everyone busy these days. Right now he is trying to mend his fences with the House of Saul. Today he wanted to know if there was anyone in the House of Saul that he should help 'for the sake of Saul's son, Jonathan?' David and Jonathan had made a covenant years ago, and David was trying to be faithful to that agreement and care for Jonathan's family. So we summoned Ziba, a servant in the House of Saul, and he was helpful. He told us about Meribbaal, the crippled son of Jonathan. Then David called Meribbaal and returned to him all of Saul's land. Also, David said to him, 'You shall always eat at my table.'"

Jonathan said, "It sounds as if you were busy. Did you tell Meribbaal that your son-in-law did not care much for David's table?"

"No. I forgot to tell him that."

I said, "If Meribbaal has all of Saul's land, he does not really need to eat at David's table, but let's sit down at ours."

After we finished the meal, Jonathan said, "Gad did you get to see Keziah's poem about the birth of a poem?"

"Yes. She let me see it when I came home this afternoon. She said that the two of you had been discussing the subject for some time. She gives some credit to you, but I have discounted most of what she said about that," father said with a smile, which at first he tried to hold back.

Jonathan said, "There is no doubt that the poem is hers. She created it just as God formed our world. She took the pieces of our chaotic conversations, and she put them together; she gave them their form. Since Keziah has given us this work on the birth of a poem, I thought I would bring home a little piece on the birth of a proverb. It goes like this:

> I passed by the field of a lazy man,
> And by the vineyard of a senseless man.
> Here, thorns climbed up all over it.
> Its surface was covered with weeds,
> And its stone wall was broken down.
> I observed; I took it to heart.
> I saw; I studied [this] lesson:
> A few naps, a few drowsy times,
> A few times of folding the hands to rest,
> And your poverty will come marching on,
> Even as a [charging] warrior your dire straits."
> (Proverbs 24:30–34)

"I like that. It really gives me some new ideas. It deals with the subject by using an intriguing example. It is easier to understand than what I wrote about poetry."

Jonathan said, "You can always deal with your subject again and again and view it from many angles. The real key, as this text says, is to observe, to consider, and to learn. This is how we stay alive."

"Where do you find all these texts that you bring home?" I said.

"I usually find them when I am looking for something else. This reminds me; I have to look for something on how Noah brought to the new world all the pre-flood knowledge. Gad, have you ever seen such a text or heard a singer deal with Noah in that way?"

"I have not seen or heard such a thing. But after the flood, our stories assume that Noah brings with him all knowledge. After all, the first couple gave up immortality or life in the 'garden' for all knowledge. That's one thing the humans want to keep."

Jonathan said, "You're correct. I'll ask Heman about a Noah tradition that assumes such a role for Noah. After the flood and after God brings order out of chaos again, things get much better. Noah takes the place of Cain and civilization develops for the second time. Hopefully, he will leave some of the vengeance of Cain and Lamech behind."

"Does he leave it behind?" I said.

"I'm afraid it is still with us, but at least, according to the story we don't have to worry about another flood."

Meribbaal and Gad

Father said, "I don't want to break this up, but I must get to bed. I have an appointment to see David in the morning. We have to deal with this food shortage business."

"Jonathan and I will clean things up. You go to bed. We will be going to bed soon. I'm getting tired these days. This baby wears me out."

Father left the house early the next morning. Even though it was still early, David was waiting for father, and David started talking at once. He said, "You have been sending these reports to me about our shortage of food, and you have said in some parts of our country there is in fact a famine. Just to our north the Gibeonites have been complaining of a famine, which was caused by Saul's murder of some Gibeonites, and they have been hurting for three years. Has the famine been going on for three years?"

Father said, "It has in some areas, but I must say I did not talk to the Gibeonites."

"I know, but I talked to them three days ago."

"What did they want you to do about their situation?"

"They wanted me to hand over seven of Saul's sons to them. They wanted to 'impale them before Yahweh' (2 Samuel 21:6 and 9). I wanted you to know about this, and to know I have already sent the seven. I received word last evening that the seven had been impaled; they all died at once."

"This is human sacrifice! We don't do this!"

"Yes, but it just may work; Yahweh may listen to the cry of the land."

"I wonder if he heard the cry of the seven?"

"Now Gad, let's keep an open mind. Now, my question to you has to do with the burial of the seven. I think I should go and gather up the bones of the seven for burial. At the same time, I'm wondering if it would help to gather the bones of Saul and Jonathan for proper burial. My relationship with the House of Saul goes up and down. It helped to deal kindly with Meribbaal but giving the seven to the Gibeonites puts me at an all time low. It might help if I gave a big and proper funeral for Saul and Jonathan."

Father said, "I have to say that you have sinned in sacrificing the seven, and you are politically ignorant with your intent to give Saul and Jonathan a 'proper burial.'"

"Ignorant?"

"That's correct. If you give Saul and Jonathan 'a big and proper funeral,' you will create a place where the House of Saul can go to receive the blessings of Saul. You will create the hope that Saul's line could be continued. You may have to do something for the House of Saul but don't do this. Some rebel will end up going to Saul's tomb and declaring himself the king of the House of Saul, if not of all Israel."

"Gad you're getting too old; you're out of your mind."

"I may be old, but my mind is still good enough to remember that Sheva and Jonathan had a long conversation about such things just before your second coronation. They were afraid that some people from the north might think that Saul and Ish-baal, as recently departed kings, should be summoned in the funeral ritual which was a part of your coronation. But, they said this would not work. Jonathan said that Sheva told him there were two basic reasons to avoid such a thing:

1) King lists, which are used in funeral rituals and at coronations in most city-states, do not include all the kings. There are many reasons for this, and most of them are political.
2) In this case, Yahweh took the kingdom from Saul, and in the coronation Yahweh proclaimed that you, David, are his son. Here we had the beginning of something new. It would not be appropriate for us to re-install Saul as a departed 'king' from a defunct line.

"Therefore, it is not appropriate for you to give Saul a new burial and to renew the hopes of his house. Kings who want to destroy dynastic lines scattered the bones of departed kings; they do not bury the departed kings again. But, I think you know this, and yet you are the one who buried the head of Ish-baal in Abner's grave!"

David said, "Gad, get your ass out of my quarters and don't come back here again. My prophet, Nathan, will handle everything from now on."

Father left without a word. He felt relaxed as he walked home, but he was not happy about what David had done to those poor souls. He thought, "David does not need any of my information on our food problems. He now solves such problems by offering up humans!"

When he got home, he found Jonathan and me having lunch. He said to us, "You will be seeing a lot more of me from now on. David told me to get out of his quarters and to never return. He was mad."

Jonathan said, "So now, you will need that office."

"Yes, I'll need it."

I said, "Why did he get so mad?"

"Because, he wanted me to approve of something he wanted to do. I told him it was wrong, and he should not do it. He does not like the word 'no.' If you can spare the time, I'll tell you the story."

Father told us everything David did, and he quoted all that he said. Then Jonathan said, "I'm glad you stood up to him. I don't think he will do anything to you for calling him a 'sinner.' In fact he should know he is wrong. He certainly did not listen to the story about Abraham and Isaac that was sung at his coronation. Human sacrifice cannot be allowed. The re-burial of Saul and Jonathan is a foolish move on David's part. We worked through that whole business with great care, and he just blunders along. The foreign diplomats in this city will think David is out of his mind."

"Here, father, have some lunch unless you don't feel well."

"Keziah, I have never felt better. You know that for some time, I have wanted to quit, and now I can. I'll help spoil the baby, and I'll help you. I don't want to work on my book all the time."

After father left David's quarters, David sent some of his men to get the bones of the seven and of Saul and Jonathan. He said to himself, "We are going to have a big funeral for Saul and Jonathan." David looked through his things, and he found the short funeral dirge, which he had written for Saul and Jonathan when he was still in Ziklag. He began at once to re-write it. He wanted to make it longer, and of course, much better.

About two weeks later, David and his men "buried the bones of Saul and Jonathan, his son, in the land of Benjamin, in Zela, in the tomb of Kish, his father..." (2 Samuel 21:14). They had the "big and proper" burial and David sang the new dirge:

> *The Song of the Bow*
> The gazelle, O Israel,
> Upon your hills was run through.
> How the heroes have fallen!
>
> You shall not tell it in Gath;
> You shall not proclaim good news,
> In the streets of Ashkelon,

The Jerusalem Academy

Lest they become ecstatic,
Those young Philistine women,
Lest they become jubilant,
Daughters of foreskinned bastards.

O mountains of Gilboa,
Let there be no dew on you,
Let there be no rain on you,
Nor overflow from the depths.
For there it was cast aside,
A shield of the great heroes—
The shield of Saul will not be,
Never anointed with oil.

From the blood of those run through,
From the fat of the heroes,
Jonathan's bow did not turn,
Nor did Saul's sword return clean.

Saul and Jonathan, they were:
Beloved and so delightful.
In their life and in their death,
These two were never parted.
They were swifter than eagles;
They were stronger than lions.

O daughters of Israel,
Weep for Saul, yes, weep for Saul.
He is the one who clothed you
In crimson with luxuries.
The one who adorned your robes
With ornaments of fine gold.

How the heroes have fallen
In the midst of the battle.
Jonathan, [O Israel,]
Upon your hills was run through.
Grief is mine on your account,
O my brother Jonathan.

You were very good to me;
Your love was wondrous to me,
More than the love of women.
How the heroes have fallen;
Weapons of war have perished.
   (2 Samuel 1:19–27)

After the funeral David sent his *Song of the Bow* to Sheva and asked him to record it in *The Book of Jashar*.

33

Noah's Sons

It was a beautiful day in Jerusalem. The rains had ceased, the grain harvest was better than last year's harvest, and the work on the royal epic was moving along at a much better pace since Sheva had agreed not to give work to the scribes that students could do. Jonathan was sitting in Sheva's office and waiting for him to return, because Sheva had asked Jonathan stop by on his way to work. Sheva was soon there, and he asked Jonathan to read David's *The Song of the Bow*.

Sheva said, "David just sent this song to put in *The Book of Jashar*. I have been mad at David ever since he got rid of Gad, but I have to say that he has written a good song, and you should read it. I see that Gad spends a lot of time in his office, and I am glad we had an extra office for him. However, we should not say too much about Gad and his office."

Jonathan said, "I don't say much about anything to anybody, but it worries me that you had to say something about this. Gad's work is too important to spend any time worrying about what David thinks. David does not care much about what any of us are doing, and I don't want to read David's *The Song of the Bow*."

"Sorry. I guess I was being overly cautious. The other day, I was talking to Zadok, and he said he has been working on the story of Joseph in Egypt. You should add him to your group. It would also equalize the group: you and Elimelech from the south and Elishama and Zadok from the north."

"I will be happy to have Zadok join us. I thought he would be too busy, since he is now the director of the Old School. How is he doing?"

"He's doing well, and he is the first to say that Ahban still helps him with important decisions. Zadok will be coming by here today, and I will ask him to stop by your office, and you can talk to him about this."

Noah's Son

"That will work out fine, and it gives me time to speak to the others concerning what Zadok is doing before he gets here. So, I should get to my office now."

When Jonathan got to his office, Elimelech and Elishama were already there. They reported to him that they were getting a lot more done on the stories of the fathers since their workload for the school was lighter. Then, Jonathan told them that Zadok had been working on the Joseph material, and he might be willing to help them work on it.

Jonathan said, "Would it be helpful for Zadok to join us?"

Elishama said, "Yes. It would be helpful, and I would like to see what he has done. You will remember that when Joshua and I first arrived in Hebron, we brought a new text of the story of Joseph. It will be interesting to see if Zadok has used our Shechem text."

Elimelech said, "Ask him to join us. We need all the help we can get."

"Well, until he shows up we can try to make some decisions on the material we'll need for the period from the flood to the stories of Abraham. I have been working on this for about ten days, and I have not found a text which deals with how Noah brought to the new world the old world's store of knowledge. However, there are stories where it is assumed that Noah provided our world with the necessary knowledge for the spread of a new civilization. The best example is one that Heman sang for me the other day. I copied as he sang. He also reminded me that when our epic is used at the dedication of David's palace, the minstrels would not always follow our text. So, we should not be surprised about that, but here is the story as I copied it:

> The sons of Noah, who came out of the ark, were Shem,
> Ham, and Japheth—Ham, he was the father of Canaan.
> These three were the sons of Noah,
> and from these all the earth was populated.
>
> Noah became a farmer.
> He planted a vineyard.
> He drank of the wine.
> He became drunk.
> He uncovered himself within his tent.
> Ham, the father of Canaan, saw the nakedness of his father.
> He told his two brothers outside.

> Shem and Japheth took the garment;
> They put it on both their shoulders.
> They walked backwards.
> They covered the nakedness of their father.
> Because their faces were turned the other way,
> The nakedness of their father they did not see.
>
> When Noah awoke from his wine, he knew what his lesser son had done to him.
> He said:
> > "Cursed be Canaan;
> > A slave of slaves
> > Shall he be to his brothers."
>
> He said:
> > "Blessed be Yahweh,
> > The God of Shem;
> > Let Canaan be a slave to them.
> > May Elohim enlarge Japheth,
> > Let him dwell in the tents of Shem;
> > Let Canaan be a slave to them."
> >
> > (Genesis 9:18–27)

"In this story, Noah is a farmer with a great deal of knowledge. He not only has to know how to plant and care for a vineyard, but he also knows how to make wine. This story assumes that he brought a great deal of knowledge to his first project in the new world."

Elishama said, "I can understand what you are saying, and if this the best story we have then we will have to use it. However, there is something here I don't understand. I don't understand what Ham did to Noah."

Jonathan said, "I don't know what he did either. Perhaps it was bad enough just to see 'the nakedness of his father,' but most people think he did something sexual to his father. Remember how Lot's daughters had sex with their father when he was drunk? Whatever happened, it was enough to earn the curse, but instead of Ham being cursed, his son, Canaan, is cursed. On this point, I'm certain the storyteller wants to show why we should defeat and enslave the Canaanites. But there is a more immediate reason for telling this story, and we should include it. It is the introduction to the general theme of this post-flood material, which is how the people spread throughout the world after the flood. All of these people are

Noah's Son

classified in the next text; they are classified into three groups: the friends of Israel, the enemies of Israel, and the kinfolks of Israel. Also, all of this begins a new section:

> *These are the stories of the sons of Noah, Shem, Ham, and Japheth*
> (Sons were born to them after the flood).
> The sons of Japheth: Gomer, Magog, Madai, Javan, Tubal, Meshech, and Tiras.
> The sons of Gomer: Ashkenaz, Riphath, and Togarmah.
> The sons of Javan: Elishah and Tarshish, Kittim and Dodanim.
> From these were populated the maritime states with their lands ---
> each with its own language according to their clans within their states.
>   (Genesis 10:1–5)

"Here, we have the friends of Israel."

Elimelech said, "Perhaps they are friends, because many of them live in the far west. We never see them!"

Jonathan said, "Don't be too hard on us. It's true that some of these are from the far west. Tarshish is probably at the other end of our western or great sea. Javan is not quite so far (the Ionians). Elishah is pronounced, 'Alashiya' in our Babylonian texts (Cyprus), and it is a large island, which was in constant communication with ancient Ugarit and Egypt. It is not so far. The Sea Peoples, who invaded the coast of Canaan about two hundred years ago, were made up of some of these groups. However, one of the main groups that made up the Sea Peoples is not listed here; they were the Caphtorim. They were put into the next list because the Philistines were from there, and the Philistines are our enemies. But the Caphtorim, or Kaptaru in Babylonian texts (Cretans), should be listed here, because David's mercenaries or honor guard, the Cherethites and the Pelethites, also came from there. But we don't need to correct this. I should give you the section on our enemies:

> The sons of Ham: Cush, Mizraim, Put, and Canaan.
> The sons of Cush: Seba, Havilah, Sabtah, Raamah, and Sabteca
> (The sons of Raamah: Sheba and Dedan).
> And Cush fathered Nimrod;
> he was the first to be a hero on the earth;
> he was the hero of the hunt in the sight of Yahweh,
> hence, it is said:

> 'Like Nimrod the hero of the hunt in the sight of Yahweh.'
> The heads of his kingdom were Babel, Erech, Accad,
> and Calneh in the land of Shinar.
> From that land Asshur went out; he built Nineveh, Rehoboth-Ir,
> Calah, and Resen between Nineveh and between Calah,
> she is the great city.
> Mizraim fathered Ludim, Anamim, Lehabim, Naphtuhim,
> Pathrusim, Casluhim, the place from where the Philistines came,
> and Caphtorim.
> Canaan fathered Sidon, his first born, Heth,
> the Jebusites, the Amorites, the Girgashites,
> the Hivites, the Arkites, the Sinites,
> the Arvadites, the Zamarites, and the Hamathites.
> Later the Canaanite clans were dispersed.
> The borders of the Canaanites were from Sidon
> until you reach Gerar,
> as far as Gaza, and until you reach Sodom, Gomorrah,
> Admah, and Zeboiim, as far as Lasha.
> These are the sons of Ham according to their clans and languages,
> within their lands and their states.
>
> (Genesis 10:6–20)

"This list of enemies is longer than the list of friends. It has its problems, but again we don't need to correct it. For example, this list makes it seem as if the Philistines came from Casluhim. This must be wrong. But, these lists were made at an earlier time, and we should keep them as they are. It is interesting to know what the early scribes thought. Also, we are mainly interested in the spread of the world's population from the three sons of Noah."

Elimelech said, "I wonder why they list Sidon but they do not list Tyre?"

Jonathan said, "I did ask Magon about that, and he said Tyre was not the leader of the coastal cities until quite recently. The use of Sidon represents an old tradition. If we were writing these lists today, we would include Tyre but within the list of friends."

Again, Elimelech said, "I noticed that the Jebusites are listed. This may be another sign that this list is old, because under their king Adonizedek, they were enemies, but as we now know, in our time, they have not been enemies in any substantial way."

Jonathan said, "That's a good point. One other problem we will soon note is that some of these 'enemies' will also be included in the list of kin. I guess that such a thing does not have to be a problem. I have some relatives who are my enemies."

Elishama said, "It seems to me this section is full of interesting problems. With the sons of Ham you are basically dealing with the kingdom of Egypt and the countries Egypt ruled. But, it also deals with Babylon and Nineveh. The list goes everywhere."

Jonathan said, "That it does, but it does make for interesting questions. Now let's have a look at the kinfolk:

> Also to Shem [sons] were born;
> he was the ancestor of all the sons of Eber,
> the brother of Japheth, the elder.
> The sons of Shem: Elam, Asshur, Arpachshad, Lud, and Aram.
> The sons of Aram: Uz, Hul, Gether, and Mash.
> Arpachshad fathered Shelah, and Shelah fathered Eber.
> To Eber, two sons were born; the name of the one was Peleg,
> for in his days the earth was divided (*niphlegah*),
> and the name of his brother was Joktan.
> Joktan fathered Almodad, Sheleph, Hazarmaveth, Jerah,
> Hadoram, Uzal, Diklah,
> Obal, Abimael, Sheba,
> Ophir, Havilah, and Jobab; all these were the sons of Joktan.
> Their settlements were from Mesha until you come to Sepher,
> the mountain of the east.
> These are the sons of Shem according to their clans
> [and] languages,
> within their lands [that belong] to their states.
>
> These are the clans of the sons of Noah,
> according to their stories from their states,
> and from these, the states were populated on the earth after the flood.
>   (Genesis 10:21–32)

"So, this is how the world was populated after the flood. Something like these last lines should also be used to introduce this entire section. We should put them just before the line 'Noah became a farmer.' It would read like this:

The Jerusalem Academy

> The sons of Noah who came out of the ark were Shem,
> Ham, and Japheth—Ham, he was the father of Canaan.
> These three were the sons of Noah,
> and from these all the earth was populated.
> (Genesis 9:18,19)

"So, we begin with the theme of how the earth was populated after the flood, and next, we deal with Noah and the curse of Canaan. Then, we note the classification of the population into three sections, which are made up of the traditional seventy groups or states. Lastly, we repeat the theme. Now there is another story about the scattering of the population after the flood. It is a story about a tower, but if we use it, we will be faced with a new set of problems."

Just at that point Zadok showed up, and Jonathan said to Zadok, "We are glad to see you. We need a break, because we have had a long session dealing with Noah's sons."

Zadok said, "I'm glad to be here. I find I have to take a break once in a while. Looking after the Old School takes too much time. But, Sheva said you wanted to talk with me."

"When Sheva told me you were working on the Joseph story, I said to him that perhaps you could help us, because we are going to deal with it in our royal epic. I have been working on the pre- and post-flood materials down to Abraham, and Elimelech and Elishama have been dealing with the fathers. We have taken a lot of time on the early material, and we hope it moves a little faster from Abraham through Joseph. We don't want to hurry too fast, but it would be nice to have this done for the dedication of David's palace. Would you be able to help us?"

"I would like to help you, and I'll share the work I have done on Joseph. Elishama will be pleased to know I have used the text he helped to develop at Shechem. However, I have made some changes in the interest of unity. I want both Israel and Judah to like this story. Most of my changes are additions. I'll not be able to be with you every day, but I could work with you at least once a week."

Jonathan said, "We want you whenever you have the time. Actually, we don't meet every day. Sometimes our meetings are short, and other times they last all day. When you can be with us, we will make a day of it, or we will meet for the time you have. Also, you should know we need you for more than your work on Joseph; we need your views on lots of things.

It is not easy to put together an epic that will bring unity and identity to a people and their king, but it is an interesting task, and from what you have said, you are also dealing with this problem."

The others agreed, and Zadok's promise helped everyone's attitude. He was not prepared to stay long, so everyone thanked him again. Then Jonathan said to him as he was leaving, "We will make you a copy of what we have put together up to now. We are also having Magon come to one of our meetings real soon. He wants to see what we have done, and it would be great to have you at that meeting as well."

After Zadok left, they got back to work, and Jonathan said, "Now about this story of the tower. Remember, I said it was a great story, but it would present us with some problems if we decided to use it. Here is the story:

> Once everyone on the earth had one language
> and the very same vocabulary.
> During their journey from the east,
> they found a valley in the land of Shinar;
> they settled there.
> They said to one another:
>   "Come, let us make bricks,
>   and we will fire [them] with extreme heat."
> For them, the brick (*lebenah*) was stone (*le'aben*);
> the bitumen (*hemar*) was for them mortar (*homer*).
> They said:
>   "Come, let us build for ourselves a city
>   and a tower with its top in the heavens;
>   let us make for ourselves a name,
>   or we shall be scattered upon the face of all the earth."
> Yahweh came down to see the city
> and the tower that the sons of the humans had built.
> Yahweh said:
>   "There is one people and one speech for all of them!
>   This is their first endeavor,
>   and now, nothing will be withheld from them
>   that they purpose to do.
>   Come, we will go down; we will confuse their speech,
>   so that, they shall not understand one another's speech."

>   Yahweh scattered them from there upon the face of all the earth;
>   they ceased building the city.
>   Therefore, [Yahweh] called forth the name [of the city], "Babel,"
>   because there Yahweh confused (*balal*) the speech of all the earth,
>   and from there Yahweh scattered them upon the face of all the earth."
>   (Genesis 11:1–9)

After Jonathan finished reading, Elishama said, "I'm not so sure about this story. It is interesting, but is it needed? In the other material we have already established the spread of the population along with their many languages, and this story takes us back to where we began."

Jonathan said, "I told you it would cause us some problems."

Elimelech said, "It is still a more interesting account than the listing of 'friends, enemies, and kinfolk.' This is a good story."

Elishama said, "If we want to use it, perhaps we could drop the other material."

Jonathan said, "I think we should use this story of the tower and keep the other material. It could be argued that this story should come first, because it represents the time before the spread of the population of the earth. But it contains a more powerful punch if it is used after we have established the spread of the population and the fact of the many languages. It is at this point that some one or several in the audience will be thinking, how and why did all these people who came from the sons of Noah get so scattered and develop so many languages? In this position, the story of the tower can answer these questions. It looks back to the time before the scattering. It is a good story, and as it looks back, it not only tries to account for the many languages, but it shows that the 'scattering' was a part of Yahweh's plan."

Elishama said, "Do you mean it is Yahweh who brings confusion to earth?"

Jonathan said, "That's what the story says, and in our royal epic, I want to use what the people will understand. They can understand that too much cooperation will produce projects wherein humans try to reach too high and become too famous. My personal views are quite different, but they are also not important."

Elishama said, "What are your unimportant personal views?"

"I see no reason to think there ever was a time when there was one language. Many countries have their flood heroes, and they are forced, in the telling of their stories, to see the development of civilization as a movement from one to many. It is a natural way to think about such things, but it can be wrong. Even so, these flood stories are important. As to Yahweh coming down to confuse us, it is not necessary. In fact, we as scribes should know that there are many languages, and if we study hard, we can learn a few of them. So, we can have some cooperation between our countries. But, Yahweh and his assembly should have no fears. They need not come down, because we will never have the power of one language. We will remain confused, human, and mortal.

"There are other reasons for us, as scribes, to enjoy this story. It is obviously a story about Babylon. It may be too critical of Babylonian religion, but note the city's name is 'Bab-el,' which means 'the gate of god.' This story deals with that city's famous tower or ziggurat. This also reminds me of Jacob. In Jacob's famous dream at the sanctuary of Bethel it says:

> There a stairway was built to the earth;
> its top reached to the heavens.
> There the messengers of Elohim
> were ascending and descending on it.
> (Genesis 28:12)

"This stairway or ramp is for the gods; it is not for the humans. Also, note what Jacob says after his dream:

> How awesome is this sanctuary.
> This is none other than the house of Elohim.
> This is the gate of the heavens.
> (Genesis 28:17)

"I'm afraid my views got us off the subject, but I would like to use this story."

Elishama said, "That's fine. Use it."

Then Jonathan said, "I only have one more text that I want to use before we take up your work on the fathers and in some ways it is the perfect transition to your work. We can call this text *These are the Stories of Shem*:

> Shem was a hundred years old;
> he fathered Arpachshad, two years after the flood.
> Shem lived, after he fathered Arpachshad,
> five hundred years; he fathered sons and daughters.
> Arpachshad lived thirty-five years; he fathered Shelah.
> Arpachshad lived, after he fathered Shelah,
> four hundred and three years; he fathered sons and daughters.

The Jerusalem Academy

> Shelah lived thirty years; he fathered Eber.
> Shelah lived, after he fathered Eber,
> four hundred and three years; he fathered sons and daughters.
> Eber lived thirty-four years; he fathered Peleg.
> Eber lived, after he fathered Peleg,
> four hundred and thirty years; he fathered sons and daughters.
> Peleg lived thirty years; he fathered Reu.
> Peleg lived, after he fathered Reu,
> two hundred and nine years; he fathered sons and daughters.
> Reu lived thirty-two years; he fathered Serug.
> Reu lived, after he fathered Serug,
> two hundred and seven years; he fathered sons and daughters.
> Serug lived thirty years; he fathered Nahor.
> Serug lived, after he fathered Nahor,
> two hundred years; he fathered sons and daughters.
> Nahor lived twenty-nine years; he fathered Terah.
> Nahor lived, after he fathered Terah,
> a hundred and nineteen years; he fathered sons and daughters.
> Terah lived seventy years; he fathered Abram, Nahor, and Haran.
> (Genesis 11:10–26)

"You may wonder why we need another list of names, so I want to explain the importance of this list for us."

"You might also explain why these post-flood fathers live so long," Elimelech said in disbelief.

"Again, the ages have to do with the traditional number of years from Noah to Abraham, but what is more important is that even as we had ten generations from Adam to Noah, we now have ten generations from Shem to Abraham. I would like to show you by the means of a chart why we need another list of ten. Take a look at this:

1) The formation of our world (order out of chaos).
2) Humans gain knowledge, and they are mortal.
3) The development of cities and civilization.
4) The ten generations from Adam to Noah.
5) The flood as a return to chaos and a re-ordering of our world.
6) Noah has knowledge, and he is mortal.
7) The spread of population and civilization.
8) The ten generations from Shem to Abraham.

Noah's Son

"The parallels between 1-4 and 5-8 are striking. In both cases we could go into more detail, but it is not really necessary. We need this new list of ten to round out the parallel, and we also need it in order to move on to the next section of our work which is *These are the Stories of Terah* wherein we will be dealing with Abraham."

Elimelech said, "Jonathan, you were well prepared on this one. Now, can we take up the work on the fathers?"

"It will not be long, before we can do just that. But, we do need to have a meeting with Magon on this first part. Then, if Elishama and I don't become fathers, we will be ready to start. Let's call it a day."

Before Jonathan left for home, he gathered up the texts for the first section of the epic. He took them to Magon who was still in his office. Magon was pleased to get them, and they agreed that in two or three days Magon should meet with the group. Also, Magon had a letter from his sister, Elissa, for Keziah, and he had already made a translation of it. He said to Jonathan, "Have Keziah try to read the original, but if she has a difficult time, you can give her the translation."

When Jonathan got home, the evening meal was ready, and father and I were in a good mood. Jonathan gave me the letter from Elissa, and I was happy.

"Do you think I can read it?"

"You'll probably do fine. At least, you should try it. As promised, Magon sent along a translation if you need it, but the two languages are not so different."

"I'll try it but after dinner. Let's eat first. Also, I'll have to write another letter to her. I have had some second thoughts about my poem; I might not send it."

We began our dinner, and Jonathan asked father how his work was going. Father said, "I'm doing well, but the records about David are really in a mess. I'm working on the records more than my writing about David. It may be for the best, because I still feel a lot of anger for David. In a few months, I will be a better historian."

Jonathan said, "Keziah this bread is special tonight."

"I'm glad that you like it. Remember that it is harvest time. The new grain crop always gives us better bread."

Just as I said this, I grabbed Jonathan's arm. I tightened my grip on his arm and said, "This is real pain."

Father said, "Shall I get Sarah?"

"Not yet. We'll have to see if it happens again. Let's try to finish our meal."

Jonathan said, "This may be the moment that we have been waiting for, but now that it is here, I feel helpless."

"But, you have a strong arm for me to grab; just keep it handy."

We did finish our meal, but then I had another severe pain. This time I said to father, "Now, you can get Sarah."

Father left at once, and Jonathan took me to the bedroom. As he put me on the bed he thought, "We wanted this child, but did we consider the amount of pain involved?"

I was thinking as well. "God, I hope that I can handle this."

Soon the pains were more often, and I did not have time to think such thoughts. Jonathan stayed close to me until Sarah arrived. After that, he joined father in the kitchen, and they began to heat some water and locate the salt. Every once in a while, they could hear me cry out. What they did not know was that between the crying there was still a lot of pain. It was getting late in the evening, and Sarah came out of the bedroom and told them that it would still be some time before the baby was born. Jonathan wanted to know if there was anything he could do. Before Sarah could answer, I called out from the bedroom. I called out for Sarah and Jonathan. They ran to me, and I said, "I just relaxed a bit, and then I tried again. It's coming this time."

Jonathan held me, and Sarah got ready to receive our child. As soon as the head appeared the baby came out with less effort. Sarah tied and cut the umbilical cord, and then she took the baby and started to clean it off. She looked at Keziah and Jonathan and said, "The two of you have a son!"

I held out my arms. Sarah gave me my baby, and she said, "I'll go and get the water and the salt. We'll clean him and rub him with salt. By then, he will need a drink of his mother's milk."

After Sarah left, Jonathan said, "Keziah, you have done it. What a beautiful baby. I'm glad you called for me. It is not according to our customs for me to be here, but then, you have always done things your way. The two of you look so wonderful, but we don't even have a name for our son."

"We'll get a name. We can wait a few days for the naming ceremony, or we can wait until the eighth day when he is circumcised."

Just then Sarah returned with the salt and father brought the water.

I said, "Come here father. Look at your grandson."

"I'll just do that. Let me set this water down."

Father sat the water down, spilling some on his foot and came over to the bed. He looked at his grandson, and a tear ran down his cheek, disappearing into his beard. He said, "How I wish your mother could see this boy. What a wonderful baby."

Sarah took the baby and began to wash him. He cried, and he cried some more when she rubbed him with salt. Then she wrapped him in a soft cloth and brought him to me for his first meal. Father and Jonathan went to the kitchen, and Sarah helped me get myself cleaned up.

Jonathan said, "Let's have some wine and cheese. We need to relax. Keziah is the one who did the work and suffered the pain, but I must say that I was getting worried."

"I was also worried. She was in labor for a long time. In fact, I need something to eat. Let's have some bread with that wine and cheese."

Just then Sheva arrived. He said, "I thought that I should get Sarah or at least find out what was happening."

Jonathan said, "Keziah just had a wonderful baby boy. Sarah is not quite finished, so you should join us. We were just getting ready to eat, and now we have a party."

"I'll be glad to join you. So you have a son! Do you have a name?"

"Not yet, but we'll have one soon. Until then, we'll just call him 'Ben.'"

"That's a good idea. Gad, have you seen the baby yet?"

"O yes! I've seen him, and he is the best looking baby I have ever seen."

"Well, I'll just have to take a look at him before Sarah and I leave."

Jonathan, Gad, and Sheva had a good time for the next hour. Then Sarah came out and said that all was in order, and she needed to go home. But she did bring Sheva in to see our baby. He was impressed. After they left, father also went to bed. Jonathan came in to the bedroom to be with me. When he got there, the baby and I were asleep, so he just lay down beside us. After about two hours, the baby started crying, and I nursed him again.

The next morning our baby was still sleeping and when Jonathan and I went out to the kitchen, there was father, and he had everything ready to eat.

"Father, thank you so much. We are both tired, and this really helps."

The Jerusalem Academy

"I will help you for a few days, because I know that you have gone through a tough time, and Jonathan is supposed to get ready for a meeting with Magon."

"That reminds me. I want to look at my letter from Magon's sister, Elissa."

Jonathan said, "The letter is right here, but it can wait until you feel a little better."

"No, I want to see it now. I may not finish it now, but I want to see it."

Jonathan handed the letter to me, and I began to read, but I did not understand all of it. The letter read as follows:

> To Keziah, my sister, speak!
> The message of Elissa, your sister.
>
> ――――――――――――――――
>
> At the feet of my sister, I bow down.
> May the gods guard you and preserve you.
>
> ――――――――――――――――
>
> And now, I will tell you that I have a
> daughter. Her name is Naomi. As her name
> says, she is a very good girl. If I had a boy,
> I would name him Naam. He would be a good boy.
> If you have a boy, call him Naam.
>
> ――――――――――――――――
>
> And now, I hope that we can meet face
> to face. Some day we will. You should come
> here. At this time, it is hot here by the sea,
> but the sea is always very beautiful.
>
> ――――――――――――――――
>
> And now, may you know it;
> I want to read your poem.
> Please send it to me.

After I read this, Jonathan gave me the translation Magon had made. I read the translation, and I said to Jonathan, "I understood most of it. The real problem was at the beginning. The form was different than the one I used."

Jonathan said, "The people of Tyre still use some of the older forms that we see in Babylonian letters and also in letters from Ugarit. But what did you think of her suggestion for a name? In the language of Tyre, *Naam* is used for "good" where we would use *tov*, but I like it."

"I like it too. Let's name our son Naam."

Father said, "It's a fine name."

"Jonathan, I know you'll be meeting with Magon soon, but try to get home early today. I want us to both enjoy Naam during these first days."

"I'll be here. I want to be with you. This is our great event."

After Jonathan left, I nursed Naam, and I shed a few happy tears for him and a few sad ones for mother.

34

The Meeting with Magon

JONATHAN LEFT FOR WORK later than usual. The first thing he did was to find Elishama and tell him about the baby. Elishama said, "I thought Deborah and I would have our baby first. Deborah is certainly ready. We hope it is soon. Did everything go well?"

"Everything was fine, and Sarah was a great help. But, it did take a long time, and I was worried."

"Do you have a name for your baby?"

"Yes, we do. His name will be Naam. Actually, Magon's sister suggested this name to Keziah in a letter."

"It's a good name, and the pun was intended. Several ancient scribes used the element Naam along with some divine name."

"We will have a naming ceremony in a few days, and I hope that you can be there. Right now, I suppose we should get to work."

Jonathan and Elishama were on their way to Jonathan's office when Elimelech caught up with them. He said to Jonathan, "I heard that you are now a father. Sarah told me this morning; she saw me when I was walking to work. You look tired. Were you up all night?"

"No, but we were up most of the night. Keziah endured the pain, and yet she is in better shape than I am."

Elimelech said, "I saw Magon this morning at breakfast. He will meet with us tomorrow if that will be good for us."

Jonathan said, "That will be great. Elimelech, you tell him at noon that we will expect him tomorrow. Also, you should get word to Zadok about this special meeting."

That day, the three of them went over all the material that they were going to discuss with Magon. Jonathan came home for lunch, and he couldn't wait to see Naam and me. When he went back to the office, he

The Meeting with Magon

announced that they would not work late. He needed to get home early. When he got home, father was ready with the evening meal, and Jonathan was able to hold Naam. I was resting and doing fine. I was thankful that all was well.

I said to Jonathan, "Last night when I was in so much pain, I cursed you for giving me this baby, but as soon as it was over, I was so glad that you had sown your seed."

"Curses and blessings really get mixed up for most of us, especially when there is a lot of pain involved. By the way, Elishama and Deborah are still waiting and hoping that their baby will arrive soon."

Father said, "Let's come to the table and get started with this meal."

The meal was not fancy but good. Best of all, father did all the work.

Father said, "I can't wait until Naam is old enough to eat with us at this table, but for now, I guess we need to eat in case he wakes up."

"He will sleep a bit longer. He ate a lot when I nursed him."

Then father said to Jonathan, "I heard something very interesting today. On my way to the market, I met Ahban. He told me that my position on David's re-burial of Saul and Jonathan was a solid position. He noted that since the big funeral, some members of Saul's family have been holding funeral rituals at the tomb of Kish for Saul and Jonathan on a regular basis. Someone wants Saul's line to continue and is seeking Saul's blessing. Someday a rebel will go to Saul's tomb and declare himself to be the king of the House of Saul."

Jonathan said, "That is interesting, and you may be correct. Someone should keep a watch on such developments. Perhaps, Ahban will do it?"

Just then Naam began to cry. As soon as I heard him, the milk seemed to rush to my breasts, and I left the table at once. Naam was hungry. After he finished nursing, both father and Jonathan took turns holding him. He was a good baby.

Jonathan said, "I'm sorry to say that we'll be meeting with Magon tomorrow, but I'll try to get back here as soon as possible. I don't want to miss out on my share of holding Naam.

The next day, both Magon and Zadok were at the meeting to review the first part of the epic from the formation of the world down to the stories about Abraham. This was really quite a group. Magon was from Tyre. Elishama was from the north/Israel and Zadok from Jerusalem. Both Elimelech and Jonathan represented the south/Judah. In earlier discussions Elishama may have felt all alone, but today he certainly had no reason to feel that way. Jonathan suggested that Magon should start the conversation. Magon said that he would be willing.

"A few days ago, Jonathan asked me to look at this material. I was glad to note that you have filled out the outline that I suggested in the early days of your work. My suggestion about the outline was not because it was my outline, but rather because this outline belongs to our world. It is what most scribes would expect in a royal epic. The stories of David's ancestors will be different in your epic from the background stories of other kings in other countries, but in the material before the time of the direct ancestors, everyone will expect you to make the points that you have made. In fact, you have given the whole matter an important new twist. In your work, the flood is not just the fifth point but rather it is the pivot around which the entire process starts again. I did not really understand this until I looked at Jonathan's chart. Here take a look:

1) The formation of our world (order out of chaos).
2) Humans gain knowledge, and they are mortal.
3) The development of cities and civilization.
4) The ten generations from Adam to Noah.

5) The flood as a return to chaos and a re-ordering of our world.
6) Noah has knowledge, and he is mortal.
7) The spread of population and civilization.
8) The ten generations from Shem to Abraham.

"My point is that number 5 is also number 1 of the parallel post-flood development in your expanded outline. In it there is God's promise that the world from now on will be safe from such destruction, and there is an expressed hope, in this arrangement, that this world will not be cursed again with another flood. Instead of that, there is a blessing for our world in the following stories of the ancestors, which lead to the kingdom of David. It is a nice arrangement. As I have told some of you before, some of the contradictions and inconsistencies in the materials that you have used to fill out the outline do not bother me at all. This will bother the empty-headed who will want a narrative with no holes. What they do not understand is that when our minstrels sing of our beginnings and when we write of our beginnings, it is done from where we stand. In order to speak about that distant past, we are forced to use our language, our terms, and our values, which cannot describe or adequately express those early experiences. But our efforts are able to give a general impression of our beginnings, and we can use these stories to express some basic things.

"One of the most basic things is that humans are mortal. You have made this clear in your story of the first human and his wife, Eve. Also, you account for the fact that humans have knowledge. These are the same points that the Babylonians make in *The Story of Adapa*. They stress all of this again in *The Gilgamesh Epic*. However, in Tyre we have inherited even a stronger tradition on the mortality of humans. In Tyre we are fond of *The Story of Aqhat*, which we inherited from our ancestors of Ugarit. No one has to teach Aqhat about the fact that humans are mortal. Notice his response when the goddess Anat offers him immortality:

> And the maiden Anat answers:
> "Request life, O Aqhat, the hero!
> Request life and I'll give [it to] you!
> Immortality and I'll hand [it to] you!
> ..."
> And Aqhat the Hero answers:
> "Do not lie to me, O maiden!
> To a hero your lies are snares!
> Man, what does he get in the end?
> What does man get as his fate?
> Lime is poured [on] the head,
> Plaster on top of my crown,
> [And] I'll die the death of everyone.
> Yes, I shall surely die!"
> (2 Aqhat: VI, 25–38)

"The Egyptians are the only people who will not accept the reality of death. But, even in Egypt there are those who have said 'no' to immortality. The ones who have said 'no' were usually the Harpers or Singers who sang their songs at the tombs and had their songs carved in the tomb walls. The remarkable thing is that these skeptical songs were allowed. Along with the skepticism was the advice that we should all have fun here and now. The word is 'Make holiday!' In your stories you have made this point on human mortality again and again. The fact that the flood hero, Noah, remains mortal is also a real plus. When you discuss the rise of civilization and the development of the various occupations, you did not give many examples. In our traditions at Tyre, we talk about many more occupations."

Jonathan said, "I want to thank you for all of your comments. On your last point, I knew we should deal with more occupations, but I could not find any texts that dealt with more. They all just talked about 'the shepherds,' 'all who are skilled with lyre and pipe,' and 'all who are workers with copper and iron.' We could have written some text with more, but it would not work. The people know that we have not dealt with many occupations in our stories. We should only write new texts if we have lost something the people would miss.

"I'm certain that Elimelech and Elishama will join me in thanking you for all the help that you have given us along the way and of course for these comments today. It is important for us to know that we will be understood in distant lands as well as here at home. Who else wants to add something at this point?"

This discussion went on for some time. Everyone was interested in this work, and they all made some comments. Even Zadok knew about most of the stories, because Ahban had exposed him to the material over the years.

Zadok did say one disturbing thing concerning the first story. It seems that Abiathar who gave Jonathan the seven-day ritual text to use now does not want it used. Abiathar says that the formation of the world in seven ritual days contradicts the Sabbath commandment where it says, "For in six days Yahweh made the heavens and the earth and the sea and all that is in them; he rested on the seventh day. Therefore, Yahweh blessed the day of the Sabbath; he made it holy" (Exodus 20:11). Ahban told Zadok that Abiathar would try to re-write the first story and bring it in line with the Sabbath commandment. Jonathan could feel himself getting angry, but he only said that Abiathar should not get involved in this question.

This discussion was brought to a sudden halt when Sheva came in and got Elishama. Sheva said, "You will have to excuse this man. He is about to become a father."

As the meeting was breaking up, Jonathan thanked Magon again, and he told him about Naam. "Your sister suggested to Keziah the name Naam, and we decided to use it."

Magon said, "It is a great name. Many of our heroes were named Naam, and the longer form, Naamanu, was used to describe our epic heroes who were always 'good singers.' Naamanu can mean a 'singer.' I hope that Elishama's wife will have an easy time. We will have to check on them a bit later."

Jonathan said, "I'll check in on them before I go home. I supposed that you noticed that it bothered me when I found out that Abiathar wants to change our work before it is even finished."

"I would suggest that you should not worry about that at this point. You will be able to keep it as it is for the dedication of the palace. After that if the priests want their own edition, you will probably not be able to stop them. They always want to harmonize everything."

"I do not intend to worry too much about it, but I do want to give Abiathar a hard time if he tries to change it now. What bothers me the most is how some of our scribes seem to be the servants of both king and priests. For our system to work, we must always put pressure on other groups in order to form some kind of balance for the future."

35

Work on the Ancestors of the Kings and the Naming of the Babies

AFTER JONATHAN LEFT THE meeting, he went directly to Elishama's house. Sheva was there, and Sarah was helping with Deborah. They were still waiting for the birth. As they were talking, Sarah came out and said, "Jonathan, I could use some extra help. If you are free to go home, ask Keziah to come over here if she is able."

"I'm on my way."

Elishama said, "Does that mean we have a problem?"

"No, but when I delivered Keziah's baby, I really needed a little more help. I will feel better if Keziah is here."

Jonathan ran home, and he told me what was going on. He said, "Do you feel well enough to help?"

"Yes I do," and I left at once. Father was preparing the evening meal, and he said to Jonathan, "Naam just finished nursing, so he should sleep for a while. So you should sit down and rest a bit. How did your meeting go?"

"The meeting was good. Magon was pleased with our work, and we had a good discussion. But, I was disturbed when Zadok told us that according to Ahban, Abiathar does not like our use of the seven-day creation ritual, because the commandment to observe the Sabbath has God creating for six days. It sounded as if he wanted to change our text, but for now I do not want that to happen even if it happens later on."

Father shook the spoon that he was holding and said, "I used to do a lot of things with old Abiathar, and he was a good worker. Now he has a much higher position, and he has to show everyone that he has a lot of power. I'll look him up in a few days and tell him to back off. I could even

Work on the Ancestors of the Kings and the Naming of the Babies

put it in the form of a word from Yahweh. That would shake him up, but I do not do such things anymore."

When I got back, I was all smiles. I said, "Elishama and Deborah have a wonderful little girl. Her name is Rachel. We should have a naming ceremony for both babies."

Father said, "This is great. I take it that all went well."

"Yes! In fact, Deborah didn't take as long as I did."

"Now, I just want you to sit down there by Jonathan, and I will serve you some of this lamb that I cooked. It will be better than some of the sacrificial meat that Abiathar used to bring to us when we were still in Ziklag. At least, I hope it will be better."

I sat down and said, "Jonathan, this is really nice to have our very own cook."

"And, he also takes care of kids."

"So how did your meeting go?"

"I was just telling Gad that everything went well. Now we will concentrate our work on Abraham, Isaac, Jacob, Joseph, and Judah. We have a lot to do, but on this section we at least know where we are going and what to do. We can finish it before the dedication of David's palace, and even if we didn't finish the last part, the minstrels could handle it. To be realistic, they may not sing any of this exactly as we have presented it."

Father said, "From the looks of the building project, you will finish first."

I said, "Everyone is busy, but we have to find some time for naming the babies, and I will need some help in answering Elissa's letter."

Jonathan said, "We can find time for those things. I'll talk with Elishama about the naming. If we wait until the eighth day we could do the circumcising for Naam at the same time. Naam is two days older than Rachel, so that would probably work out quite well for Rachel's naming ceremony."

"That sounds good, but you should talk to Elishama about such a plan. I'll talk to Deborah, because I'm certain that I'll see her tomorrow."

Father said, "I would offer you more lamb, but both of you have not started to eat. Let your plans go for a moment."

"Sorry, father, I guess we got carried away."

"That's all right, but I do want you to eat. Also, I have a question for Jonathan. Do you now have enough material for your work on the fathers? I ask this, because when you were preparing the second corona-

The Jerusalem Academy

tion for David, I thought that you were short on some things concerning the fathers."

"We were, but Elishama and Elimelech have been collecting texts ever since we started this project. Now we have enough. We may have too much. Our main goal is to put it all together in such a way that all the people will recognize this epic as their story. We must have traditions from Israel and from Judah. We want to bring people together and at the same time present the line that leads to David."

I said, "If you have two stories concerning one father and you can only use one of them, how do you make a choice? Does the story have to be entertaining or does it have to teach something useful?"

"First, the story must be a favorite story of some group who makes up our greater Israel. Second, it must be entertaining. Third, it needs to fulfill a slot or function in our outline. We will not make such a choice based on some useful teaching. In the first part of our epic, we did want to teach some things. For example, humans are mortal, and they are also imperfect. When we deal with the lives of the ancestors, we are more interested in where they are going and what they are doing than we are in 'useful teachings.'"

Then Jonathan added, "The two of you have been asking me questions. You have been eating, but not me. Is this some kind of a plan?"

I said, "Never! But, I'm finished now, and I can take care of Naam while you eat."

Father said, "At least, we got Keziah fed."

"That we did."

Jonathan wrote most of this next part for me. It concerns an important meeting, and I wanted to get it just right.

When Jonathan saw Elishama the next morning, he said, "Let's plan a double naming ceremony for our babies. It should be five days from now for Naam. I hope this will fit into your schedule for Rachel."

"It will, and we should do it. We will have to make some plans during the next few days. We can work it out."

"Good. Keziah told me that she would be seeing Deborah today, and they will also be making some plans."

"It sounds as if all is under control."

Work on the Ancestors of the Kings and the Naming of the Babies

Just then Elimelech arrived, and Jonathan said, "*Boqer tov*! Before we get to work, I wanted to ask about Danel and Noah. I have not seen them for some time. What are they doing now?"

"Elimelech said, "They work some for Zadok and Sheva, and they are also teaching a few classes. They are having some problems with some of the students who follow their teachers in everything."

"So what's wrong with that?"

"The students of such teachers don't think. They believe the old traditions that say if you are righteous you will have a long and good life, but if you are wicked you will be cut off from the land. But, when you look around, this is just not the case. Jonathan, you should read your poem on Job to such students."

"Perhaps I can do that if we ever finish this epic, and if I can find the time to teach. So, let's get on with our work. Today, you need to tell me what you have done, and then we need to talk about how to organize the material."

Elishama said, "We have collected a lot of texts, and we should not use all of them. We have already mentioned to you that we are prepared to deal with Abraham, Isaac, Jacob, Joseph, and Judah at length, but we can not see the point in dealing at any length with Ishmael or Esau."

Elimelech agreed and said, "There is another place that we could cut out some material, and that is from the cycle *These are the Stories of Abraham*. This material contains a lot of stories about Isaac, and Isaac is really not a favorite father among the people of Judah or Israel. We will have enough if we select only what the people really want."

Jonathan answered with a slight frown, "I disagree with this last point. I find some of the Isaac stories very interesting, and how do you know that the people are not interested in Isaac?"

"I noticed a lack of enthusiasm for Isaac during the second coronation. The people were really interested in Abraham, Jacob, Judah and Joseph. Since then I've asked around, and I have even asked some of the singers. The Isaac material is dull, and they don't use it very much at the tombs in Hebron. Isaac was overly protected as a child. His wife, Rebekah, was given to him and he said, 'I do.' Isaac is just a means of getting to Jacob."

"Does this mean that you don't want to use any of the Isaac stories?"

"I'll let Elishama answer that."

The Jerusalem Academy

"Elimelech has turned this over to me because he knows that I have been working on an outline of these materials. We both agree that in the first part of our epic the outline was important. Plus, when we were working on this material for the coronations we heard you discussing a certain pattern to these cycles concerning the fathers. We need to look at some of these things, and then I can show you where we could use some Isaac stories. At the present time, we have collected the stories into cycles, and we have followed our earlier practice of giving the usual titles.

"The titles that we gave to the materials that we have completed can be seen on this chart:

1. *These are the stories of the heavens and the earth since their formation* (Genesis 2:4a).
2. *This is the document of the stories of Adam* (Genesis 5:1a).
3. *These are the stories of Noah* (Genesis 6:9a).
4. *These are the stories of the sons of Noah* (Genesis 10:1a).
5. *These are the stories of Shem* (Genesis 11:10a).

"We have another chart for the materials that we have collected about our more immediate ancestors, and they are entitled:

6. *These are the stories of Terah* (Genesis 11:27a).
7. *These are the stories of Abraham* (missing except for Genesis 24 and 26).
8. *These are the stories of Ishmael* (Genesis 25:12a).
9. *These are the stories of Isaac* (Genesis 25:19a).
10. *These are the stories of Esau* (Genesis 36:1).
11. *These are the stories of Jacob* (Genesis 37:2a).

"Sections 8 and 10 are brief. As you know, each section contains material for the most part about the heir of the person named in the title. This means that in section 6 (Terah), we have the Abraham material. In seven (Abraham), the Isaac texts are collected, and in nine (Isaac), we have the Jacob material. Eleven (Jacob) gives us the Joseph story plus whatever we do on Judah. I have to go into some detail concerning the way in which each section is organized. Here we have our outline for our main sections:

1) All are interested the birth of an heir, but great difficulties are always present (famine, seduction [Sarah, Rebekah, and Joseph], and infertility).

Work on the Ancestors of the Kings and the Naming of the Babies

2) There is always the point made that the "elder shall serve the younger." This is not the normal custom for our people, but in our epic many things are not normal.
3) The hero either buys or receives land (e.g. the burial cave that Abraham buys and Jacob's holdings in Shechem).
4) Similar conclusions containing three scenes: a burial scene, additional material on the heir(s), and a death scene.

"This last part (4) of these stories is very important. It is clear that proper burial was important for the blessing of the next 'father.' Without such a blessing there would not be another heir. Plus by means of proper burial the next 'father' took his place of leadership among his people.

"So, Jonathan, if we did away with section seven (These are the stories of Abraham), we could still use some of the Isaac material. For example we could use the story of Abraham's servant bringing Rebekah to Isaac in the last part of section six. This last part would then contain the story of Sarah's burial, additional material on how Isaac obtained his bride, and then the death of Abraham. Also you will soon see that we will have some Isaac material in section nine just as there are some Jacob stories in section eleven. I'll have to go along with Elimelech on his evaluation of the material, and if we can delete section seven, we will just have five sections dealing with our immediate ancestors and only three of them will be major sections or cycles."

Jonathan said, "When I asked my question I did not know that you would hit me with all that. I must say that you two have really been working. I'm not going to vote for or against your proposal at this time. I need more time. I'm impressed with your work, and I'll want to see how this all turns out. I like the way you went at your work. You tried to find out what the people were interested in, and you have organized the materials in order to bring out the most important points. In your outline, I see what is most important to me. These are stories about birth, burial and blessing. This should not be a great surprise, since most of the stories took their form in the context of the tomb where proper burial brings blessing and that results in the birth of an heir. But, I will have some more questions. The first one that comes to mind is what happened to the section *These are the stories of Judah*?"

Elimelech answered, "I told Elishama that you would ask that question, and I must say that we are not as certain concerning our suggestions on Judah as we are about our stand on Isaac. However, you should note that we have not only left out *These are the stories of Judah* but we have also left out *These are the stories of Joseph*. Also, note that we will have a lot of Judah and Joseph materials in section eleven ('These are the stories of Jacob'). We felt that if we were interested in the unity of Israel, we should give both Joseph and Judah important roles in our last section. If we deal with *These are the stories of Judah* and *These are the stories of Joseph*, we will just be showing how Perez and Ephraim went their separate ways at a later time. For our Royal Epic, this would not be good. Also, if we ever expand our epic to include the exodus from Egypt, we would want our people to be in Egypt at the end of this first part. We have stopped at the right place."

Jonathan said, "I just have to repeat myself. You guys have really been working and thinking this through. I am pleased with what you have done. Your answer to my last question is also interesting, and your last point about stopping while our people are still in Egypt is your best argument for not dealing with either *These are the stories of Judah* or *These are the stories of Joseph*. It is important that you have already thought about a Part Two of our epic.

"What I need at this point is a complete list of materials that you will use after you take out the things that you have suggested we remove. If the two of you could make that up during the next few days, then it would be much easier to make a decision and defend it. Can you do that?"

Elishama said, "We can have the list ready in two or three days."

Jonathan said, "That will be great, but I must say that I can't spend all of that time thinking about your proposals, because I also have to think about the naming ceremony for the babies. We will just have to see how all of this works out, because I will need your help, Elishama, on this ceremony. In fact, we will have to get together one evening, because I know that Keziah and Deborah will have some ideas about naming the babies."

Jonathan came home for lunch. Naam was sleeping, and father and I were putting lunch on the table. Jonathan kissed me and said to me, "I have some good news. Elimelech and Elishama have been working hard on all the stories of the fathers. They are going to make a list of the materials for their work for our next meeting, and they will need a few days for that task. Therefore, I'm going to have some time during the next few days to make plans for the naming of the babies and to help you with your letter."

Work on the Ancestors of the Kings and the Naming of the Babies

"That is good news. This will give me a little time to plan a celebration for father's birthday. He will be seventy in five days."

Jonathan said, "That is the same day that we will name the babies! We can have a birthday party in the evening."

Father said, "We don't have to have a birthday party, but I do have a few things to share with you at that time. I've written some things about turning seventy."

"You can read them for us at your party," I said. "We must have a party."

"That's right! We must have a party," Jonathan echoed.

They sat down to eat. Since Naam was sleeping, I was able to eat with Jonathan and father for a change. I said to Jonathan, "I would like for you to help me with the letter to Elissa before you go back this afternoon. I have decided not to send that first poem I wrote. I have another one that I will send in the letter, and we can also use it in the naming ceremony for Naam."

"I will help you before I go back to the office. It will also help me to have the poem before I work on the naming ceremony."

Father said, "I will clean things up after our lunch, and the two of you can take a look at the letter."

After lunch, I brought out my new poem. In fact, I read it for Jonathan and father, after saying, "It makes me very nervous to read my poetry."

When I finished reading Jonathan said, "Your poem will be just right for the naming ceremony, and it will be good for your letter. Elissa suggested the name, and she will be pleased that we have followed up on her suggestion."

I said, "This poem may not be as thoughtful as the first one, but I feel better about it. Also, if we use it at our naming ceremony, it will become a real part of our lives. I want to share it."

Father said, "It's great, and as you say, it flows from your experience. That makes it meaningful."

"That's right, but I still like the first poem," Jonathan added. "The first one should go into our 'Minority Report.' The second one will really add to our naming ceremony. So, let's look at the letter."

Jonathan read it aloud:

> To Elissa, my sister and friend,
> Thus says Keziah, your sister and friend:

The Jerusalem Academy

Shalom to you, *shalom* to your house,
and *shalom* to all that is yours.

And now, I am sending you my poem
that we will use in our naming ceremony
for Naam. It reads:

"'Naam,' we called forth his name.
He will give us pleasant days;
He will fill them with great songs.
Goodness was ours, when he came.

We gave him a hero's name;
Lives touched by him will be changed.
He will sing of great events;
We will never be the same."

And now, I want to thank you
for suggesting the name. Someday
you will have to see Naam.
We all want to meet you.

And now, your brother, Magon, is fine;
he has helped us in so many ways,
and may you know it.

Jonathan said, "Your letter is fine. I'll take it to Magon on my way back to the office. Do you still have some writing material? In any case, I will bring some papyrus when I come home this evening. Magon just got some for us from Tyre."

"That would be great. Be sure and thank him for all that he does for us."

Before Jonathan went to his office he stopped in to see Magon. Magon was glad to get Keziah's letter, and as he was getting some papyrus for Jonathan, he said, "I hope that you will make every effort to go with me to Tyre as soon as Naam is old enough to travel. I really want Keziah to meet my sister, and I would like to show you around."

Work on the Ancestors of the Kings and the Naming of the Babies

"I know that both Keziah and I want to go, so we will start thinking about it. We should try to do it after the dedication of David's palace and of course before next winter."

"Just after the dedication would be a great time," Magon said. "There will be people here from Tyre, and we could go with them on their return trip. It would be safe and a lot of fun. Talk it over with Keziah, and let's keep that time in mind."

"I'll keep it in mind and *todah rabbah* for this papyrus."

"Your thanks is welcomed, but I guess that you should really thank David. The papyrus was purchased for the school. When the builders brought in more supplies for the palace, I had them bring the papyrus. There is always a supply in Tyre. It comes straight from Egypt."

"On the one hand, I am thankful for this school, but on the other, I really hate to thank David for anything. It may seem strange, but I am quite certain that every gift from David is really a demand. I don't give thanks for demands."

"Your words are really not strange. Scribes who work for kings have such feelings provided that they think. Some of them only copy and say, 'Yes.' However, if one likes to think, one may prefer silence rather than many words."

"You're right, and I need to get to work. In five days, we will have a naming ceremony for Naam and Rachel. I hope that you can be there. We will also have a birthday party for Gad in the evening. He'll be seventy on that same day."

"I'll be there."

Jonathan went to his office, and he had just started his work when Elishama came by. He said, "Jonathan. I've been thinking about our work; we will not be ready with the list of materials until after the naming ceremony."

"That will be fine. I didn't mean to push you. I can tell that you have worked hard on this, and we will do it when you are ready."

"We will be ready soon. Deborah and I will be extra busy with this naming ceremony, because my mother and father will be arriving soon. They have not seen Rachel yet."

"That will be nice. I'm glad they can be here. On the evening of the ceremony, Keziah and I will have a birthday party for Gad. You and your family are invited, and since you and your family will already be there, we would like for you just to stay on for Gad's party."

"We might just be able to do that."

The next few days were busy for all of us. Jonathan and I had circumcised Naam on the seventh day instead of the eighth, because we decided that a private ceremony for such surgery would be much better. Also, we did not want anything to take away from the happy occasion of the naming, and we did not care that much about having the circumcision on the traditional eighth day. On the evening of the seventh day, when Naam was feeling better, father, Jonathan, and I were discussing the plans for the next day. We were still at the table, and I said, "I'm ready, but I'm going to need both of you to help with the food tomorrow morning. The ceremony will not be until the middle of the afternoon, so you can help me in the morning."

Father said, "You can count on me, but I might have to hold Naam if he is not sleeping."

Jonathan added, "It looks like I can help, and I guess I will not need to hold Naam."

I smiled and said, "I knew that you both would be willing, if we just had two babies, you both would have an excuse to rest once in awhile. We will also spend some of our time tomorrow morning getting a few things ready for the party in the evening."

"I'm ready for that," father said. "In fact, I've been preparing for the last seventy years for tomorrow night, but I must say that I'm having the same problem that I had at your wedding."

"What's that?"

"Keziah, my problem is always the same. Your mother is not here."

I kissed father and said, "I know that all of this is difficult for you, and so it is for me. We'll take time tomorrow to remember her."

Just then Naam began to cry, and I went in the bedroom to feed him. Jonathan and father cleaned things up from our meal, and then both of them were ready for bed. Tomorrow would be a long day.

Everyone was up early the next morning. Jonathan was sitting in the kitchen, and I was getting some food prepared. At one point, Jonathan took my hand and pulled me to him and sat me on his lap. He said, "Why are you so beautiful this morning?" Between his kisses came my answer: "You're just stalling."

Work on the Ancestors of the Kings and the Naming of the Babies

"Not at all. You are beautiful, and your beauty has to do with your whole being. You are beautiful to behold and beautiful to be around. You know that some beauties would be impossible to live with."

"You have a good line. In fact, I almost believe you, and I will believe you, if you will go out and butcher the lamb that I got for today. That should be easy for you with all your experience as a shepherd."

"Now, who is it that's making fun? I'll butcher the lamb as soon as we eat."

"That will be just fine. We are ready. You call father for me. He needs to get started as well."

Everyone worked hard all morning, and by noon, we were about ready. We still had some time to get ourselves ready. The first people to arrive, about mid-afternoon, were some of the single scribes. Jonathan greeted Elimelech, Danel, and Noah; he said, "I thought that you three would be first. You must be hungry? But, the food comes later."

Noah said, "We know, but we thought Keziah could use some last minute help with the food. If so, she would at least let us taste just a bit."

Jonathan said, "Maybe, but she would not allow me a taste of anything."

Soon others arrived. Sarah and Sheva were among the first, and Ahban, Zadok, and Magon came together. They were engaged in a spirited conversation as they entered the yard. Elishama, Deborah, and their family were the last ones to arrive. Everyone was having a good time, and both Deborah and I withdrew in order to feed our babies just before the ceremony.

The ceremony was to be outside, and the weather was wonderful for this event. As soon as Deborah and I re-joined the group, everyone was ready to start. The others were seated. Jonathan and I were standing before the group, and I was holding Naam.

Jonathan said, "Keziah and I want to welcome all of you to this ceremony. We want Elishama, Deborah, and Rachel to join us as we stand before you, and Elishama will speak first."

"I am happy to see all of you, and after this ceremony, I want you to meet my father and mother who have joined us for this occasion. Deborah and I are glad they can be here and meet our friends. You all have helped us in many ways, and now you are here to witness the naming of our daughter. Her name is a popular name in Shechem, because when

233

we remember Joseph at his tomb, we never forget Rachel, his mother. The mother of Joseph lies alone in her grave, but she is never alone in Israel."

Then Deborah held her daughter and said:

> "We call forth her name, 'Rachel,' saying:
> She is like a lovely ewe lamb,
> one to keep and to cherish."
> Elishama said,
> "Now we will bless Rachel:
> Our daughter, surely you are.
> Be thousands and myriads.
> May your descendants be kind;
> May they grant wisdom to all."

I said, "I would like to read my poem about Naam:

> 'Naam,' we called forth his name.
> He will give us pleasant days;
> He will fill them with great songs.
> Goodness was ours, when he came.
>
> We gave him a hero's name;
> Lives touched by him will be changed.
> He will sing of great events;
> We will never be the same."

I held my son and said:

> "We call forth his name, 'Naam,' saying:
> He will give us good and pleasant days,
> and he will fill them with song."

Jonathan said, "Now we will bless Naam:

> The God of our fathers,
> May this God bless Naam.
> Our names and our fathers' names,
> Shall be called forth by Naam,
> And he will become many,
> A multitude in the land."

Work on the Ancestors of the Kings and the Naming of the Babies

Jonathan continued, "We have named and blessed two children. It is going to be interesting to watch them as they grow in stature and favor with our God and with our people. And now, we need some time for wine and conversation. The food will be ready soon."

Elishama's mother came over to take Rachel, and father took Naam. We, the young parents, turned our attention to the food. We did have some help from Sarah, and of course from Noah who had volunteered earlier for food duty. Ahban was entertaining Danel, Elimelech, Elishama's father, Sheva, Magon, and Zadok. He was saying that if one listened to the blessings given by these two new fathers, one just might get the impression that they were working on the stories of the fathers. Elimelech said, "How did you guess? And I should add that we have been working so hard that there was no time for them to come up with anything new."

Danel said, "Probably I should not say this, but they really don't work that hard. They just sit and talk. Some of their meetings last all day!"

Elimelech said, "I'll take Danel over to the food table and get him something. He's a bit faint, and he gets confused when this happens."

They went over to the table, and the others laughed. Sheva said, "They had that little act planned. At any rate, they have worked their way over to where we should be."

Just then everyone was invited to the table. In the center of the table was the lamb surrounded by several kinds of bread and bowls of honey. There was cheese, cake, fruit and plenty of wine. Everyone had plenty to eat and drink, and the conversation was rich. This was to be expected; after all it, was father's table.

Ahban said to Magon, "I remember when we interviewed you that you said that you liked to teach, because you were able to open up 'new worlds' for students. You also added that only a few students take advantage of these 'new worlds.' Then you said, 'Those few are the voices of the future.' Have you found any 'voices of the future' in your classes?"

"I can't tell yet. I'm sure that you also remember that I said that a person has to have a degree of freedom in order to be among the few. My students are not free as yet. But, I'm still hoping there will be a few voices of the future."

Ahban asked, "Why are they not free?"

"It is because they are religious, and they are also devoted to a few teachers in the Old School who are orthodox. These teachers believe the righteous will prosper and evildoers will be punished. Since 'new worlds' might not be righteous worlds, they hold back, but this has been the case in scribal schools from ancient Babylon to Ugarit. The problem is not unique to our times or to the Jerusalem Academy. Even with such problems, I can say that I'm glad that I came here, because this is a place where there are voices of the future, and most of them are around this table."

Jonathan said, "You are kind, and we are happy that you are here. Now I'll change the subject. Gad is seventy years old today. We want to celebrate his day, and I want to thank him for being such a great father-in-law for me and the best kind of grandfather for Naam."

I said, "Jonathan and I could not get along without him, and my dear father has some words for us."

Father stood up and said, "I am 'Gad;' I am 'fortunate.' Also, I would like to note that I am not as old as Ahban, but I am running a close second. I found the following lines in a psalm the other day, and I would like to read them for you:

> 'The days of our years add up to seventy years,
> And perhaps with the strength of heroes, eighty years.
> And the best of them have been travail and trouble,
> But the best did pass quickly; "We have flown away." '
> (Psalm 90:10)

These lines are pessimistic. The best years were 'travail and trouble!' But these 'best' years did pass quickly. This is considered a plus, and the poet allows the so-called best years to sing tauntingly: 'We have flown away.' I may be pessimistic at times, but these lines go too far in that direction. My seventy years have been difficult, but they were not all bad. I can remember some good days, and this day will take its place among them. So, I would like to express my thoughts with some of my words:

> It seems like it was yesterday;
> When I was so young, just twenty,
> And today, I am seventy!
> Fifty years gone by in a day!
>
> What happened to those days and years?
> Filled with work, food, rest, sleep, and thought;
> Some were dull, empty and thoughtless.
> Not treasured were those days and years.

Work on the Ancestors of the Kings and the Naming of the Babies

So fast the future becomes past.
It comes running, rushing to us.
Who can look to or prepare for?
My future vanished; it didn't last.

My children, they have found a way.
For most of us it's not easy;
We all crave instant approval.
The way: live the future today.

"When I prepared these words, I did not know that Magon would discuss 'voices of the future,' but I am glad that he did. It is exciting for an old man to participate in the future by helping to name and to raise his grandson. This is a great day for Rachel, for Naam, and for me."

Everyone wished father the best, and Ahban said to him, "I have never liked prophets, but I have always liked you. Perhaps I'm wrong in my view of prophets."

"The other possibility is that I was never a real prophet. One thing is certain; I'm no longer a prophet."

Ahban smiled and said, "Right, but I won't hold that against you."

Everyone visited and drank a lot more wine until late in the evening. None of the guests had to go any distance to get home, and that made it all convenient. After everyone had left, Jonathan, father and I cleaned things up, and as usual, we had a good time doing it.

36

The Ancestors of the Kings
These are the Stories of Terah

THE NEXT MORNING FATHER, Naam and I slept late, but Jonathan had a meeting with Elishama and Elimelech. Once again he helped me write this part of my story.

When Jonathan got to his office, the others were already there, because they had a lot to do. They wanted to finish the list of materials on the fathers before Jonathan called them in for the meeting. However, Jonathan called them to his office before they were finished. He told them that he appreciated their efforts, but he said, "You don't have to have it all done. We can start with what you have completed."

Elishama said, "You're right. We could do it that way. Let's start with *These are the Stories of Terah*. I'll give you our basic list of materials for this section, and then we can discuss if we should add to or subtract from this list. In other words we have more materials than just this list, but this list does cover the things that we need according to our outline that we discussed at our last meeting."

Jonathan said, "I would like to suggest one change in your plan. Instead of giving us the entire list and then discussing it, I would like to discuss each section of the list as you give it. When we get done, we can talk about adding or subtracting, but even this subject might come up before we are finished."

"That will be fine."

Then Elimelech said, "We should stop our discussions soon enough so that Elishama and I will have some time each afternoon to get ready for the next day. This will be essential."

Jonathan agreed, and Elishama turned to the first part of the list. He read:

The Ancestors of the Kings

> *These are the stories of Terah*
> Terah fathered Abram, Nahor, and Haran, and Haran fathered Lot.
> . . .
> Abram and Nahor took for themselves wives;
> the name of the wife of Abram was Sarai,
> . . .
> Now Sarai was barren; she had no child.
> Terah took Abram, his son, Lot, the son of Haran, his grandson,
> and Sarai, his daughter-in-law (the wife of Abram, his son);
> he set out with them from Ur of the Chaldeans
> to go to the land of Canaan.
> They came as far as Haran; they settled there.
> The days of Terah were two hundred and five years;
> Terah died in Haran.
> Yahweh said to Abram:
> > "Go, yes you,
> > From your land,
> > Your kindred,
> > And your father's house,
> > To the land that I will show you.
> > I will make of you a great people;
> > I will bless you.
> > I will make your name great;
> > It will be a blessing.
> > I will bless those who bless you;
> > Those who curse you I will curse.
> > They shall bless themselves through you,
> > All the families of the ground."
> Abram went as Yahweh had commanded him; Lot went with him.
> Abram was seventy-five years old
> at the time of his departure from Haran.
> (Genesis 11:27—12:4)

Elimelech said, "In this passage, we start with the title, and then we have a good introduction. I say good, because: 1) it uses the early form of Sarah and Abraham's names, 2) it establishes an important point in our outline, Sarah is barren, 3) it mentions their intended trip to Canaan, and 4) we are informed of Terah's death. This passage does not mention the burial of Terah, but the burial is presupposed, because the next thing that we have is the blessing of Abraham plus Yahweh's commandment."

Jonathan said, "This is no doubt an excellent introduction, and you are correct in assuming the burial of Terah. Note that when Abraham is blessed Yahweh says that 'I will make of you a great people.' This is the reward for taking care of the dead, as we know from the other accounts. Of course, it is also important that Abraham listened to Yahweh's command. Yes. I like this."

Elishama said, "After the introduction, we have arranged three journeys, one after the other. The first one is Abraham's journey from Haran to Canaan. When he first arrives here, one of his first stops is Shechem; we think that this is important for our epic. The people from Shechem will like this. It goes like this:

> Abram passed through the land as far as the sanctuary of Shechem,
> as far as the oak of Moreh
> (The Canaanites were then in the land).
> Yahweh appeared to Abram; he said:
> > "To your descendants I will give this land."
> He built there an altar for Yahweh,
> the one who had appeared to him.
> > (Genesis 12:6–7)

"It is also important that during this first journey Abraham also goes to Bethel and on toward the Negeb. In other words, Shechem is important but so is the land to the south. Both Elimelech and I thought that this was a good way to interest all of the people from the start."

Jonathan said, "I'm pleased with what you have done. We must bring all the people together as one in this epic. So what is the second journey?"

Elimelech answered, "The second journey is to Egypt. For some, this story may just point ahead to Jacob's journey to Egypt under similar circumstances, but we are using it for another reason. In our outline of these cycles from the other day, the first point to make is that even though there is this interest in the birth of an heir by Sarah, this may be delayed. In the introduction, we have already discovered that Sarah is barren. Now, our lead characters encounter a famine, and they must go to Egypt. In Egypt, Sarah becomes the wife of the Pharaoh. This seems to ruin the story. How will Abraham and Sarah produce an heir? The people will be interested in the answer to this question. Here is the story:

The Ancestors of the Kings

> Now there was a famine in the land.
> Abram went down to Egypt to sojourn there,
> for the famine was severe in the land.
> As he was about to enter Egypt, he said to Sarai, his wife:
>> "Look now, you know that you are a good looking woman.
>> When the Egyptians see you, they will say,
>> 'This is his wife!'
>> They will kill me,
>> and they will let you live.
>> Please say that you are my sister,
>> so that it will go well for me because of you;
>> I will live on account of you."
>
> When Abram entered Egypt, the Egyptians noticed the woman,
> because she was very beautiful.
> The courtiers of Pharaoh saw her; they praised her to Pharaoh.
> The woman was taken to the house of Pharaoh.
> He treated Abram well because of her;
> soon he had flocks, cattle, male asses, male slaves, female slaves, female asses, and camels.
>
> Yahweh plagued Pharaoh and his house [with] great plagues,
> on account of Sarai, the wife of Abram.
> Pharaoh summoned Abram; he said:
>> "What is this you have done to me?
>> Why did you not tell me that she was your wife?
>> Why did you say, 'she is my sister,'
>> so that I took her for my wife?
>> And now, here is your wife. Take [her] and go!"
> Pharaoh put [his] men in charge of [Abram];
> they deported him, his wife, and all that he owned.
>> (Genesis 12:10–20)

"After this the people will really wonder if an heir will ever be born."

Jonathan said, "Your outline needs the points made in this story, and the epic needs the suspense. In addition, I would suggest that there is a point that you have not listed in your outline, which is made here. I note that the hero in these epic stories is usually successful; he becomes rich

241

The Jerusalem Academy

even in the most difficult of circumstances. We may have some arguments later on about your selections, but so far you are doing great."

Elishama said, "The third journey is the journey back to Canaan from Egypt. The text that we have shows how Abraham and Sarah came back to Bethel. Then it deals with Lot's separation from Abraham. Next it says:

> Yahweh said to Abram, after Lot separated from him:
> "Please, lift up your eyes and see,
> From the place where you are,
> To the north and to the south,
> To the east and to the west,
> For all the land that you see,
> To you I give and to your descendants forever.
> I will make your descendants as the particles of the earth;
> If one were able to count the particles of the earth,
> Even your descendants could be counted.
> Arise, walk around the land,
> Unto its length and unto its breadth,
> For I give it to you."
> Abram tented; he came;
> he settled at the oaks of Mamre that are in Hebron.
> There he built an altar for Yahweh.
> (Genesis 13:14–18)

"We decided to end this third journey in Hebron. We began the series in Shechem and brought them back to Hebron."

Jonathan said, "That is nice, and in addition Abraham, himself, looks to the north and to the south, to the east and to the west. He unifies the entire land in just the way that we are trying to unite a greater Israel in our epic."

Elimelech said, "We are pleased that you seem to go along with us so far. However, the next few sections of this cycle are not so easy. Our main interest in the next four parts is to maintain the suspense. The people will wonder if there will ever be an heir. In fact, in the first one of these parts Abraham has given up. Elishama and I wonder if we are using too much material at this point. We hate to throw out things, but perhaps we should do just that."

Jonathan said, "Well, we will just have to take a look at the stories and see what to do. When we delete material, we will have to be prepared

The Ancestors of the Kings

to see it return some time in the future. It is possible that later scribes will put it back in place, or the singers may put it back during the first performance, provided it is a popular piece, and they know it well."

Elishama said, "The first of these sections shows how worried Abraham was, but God tries to encourage Abraham; he makes a covenant with him. The first part of it starts in this way:

> After these events, the word of Yahweh came to Abram in a vision saying:
> "Do not be afraid, Abram;
> I am your benefactor;
> Your reward shall be very great."
> Abram said:
> "Lord Yahweh, what will you give me?
> Am I going about destitute?
> Now the steward (*mesheq*) of my house,
> he is Dammesek Eliezer."
> Abram said:
> "Since you have not given me a descendant,
> surely, my steward will be my heir."
> Then the word of Yahweh [came] to him saying:
> "This one shall not be your heir;
> Rather one who issues from your organs,
> He shall be your heir."
> He took him outside; he said:
> "Please, look towards the heavens.
> Count the stars if you are able to count them."
> He said to him:
> "So shall be your descendants."
> He trusted Yahweh; [Yahweh] counted it to him [as] a rightful act.
> (Genesis 15:1–6)

"I won't read all of this. This much shows you how Abraham is worried. After this, Yahweh makes the covenant with Abraham, and he grants him all of the land and its people. So is this a necessary piece?"

Jonathan said, "Yes. It is necessary. Abraham is discouraged, but he cannot just change the rules. His son will be his heir. He will have to wait, and we will have to wait. However, you just said that Yahweh granted him all the land. We should read that part, because it is important."

Elishama said, "That's easy it is right here:

The Jerusalem Academy

> On that day, Yahweh cut with Abram a covenant as follows:
> "To your descendants I have granted this land,
> from the river of Egypt to the great river (the river Euphrates):
> the Kenites, the Kenizzites, the Kadmonites,
> the Amorites, the Canaanites, the Girgashites,
> the Hittites, the Perizzites, the Rephaim,
> and the Jebusites."
> (Genesis 15:18–21)

"Is that the part you wanted?"

"Yes. That's it. This is important, and we should have used it at our second coronation. When the fathers blessed King David in Hebron, David established himself in the correct line; he claimed his kingship; and he inherited the land and the people who were given to the fathers. This would have been the perfect way to point to the greater Israel on that occasion. But now we have another chance to use this text. This will be helpful."

Elimelech said, "Before this last part that we have just read, there is a reference to Abram's descendants becoming slaves and then returning in the fourth generation. This is the reason that we said earlier that our epic will need a second part, namely the exodus from Egypt."

And Jonathan added, "I remember your point on this, and you also said that this was why we must end part one in Egypt."

At that point in the conversation, Zadok came to the doorway. He said, "I'm sorry to interrupt your meeting, but I must speak to Jonathan."

Elishama and Elimelech got up to leave, and Jonathan said to them, "We have done enough for today. I'll see you in the morning."

After they left, Zadok said, "Thanks for seeing me. I need to talk to you about Ahban. He is in my office resting. He will need more than a little rest. Can you come over and see him?"

It did not take long to walk to Zadok's office. Ahban was sitting in one corner with his head against the wall. He raised his hand when Jonathan entered the room, but he said nothing.

Jonathan said, "Zadok has told me that you are not feeling well. Is there anything that we can do for you?"

"I don't think so. I have been weak and sick several times during the last few months. The other evening at your party for Naam and Gad, I felt good, but lately I have not had many good days. Today things are much worse, because I have a toothache. My teeth give me unbearable pain."

Jonathan said, "I wish we knew how to cure such things"

The Ancestors of the Kings

Ahban answered, "We know a great deal about healing horses and mules; they are valuable. We do not know much about caring for humans. But in either case, when our physicians come to the end of their knowledge, they all resort to religion and magic—to prayers and incantations. The Babylonians and Hurrians had some great incantations for a toothache. I wonder if their incantations ever helped anyone? What do you think Jonathan?"

"I doubt it, but sometimes I dislike the prayers more than the incantations. The incantations are empowered by the personal authority and the gods of the magician. All of this is a hoax. But prayers are even more distasteful, because the pious, who put God in charge of the world, dare to ask God to neglect the rest of the world and turn his attention to their needs and problems. The same people care nothing for the suffering of others, because suffering is the offspring of sin. I can sometimes understand priests who think in these terms, but it is still difficult for me to see how scribes can support such views. Magon said the other night at the party that such scribes were not free. I suppose he is correct, but he has more patience than I have."

Ahban said, "I agree with you. What is difficult for me to understand is this: I don't think that we should pray, but when the pain is unbearable, I scream, 'God help me!' It seems that we are never completely free from the things that we disavow."

Zadok said, "That is exactly right."

"Here is another interesting point. When the two of you came into this office, I hurt so much that I couldn't speak, but in this short conversation, I forgot about the pain a couple of times. I also forgot why I was here. Jonathan, I actually dropped by to see if you might want to use a text that deals with Abraham. This text has been in the library of the Old School for at least fifty years. It deals with a battle between two groups of kings. Someone who didn't know Abraham wrote it. The author calls him 'Abram, the Hebrew.' At any rate Abraham, helps to defeat the enemies who had also captured Lot. At the end of this story, Melchizedek, the king of Jerusalem, blesses Abraham. Here is the scroll; read the last part."

> Melchizedek, king of Salem, brought out food and wine;
> he was a priest of El-Elyon.
> He blessed him; he said:

The Jerusalem Academy

> "Blessed be Abram of El-Elyon,
> Procreator of heaven and earth.
> Blessed be El-Elyon,
> Who gave your foes into your hand."
> [Abram] gave him a tenth of everything.
> (Genesis 14:18–19)

After reading this, Jonathan said, "I'll show this to Elishama and Elimelech tomorrow. They have the stories of the fathers well thought out. They have thrown out some material, but this is interesting. It certainly is not a well-known story in Israel or Judah and being well known is important to us for the peoples' epic, but it does connect Abraham to Jerusalem, David's royal city. We'll talk about it, and I thank you for bringing it to me.

"But now you need to get some rest. You are welcome to come home with me, or Zadok and I can get you to your quarters."

"You go on home. I'll rest a bit, and then Zadok can help me get back to my quarters. Sometimes I wish I was back here at the school."

"We would welcome you back at any time. So thanks again and take care."

After this Jonathan came home, and he brought the old scroll with him. He was a bit late, and I said, "We are ready to eat, so come and sit down. Naam is asleep, and I'll call father."

During the meal, Jonathan told us about his day and about Ahban. "Perhaps you should have brought him here," I said.

"I suggested that, but he didn't want to do it. Zadok will get him home before long. I wonder if his son or his granddaughter, Bathsheba, know that he has been ill."

Father said, "Bathsheba is probably worried about her father and her husband. Both of them are off fighting David's wars. She might not know about Ahban, and he would not want to give her another worry."

Jonathan said, "Ahban did not even want us to know about his illness. What he wanted was to share an old scroll with us that was found in the library of the Old School."

Father said, "Do you know who wrote it?"

"No. We know almost nothing about it, and my first thought was that we should not use it. We have enough material, and the stories that we use should be well known by some group within our larger Israel. But it does show that a king Melchizedek, who was king of Jerusalem, blessed Abraham. Jerusalem was known, as Salem or Urusalem, in those days.

The Ancestors of the Kings

This connection between Abraham and Jerusalem could be useful to us as we try to relate to our friends in the Old School."

Father said, "You should use a text like that."

"I'll record your vote. And Keziah, what is your vote?"

"I have not seen the text, but I would vote to use it."

"This text has almost made it!"

"So how was Naam today?" asked Jonathan.

I said, "He was a little upset. Our party for him may have tired him, but he'll be fine. You'll be able to see him soon. It's almost time for him to eat."

Later that evening, Jonathan told me about Magon's invitation to go to Tyre after the dedication of David's palace. I was interested in the idea, but the problem was that no one seemed to know when the dedication would take place. I said, "I hope that it is late in the fall, but of course not in the winter. Naam could travel by fall."

Jonathan said, "I'm going to be spending more time at the office. We must finish the epic and have it ready for the dedication."

Jonathan was in his office by dawn. He reviewed what they had done at the last meeting, and he looked at the Abraham/ Melchizedek text again. When the others arrived, he shared the text with them.

Elimelech said, "If we used this text where would we put it?"

Jonathan answered, "Just after Lot's separation from Abraham. Lot goes his own way, and then he gets captured. In this text Abraham saves him. It would work well following the separation."

Elishama added, "I'll go along with that. It should go after the separation, and it must be inserted before the destruction of Sodom."

Elimelech said, "I note that at one point Abraham says, 'I have lifted up my hand to El-Elyon.' This means that Abraham has sworn to El-Elyon. Shouldn't we change this and replace 'El-Elyon' with Yahweh?"

Jonathan said, "No. We should leave it as is. We should not assume that Abraham believed in only one God. Also this author has just told us that Abraham was blessed by El-Elyon, and this author knows nothing about Yahweh. We should leave it alone."

"That's fine with me, but I'll bet that some priest or singer will add 'Yahweh' to our text at some later time."

"I would not bet against you on that. Well, we can now start on the work that you have prepared for today. As I recall, you had several more texts to deal with before the birth of Isaac."

Elishama said, "Yes. I would like to use four more stories before we get to the birth of Isaac, but Elimelech only wants three. The four are: 1) The Birth of Ishmael, 2) Covenant and Circumcision, 3) A Promise of a Son and the Destruction of Sodom, and 4) Abraham and Sarah in Gerar. This fourth one, Elimelech says, is not needed."

"Elimelech, why do you object?" asked Jonathan.

"Because it is redundant. We have already dealt with a king who takes Sarah as his wife when we told the story of the trip to Egypt. Granted, it prolongs the suspense, but we have already satisfied the need of our outline for such a story (that is, a seduction scene for our barren 'mother'). Also, this story is not as good as its Egyptian counterpart. It has been cleaned up. Here Abimelech, king of Gerar, takes Sarah, but the act is not consummated. In fact, God says to Abimelech, '. . . I did not allow you to touch her' (Genesis 20:6b). We should use a variation of this account in our story about Isaac and Rebekah, but not here."

Jonathan said, "I agree with Elimelech, but I want us to remember an important fact. Most of these stories took their form at the tomb. When the minstrels sing about the life of Abraham at the tomb, they do not use all the stories that they know for any one ritual occasion. A good minstrel will vary his selections from time to time. Our problem is that we will not have the opportunity to re-do our work for some later event. We must take these stories and make our selections for this royal epic. So, Elishama, if we don't use this story, it does not mean that you are wrong. It means that we have left it out of our royal epic. It may be that the singers will insert it and leave out the Egyptian story. But that is not our problem. I also agree with Elimelech about using this story in connection with Isaac and Rebekah."

Elishama said, "My position on this was based on my past experience. My friends used this story rather than the Egyptian story, and they put it just before the birth of Isaac. But I can go along with deleting it from our work."

Jonathan said, "As we have all noted from time to time, this may be one of those texts that finds its way back to this place. But now we still have the other three stories to discuss."

The Ancestors of the Kings

Elishama said, "The first one deals with the birth of Ishmael. This is a useful story in that it continues the suspense and at the same time it shows how Sarah and Abraham once again try to obtain an heir by an alternate route. Let me read a few lines for you:

> Now Sarai, the wife of Abram, had not given birth for him,
> and she had an Egyptian maid, and her name was Hagar.
> Sarai said to Abram:
> > "Note that Yahweh has kept me from bearing.
> > Please go into my maid;
> > Perhaps I will reproduce through her."
> Abram listened to the voice of Sarai.
> Sarai, the wife of Abram, brought Hagar, the Egyptian, her maid
> (after Abram had been settled for ten years in the land of Canaan);
> she gave her to Abram, her husband, for a surrogate.
> He went in to Hagar; she conceived.
> She saw that she had conceived;
> her mistress was diminished in her eyes.
> > (Genesis 16:1–4)

"The text goes on to tell about how Hagar ran away form Sarah, and it gives some details on the birth of Ishmael. Now, as we know, this is a legal way of obtaining an heir, but as we will soon find out, this was not the way that God meant for them to do it. For Sarah and Abraham it was plan B. The next two stories will show that Hagar did return after the birth of Ishmael. Elimelech, you had better take over on the second story."

"In this account we have a renewal of the covenant, the introduction of circumcision, the name changes (Sarai to Sarah and Abram to Abraham), a promise by God that Sarah will produce a son, and a promise that both Abraham and Sarah will produce kings. The mention of 'kings' at this point is important; it is important for David whose line comes from Sarah and Abraham. This story also makes a place for Ishmael. He will be a great leader, but he will not be in the line, which leads to David. Note the following:

The Jerusalem Academy

> Elohim said to Abraham:
>> "Truly, Sarah your wife shall bear for you a son;
>> you shall call forth his name, 'Isaac.'
>> Then I will establish my covenant with him
>> as an eternal covenant for his descendants after him.
>> As for Ishmael, I have heard you; as of now,
>> I have blessed him: so I will make him fruitful;
>> I will increase him more and more.
>> He shall father twelve princes;
>> I will grant him a great state.
>> But my covenant, I will establish with Isaac,
>> whom Sarah shall bear to you at this time next year."
>
> (Genesis 17:19–21)

Jonathan said, "So this story seems to clarify the situation. A discouraged Abraham first thinks that his 'steward' will be his heir. Then he sets his hopes on his son by the surrogate Hagar, namely Ishmael. But God says, 'No' to both of these alternatives. Sarah will bear a son, and they are instructed to name him Isaac. So if we do not use the story of Abraham and Sarah in Gerar, we should be ready for the birth of Isaac?"

Elimelech said, "Perhaps that should be the case, but it is not that easy.

The problem is that there is a group of people out there who dearly love another story concerning a mysterious appearance of Yahweh, which makes about the same point as the story that we have just discussed. Several singers have told us that we will have to use this story even if we repeat ourselves. In this account Abraham entertains three guests, apparently gods, and one of them is Yahweh. Finally, one of the three speaks,

> He said:
>> "I will certainly return to you at the time of life;
>> There will be a son for Sarah, your wife."
> Now Sarah was eavesdropping at the entrance of the tent,
> which was behind him.
> Abraham and Sarah were old, advanced in days;
> the way of women had ceased to be for Sarah,
> Sarah laughed, saying [sarcastically] to herself:

> "After I was withered,
> And my husband was old,
> Passion was mine."
>
> Yahweh said to Abraham:
> > "Why did Sarah laugh, saying,
> > 'Really now, shall I be a mother? I am old.'
> > Is anything too difficult for Yahweh?
> > To this place, I will return to you at the time of life;
> > Sarah shall have a son."
>
> Sarah lied saying:
> > "I did not laugh" (for she was afraid).
>
> He said:
> > "Not? But you did laugh."
>
> (Genesis 18:10–15)

"The people like the way this story is told. It has some wonderful lines such as Sarah's sarcastic remark, 'Passion was mine.' Elishama and I do not mind the repeats, but the bad thing is that this story is tied to a long story about the destruction of Sodom and Gomorrah, the rescue of Lot and his daughters, and the subsequent descendants of Lot. So what do we do?"

Jonathan said, "It is a great deal of material, but I would take the word of the singers. They know what sells. We must always remember the entertainment factor. We cannot take away the fun parts of these stories. The people always talk about Mrs. Lot, and how she became a pillar of salt. Also you cannot take away the tale about how Lot's daughters got him drunk and slept with their father. Then it says, 'The two daughters of Lot were pregnant by their father' (Genesis 19:36). These are things that the people will not allow us to delete. But now we can deal with the birth of Isaac."

Elishama said, "That we can, but it will have to be tomorrow. We need to organize the material for that discussion."

Jonathan said, "That will be fine. I need to go home and play a bit with Naam. How's Rachel?"

"She's doing well. She's a good baby."

Jonathan said, "Elimelech, are you still seeing your girl friend who came to our wedding?"

The Jerusalem Academy

"No. She's still in Hebron, but I have been told by Danel and Noah that there are some beautiful girls here in Jerusalem. But I wouldn't know. I'm too busy with this epic."

Jonathan said, "When this is finished, we will have to give you some time off. The Jerusalem girls don't know what they are missing."

Jonathan got home just after father returned to the house. Father had been gone all day. He had been visiting Ahban. So he was full of news. He said, "I want both of you to know that Ahban is feeling much better. He still needs some rest, but he is getting better. We had a good talk. He will probably leave Jerusalem for a few days. He will go to Giloh, which is his town. He has lived there for a long time, but now David has given the town to him in a royal grant. David has also granted land to his son Absalom, and next to Absalom's land, he has granted a large estate to Joab. That is hard to understand. The old question keeps coming up. Why does David treat Joab like a precious person?"

Jonathan said, "I don't know, but it is a bad sign. David is being used by Joab."

I said, "It makes me angry to hear that Joab has land of his own, but it is good that Ahban received his grant. So what else did you hear?"

"There is some bad news. Amnon, David's first-born, is in real trouble. He raped Tamar, his half-sister and the sister of Absalom. Tamar is now living with Absalom, and it is clear that Absalom hates Amnon. Everyone is asking, 'What will Absalom do and when?' It is difficult to know exactly what happened. It may be that Amnon is just like Joab. He sees something that he wants, so he takes it. Or did Absalom and Tamar set a trap for Amnon? After all, Amnon is the first-born, and it is clear that David's second son is not able to take over. Absalom, the third son, is really the next in line. Is Absalom looking for a reason to get rid of Amnon? Who knows? One thing that we do know is that Tamar is in mourning. She rent her *ketonet passiym*, her 'royal robe,' and she went screaming through the streets."

I said, "That is sad. Either way you take it, one of those two took advantage of Tamar, either Amnon or Absalom."

Jonathan added, "And either way, we have not heard the last of this story."

Father said, "Since Naam is sleeping perhaps we should eat, and then I will tell you about another part of my conversation with Ahban."

The Ancestors of the Kings

I said, "I would like that. It has been so hot today; I am wondering how Naam can sleep, especially with all these flies. I need to get something to cover his face."

After their meal, the men cleaned up the kitchen area, and I started to nurse Naam. Then father continued his story about his day with Ahban, and he said, "You will recall that during the last few months on several occasions, we have discussed with Magon and Ahban the fact that from all the scribes who come out of our school not many become 'voices of the future,' to use Magon's phrase. I guess that Ahban has been thinking about this fact, and he shared some of his thoughts with me. He says it is easy for us to judge the present as being dull. Many of the students are dull, and other aspects of our daily lives seem boring. But perhaps we need to open our eyes. Since greatness does not seem to surround us, it seems easier to assign greatness to the past. He gave me a copy of the following lines, which do just that:

> To the ancients, came God's word;
> In the present, there's no word.
> Yes. He spoke to Samuel,
> But then only a few words,
> And for king Saul, not a word.

"He gave me another short poem, which makes the same point, but it does it in terms of scribes and sages:

> Before scribes there were Sages,
> Oh yes, seven before the flood.
> And after? A few from out the mud.
> But now, scribes by the myriad.
> And the Sage? What? Oh, gone for ages.

"He said that he liked this second poem, and that it did make some needed points for an audience of scribes. However, he was beginning to see that there was something lacking in any poem that did not point to the importance of the present. Or to put in another way, Ahban thought that Magon's observations about his students were right on the mark. He valued the present, because he still had hopes for his students, and then he said, 'I'm glad that I came here, because this is a place where there are voices of the future, and most of them are around this table.' At that point, I said to Ahban that his voice was certainly one of the ones that Magon was talking about. Then Ahban said, 'Perhaps, but we won't really know if he is right until the future is present. Then I had to say that he was backing away from his praise of Magon's observations, and I added, 'You will have to agree the sage has returned, and that sage is you!' At that he laughed, and we both escaped from the heavy conversation. But I still say that he is a sage; he is so wise."

Jonathan said, "I agree with you."

I said, "You put Naam to sleep, but I was really taken by this. I am so glad that you went to see him."

Jonathan added, "That goes for me as well. It was a good thing to do, and it sounds as if you had a good time. That is also important. The subject of your discussion will always be with us. We have talked about it many times, and we will talk about it again. We must give the past its due, but we also must rethink everything in the present if our thought is going to make a difference. But most of us are not bold enough or certain enough to stand by our best thinking. But when you were a prophet, you were forced to take such a stand."

"That's right. But it is better not to be 'forced' to take such a stand when you don't have time to really think things through."

"You're right, and that's why some prophets seem to talk from the belly and not the heart/mind."

I said, "You should talk from both; the gut and the heart will correct each other."

Jonathan said, "You're right. Also, I want to go to bed. For once we will go to bed before Gad. I must get up early and get to work. I want to finish this epic. We finally got to the birth of Isaac. I thought we would never make it."

Jonathan was in his office when the sun came up. He was thankful for the light, but he hoped that it would not get too hot. He decided that he would get started on the days work before the others arrived. So he turned to the next text:

> Yahweh visited Sarah as he had said;
> Yahweh did to Sarah as he had spoken.
> Sarah became pregnant; she bore a son to Abraham for his old age
> (at the appointed time of which Elohim had promised him).
> Abraham called forth the name of his son
> (the one born to him, that is whom Sarah had borne to him), "Isaac."
> Abraham circumcised Isaac, his son, [when] he was eight days old,

The Ancestors of the Kings

as Elohim had commanded him.
Abraham was a hundred years old when Isaac, his son, was born to him.
Sarah said:
> "Elohim has made laughter for me;
> Everyone who hears will laugh with me."

She said:
> "Who has said to Abraham,
> 'Has Sarah nursed children?'
> Yet I have borne a son for his old age."

(Genesis 21:1–7)

Jonathan thought to himself, "This is the passage that I discussed on an earlier occasion with Elimelech and Elishama." Just then the two of them came in the office.

Jonathan said, "I thought I would get started, because I knew that both of you had read about the birth of Isaac during your preparations. Well he was just born and named. They really dwell on the 'laughter,' which of course is the meaning of 'Isaac.' Also, I just remembered that I had mentioned this passage to you some time ago. I told you that I thought that God was the real father here. I suppose this is not the only interpretation of this passage, but it is the most obvious one. In any case, Sarah conceives, and the child is born."

Elishama said, "We both remembered your earlier discussion of this, and we took it in that way. We also wanted to discuss a few additional lines in this text. After the part that you have just read, Sarah gets angry with Hagar and her son. She told Abraham to get rid of Hagar and Ishmael. Abraham did not want to do this but God spoke to him:

Elohim said to Abraham:
> "Do not be displeased in your eyes
> because of the boy and your servant girl.
> Whatever Sarah demands of you, listen to her voice,
> because through Isaac descendants will call forth to you.
> As for the son of the servant girl,
> I will make him into a state,
> for he is your descendant."

(Genesis 21:12–13)

The Jerusalem Academy

"We knew this part was important, because here we have the first passage in these stories, which looks to future in terms of tomb ritual. Isaac's descendants will call forth to Abraham at his tomb. This is like the story that we used in the second coronation where Jacob blesses Joseph and his sons. You used this in your blessing of Naam the other day. I remember that you liked this blessing, because the sons were to call forth the names of Abraham, Isaac, and Jacob in order to be blessed. And of course, we called forth the names of the fathers during the coronation."

Jonathan said, "You're right! This is the same idea, and it is important for us. Also I have been doing some more thinking about such tomb rituals. The heir receives a blessing at the tomb from the departed, but he also assumes his role as the leader of the community; the people bless him. In addition to these things you have mentioned, it is also important to note that when Isaac is born, Ishmael is sent away."

Elimelech added, "So the pattern is established. As in later cases, the younger will rule. Abraham and Sarah finally have the correct heir, but the audience must not relax just yet, because next comes Abraham's great test."

Jonathan said, "I was expecting this. He finally got his rightful heir, and now he is asked to sacrifice him. This should be almost too much for the audience."

Elishama said, "We thought about throwing this story out. It is 'too much,' and we don't really need to convince anyone that human sacrifice is not right."

Jonathan said, "I can share your mood, but you are mistaken about human sacrifice. I can't believe I did not tell you why Gad was kicked out of his position in David's administration. At any rate, David heeded the requests of the Gibeonites, and he sent them two of Saul's sons and five of Saul's grandsons. The Gibeonites sacrificed them 'before Yahweh' to stop a famine. When Gad objected to this and a few other things, David threw him out. We must keep this story of Abraham's test. David should be forced to hear it again and again."

Elishama said, "Sorry. I did not hear the story about Gad. However, I only said that we thought about throwing it out."

Elimelech said, "I had heard that David was mad, but I didn't know why."

"It is just as well that the story is not known by many. Gad told Keziah and me the day it happened. It has been a good thing for Gad. He was tired of working for David. But again, the real problem is David.

The Ancestors of the Kings

Sometimes I cannot imagine the David that I grew up with doing such things. Not only does David need this story, but also the people did like it at the second coronation. When Abraham took the knife to kill his son, I heard someone say, 'Oh no.' There was great relief in the crowd when the messenger of Yahweh said to Abraham, 'Do not move your hand to the boy!' (Gen 22:12a). David did his horrible deed before anyone could say, 'Do not move your hand to the boys!' I wonder when I'll quit working for David?"

Elishama said, "I don't know, but don't quit yet. Now we are ready for section 4 of the stories of Terah. But we should review our outline for each cycle on our chart. Hand me the chart Elimelech. So part 4 reads:

> 4) Similar conclusions containing three scenes: a burial scene, additional material on the heir(s), and a death scene.

In other words, we start with the burial scene. But I need to add that in this case part 3 is combined with part 4. The burial of Sarah and the purchase of the sepulchre are extremely important in this typical ending. This ending sets the location for most of the burials in part 4 of each cycle. So we want to deal with the following material: 1) the burial of Sarah, 2) How Isaac obtained his bride, and 3) the death and burial of Abraham."

At this point Elimelech took over and said, "Before we deal with Sarah's death and burial we want to show you another chart. Jonathan, we know that you like charts so here is one that shows part 4 of each cycle:

Cycles:	Terah	Abraham	Isaac	Jacob
1) Burial:	Sarah	Rebekah	Rachel	Jacob
2) Heirs:	Isaac	Jacob & Esau	Jacob's sons	Joseph's brothers
3) Death:	Abraham	Isaac	Leah	Joseph

"This all works out nicely, but we are taking out the cycle or Stories of Abraham. This means that we have to make some changes, and thus we are left with the following chart:

Cycle:	Terah	Isaac	Jacob	
1) Burial:	Sarah	Rachel	Jacob	
2) Heirs:	Isaac	Jacob's sons	Joseph's brothers	
3) Death:	Abraham	Isaac	Joseph	

We were forced to leave out of this pattern both Rebekah and Leah. However, Jacob, on his deathbed, mentions both Rebekah and Leah among those buried in the cave that Abraham purchased. This is helpful if some one wants a full count. So this is the pattern that we will follow."

Jonathan said, "This discussion has been very helpful, and I do like charts. We should keep them handy at least for me. Let's take up Sarah's burial."

Elishama said, "In this text, Sarah dies in Hebron and Abraham laments, but most of the text deals with Abraham's negotiations with Ephron. Abraham cannot use a sepulchre or accept the gift of one; he must own it out right. Finally, they agree, and Ephron speaks:

> Ephron answered Abraham as follows:
> "Pray my lord, hear me!
> The land is four hundred shekels of silver!
> Between me and between you, what is that?
> So bury your dead!"
> Abraham listened to Ephron; Abraham weighed out for Ephron
> the silver of which he spoke in the hearing of the sons of Heth—
> four hundred shekels of silver at the exchange rate of the merchants.
> The field of Ephron that was in the Machpelah, before Mamre,
> the field and the cave that was in it and all the trees that were in the field
> (that were within all its boundary lines) was deeded
> to Abraham as a purchase in the presence of the sons of Heth,
> from all who entered the gate of his city.
> After that, Abraham buried Sarah, his wife,
> in the cave of the field of the Machpelah,
> before Mamre (that is, Hebron), in the land of Canaan.
> The field and the cave that was in it was deeded to Abraham
> for [his] own sepulchre from the sons of the Hittites.
> (Genesis 23:14–20)

Jonathan said, "This is a great text. The people will like the drama of the negotiations, and it gives everyone a feel for the importance of Hebron for our first two coronations. Let's move on. We should complete this last part of the Terah cycle."

Elimelech said, "It's my turn once again. I always get the difficult ones. The second scene of this fourth part has to do with the heirs or the descendants. At first, in this spot, we just had a small note about Abraham's descendants from his 'concubines' (Genesis 25:1–6), but when we decided to delete the Stories of Abraham (meaning most of the Isaac material), we thought that this would be the place to add from the Isaac material the long story about how Abraham's servant found the right wife for Isaac. It contains Rebekah's journey and her marriage to Isaac."

Jonathan said, "I'm glad that you found a place for this, because as you well know, it is one of my favorite stories; it is the ideal wedding. As you were talking, I thought that the people would like this text even if they were not interested in Isaac. For example, when Abraham's servant first meets Rebekah the text reads:

> This girl was very good looking,
> a young woman whom no man had known.
> She went down to the spring; she filled her jar;
> she came up.
> The servant ran to meet her; he said:
>> "Please give me a little swallow of water from your jar."
> She said:
>> "Drink, my lord."
> She hurried; she lowered her jar upon her hand;
> she gave him a drink.
> She had finished giving him a drink; she said:
>> "I will draw for your camels as well,
>> until they have finished drinking."
> She hurried; she emptied her jar into the trough;
> she ran back to the well to draw; she drew for all his camels.
> (Genesis 24:16–20)

The minstrels will have great fun with this text. What a girl! According to the story, she carries water for ten camels."

Elishama said, "It is a good story, and it is really needed in this spot. Since we have left out so much of the Isaac material, we will be forced near the beginning of the next cycle to deal with the birth of Jacob and Esau. So we had to bring Rebekah and Isaac together here. Next we can deal with the last scene in the stories of Terah: the death and burial of Abraham. This is short so let's read it all:

> These are the days of the years of the life of Abraham,
> who lived a hundred and seventy-five years.
> Abraham expired; he died at a ripe old age, old and satisfied.
> He was gathered to his people.
> Isaac and Ishmael, his sons, buried him in the cave of the Machpelah,
> in the field of Ephron, the son of Zohar the Hittite, that was before Mamre,

> the field that Abraham purchased from the sons Heth;
> there Abraham was buried and Sarah his wife.
> It was after the death of Abraham that Elohim blessed Isaac, his son,
> and Isaac settled near Beer-lahai-roi."
>
> (Genesis 25:7–11)

Jonathan said, "In this last scene, it is interesting that it was both Isaac and Ishmael who buried their father. This means that they were both blessed, but of course our text only mentions that Isaac was blessed. It feels good to me that we have finished this first cycle. Now we can take up the Stories of Isaac but not today. This has been along session."

Elimelech said, "Are we going to show any of this material to Zadok and Magon like we did with the earlier material?"

Elishama said, "I have talked with Zadok, and he still wants to come back. However, he always asks if we have arrived at the Joseph story. He is waiting for that."

Jonathan said, "I certainly hope they both return."

Elimelech said, "I talked with Magon last night at our evening meal, and he wants to discuss with us a common pattern for a journey. He was talking in terms of Jacob's journey to obtain a wife."

Jonathan said, "It sounds like they will be back, and especially when they have something special to contribute. I will see you both tomorrow. Have a good evening. We forgot our lunch break."

As Jonathan approached our house, he saw me in the yard. He was in a happy mood. I was glad that he was feeling good, but I wondered why he had not come home at noon. He said, "We were getting so much done we could not stop. I'm pleased we did so well. We have finished *These are the Stories of Terah* with all of the Abraham stories. Both Sarah and Abraham are dead, but there is hope. Rebekah and Isaac are married, but as usual in these accounts, she is barren. We will have to wait and see if God will open her womb."

"Do you think he will?"

"Only after everyone in the audience asks that question. Actually most of the mothers of Israel were seduced by powerful kings, but that was not too bad because they were all barren."

"So I guess I'm not a 'mother of Israel.' I was not taken by a king."

"And you were not barren. How is Naam of the not-so-barren?"

"He's fine. It's about time for him to get up. You are late for lunch but a little early for dinner. Perhaps you can entertain Naam, because I need to finish a few things. I don't know where father is."

We went inside the house, and Naam was awake. Jonathan enjoyed these moments with Naam and promised himself that when he was finished with this *Royal Epic*, he would slow down. He wanted to spend more time with Naam.

37

These Are the Stories of Isaac

It was difficult to get started on the stories of Isaac, because Jonathan and the others had to deal with Isaac and Rebekah in Gerar. They recalled that they had deleted such a story when they were dealing with Abraham, and they intended at that time to include it in the Isaac material. But this called for some changes in the story plus the name changes. At the next meeting Jonathan was suppose to deal with some of these things, and I decided to go with him. It seemed like an interesting topic, so I took Naam over to stay with Deborah and Rachel for a little while.

Jonathan said to us, "If we use the story about Abraham and Sarah in Gerar, we will have to change the names to Isaac and Rebekah, and we will have to insert it before the birth of Jacob and Esau. For our discussion we can call this one 'story A.' I still think we should do this, but I must say that I have discovered another variant of this story within the Isaac material, 'story B,' which was discarded when we eliminated *These are the Stories of Abraham* at the beginning of our work. This variant is really watered down. Here the king, Abimelech, is not even interested in Rebekah, but he is afraid that 'one of the men' might have taken her. I'll read a little of it for you:

> Now there was a famine in the land,
> in addition to the first famine that was in the days of Abraham.
> Isaac went to Abimelech, king of the Philistines, in Gerar.
> . . .
> Isaac settled in Gerar.
> The men of the place asked concerning his wife. He said:
>   "She is my sister,"
> for he was afraid to say, "My wife," [for he thought]:

> "The men of the place might kill me on account of Rebekah,
> for she is good looking."
> Now after he had been there for many days,
> Abimelech, king of the Philistines, looked down from the window;
> he saw Isaac making love with Rebekah, his wife.
> Abimelech summoned Isaac; he said:
> > "So she really is your wife!
> > How could you have said, 'She is my sister?'"
> Isaac said to him:
> > "Because I thought that I might die on account of her."
> Abimelech said:
> > "What is this you have done to us?
> > Just a little longer and someone might have laid your wife;
> > you would have brought guilt upon us."
> Abimelech charged all the people as follows:
> > "The one who touches this man or his wife shall be put to death."
> > (Genesis 26:1–11)

In this version, the king does certainly not endanger the ancestress. I'm glad that we are not using 'story B.' Now with the appropriate changes, 'story A' which we will use is as follows:

> Isaac journeyed from there to the land of the Negeb;
> he settled between Kadesh and Shur;
> he sojourned in Gerar.
> Isaac said of Rebekah, his wife, "She is my sister."
> Abimelech, king of Gerar, sent and took Rebekah.
> Elohim came to Abimelech in a dream that night;
> he said to him:
> > "You are dead, because of the woman whom you have taken.
> > She is a married woman!"
> . . .
> That same God said to him in the dream:
> > "Indeed I knew that in the integrity of your heart you did this;
> > indeed I kept you from sinning against me.
> > Therefore I did not allow you to touch her.
> > Now restore the wife of this man, for he is a prophet."
> . . .
> Abimelech summoned Isaac; he said to him:

> "What have you done to us?
> What sin have I perpetrated against you
> that you should bring a great sin upon me
> and upon my kingdom?"
>
> . . .
>
> Isaac said:
>> "I said that only because
>> there is no fear of Elohim in this place;
>> they will kill me because of my wife.
>> Besides, she really is my sister—"
>
> . . .
>
> Abimelech took flocks and cattle, male slaves and maidservants;
> he gave them to Isaac; he restored Rebekah, his wife, to him.
> Abimelech said:
>> "Here, my land is before you;
>> settle where it is good in your eyes."
> To Rebekah he said:
>> "Note that I have given your brother a thousand pieces of silver;
>> this is your compensation for everything that you experienced.
>> From everything you are vindicated."
> Isaac prayed to the gods.
> Elohim cured Abimelech, his wife, and servant girls; they gave birth.
> For Yahweh had completely closed every womb of the house of
>   Abimelech because of Rebekah, the wife of Isaac.
>   (Genesis 20:1–18, with name changes)

"By using 'story A' here we have the endangerment of Rebekah before the birth of Jacob and Esau, and according to your outline it is needed here. Also, in order to delay the birth of the heir a little longer, I suggest that we add the material which follows 'story B.' This material explains how Isaac became rich and about his subsequent relations with Abimelech" (Genesis 26:12–33).

Elimelech said, "Jonathan, you keep bringing in more Isaac material that we have previously discarded."

Jonathan responded, "I know, but in this case it is needed. Plus, it continues the suspense until we get to the birth story."

I said, "What I will miss is the love scene in 'story B.' This scene actually makes Isaac and Rebekah seem like real people."

These Are the Stories of Isaac

Elishama said, "What Keziah has just said is true, but we can't include everything.

"I didn't say that you should include it. I said that I would miss it."

After that exchanged, I wondered if Elishama was flustered, because I had mentioned the love scene as being important.

Elishama said, "I just hope that our changes hold up. There are some minstrels and scribes who will have a difficult time with our name changes and placing 'story A' at this point. But now we do need to get on with the birth of Jacob and Esau. We don't want to drag it out as much as we did with the birth of Isaac. We will have to move our title, *These are the stories of Isaac*, and we can place it before 'story A' that we have just discussed."

Elimelech said, "Jonathan, I have a question for you. Do you think in our 'story A' it will bother the priests or the prophets for Isaac to say, 'So when the gods caused me to wander from the house of my father, . . .' or at the end of the text where it says, 'Isaac prayed to the gods'? I'm asking about 'the gods,' because some people would rather have Isaac or Abraham praying to Yahweh? Right?"

Jonathan answered, "This may bother some people, but it will not bother the audience who hears it at the dedication of David's palace. In any case, I would not want to change this text in order to express loyalty to Yahweh. We can't do that. Also it is clear at the end of the text, Isaac must be praying to more than one god, because Elohim cures the illness that was inflicted by Yahweh. Our fathers didn't worry about such things; David might be concerned but not our fathers."

Elishama said, "I agree. I would not want to change such things. In fact, it bothers me to change the names in 'story A,' but I know that we have to if we use it. Let's go on to the next birth story."

I said, "I must leave now and pick up Naam, but I wish that I could hear about the birth of these twins. I'll have to hear about it later."

With that I left and Elishama read:

> Abraham fathered Isaac;
> Isaac was forty years old when he took for his wife Rebekah,
> the daughter of Bethuel the Aramean from Paddan-aram,
> the sister of Laban the Aramean.
> Isaac made a petition to Yahweh on behalf of his wife,
> for she was barren.
> Yahweh responded to him; Rebekah, his wife, conceived.
> The children were being crushed inside her; she said:

> "If this is the case, why me?"
> She went to seek Yahweh.
> Yahweh said to her:
>> "Two states are [now] within your womb;
>> Two peoples shall come from your body.
>> One shall be stronger than the other,
>> And the elder shall serve the younger."
> Her days were fulfilled to give birth;
> there were twins in her womb.
> The first one came out red, all of him like a hairy mantle.
> They called forth his name, "Esau."
> Next his brother came out with his hand
> grasping the heel of Esau.
> He called forth his name, "Jacob."
> (Genesis 25:19b–34)

"This story is delightful and it speaks to the second point of our outline: 'And the elder shall serve the younger.' It seems that it was not enough just to say it. The story goes on to point out how Jacob is the 'complete man,' and then it relates how Jacob made it all 'legal.' When he bought Esau's birthright, he became the firstborn, and he was due a double portion of any inheritance."

Jonathan said, "I like the story, and of course it is like the birth story of Perez and Zerah in *These are the stories of Judah*. Also, I know that the people really like this story."

Elishama said, "We need a lot of favorite stories in our epic. For this reason we are suggesting that we follow this birth story with another favorite which reinforces this idea that it was Jacob or the younger who was the heir; it was Jacob and his mother who were clever and were able to rule, and they obtained Isaac's blessing for Jacob. Here is the story:

> When Isaac was old, his eyes were too dim to see.
> He called Esau, his elder son; he said to him:
>> "My son."
> He answered him:
>> "Yes."
> He said:
>> "Notice that I have grown old;
>> I do not know the day of my death.
>> Now then, take your gear, your quiver and your bow,

These Are the Stories of Isaac

    and go out in the wild and hunt some game for me.
    Prepare for me the tasty food that I love,
    and bring it to me. I will eat it,
    so that my very being may bless you before I die."

Rebekah was listening when Isaac spoke to Esau, his son.
Esau went into the wild to hunt game to bring back.
Rebekah said to Jacob, her son, as follows:
    "I just heard your father speaking to Esau,
    your brother, saying:
    'Bring me game, and prepare for me tasty food.
    I will eat it; I will bless you
    in the presence of Yahweh before my death.'
    Now, my son, listen to my voice,
    to what I command you.
    Go to the flock, and from there get me
    two fat young goats;
    with them I will prepare the tasty food
    for your father that he loves.
    You shall bring [it] to your father; he will eat,
    so that he may bless you before his death."
Jacob said to Rebekah, his mother:
    "But Esau, my brother, is a hairy man;
    I am a smooth man.
    What if my father touches me?
    I will be in his eyes as one who mocks.
    I will bring upon myself a curse and not a blessing."
His mother said to him:
    "Be upon me your curse, my son!
    Just listen to my voice.
    Go and get [them] for me."

He went and got [them]; he brought [them] to his mother.
His mother prepared the tasty food that his father loved.
Rebekah took the finest clothes of Esau, her older son,
which were with her in the house;
she outfitted Jacob, her younger son.
She put the skins of the young goats on his hands
and on the nape of his neck.

She placed the tasty food and the bread that she had made
in the hands of Jacob, her son.

He went to his father; he said:
"My father."
He said:
"Yes, who are you, my son?"
Jacob said to his father:
"I am Esau, your firstborn. I have done as you told me.
Come now, sit up and eat of my game,
so that your very being may bless me."
Isaac said to his son:
"What is this? You have succeeded so quickly, my son."
He said:
"Because Yahweh, your god, made it happen before me."
Isaac said to Jacob:
"Come closer. I will touch you, my son."
Are you my son, Esau, or not?"
Jacob came close to Isaac, his father. He touched him; he said:
"The voice is the voice of Jacob,
but the hands are the hands of Esau."
But he did not identify him, for his hands were hairy,
like the hands of Esau, his brother.

[Isaac] blessed him; he said:
"Are you my son Esau?"
He said:
"I am."
He said:
"My son, serve me, and I will eat game, so that
my very being may bless you."
(He served him; he ate. He brought wine for him; he drank.)
Isaac, his father, said to him:
"Come closer, and kiss me, my son."
(He came close; he kissed him; he smelled the odor of his clothes.)
He blessed him; he said:
"Yes! The odor of my son
Is like the smell of a field—
A field that Yahweh has blessed.

> And may that God grant to you,
> From the dew of the heavens,
> And from the fat of the earth,
> Abundance of grain and wine.
> Peoples shall serve you;
> States shall bow down to you.
> Be the ruler of your brothers;
> The sons of your mother shall bow down to you.
> Cursed be those who curse you;
> Blessed be those who bless you."
> (Genesis 27:1–29)

"I don't need to read the rest of this text. You will recall that Esau becomes very angry, because Isaac cannot bless him! Jacob has the blessing, and he will rule over Esau. Esau hates Jacob, and he even threatens to kill him. So both Isaac and Rebekah send Jacob away. Isaac says:

> "You shall not take a wife from the daughters of Canaan.
> Get up! Go to Paddan-aram, to the house of Bethuel,
> Your mother's father and take from there
> a wife for yourself,
> from the daughters of Laban, your mother's brother."
> (Genesis 28:1–4)

Jonathan said, "This is an important point. There can be no doubt as to Jacob's future, but first he must find the right wife."

Elishama said, "So this brings us to Jacob's journey. Elimelech mentioned the other day that Magon was interested in Jacob's journey. We should stop for today, and Elimelech, you should try to get Magon to join us for our next meeting."

"I'll do it."

Jonathan realized that once again they had worked all day without a lunch break. He got home, and father and I were ready to eat. I said, "You are late, but I can understand why. I hated to leave. After I got home, I had a visitor.

"And who was your visitor?"

"Come and sit down, and I'll tell you all about our visitor while we eat."

The Jerusalem Academy

Father said, "Yes! Sit down. I want to hear about this. Keziah has made it all sound so mysterious."

"It was not so mysterious. But it is important, and I'm usually not the one in this family who brings home the news. I need to have my day. I was outside playing with Naam, and Magon came by. He was on his way to check on the progress of the builders. I asked him to stop by on his way back and let me know how the palace was coming along. After some time, he was back, and you will be glad to know that all is well. However, his countrymen told him that they could not finish the building until late in the fall. Magon said that such a late date might mean that our trip to Tyre would have to be delayed. It might get too cold to travel with Naam. But, there is also some good news. He had a letter from Elissa (she has not answered mine yet), and she told Magon that she might come to Jerusalem for the dedication of David's palace with the royal party from Tyre. If she does that, we will still get to meet her even if we don't go to Tyre."

Jonathan said, "That is good news, because I was a bit worried that Naam would be too young for the trip this fall."

"Elissa's visit will be interesting for everyone. She told Magon that she was going to bring a tablet for him to translate. It seems that King Hiram was renovating his palace, and the builders found some old records. The tablets were taken to the scribal school, but they were having some trouble reading them. The scribes wanted to send one to Magon, because they knew that he could get them started."

Jonathan said, "This is exciting. The tablets are probably written in Babylonian. At least, most of the correspondence in the past was written in Babylonian. At any rate, if the scribes could not read these tablets, the language was not their own."

Father said, "So, now we have something to look forward to. I like such times, but I have probably said before that when looking forward to a great event time seems to slow down and then when the event happens everything goes so fast. It is finished. So Jonathan how did your work go today?"

"It was an interesting day, and I was glad that Keziah was there for the first part of it. Things will go faster from now on. Also, both Elishama and Zadok have recently worked on the Joseph material, and this means that the last part of our epic will be almost finished before we get to it. Today we dealt with clever Jacob. The entertainment value of such stories is great. Jacob was clever, sneaky, and successful. It appears that such characteristics are necessary in a great leader."

Father said, "That's right, but it also makes great leaders unbearable."

Jonathan said, "They are unbearable to those who are close to them, but they are heroes to the people who are distant from them in time or geography. David is a prime example."

I said, "I want to change the subject. Jonathan, I've wanted to see your poem on Job for some time. When will you show it to us?"

"I really don't know. I'm not trying to be difficult, but it needs a lot of work. I have been stalled on it for a number of years."

"But several months ago when we were talking about God, you recited the last seven lines of it, and I remember the last two lines:

> 'What a whisper of a word we hear from him;
> Who can understand the thunder of his might?'"
> (Job 26:14b–c)

"And those lines will be the last lines, but the main part needs to be changed. I know what I can do. Some evening in the near future, I will tell you the old story of Job. I will explain in some detail why it is an awful story and full of errors. After that, you will understand why I must go slowly on my poem. The poem has to be good enough to completely destroy the thrust of the old story. I need to know more, to live more, and have more time to put it all together. You will see, and you can help."

"I accept your points, but I will not accept a long delay. I want you to make the 'near future' soon."

Just then Naam started to cry, and Jonathan and father were left alone to clean up after dinner. Jonathan said, "We will have an interesting day tomorrow, because Magon will be with us. We'll be working with Jacob's journey to obtain a wife, and Magon wants to tell us about such journeys in epic literature."

"Would you mind if I came to your meeting? I would like to hear what Magon has to say."

"You are more than welcome."

When father and Jonathan arrived at Jonathan's office the next morning, Elishama, Elimelech, and Magon were there. Jonathan said, "Sorry. We are late. Gad wanted to join us today, so I helped him with some of his morning chores. I did not know that he did so much for us every morning. He fixes the breakfast, puts away the food, washes our plates, and makes

The Jerusalem Academy

a list for our rations. Elishama, I really don't understand how you and Deborah manage without a Gad. I know that without him Keziah and I would live in utter chaos."

Elishama said, "Perhaps you and Keziah would be willing to share Gad? Don't answer the question, but think about it. Now we turn to the story that will be the center of our discussion:

> Jacob set out from Beer-sheba and went towards Haran.
> He came upon a sanctuary and lodged there, for the sun had set.
> He took [a stone] from the stones of the sanctuary.
> He placed [it] at his head.
> He lay down in that sanctuary.
> He dreamed:
>> There a stairway was built to the earth;
>> its top reached to the heavens.
>> There the messengers of Elohim
>> were ascending and descending on it.
>> There Yahweh stood upon it.
> He said:
>> "I, Yahweh, am the god of Abraham,
>> your father, and the god of Isaac.
>> The land on which you are lying,
>> I will give to you and to your descendants.
>> Your descendants shall be as the particles of the earth.
>> You shall spread out to the west and to the east,
>> to the north and to the south.
>> They shall bless themselves through you and your descendants,
>> all the families of the ground.
>> Yes! I am with you; I will guard you wherever you go;
>> I will bring you back to this ground,
>> for I will not leave you until I have done what
>> I promised to you."
> Jacob awoke from his sleep; he said:
>> "Surely, Yahweh is in this sanctuary,
>> and I did not know it."
> He was afraid; he said:
>> "How awesome is this sanctuary.
>> This is none other than the house of Elohim.
>> This is the gate of the heavens."

These Are the Stories of Isaac

> Jacob got up in the morning.
> He took the stone that was there at his head.
> He set it up [as] a sacred pillar.
> He poured oil on its top.
> He called forth the name of that sanctuary, "Bethel"
> but Luz was the name of the city at its beginning.
> Jacob vowed a vow saying:
>> "If Elohim will be with me,
>> if he will guard me on this journey that I am making,
>> if he will give me food to eat and clothing to wear,
>> if I return in health to the house of my father,
>> and if Yahweh will be for me, O Elohim,
>> then, this stone that I have set up [as] a sacred pillar
>> shall be the house of Elohim,
>> and of all that you give to me, a tenth I will give to you."
>
> (Genesis 28:10–22)

"Magon, Elimelech told us the other day that you would be interested in our discussion of Jacob's journey to obtain a wife."

"I'm interested. This all came about, because Elimelech and I were talking about Jacob and his journey the other evening. I told him that our ancestors at Ugarit had such a story about one of their fathers, who took a similar journey. We do not have a written copy, but a few older singers remember it as do a few of our scribes. The story was about a man named Keret. This story was used in tomb rituals and coronations just as you have used the stories of your fathers. He was the greatest of all the early fathers."

Jonathan said, "Do you mean that the two stories are similar?"

"No. The two stories are quite different, but they are both used in 'royal epics.' What I said was that they both dealt with similar journeys. As the story begins, Keret has just lost his entire family. Without an heir, his dynasty will end. While mourning this loss, Keret sleeps and dreams. The god El appears to him in his dream. El gives Keret detailed instructions for a journey. The purpose of the journey is to obtain a wife in order to produce an heir. Keret follows these instructions, and he sets out on his journey. However, on the third day of the journey (epic journeys usually take seven days), Keret stops at a shrine of Asherah, goddess of Tyre and Sidon. This was not in the plan for the journey. At this shrine Keret makes a vow to Asherah, and he asks for success in finding his rightful wife. If he is successful, he vows to give Asherah silver and gold. Keret does have a successful journey, but he forgets to keep his vow. This causes him to have some great problems, but we do not need to pursue those details."

Jonathan said, "This is interesting. The journeys are not exactly the same, but they are close enough. Jacob received his instructions from Isaac. He was told not to marry a Canaanite woman. Rather he was to choose a wife from the daughters of Laban. I should add that with Jacob there is a second reason for the journey and that is to escape the anger of Esau. But as it turns out the main reason is to obtain a wife. As we have just read, Jacob also stopped at a shrine, and he made a vow. It is here that Jacob had his dream, and in that dream Yahweh promised to be with him; Jacob will be successful. What is most interesting to me is that in both stories, the promise of El and the promise of Yahweh were not enough for Keret or Jacob. Keret wanted some additional help from Asherah, and Jacob wanted additional help from Elohim. Jacob wanted Elohim to not only grant him success, but it appears that Jacob wanted Elohim to remind Yahweh of his promise to be with Jacob. If all of this comes to pass, then Jacob will worship Elohim at this shrine and he will give Elohim a tenth of all that Elohim gives to him. In our story, Jacob does remember his vow."

Magon said, "When I compare these two journeys, I'm not trying to draw any conclusions which would show that someone borrowed from another tradition or that one story was better than the other or anything like that. The story of Keret is older than the Jacob story, but that is not the point. What is important about all this is to note that in royal epics this is what one would expect. If there is a journey to obtain a wife, this is how you do it."

Elishama said, "It is important for us to know that this story will be understood by the people of Israel and Judah, plus the people who are here for the dedication of David's palace from other countries will understand it as well. Our singers who preserved this story knew how to tell a story."

Father added to Elishama's thoughts, "It is nice to know about these things, but I would like to suggest that none of this is really surprising. We are from Jerusalem and Tyre. Our languages are similar and so are our cultural backgrounds. It would be difficult for us to come up with completely new ways of saying things, and if we did, there would be no communication. This does not mean that we are all identical in our thinking. No. We are quite different, and it is always a struggle to communicate our differences in this common tongue. However, it seems to happen, because we seldom agree on anything."

These Are the Stories of Isaac

Magon said, "With that, I agree!"

Elimelech said, "Gad, I would like to ask you a question. It is a question that we have discussed several times in our meetings, but I would like to bring it up again since you are here today. Jacob seems to be dealing with at least two gods in the story of his journey; perhaps more since Elohim is plural. Will that bother someone who only worships Yahweh in Jerusalem?"

"I suppose that it might bother some priests, but I certainly don't think that it will bother most of the people who will hear this epic at the dedication. Most of them believe in more than one God."

"That's what I thought, and as Jonathan has reminded us many times, we should not change these traditions in order to make them more pleasing or current."

And Jonathan added, "All of us have reminded ourselves again and again that the minstrels may depart from our copies of this epic as to the order of the stories and the exact wording, but we may be surprised. Heman asked me the other day for a copy of the epic and for a list of 'first lines' of each story. This may mean that the order has a better chance of survival than the exact words."

Magon said, "Even if your epic suffers such changes, it is an important thing that you are doing. You are using, as Gad says, common forms in order to communicate; you are creating a foundation for David to stand on and an identity for his people. Also you seem to realize that you are not free to just write up new material. The fathers have been remembered at their tombs, and these stories have become popular. These stories may not tell you much about the past, but they do present you with your 'fathers' and unite you in the present. This is an important occasion for this new state. No one in my country is trying to do such a thing. What you are doing will be also be important for your future."

Jonathan said, "Magon, you are kind, and we thank you for your help. At this point, I would like to ask Elishama to tell us briefly about Jacob's success on his journey and about his return. You can do this by giving us a list of the stories that you plan to use. I am certain that Magon will be interested in these subsequent details. Also if you can do this, we will be able to conclude 'These are the stories of Isaac' at our next meeting.

"I can do it, and it will help us to think in terms of the full story, but I'll bet we'll want to talk about some of these items. In other words, I'm not so sure we will be ready to conclude this cycle at our next meeting."

275

Jonathan said, "I understand but give it a try."

Elishama said, "Since Elimelech gathered some of this material he will have to help me on some of it. I have just counted the stories that we will probably use. There are nine, and I will refer to them by their first lines. The first is 'Jacob directed his feet to the land of the Bene-qedem' (Genesis 29:1). This says nothing concerning his journey to the east, but it goes into some detail about his arrival. Jacob met Rachel, the daughter of Laban, at the well where she brought her father's sheep for water. Usually the shepherds watered all the sheep at the same time. They would roll the stone from the mouth of the well, but as soon as Jacob saw Rachel coming with the sheep, he broke with the custom, and he rolled away the heavy stone by himself and watered the sheep. He also kissed Rachel and wept for joy. For Jacob it was love at first sight. Laban invited Jacob, his nephew, to stay with them. I cannot just tell you about the next part. You must hear it, and I know that the people will love it. Listen:

> Laban said to Jacob:
> > "Just because you are my kinsman,
> > should you serve me for nothing?
> > Tell me, what is your wage?"
> Laban had two daughters: the name of the older one was Leah,
> and the name of the younger one was Rachel.
> Leah's eyes were soft, and Rachel was well built and good-looking.
> Jacob loved Rachel.
> He said:
> > "I will serve you seven years for Rachel,
> > your younger daughter."
> Laban said:
> > "It is better that I give her to you
> > than that I should give her to another man;
> > stay with me."
> Jacob served seven years for Rachel.
> In his eyes they were as a few days—
> he was in love with her.
> Jacob said to Laban:
> > "Give me my wife for my time is fulfilled;
> > I want to go in to her."
> Laban gathered all the men of the [home] place. He prepared a feast.
> When evening came, he took Leah, his daughter;

These Are the Stories of Isaac

> he brought her to [Jacob].
> He went in to her.
> (Laban gave Zilpah, his maidservant, to Leah, his daughter,
> for her maidservant.)
> When morning came, there she was, Leah!
> He said to Laban:
> > "What is this you have done to me?
> > Was it not for Rachel that I served you?
> > Why have you deceived me?"
> Laban said:
> > "It is not done so in our place to give the younger
> > before the firstborn.
> > Complete the seven [day feast] of this [one].
> > In addition we will give you this [other one]
> > for service that you will render me for another seven years."
> Jacob did so. He completed the seven [day feast] of this [one];
> [Laban] gave Rachel, his daughter, to him for a wife.
> (Laban gave to Rachel, his daughter, Bilhah, his maidservant,
> for her maidservant.)
> [Jacob] also went in to Rachel.
> Moreover, he loved Rachel more than Leah.
> He served [Laban] yet another seven years.
> > (Genesis 29:15–30)

Jonathan said, "I always enjoy that account, but I really did want you to tell us about these stories with only a few descriptive terms. We must move along."

Elishama said, "Jonathan, you are a poet, and you can do that sort of thing, but I can't. How would you summarize these lines?"

"Perhaps I was too critical. After all, many of these stories are already summaries and it is difficult to reduce them. I did not want a detailed description or a poem. I suppose that I would say that Jacob fell in love with a beautiful girl, Rachel. He was so happy at the time of the wedding that he did not remember that Laban was a clever man. Laban was able to marry off Leah and at the same time extract another seven years from Jacob. I also remember that on the day of my wedding, Noah suggested that I look under Keziah's veil just to make certain that Gad had not tricked me. As it turned out Gad did not have a Leah."

277

Elimelech said, "I'm no poet nor the son of a poet, but this is my summary:

> Isaac was blind.
> Jacob was blind,
> Blindly in love,
> Working and waiting,
> And wanting in.
> A wedding night
> Filled with delight.
> When morning came,
> With semen spent,
> There was Leah!
> Where was Rachel?
> The deceiver was deceived.

Everyone laughed and all the tension was gone. Elimelech said, "And I would like to strike the above words from the record."

Magon said, "From the record, yes, but not from our thoughts. It is important in our epics that certain themes and situations are repeated as we go along, and we should remember this fact. 'The deceiver was deceived.' It is a nice story."

Elishama said, "Now I will move to the second part and my summary. The first line of this text is 'Yahweh saw that Leah was unloved; he opened her womb (Rachel was barren)' (Genesis 29:31). This entire story is devoted to the birth of Jacob's children. First, Leah gives birth to Reuben, Simeon, Levi, and Judah. Rachel gives her surrogate to Jacob and she has Dan and Naphtali. Then Leah uses her surrogate and produces Gad and Asher. Once again Leah begins to produce for herself. She gives birth to Issachar, Zebulun, and Dinah. Finally, Rachel's womb is opened, and she gives birth to Joseph. So, the total number is twelve.

"The third account is 'After Rachel had given birth to Joseph . . .' (Genesis 30:25a). In this part, we learn of Jacob great success. He became rich with flocks and it concludes: 'The man became very prosperous' (Genesis 30:43a).

"In the fourth part ([Jacob] heard the following words of the sons of Laban: 'Jacob has taken everything that belonged to our father; . . .' [Genesis 31:1a]), and we have the account of Jacob's flight and Laban pursuit. Laban and Jacob finally settle their problems and make a covenant. This is a long section, and I have left a lot of things out."

These Are the Stories of Isaac

Elimelech continued at this point, "The fifth story deals with Jacob's fear of Esau ('Jacob went on his way; the messengers of Elohim met him.' [Genesis 32:2]). He feared Esau so much that he prepared gifts for Esau. At the end there is a short poem:

> I will change the expression of his face,
> With the gift that goes before my face.
> Afterwards when I shall see his face,
> Perhaps he will lift up my face.'
> (Genesis 32:21)

This poem is important, because the word 'face' introduces the next section, the section on Jacob's ordeal at Peniel ('the face of god'). The first line reads, 'The gift went on before his face; . . .' (Genesis 32:22a). Here is a story that is difficult to understand. It seems that Jacob wrestled with Elohim and men, and Jacob prevailed. Also his name was changed to Israel."

Jonathan said, "I now understand why Elishama wondered if we could finish this task. It is difficult to summarize what is unclear. We need to look at this text."

Elimelech read:

> During that night, he got up and took his two wives,
> his two maidservants, and his eleven children;
> he crossed the ford of the Jabbok.
> He took them; he brought them across the stream;
> and he brought over his possessions.
>
> Jacob was left alone;
> a man wrestled with him until the break of the dawn.
> He saw that he could not prevail over him;
> he struck the socket of his hip—
> Jacob's hip socket was dislocated,
> as he wrestled with him.
> He said:
> > "Let me go, for the dawn has broken."
>
> He said:
> > "I will not let you go, unless you bless me."
>
> He said to him:
> > "What is your name?"

He said:
> "Jacob."

He said:
> "Your name shall no longer be called Jacob, but Israel,
> because you have wrestled with Elohim and men;
> you have prevailed."

Jacob asked and said:
> "Please make known your name."

He said:
> "Why is it that you asked for my name?"

He blessed him there.
Jacob called forth the name of the sanctuary, "Peniel," because [he said]:
> "I have seen Elohim face to face, and my being
> has been preserved."

The sun rose on him as he passed Penuel;
he was limping on account of his hip.

(Genesis 32:23–32)

Elishama said, "I'm not sure what this means, but I know that it is important for my people in the north. They like the story, and it makes the name Israel important."

Magon said, "I would like to make a comment on this text. It is not clear at all what happens, and Jonathan, I'm glad that you had it read. It is clear that Jacob is fearful of Esau. It is also clear that Jacob wrestles with 'a man,' but who wins? Is it a draw? As most of you know, in some courts, when the judge cannot decide a case, the two parties were commanded to wrestle. The winner of such a contest was declared innocent. In this case, Jacob is crippled, but his opponent is held down. Nevertheless, Jacob is blessed and his name is changed to Israel. This name means that 'God prevails.' These comments do not help much, because it also says that Jacob wrestled with 'Elohim and men,' and he prevailed. Somehow Jacob wins and is blessed, but the hearers know that it is really God who wins; it is Israel. I don't really understand this, but we can understand the outcome. Jacob is ready to face Esau."

Jonathan said, "Yes. That must be the point. Jacob has faced Elohim, and he is still alive; he will be able to face Esau."

Elishama said, "I have some other questions about this, but we should move on. The next story begins, 'Jacob lifted up his eyes; he saw:

These Are the Stories of Isaac

. . .' (Genesis 33:1a). In this text Jacob meets Esau. Esau comes with his troops. Jacob wants Esau to accept his gifts. At first Esau politely refuses. Then Jacob says, 'If I have found favor in your eyes, you shall accept my gift from my hand, for I saw your face—it was like seeing the face of Elohim' (Genesis 33:10a). Well Esau finally accepts the gift, and all seems well. However, Jacob wants Esau to move on. This will not be a lasting relationship."

Magon said, "I would like to point out that your first line is exactly the way we begin new sections in Ugaritic stories."

Jonathan answered, "Once again we must say that we are late comers compared to our neighbors, and it seems that we have looked to the past and to others in order to find the best way to tell a story. We may want to say something new, but we write according to the best of ancient styles."

"The next part is about Jacob's visit to Shechem. The first line is 'Jacob came in peace to the city of Shechem'" (Genesis 33:18a). Elishama continued, "This story is not the most important story of our work, but we could never leave it out. There would be a great uproar from today's citizens of Shechem. It is also important for our outline. It is here that Jacob buys some land, and of course it is here that Joseph is buried. However the story also causes some confusion. Most of the story is about the rape of Dinah, and the subsequent punishment of the citizens by Jacob's sons (Simeon and Levi). Of course the text is not clear concerning the rape, because she was also loved. But they defeated and demolished the city, and this may have started another tradition about Jacob taking Shechem by the sword. But the first tradition wherein Jacob buys his land is more important for those of us who come from Shechem. We applaud the fact that Jacob scolds his sons for their actions."

Jonathan said, "That was a good summary, and you are the only one here who could have given it. I wonder if the description of the rape of Dinah will be of interest to our people in light of the recent rape of Tamar? We don't need to answer the question, but we should keep our ears open for any post-dedication remarks on this subject."

Elimelech took over and said, "The last part before the conclusion of this cycle begins, 'Elohim said to Jacob: "Arise, go up to Bethel; settle there, and make there an altar for El . . ."' (Genesis 35:1a). With this text we have come full circle. We are back in Bethel, and in the sanctuary where Jacob made his vow. In this story, Jacob's name is changed, once again to Israel. Also Elohim renews his promise of land and says, 'Kings shall come forth from your loins' (Genesis 35:11b). This is important for our epic and for the dedication of David's palace."

Jonathan said, "Well, this gives us a picture of Jacob's or should I say Israel's journey. I want to thank both Elishama and Elimelech for their work. They have spent a great deal of time on this. So, we can do the conclusion of this cycle at our next meeting, and then we need to get Zadok to join us for the Joseph material. Magon and Gad, we were glad you were with us today, and I hope that both of you can be with us when we deal with Joseph."

On the way home, father said to Jonathan, "I enjoyed being at the meeting, but I must say that I'm a bit hungry. I wonder if Keziah will let us have a piece of bread before dinner?"

"She will if we make the dinner."

The first thing I said as they came in the door was, "I'll bet you are both hungry after such a long day. I thought you would be home about now, so I have fixed our dinner a little early. It is ready now."

"What a wonderful wife! And Gad, you just forget what I said when you said that you were hungry."

"I won't ask what you said. Did you have a good day?"

"We had a good day. We are now ready to finish the Isaac cycle. We will do it tomorrow, and then it will be the Jacob cycle with the story of Joseph."

Father said, "They did well, and now I am certain that they are going to be ready for the dedication of David's palace."

I said, "If tomorrow is an easy day, I will expect both of you to be home for an early dinner. After dinner, I want to hear the old story of Job that my dear husband promised. Will that work, dear husband?"

"It will work. But I must warn you that after telling that story, I may be in an angry mood. I will try and control myself, but you have been warned."

"We can handle the story and your mood," I replied.

Jonathan said to father, "I may need you to help me if I forget any of it."

"I'll be here, but I don't know if I'll be much help. I have another idea. If you finish the Isaac cycle tomorrow everyone will be happy. Perhaps we should invite some others to hear the old story of Job. What do you think, Jonathan?"

"I'm not sure. Some people like the story, and they would not be happy with my attitude. But if you are thinking of Elishama and Elimelech, that would be fine. If it's alright with Keziah, I'll ask them tomorrow."

"It's fine with me."

The next day Jonathan, Elishama, and Elimelech didn't have much to do, but they all wanted to do it early. They reviewed the fourth part of their outline. So, they needed to deal with Rachel's death and burial, the heirs of Jacob, and the death and burial of Isaac. They did not have much material for these last three scenes, but they had enough. Rachel died just after Benjamin was born. "She was buried on the road to Ephrath (that is Bethlehem)" (Genesis 35:19b). Elimelech noted that she was the only one that was not buried in Hebron. For the second scene, they just listed Jacob's twelve sons. The final part was also brief. They said, "Isaac expired. He died; he was gathered to his people, old and full of days. Esau and Jacob, his sons, buried him" (Genesis 35:29b). This was, in many ways like the burial of Abraham, because both Isaac and Ishmael buried him. Earlier when they had worked on the burial of Abraham, the mention of Ishmael reminded them to arrange a small section (names of the heirs) just after the burial of Abraham with the title, *These are the Stories of Ishmael*. After the burial of Isaac, they followed the same pattern and put in *These are the Stories of Esau*. The note as to where Isaac settled after the burial of Abraham came before the material on Ishmael, but with the burial of Isaac, the note as to where Jacob settled was put in after the Esau material: "Jacob settled in the land where his father sojourned—in the land of Canaan" (Genesis 37:1). After they read, this note they all shouted, "finished!"

Jonathan said, "Now we are ready to start *These are the Stories of Jacob* (Genesis 37:2a), with all the Joseph material. We will have to make sure that Zadok can attend our first meeting for this new section. I hope that he has it all worked out. This will be an important and sensitive task for us. We know that most of the material will be about Joseph, but somehow we have to make certain that there is enough focus on Judah but not too much. This must be the peoples epic."

Both Elimelech and Elishama agreed, and then Jonathan said, "Keziah, Gad, and I would like for both of you, and of course Deborah and Rachel, to come to our house tonight after dinner. We will celebrate with good wine the burial of Isaac. Not only will our house become a Bet

Marzeah, a house of mourning, but I am going to tell the ancient story of Job. Keziah has wanted to hear this for some time. I told her that the story makes me angry, but she has decided to chance it. It may not be the ideal way to celebrate the burial of Isaac and the conclusion of our work on his cycle, but we will have some fun. I know that there are many in our school who would not care for my attitude concerning the old Job story, so we are keeping the group small."

Elishama said, "We are through with our work before noon, so we will be able to make it. Thanks."

Elimelech said, "I'll be there, but let me bring Magon. He won't give you a bad time."

"That will be fine. Bring Magon."

After they left, Jonathan thought, "I'll go home and have some lunch. Then I should come back here and try to review the story of Job and my thoughts about it."

Jonathan came home, and he informed me that we would be having guests. I said, "We should have invited Ahban, but I suppose he is still at his home."

After lunch, Jonathan went back to his office. As he was working he thought, "Perhaps we should have invited Sheva and Sarah, but I really don't know where Sheva stands on some of these issues." He got out some of his notes on Job, and went over the old story several times. He finally decided that he was ready for the evening story time, and he walked over to the old school to see Zadok. He found Zadok is his office.

Jonathan said, "*Shalom*, my friend. How are you these days?"

"I'm fine, but I still worry about Ahban. He is better, but he still is not back at work."

"How are things here in the school?"

"We are doing alright, and I must say that we are thankful for your support. Noah and Danel have helped us in many ways."

"And how is your work on the Joseph story coming along?"

"Most of the work has been finished, and it is ready for review. I want to say that I really did not do much. I followed Elishama's text, and Ahban helped me at every turn. He suggested the project to me, and he has guided me all the way to the finish."

"This is great news, because we are ready to deal with this material for our royal epic. Can you meet with us any time soon?"

"I can't meet tomorrow, but after tomorrow I could be with you for the rest of the week. I'll give you my copy of the text, and tomorrow you can go over it with Elishama and Elimelech."

"This is the good news—like meat for starving nomads."

"Here take this copy, and I'm leaving now to visit Ahban. That's where I'll be tomorrow."

"*Todah rabbah*. I hope that I have not delayed your departure."

"No."

Jonathan took the text back to his office, and then he came home. He had to tell me the good news about the Joseph text.

38

The Story of Job

JONATHAN SAID TO ME, "This was a wonderful day. We finished the Isaac cycle and talked about what we had to do next with the Joseph story. We mentioned that we would have to get Zadok to come to our meetings. When I went to see Zadok, I did not know that he was finished. He cannot meet with us tomorrow, but he will be with us during the rest of the week. This is great. Tomorrow we will go over the text, and then we will be ready to discuss it when Zadok gets back. Today he went to see Ahban, and he will spend most of tomorrow with him. Also today as we were finishing the Isaac cycle we had to deal with the burial of Isaac. So I told the others that tonight we would have lots of wine and celebrate the life of Isaac in our own little Bet Marzeah. I added that I did not know how to make the story of Job fit into a funeral-drinking feast, but the others thought that we could solve that problem. In any case the mood for tonight is going to be happy."

I said, "But how will you solve the problem? I'm glad you are happy, but you warned us that the Job story would make you angry."

"I'm going to let the wine help me stay happy. I warned you and Gad when I thought that we would be three, but with guests I will not be angry. I may be caustic but not angry. Even so the Job story may not fit the occasion. But wait, it does fit, because Job mourns the death of his children for seven days and seven nights. So we will have a wake for Isaac and for Job's children."

"Jonathan, you always work your way out of such problems. Why don't you call father, and then we will eat. We need to get finished and on with the party."

We ate, and father and Jonathan cleaned things up while I nursed Naam. He was really growing. I thought, "I hope that Naam goes to sleep before the guests arrive. Perhaps Deborah can also get Rachel to sleep."

The Story of Job

Soon everyone was here, and both babies were asleep. Jonathan made certain that everyone had a full cup. Elimelech said, "Well we buried Isaac today, and now lets drink to him. We should do this for seven days. Right?"

Jonathan said, "You may be right, but we don't have time. I got the Joseph material from Zadok today. We will look at it tomorrow but later in the morning than usual."

Elishama said, "That is good news. Let's drink to Joseph."

Elimelech said, "This means that we will finish before the dedication. At that point, we can drink for seven days!"

Jonathan said, "I'll drink to that. Now, at Isaac's funeral we should really read or sing about Isaac, but since we have heard enough just lately about Isaac, and because Keziah has requested it, I want to tell you about another funeral. The funeral that I am talking about is the funeral for Job's children. So, in just a moment we can fill our cups again.

"The story of Job is old, and I know it has many forms. The way I will tell it is of course the best, and that makes it the worst. This may sound confusing, but you will soon get the point. The story goes this way:

> There was a man in the land of Uz; his name was Job. That man was perfect and upright, one who feared Elohim and avoided evil. Seven sons and three daughters were born to him. His property was seven thousand sheep, three thousand camels, five hundred donkeys, five hundred yoke of oxen, and many servants. That man was greater than any of the Bene-qedem. His sons would go and make a feast in the house of each one on his day. They would send and invite their three sisters to eat and drink with them. When the days of the feast had gone around, Job would send [a message]; he would sanctify them. He would rise early in the morning; he would offer burnt offerings, as many as all of them, for Job said: "Perhaps my children have sinned and cursed Elohim in their minds." Thus would Job do all the time. (Job 1:1–5)
>
> [One day Yahweh decided to test his servant Job. He said, "If I take from my servant Job all that I have given to him, will he remain perfect and upright? Or will he curse me to my face?"]
>
> One day when his sons and his daughters were eating and were drinking wine in the house of their firstborn brother, a messenger came to Job; he said:

"The oxen were plowing,
And the donkeys were grazing beside them.
The Sabeans attacked; they took them,
And they devoured the plowmen with the sword.
I have escaped, only I alone, to tell you."
This one was still speaking, and another one came;
he said:
"The fire of Elohim fell from the heavens.
It burned the flocks and the shepherds.
It consumed them.
I have escaped, only I alone, to tell you."
This one was still speaking, and another one came; he said:
"The Chaldeans formed three columns;
They raided the camels; they took them.
And they devoured the cameleers with the sword.
I have escaped, only I alone, to tell you."
This one was still speaking, and another one came; he said:
"Your sons and your daughters
Were eating and drinking wine
In the house of their firstborn brother,
When a great wind came from across the wilderness.
It struck the four corners of the house.
It fell upon the young people. They died.
I have escaped, only I alone, to tell you."
Job got up; he tore his robe; he shaved his head; he fell to the ground; he worshiped.
He said:
"Naked I came out from the womb of my mother,
And naked I shall return there.
Yahweh gave, and Yahweh took away.
Blessed be the name of Yahweh."
From all of this, Job did not sin; he did not cast reproach on Elohim.
(Job 1:13–22)

[One day, after Job had lost everything, Yahweh thought, "Job did not sin, but what if I touch his bone and flesh? Will he at that point curse me to my face? So, Yahweh afflicted Job with horrible sores from the sole of his foot to his head.]

He took a potsherd with which to scrape himself, and he was the one who sat in the midst of the ashes.

The Story of Job

His wife said to him:
> "Do you still hold fast to your integrity?
> Curse God and die."

Job said to her:
> "You speak as one of the foolish women might talk.
> Should we, indeed, accept the good from this God,
> And not accept the evil?"

From all of this, Job did not sin with his lips.

The three friends of Job heard of all this evil that had come upon him. They came each from his place, Eliphaz the Temanite, Bildad the Shuhite, and Zophar the Naamathite. They arranged together to go to console him and to comfort him. They lifted up their eyes from afar; they did not recognize him; they lifted up their voices; they wept. Each one tore his robe. They threw dust heavenward upon their heads. They sat with him on the earth, seven days and seven nights. No one spoke a word for they saw that the suffering was very great. (Job 2:8–13)

Jonathan said, "We need a break and my cup is empty. We should at least drink to the memory of the children."

I said, "I should say so. The loss of the children far exceeds the pain of Job's boils as far as I'm concerned."

Elimelech said, "The speech of a good mother. Let's drink to all good mothers."

Magon said, "When we were together last, I mentioned that Keret lost all his family, and in our story of Danel there is a similar loss. This seems to be a popular way to begin a story."

Jonathan said, "It does get your attention. I read this first part word for word. In the next section, I'll not give all of the details; it would take too long. However at the end, I can go back to reading the text."

Now Jonathan continued the story:

"[The three friends, after seven days and seven nights of silence, spoke to Job. They told him that his sufferings were unjust. They said, 'Your wife is right. Curse God and die!' Now, Job thought that they were as foolish as his wife. Job said that he would never agree with them.] His lips would never speak evil, and he would maintain his integrity (Job 27:4–5). Job must maintain his righteousness, because the impious has no hope (Job 27:8).

"At this point Job begins a long speech and then rests his case (Job 29-31). In this speech, Job recalls his former life when his children were with him, and God was his friend (Job 29:4 –5). He remembers how he cared for the widow and the orphan. He lived like a king. But then his entire world collapsed. He no longer comforts mourners. Rather he mourns; his lyre has turned to mourning (Job 30:31). Perhaps Job should not have spent so much time remembering how great he was, because the comparison with his present devastation was overpowering. Next he swears that he has never committed a long list of sins; he has always been a caring person. However, he is finally overcome by his suffering. After all, he is righteous and innocent. His lips do not curse God, but finally he did make a mistake. He demanded a hearing before God his judge. Notice these words: 'Who will give [someone] to me? Who will listen to me? Here is my signature; Shaddai answer me. My accuser has written a document' (Job 31:35). Here the ancient Job is actually not so patient. Perhaps he goes too far.

"Responding to the demands of Job, 'Yahweh answered Job from out of the storm' (Job 38:1). Yahweh takes Job to court. He tells him to 'gird up,' to put on his belt. Yahweh implies that he will defeat Job; he will strip his belt or cord from him (a fact which Job has already mentioned Job 30:11), and this wrestling victory means that Yahweh is indeed the innocent one. Job's demands proceed from ignorance. The creator asks Job a series of questions concerning the creation. Job cannot answer. He does not know how the world was ordered or how it all works. Then God asked if Job who contended with Shaddai would give up (Job 40:2). Job cannot answer, so God continues to ask questions.

"Finally Job was ready to respond. He said, 'I know that you can do all things' (Job 42:2a), and in the end Job repents 'in dust and ashes' (Job 42:6). In the face of God's power, Job repented."

After Yahweh had spoken these words to Job, Yahweh said to Eliphaz the Temanite:

> "My anger is inflamed against you and against your two friends, for you have not spoken correctly about me, as did my servant Job. So now, take for yourselves seven bulls and seven rams and go to my servant Job and sacrifice a burnt offering for yourselves, and Job, my servant, will pray for you, for I will lift up his face, so that I will not be harsh with you, for you have not spoken correctly about me, as did my servant Job."

Eliphaz the Temanite, Bildad the Shuhite, and Zophar the Naamathite went and did as Yahweh had instructed them. Yahweh lifted up the face of Job. Yahweh restored the fortune of Job when he prayed for his friends. Yahweh doubled everything that Job owned. All his brothers, all his sisters, and all his former acquaintances came to him. They ate food with him in his house; they consoled and com forted him for all the evil that Yahweh had inflicted on him. They gave him, each one, one *qesitah* and each one, one golden ring.

So, Yahweh blessed the later [days] of Job more than his former [ones]. He had fourteen thousand sheep, six thousand camels, a thousand yoke of oxen, and a thousand donkeys. He had seven sons and three daughters. He called forth the name of the first, 'Jemimah, and the name of the second, 'Keziah,' and the name of the third, 'Kerenhappuk,' and no women were to be found in all the earth as beautiful as the daughters of Job. Their father gave them an inheritance together with their brothers. After this Job lived one hundred forty years. He saw his children and grandchildren to four generations. Job died, old and satisfied with life. (Job 42:7–17)

Jonathan continued, "So here we have the old story of Job, a story of a righteous man who was tested by God. He was afflicted with evil, but he remained righteous. Not so his wife and friends. Job almost lost out when he made his demands known to Shaddai. He wanted an answer. Well God answered in his mighty role as the creator. Job was crushed beneath the weight of this encounter. He repented and was forgiven. God lifted up his face. But best of all, everything was restored and better than before. It pays to be righteous.

"There is only one good thing about this story. It does say that Keziah is one of the three, the three most beautiful women on earth. My cup is empty again."

So we took a break, and we all filled our cups. I came over to Jonathan and said, "Thanks for the compliment, my dear husband, but we will have no discussions about the meaning of my name."

"I was not going to do that, besides everyone knows what it means."

"Fine. However, when we are alone you can remind me of the meaning."

After a bit, it was clear that there were questions to be asked and opinions to be expressed. Jonathan said, "We can discuss this story, and then I want to tell you a little bit about my poem on Job."

I said, "What's so bad about being rich?"

Father said, "I should answer that one, because I see her tongue in her cheek. It's not 'so bad' to be rich, but it is a big mistake to think that if you are righteous you will be rich. The fact is that most rich people are not righteous. Also it does not follow that the pious are rewarded and the impious are punished. It is a popular theory and that's all. To move from Keziah's question just a little, I want to say that I could not count how many times people have said to me when they found out about the death of my wife, 'Perhaps God was testing you or could he be punishing you? These remarks are really out of order."

Magon said, "I have had the same experience after the death of my wife. People should know that we live in a difficult world. It may be wonderful in many ways, but it is difficult. I want to thank Jonathan for sharing this story, and some of you know that there are some remarkable parallels in Babylonian stories. We have the poem of the righteous sufferer that goes by its first line *Ludlul bel nemeqi* (I will praise the Lord of Wisdom) where a righteous man suffers, and finally Marduk restores all. There is another text about a righteous sufferer, and he has a long debate with a 'friend.' Neither text really solves the problem of why the just suffer."

Jonathan said, "I plan to write my poem in the form of a debate which will be like your second example."

Elimelech said, "It seems as if the story is everywhere. It is natural and popular to blame the gods and hence fear the gods or on the other hand to thank the gods. It will be difficult to do away with this kind of thinking."

Jonathan said, "You are correct, but we can put forward another option."

Elishama said, "That would be a worthwhile project, but you know that some people are past changing."

"I know, but as Keziah and I say such an effort can at least go into our *Minority Report*. It will be a work for the future. It will be for a few of Magon's students. Right?"

Magon said, "I am still hoping."

Jonathan said, "Let me tell you what I'm planning. This is not an easy thing. I have been working on it for a long time, and I have a long way to go. I know that my poem will be in the form of a debate or dialogue. I know how I will start it, and how I will end it, but I am not ready to complete the poem. I need more experience; I need more living; and I will need your help. Your remarks this evening make my point. You have said it will be a difficult task. This poem has to be so good; it has to be able to crush and destroy the old story of Job. In this poem I will turn everything upside down. Job will be a rebel, the friends will be orthodox and pious, and there will be no happy ending. Why? Because there is no justice in our world. In this world, the imperative is to help the one who suffers and to love."

Elishama said, "Will you turn the friend's God upside down?"

Jonathan said, "The answer is yes, but the 'yes' is a complicated one. The rebel Job does not believe in the God of the 'friends.' That God cannot be found; he does not exist. But at the same time, that God can haunt one in the dark of the night."

I said, "Jonathan, you have told me how you will end the poem, but I would like to know how it will start?"

"The poem will have to presuppose the collapse of Job's world. That will have to be shown, but I don't know how. I will respond at great length to Job's demand to confront his judge. My Job will make the same demands but with fear and stronger language, and my Job will never repent. But, the first thing that my Job will do is to curse the day of his birth. All of this curse is not worked out yet, but he begins it by saying:

> Perish the day on which I was born;
> The night that said, "A hero is conceived."
> (Job 3:3)

"The presupposition is that Job has already lost everything, and to curse his day is his first response. During this curse he asks things like, 'Why did I not die at birth?' Since you have mentioned the ending, I will give that as well. In the end my poem also speaks of God as the creator, but the results are not the same. No one is overpowered:

> By his power he stilled the Sea;
> By his cunning he smashed Rahab.
> By his wind the heavens were cleared;
> [By] his hand he pierced the fleeing Serpent.
> Lo, these are just traces of his rule;
> What a whisper of a word we hear from him;
> Who can understand the thunder of his might?
> (Job 26:12–14)

"I will accept help from any of you on this project, and I hope that it is finished before I am forced to ask Naam and Rachel for help. Whenever I work on this poem, I keep the following three lines before me:

> In the mouths of the righteous,
> In the words of the pious,
> Truth is inconspicuous.

"There's more wine, so don't run off."

Magon came over and said to Jonathan, "We'll have to keep in touch on your debate form, because the Babylonian text will help."

"I'll keep in touch."

Soon, most everyone was gone. It was late. Father said, "That was a fine evening, and I was proud of you. You didn't get angry."

"Being with friends helped me to control my anger."

I said, "After the royal epic and the dedication, I hope that you can do more work on your Job poem. You can do it. What is difficult for me is to understand how you can present it to the public, or how it will ever have the chance to crush the old story of Job?"

Jonathan said, "Your question is also mine, and I don't have an answer."

39

These Are the Stories of Jacob

As promised, Jonathan arrived at the office later than usual. The others were still not there. This gave Jonathan some time to look at Zadok's work on the Joseph materials. He thought, "It looks to me like a finished work. We may not have to do much to it. I hope that Elishama brings the Shechem text that he worked on. We will need to compare it with Zadok's work." Just then Elishama and Elimelech arrived. Jonathan said, "Zadok will not be with us until tomorrow. Elishama do you have your text of the Joseph stories?"

"No. I loaned my text to Zadok after he got started on his project. He will probably bring it with him tomorrow."

"That will be fine. We will just go over Zadok's work, and I'm certain that we will have many thoughts and questions. I expect it to be a good work, and he has already told us that most of his changes were additions that would promote the unity of Israel and Judah. So, the main question is how are we going to do this? It will take us the rest of the morning just to read it"

Elimelech said, "Just start by summarizing, and we can take turns."

"The first part deals with Joseph before he is taken to Egypt. After the title, *These Are the Stories of Jacob* (Genesis 37:2), almost every word deals with one of our main points in the outline. The elder will serve the younger. Joseph has the royal robe; he has his perfect speech, and he has dreams in which he will one day rule his older brothers. The brothers decide to kill Joseph, but Reuben objects. The murder of Joseph is at least delayed, and they throw him into a pit. Judah suggests that it makes more sense to sell Joseph to some Ishmaelite traders, but another group of traders finds Joseph, and they sell him to the Ishmaelites. Joseph is on his way to Egypt."

The Jerusalem Academy

Elishama said, "In the text we made in Shechem and that we used in the second coronation, Reuben objects, but this suggestion of Judah's to sell Joseph is new. Read that part for us:

> They sat down to eat a meal; they lifted up their eyes; they saw:[7] there was a caravan of Ishmaelites coming from Gilead. Their camels were carrying gum, balm, and resin; they were making a run down to Egypt.
>
> Judah said to his brothers, "Where is [the] profit if we kill our brother and if we cover his blood? Come, we will sell him to the Ishmaelites; our hands will not touch him, for he is our brother; he is our flesh."
>
> His brothers agreed. (Genesis 37:25–27)

Elishama continued, "This is one of Zadok's additions, and it does help to have Judah come up with such a plan. But Jacob still has to face the tragic end of Joseph. He is given the robe of Joseph, which was dipped in the blood of a goat. There is no body and no burial. This was always a sad moment in our rituals at the tomb of Joseph in Shechem."

"I can believe it," said Jonathan. "Also, I am interested in your comment that we have here one of Zadok's additions. This is an important addition, and it gives me an idea. Before we go on I would like to ask you both to think about something. I have glanced at some of the material that we will be reading. I know that Zadok has made Judah important in this story, but I still think we should at least include the first part of *These Are the Stories of Judah*, that is, the part that we used at the coronations. After all in this story of Joseph, we will learn about the birth of Joseph's sons. It would not hurt to also learn about the sons of Judah. This is important for us, because this line leads to David. My question is where would we put such a section? We could do it at the beginning, just before the section that I discussed. Or we could insert it at the end of that section. In other words, we could insert it as the next part."

Elimelech said, "If we insert it now, the story of Joseph is interrupted. Who wants to wait to see what happened to Joseph?"

Elishama said, "I would not like it at the beginning, and I also hate to interrupt the Joseph story at this point."

Jonathan said, "I can understand what you are saying, but my arguments for putting it right here before going ahead are two: 1) With Zadok's addition, Judah has just been mentioned in the story, and this insertion of the first part of *These Are the Stories of Judah* at this point would give the audience more material on Judah. 2) This would happen while Joseph was on his way to Egypt. We don't want him to get there too soon. Just think about these things. This also needs to be explained to Zadok, and I will not make any decision without him."

Elishama took over at this point. He said, "This next part is like the other cycles in that it has to do with Joseph's endangerment and success, his rise from poverty to power. His master's wife put an end to his success, at least for the time being. This part of the story reads as follows:

> Joseph was well built and good looking.
> It was after these events that the wife of his master lifted up her eyes to Joseph; she said, "Lie with me."
> He refused! He said to the wife of his master: "Here is my master; he does not have common knowledge with me [about] what is in the house; all his possessions he has put under my supervision. He is not greater in this house than I; he has not withheld anything from me except you, because you are his wife. How could I commit this great crime? [How could] I offend Elohim?"
> This was her word to Joseph day after day, but he did not listen to her [propositions] to lie beside her, to be with her. One such day, he came into the house to do his work. There was no one from the household personnel there in the house.
> She caught hold of him by his garment, saying, "Lie with me."
> He left his garment in her hand; he fled; he went outside.
> When she saw that he had left his garment in her hand (he had fled outside), she summoned the personnel of her house; she said to them the following: "See, he had to bring us a Hebrew to have sex with us; he came to me to lie with me. I called out with a terrible scream. When he heard that I screamed and called out, he left his garment beside me; he fled; he went outside.
> She kept his garment beside her until her master came home; she told him about these events as follows: "The Hebrew slave, whom you brought to us, came to me to have sex with me. When I screamed and called out, he left his garment beside me; he fled outside."
> When his master heard the words of his wife that she spoke to him, namely, "about these things that your slave did to me," his anger flared up. Joseph's master took him; he put him in prison (the place where the royal prisoners were confined). (Genesis 39:6b–20)

Elishama continued, "There is an interesting point in these lines. This is the second time that Joseph has lost his garment. When he gives up his garment he gives up his power and position. Trouble will soon follow.

"I will give a summary of the next section which covers Joseph's experience in prison. Even here, Yahweh is with him, and he is successful.

He successfully interpreted the dreams of the 'cupbearer' and the 'baker,' but the cupbearer forgot about Joseph when he was free, and Joseph remained in prison for another two years. Then Pharaoh had a dream or rather two dreams. Pharaoh was disturbed by his dreams and by the fact that none of the wise men could interpret them. It was then that the cupbearer remembered Joseph:

> The head of the cupbearers spoke with Pharaoh saying: "Today, I have remembered my offenses. Pharaoh was angry with his servants; he put me in the jail on the estate of the head of the stewards, me and the head of the bakers. We had dreams during the same night, he and I; we had [dreams, and] each one had its own meaning. A Hebrew youth was there with us, a servant of the head of the stewards; we recounted [our dreams] to him; he interpreted our dreams for us—he interpreted [for] each according to his dream. Then just as he had interpreted for us, so it was: I was restored to my position, and [the other] was hanged."
> (Genesis 41:9–13)

Pharaoh immediately summoned Joseph. The messengers brought him from the 'pit.' It is interesting that the text has the word 'pit' instead of 'prison.' This reminds the audience that Joseph has been thrown into a 'pit' two times, once by his brothers and once by his master, Potiphar. Joseph shaved, cleaned up, changed his clothes, and came before Pharaoh. Pharaoh told Joseph his dreams, and Joseph interpreted them. The two dreams were really just one. Pharaoh's dream meant that Egypt would have seven years of abundance and then seven years of famine. Then Joseph said, 'And now, let Pharaoh look for a man of understanding and wisdom and put him in charge of the land of Egypt' (Genesis 41:33). This person would see to it that the Egyptians saved their food during the years of abundance for the lean years. Now back to the text:

> Pharaoh said to his officials, "Can we find a man who has the spirit of Elohim in him like this one?"
> Pharaoh said to Joseph, "Since Elohim informed you with all this, there is no one [with] understanding and wisdom like you. You shall be in charge of my palace and on your order my troops will be armed. Only [with respect to] the throne shall I be superior to you."
> Pharaoh said to Joseph, "See, I have put you in charge of all the land of Egypt."
> Pharaoh removed his signet ring from his hand; he put it on the hand of Joseph. He dressed him in linen robes and put the gold chain about his neck. He had him ride in the chariot of his second

in-command; they called out before him, "Attention." He put him in charge of all the land of Egypt.

Pharaoh said to Joseph, "I am Pharaoh, but without your [approval] a person shall not raise hand or foot in all the land of Egypt. Pharaoh called forth Joseph's name, "Zaphenath-paneah."

He gave him Asenath, the daughter of Poti-phera (priest of On), for a wife. Joseph went out in charge of the land of Egypt. (Genesis 41:38–45)

"Well once again Joseph has a royal robe, and he is in power. Everything happened as Joseph had predicted, and the entire earth came to Egypt to buy grain. In this section there is one note that we must not forget:

> Before the years of the famine came, two sons were born to Joseph, whom Asenath, the daughter of Poti-phera (priest of On), bore to him.
>
> Joseph called forth the name of the firstborn, "'Manasseh,' because [he continued], Elohim has made me forget all my troubles and all about my father's house."
>
> He called forth the name of the second one, "'Ephraim,' because [he continued], Elohim has made me fruitful in the land of my suffering." (Genesis 41:50–52)

Jonathan said, "Elishama, you reviewed this in a masterful way. It is clear that you really know this material. So, is Zadok's text about the same as yours?"

"This seems to be identical, but I do not expect any more changes until later when Joseph interacts with his brothers."

"That makes sense. Elimelech can you take over for the next section?"

"I can, but we both know that it would go faster with Elishama."

Elishama said, "Thanks, but I will look on the text with you, and I may see some of Zadok's changes."

Elimelech said, "The next part concerns Jacob and his sons. Jacob has heard that there is grain in Egypt that they could buy. So, he sent Joseph's ten brothers to buy grain. Joseph's younger brother, Benjamin, stayed at home. Joseph was in charge of selling the grain. When his brothers came before him, he recognized his brothers, but they did not recognize him. Joseph accused his brothers of being spies, and this is their reply:

> They said, "We, your servants, were twelve brothers, the sons of one man in the land of Canaan, but the youngest is at this time with our father, and the [other] one is no more." (Genesis 42:13)

The Jerusalem Academy

But Joseph wants to test them. He keeps Simeon and sends them home with their grain and silver. They are to bring back to Joseph their youngest brother to verify their words. They must do this for the release of Simeon and to be able to trade in Egypt. But Jacob tells them that he will not consent.

> Jacob said, "My son shall not go down with you, for his brother is dead, and he alone is left. Disaster would encompass him on the journey which you are taking; you will send my white head down to Sheol in sorrow." (Genesis 42:38)

Elimelech said, "I do not know this material."

Elishama said, "That's alright. Again there are no new additions here. However, Jonathan, in light of your old story of Job, this section is interesting. The brothers say that they are guilty for what they did to Joseph, and now they are being punished. But I think you implied that the guilty usually do just fine."

Jonathan said, "Yes they do, but this kind of situation could give rise to a punishment theory. And certain acts do carry with them predictable consequences. If someone does wrong, any bad luck after that time must be punishment, so they think. Of course the opposite claim is even worse. In this second situation, the good things that happen are credited to their righteousness. This popular belief that the wicked will perish and that the righteous will prevail is everywhere. And as we said last night, it will not be an easy task to crush it. It is in the old story of Job, but that is just the beginning. It is now in all of our literature and in our minds.

"What interests me in this section is that Reuben offers his two sons to Jacob. He is obviously certain that he can protect Benjamin. But it appears that Jacob still does not trust Reuben (or perhaps anyone). Reuben certainly fractured his relationship with his father when he went to bed with Bilhah, his father's concubine or rather Rachel's surrogate. Nevertheless, Reuben has been attempting to win back his position as Jacob firstborn."

Elishama said that he wanted to do the next section. He said, "In the next section, I note some additions that are important. Also, It seems as if Jacob has forgotten the rules that Joseph had put down for them. Once again, Jacob told the brothers to go down to get food. Now in the text that I have worked with, it just has the brothers reminding Jacob of the situation, but in Zadok's text, it is Judah who speaks:

> Judah said to him: "The man threatened us, saying, 'You shall not see my face unless your brother is with you!' If you are one who is able

to send our brother with us, we will go down and buy food for you; if you are not one who is able to send [him], we will not go down, for the man said to us, 'You shall not see my face unless your brother is with you!'"

Israel said: "Why did you betray me by telling the man that you had another brother?"

They said: "The man kept asking about us and our family, saying, 'Is your father still alive? Have you [another] brother?' We were forced to answer these questions. How could we possibly have known that he would say, 'Bring down your brother!'"

Judah said to Israel, his father: "Send the boy with me! We will get ready; we will go; we will live and not die—we, you, and even our toddlers. I personally will be liable for him; you shall hold me responsible for him: if I do not bring him back to you and set him before you, I shall stand condemned before you all the days [of my life]. If we had not wasted time, we could have made two return trips by now."

Israel, their father, said to them: "If this is the case, then do this: take some of the choice products of the land in your bags; take down a gift for the man: a little balm, a little honey, gum, resin, pistachios, and almonds. Take double the silver with you; you shall take back with you the silver that was returned in the mouths of your sacks; perhaps it was a mistake. Take your brother! Get ready and return to the man. May El Shaddai grant you mercy before the man; may he set free your other brother for you along with Benjamin. As for me, when I am bereaved, I am bereaved!" (Genesis 43:3–14)

Elishama said, "Judah's first speech, in my text, was just introduced with 'They said to him' and there was nothing where Judah's second speech appears. I would say that Judah's second speech is an important one. He says that he will be liable for Benjamin, and in this case, Jacob's 'no' to Reuben is replaced by his 'yes' to Judah. This should help the south appreciate this northern story."

Jonathan said, "I agree with you. Zadok's additions here are important. Also, I think Zadok has not just invented all of these additions. I remember hearing this last speech of Judah's in a performance in Hebron some years ago. Ahban may have put Zadok on to this."

Elimelech said, "I have heard it that way as well."

Elishama said, "We are all learning something today. I will go on with this section. The brothers go to Egypt and everything seems to go quite well. In fact, Joseph puts on a big party for them, and he is overcome when he meets Benjamin. Joseph had to go into another room; he wept there. So they had a great feast, and the last words are: 'They drank; they got drunk with him'" (Genesis 43:34b).

Elishama continued, "Now Joseph still had another test for them. Later that night Joseph spoke to his man. He said, 'Fill the sacks of the men with food; put each one's silver in his sack; and you shall put my cup in the youngest one's sack.' Later Joseph's man was sent to overtake the brothers. He told them that he had to find the cup, and the one among you with whom it is found will die. The cup was found in Benjamin's sack. So they had to return to Joseph's villa; they were worried:

> Judah came closer to him and said: "O my lord, please allow your servant to speak a word [only] for the ears of my lord; do not be angry with your servant, for you are equal to Pharaoh. My lord asked his servants, 'Have you a father or [another] brother?' We said to my lord, 'We have an elderly father and [there is] a child of [his] old age, [the] youngest, and his brother is dead; he alone is left from his mother, and his father loves him.' You said to your servants, 'Bring him down to me; I will look after him.' We said to my lord, 'The boy cannot leave his father; [if] he leaves his father, he will die.' You said to your servants, 'Unless your youngest brother comes down with you, never again shall you see my face.' Then we went north to your servant, my father. We reported to him the words of my lord. [Later] our father said, 'Return and buy for us a little food.' We said, 'We cannot go down! If our youngest brother is with us, we can go down, for we cannot see the man's face if our youngest brother is not with us.' Your servant, our father, said to us, 'You know that my wife bore two [sons] for me. The one left me, I said, he must have been torn up! And I have not seen him since. You would take this one from me as well? Disaster would encompass him. You will send my white head down to Sheol in grief.' And now, when I come to your servant, my father, and the boy is not with us (his life is bound with his life), and when he sees that the boy has vanished, he will die! Your servants will send the white head of your servant, our father, down to Sheol in sorrow, for your servant has taken responsibility for the boy from my father, saying, if I do not bring him back to you, I shall stand condemned before my father all the days [of my life]. And now, please let your servant remain in the boy's place [as] the slave of my lord; let the boy go north with his brothers, for how can I go to my father if the boy is not with me? In that case I would witness the woe that would seek out my father." (Genesis 44:18–34)

These Are the Storeis of Jacob

Elishama said, "Here Judah is clearly the leader of the brothers. In my text, after they are brought back, it just says, 'The brothers entered Joseph's villa.' Here we have 'Judah and his brothers . . . .' In my text, after Joseph speaks, I am almost certain that it says, 'They said: . . . .' But once again, in this account we have 'Judah.' He is the spokesman. As for the long speech that Judah makes to Joseph, I have never seen it before. It is good, and it works."

Jonathan said, "I have heard this long speech, but I do not remember if it is exactly the same. But it must be from the same source as his earlier speech, because this long speech refers back to his vow to his father. In any case, Judah becomes extremely important in dealing with this crisis. At this point the story turns. In the very next lines, Joseph makes himself known to his brothers. I will carry on:

> And Joseph was not able to control himself before all his attendants, he cried out, "Everyone leave me!" So no one was attending him when Joseph made himself known to his brothers. (Genesis 45:1)

Jonathan said, "Next Pharaoh ordered Joseph to send his brothers back to Canaan with wagons, gifts, and supplies, so that Jacob could bring all of his family to Egypt. Then it says:

> They went north from Egypt; they entered the land of Canaan [and came] to their father Jacob.
> They told him: "Joseph is still alive!" And that he is the one who rules in all the land of Egypt.
> His mind became numb, for he did not believe them. They repeated to him all the words of Joseph that he had spoken to them. He saw the wagons that Joseph sent to transport him. The spirit of Jacob, their father, revived.
> Israel said, "Enough! Joseph, my son, is still alive; I must go; I will see him before I die." (Genesis 45:25–28)

Jonathan said, "The next part has to do with the journey to Egypt, and I want you to notice that once again the main journey departs from a shrine (as with Jacob's much earlier journey):

> Israel departed with all that belonged to him. When he entered Beer-sheba, he offered sacrifices to the God of his father Isaac.
> Elohim spoke to Israel in a vision of the night; he said: "Jacob, Jacob!"
> [Jacob] said: "Here am I."

The Jerusalem Academy

> He said: "I am the God, the God of your father. You shall not fear going down to Egypt, for I will make you into a great people there. I, I will go down with you to Egypt; I, I will even bring you up again, and Joseph shall put his hand upon your eyes." (Genesis 46:1–4)

Jonathan continued, "The rest of this section lists the names of those who belong to the house of Jacob, seventy in all. Then there is the scene where Joseph greets his father:

> [Israel] sent Judah ahead of him to Joseph to give directions before his [arrival] in Goshen. They arrived in the land of Goshen. Joseph hitched up his chariot; he went up to meet his father, Israel, in Goshen. He saw him; he fell upon his shoulders; he wept on his shoulders incessantly. Israel said to Joseph, "Now let me die since I have seen your face; [I have seen] that you are still alive." (Genesis 46:28–30)

Jonathan said, "The story of Joseph is almost over. Now we have mixed accounts of Joseph's brothers meeting Pharaoh plus Jacob's audience with Pharaoh. Also there is some material on how Joseph took care of the people, feeding them but also gaining their lands for Pharaoh. After being in Egypt for seventeen years, Jacob is close to death, but two important things happen before that event which is the beginning of the conclusion. The first event is the blessing of Joseph and his sons. We know this passage well, and we used it in our second coronation. As we have discussed before, this is the classic passage which shows how Joseph's sons were to 'call forth' the names of the fathers in order to be blessed, and we know now that they did 'call forth' the names and at the same time remembered and told many of these stories that we are collecting ('My name and the names of my fathers, Abraham and Isaac, shall be called forth by them' [Genesis 48:16b]). The second event has to do with Jacob's final words to the twelve. Some of the brothers receive only a few words from Jacob, but both Joseph and Judah have rather long passages. We should read these. First Judah:

> Judah, you really are!
> Your brothers shall praise you—
> Your hand is on the neck of your foes;
> The sons of your father shall bow down to you.
> A lion's cub was Judah;
> On prey, my son, you have grown up.
> He lay down; like a lion he crouched,
> And as an old lion, who will rouse him?

These Are the Storeis of Jacob

> The scepter shall not pass from Judah,
> Nor the staff from between his feet.
> So tribute shall be brought to him;
> His shall be [the] homage of peoples.
> He is the one, who ties his colt to the vine,
> His donkey's colt to the choicest vine.
> He washes his garment in the wine,
> In blood of grapes his robe.
> [His] eyes are darker than wine;
> [His] teeth are whiter than milk. (Genesis 49:8–12)

"And next, Joseph:

> Joseph is a colt of a wild ass,
> A colt of a wild ass by a spring—
> Wild colts by Shur.
> Archers bitterly attacked him;
> They shot and assaulted him.
> His bow was always steady;
> His arms were quickened,
> From the power of the Abir of Jacob,
> From that of the Shepherd, the Rock of Israel,
> From the God of your father, he helps you,
> And from Shaddai, he blesses you:
> Blessings of heaven above,
> Blessings of the deep, who crouches below,
> Blessings of breasts and womb,
> Blessings of your father, they are mighty.
> In addition, blessings of ancient mountains,
> Delights of eternal hills.
> May these be on the head of Joseph,
> On the pate of the leader of his brothers." (Genesis 49:22–26)

Elishama said, "These two texts say important things about each father. However, Judah is clearly the ruler, and yet, Joseph is certainly blessed. So now we just have the conclusion of the Jacob cycle starting with the death and burial of Jacob. Here the conclusion is longer than in some of the others. First we have Jacob's charge to the brothers and then his death and burial. He charged them to bury him in the cave that Abraham bought from Ephron the Hittite. So after his death they had to take him to the land of Canaan. They first went to the threshing floor of Atad that is beyond the Jordan for seven days of mourning. Then they carried him to the land of Canaan and buried him in the cave of the field of the Machpelah (Genesis 49:29—50:14).

Jonathan said, "This is the best account we have of a two-stage funeral. In many cases, the first stage of mourning is at the threshing floor and then the second stage is held at a temple or burial cave. Now after the death and burial of Jacob, you will note that we deal with the second part of the conclusion (a word about the heirs). However, this time it is mainly just a word of comfort by Joseph to his brothers. Next we come to the conclusion of the Jacob cycle, that is the death of Joseph, and of course this is the conclusion of our royal epic, at least for now. Let's read it:

> Joseph settled in Egypt, he and the house of his father. Joseph lived a hundred and ten years. Joseph saw the sons of the third [generation] of Ephraim; also the sons of Machir-ben-Manasseh were born on the knees of Joseph.
>
> Joseph said to his brothers: "I am about to die. Elohim will surely visit you. He will bring you up from this land to the land that he swore to Abraham, to Isaac, and to Jacob." Joseph made the sons of Israel swear, saying: "Surely Elohim will visit you. Then you shall bring up my bones from here."
>
> Joseph died, being a hundred and ten years. They embalmed him. He was placed in the sarcophagus in Egypt." (Genesis 50:22–26)

Elishama said, "When Jacob blessed Joseph just before his death, he gave Shechem to Joseph. He said, 'And I, I grant to you, as one above your brothers, Shechem . . .' (Genesis 48:22a). This is important for us who are from Shechem, and this is why when Joseph told his brothers to 'bring my bones up from here.' They brought his bones to Shechem, and he was finally buried in Shechem.

Jonathan said, "It is apparent that the Joseph story is important to the people of Shechem, and it is clear that your scribes and minstrels have created a great story. It is more refined than the other stories that we have used, and now I hope that we have made it even more meaningful. At least, we have made it more meaningful for Judah.

"This has been a good session and an important one. We are ready now to talk to Zadok about his Joseph text. Also, we still have the problem concerning the insertion of the first part of *These Are the Stories of Judah*. But this has also been a long session with no lunch break. I'm sorry about that, but I could not stop. We are almost finished, and it is a great feeling. We will meet with Zadok tomorrow.

Jonathan hurried home. As he entered the door, I said, "You missed your lunch, and you are almost late for dinner. You must have had a busy day."

"We had a busy day, and we are just about finished with this epic. We went through all Zadok's material on the Joseph story; we noted the places where he had made some changes, and tomorrow we will be ready to discuss all of this with Zadok. We could be finished tomorrow."

"That is good news. Here, you hold Naam, and I will call father. We all need to eat, and you must be starved."

Jonathan took Naam, and he was glad to get to hold him. He was really growing now and changing daily. Jonathan said to Naam, "Your mother must be feeding you well."

I returned with father and said, "He was taking a nap, but he woke up at once. He wants to know what you think of Zadok's Joseph?"

"Gad, I'll tell you what I think as soon as I have had one piece of Keziah's bread and one cup of wine."

As they sat down at the table, Naam was reaching for everything on the table. I took him from Jonathan and gave him just a bit of bread with a little honey. Of course he made a mess, and his little hands were sticky, but he could always grab his dad's beard and wipe them off. What joy!

Jonathan said, "Gad, Zadok has given us a good text of Joseph, and he has also made Judah important in the story. I was pleased with it. This means, as I told Keziah, that we are almost finished. We went through the story with great speed, and I noticed something for the first time. The story was really finished for me when Joseph made himself known to his brothers. He had put them through his various tests, and finally he made himself known to them, and he made arrangements for them to bring Jacob down to Egypt. After that, we have a list of the names of those coming down with Jacob (*These Are the Names*); we have Jacob's words and blessings for the brothers and for Joseph's sons and then a normal conclusion (according to our outline). It contains the death and burial of Jacob, Joseph's word of comfort to his brothers, and the death of Joseph."

Father said, "You mentioned a list, *These Are the Names*; how many names are on the list?"

"It depends on how you count it, but the intention is to have seventy names. However, I see by your smile that you knew that."

"I knew that it should be seventy. After all, there were seventy states after the flood, the goddess Asherah was the mother of seventy, and Gideon had seventy sons. Some things are always the same."

"When we end our epic, the seventy will still be in Egypt, and when we get around to writing up Part II of the epic, we should start with these words: 'These are the names of the sons of Israel, the ones who came to Egypt with Jacob, . . .' (Exodus 1:1a). Again, the number will be seventy."

I said, "I don't like to hear you talk about 'Part II.' You have other things to do. You are tired of 'Part I,' and I want you to do some of the things that are at the top of your list."

"I hear you, my sweet. Right now Part II is low on everybody's list. I don't know about Elishama, but Elimelech is planning on spending some time with the girls of Jerusalem. I have no such plans."

"I'm glad to hear that, but Naam and I want to see more of you."

"I know, and we must have some fun together. Perhaps we could visit at Ahban's place or take a short trip to Bethlehem. There is one slight problem. I do know that I will have to help plan the dedication of the palace. We will have the royal epic ready, but there are a few other things to plan. This celebration will be for seven days; our epic is too long for a one day performance."

I answered, "I would like to do those things, but I would also like for you to help me on the Minority Report. I could start to write it, because you will never have the time."

"That's a good idea, and you are probably right."

"I have to nurse this baby, so I'll let the two of you clean things up."

Father said, "Naam made a mess, but we can clean it up. By the way, you were just talking about the dedication. The building will be finished before too long. I saw it today, and they have made some progress."

"I'm glad to hear that. Zadok will be with us tomorrow. I hope that we can finish the epic, and I'll ask him all about Ahban."

"Please do."

In the morning, Jonathan dropped by Sheva's office to let him know that he hoped to finish the epic on that same day. Sheva was pleased. Then Jonathan went on to his office and the others were there including Zadok.

These Are the Storeis of Jacob

Jonathan said, "It seems that I'm late again. The first thing I want to do is to ask you, Zadok, a question. Is Ahban better?"

"Yes. He's much better. Yesterday was a great day for me. Ahban is better; his place was beautiful; and we were able to talk a lot about Joseph."

"Will he be coming back to Jerusalem soon?"

"Yes, in three or four days."

Then Jonathan said, "Zadok, we went through your text yesterday, and we have seen that you have produced a fine work. You did make Judah an important part of the story."

Elishama added, "Jonathan, I bothered Zadok early this morning. I have now checked his text against mine, and I did have the additions correct yesterday."

"It sounded as if you were quite certain at the time."

Zadok said, "Ahban says I have improved the story, and of course Joseph is still the main hero. Also, Ahban suggested that since we have mentioned Joseph's sons and their blessing by Jacob, we should use the first part of *These Are the Stories of Judah* as you did in your coronations. This would end with the birth of Judah's sons, Perez and Zerah."

Jonathan said, "I can't believe he said that, because I suggested the same thing yesterday. I was going to bring it up today. Our main problem with the suggestion was where to put it. I wanted to put it just after you mentioned Judah for the first time and during Joseph's journey to Egypt. We worried about interrupting the Joseph story, but is there a better place to put it?"

Zadok said, "I've been thinking about that and I have no answer."

Elishama said, "I have changed my mind. I think Jonathan's suggestion is the best idea."

Elimelech said, "I'm from Judah, but I still don't like the interruption. Even though I'm outnumbered, I would back up a bit and put it with the other materials on the heirs immediately before the burial of Isaac."

Jonathan said, "Elimelech, your suggestion is not bad. This material is rather long for that spot, but we did the same thing just before the burial of Abraham with some Isaac material. I don't know."

Zadok said, "I would not put it back there. In this last story of the epic the people need to be reminded that both Joseph and Judah have sons. I would follow Jonathan's suggestion."

Elimelech said, "I'm willing to go along with the rest of you, but it will confuse a lot of people in years to come."

Elishama said, "You are correct, and some will not like it, but most of the minstrels will probably make it an easy transition. If I were singing this, I would insert some comment like: 'Joseph is on his way to Egypt, and I want to tell you more about Judah. We will join Joseph in a few moments in Egypt.'"

Jonathan said, "I'm sorry that we can't fully please everyone, but this first part of the Judah story is needed. It is important for the dedication of David's palace even as it was important for the coronations. We have all agreed that the first part of the epic needs to end in Egypt, so we do not want all of *These Are the Stories of Judah* or *These Are the Stories of Joseph*. But we have made Joseph important, and Judah is almost as important. Plus we have shown with this addition how this points to David. I want to say that with Elishama's earlier work and with Zadok's more recent work, we are suddenly weeks ahead of schedule. We thank you both."

Zadok said, "And I want to say that without Ahban's help I could not have done this. In many ways, it is really his work."

Jonathan said, "We will all extend our thanks to him as well. I will see him soon and thank him. Now Zadok, I would like to ask you another favor. We need some copies of our work, and I'm wondering if some of your students could help us. Elimelech and Elishama are going to reduce their work and take partial vacations, but they could supervise some students in making copies of the royal epic. We need at least four copies: one for David, one for Heman, one for Sheva, and one for you. In addition, we need a list of first lines of all the stories that we have used in this epic, and they need to be in order. I started such a list, but it needs to be finished."

Zadok said, "I will send four students to your office tomorrow. We will get this done."

Jonathan said, "I can't believe it, but we are finished with this work. We now have a royal epic."

Before Jonathan went home, he stopped by Sheva's office to tell him that they were finished. He found Sheva, but Sheva looked depressed. Jonathan asked Sheva if he felt well. Then Sheva informed Jonathan that his son-in-law, Samuel, had been killed. Jonathan said, "This is awful. They were at our wedding. Will Naomi come here to live?"

"Yes, she will be here soon. But you had other things on your mind when you stopped here."

So, Jonathan told Sheva that they had finished the royal epic. He also informed him that Zadok would send some students to help with the copying. Then he said, "Sheva, I would like for you to tell David that we are finished, and that he can begin to make plans for the dedication of the palace, if it is almost complete. You should tell him that we will need a seven-day celebration in order to perform the royal epic. Sheva, you will finally get your seven-day celebration."

"Yes! This will be a big event. We will need to get more students to write some of the invitations, but we will let David make most of the plans. His staff will have to arrange for food, lodging, and all the rest. I want to thank you for pushing this through. I will inform David at once."

40

The Dedication of David's Palace

During the next two months things were busy in Jerusalem. The summer had been hot, but now in the fall the weather was wonderful. The dedication was only a week away. Everyone was getting ready for this event. The royal epic was complete; the copies were finished; David's staff seemed to be ready; and the palace was beautiful. The workmen had even cleaned up their mess. Some people were still trying to get the palace furnished, because some of the guests would be staying there. There would also be some guests at both the Old School and the New School. Sheva and Zadok even had the students cleaning up.

For Jonathan and me this was a pleasant two months. Jonathan was home more than before. He was able to get me started on our Minority Report, and Naam was lots of fun. Best of all, I just received a letter from Elissa, and she informed me that she would be in Jerusalem a few days before the dedication. So, I put everyone to work. I wanted everything to look good, and I wanted to have the food prepared. I sent Jonathan to see Magon, and I told Jonathan, "Invite Magon and Elissa to dinner on the day that she arrives from Tyre. I want to meet her as soon as possible."

Jonathan went over to Magon's office. Jonathan said, "I don't want to bother you, but Keziah sent me over to invite you and your sister to dinner just as soon as she gets here."

"We will be happy to come, and I'm sure that the food and conversation will be better than what I can provide. She will probably arrive tomorrow."

"We are pleased, and we will have some fun. Have you heard that we finished the epic?"

"Yes, I did. I was at Sheva and Sarah's two nights ago. I had dinner with them and their daughter Naomi, who had just arrived from Ziklag. We talked about the epic, and in fact Elishama showed me the Joseph

The Dedication of David's Palace

story. It is a really great story, and it is as good as the Egyptians produced with stories like Sinuhe. It is really a fine work. It is also interesting that we know the Joseph story took its form in the context of the tomb. The minstrels wanted to remember Joseph in this way. Also Sinuhe was composed to be read at the tomb. The only difference being that Sinuhe is in the form of an autobiography."

"It is a great story. For us it was fortunate that Elishama had just worked on it, and that Zadok, with the help of Ahban, came up with an edition, which met our needs."

With that Jonathan left and came home. He told me that Magon had accepted my invitation, and that Elissa might arrive tomorrow. Then he said, "Do you have time to take a walk? I'll carry Naam and we can go to the palace and see how it looks."

"That would be fun. It is not far."

"Right. I don't know why we haven't looked at it before. After all, we live in a small city. We should know it well, but we just stay home and work."

"So, we will change our ways."

"Right."

We only walked for about ten minutes to the north, and there it was. I said, "Jonathan, it is beautiful."

"Yes. It is."

What we saw was a large courtyard with the palace at one end. The stone walls of the courtyard were lined with cedar. The palace had a large portico, and the main doors were made of olive wood. The palace was essentially a fine stone building, and it was completely lined with cedar. The floor was made of cypress planks but everything else was cedar. Cedar planks ran from the floor to the ceiling, and then cedar beams supported the cedar ceiling planks. I said, "It is such a finished work, and the smell of the cedar is wonderful. No wonder it took so long to build."

"This will be a perfect place for the dedication. The audience can be in the courtyard and the singers on the portico."

"But where are David's quarters?"

"I've heard that he will live on the second floor. It is really a nice palace. The workmen from Tyre have done a fine job. The stones are dressed with great skill, and all the cedar fits together with no cracks; the joints are perfect. It must be about seventy-five cubits long, forty wide, and I think it must be thirty cubits high. It is a large building."

The Jerusalem Academy

We walked all around the building. In the rear of the building we saw the ovens and cooking pits. Jonathan said, "Sometimes I wish that I worked on buildings like these. These workmen take pride in their work, and it stands here for all to admire. But we write books, and no one sees them."

As we started to leave, we met David and some of the workmen who were showing David the details of the building. David said, "Jonathan, I have not seen you for a long time. What do you think of the palace?"

"It is beautiful, and the dedication will be a grand event."

David replied, "And is this your baby? He is a cute one. He looks strong."

"Naam is a fine baby," I said.

David said, "You mentioned the dedication; some people arrived today for the big event. They came here from Tyre."

After that, Jonathan and I left, and we hurried home. We knew that Elissa was probably one of those who arrived from Tyre. As soon as we got home, I started preparing for dinner. I said, "Magon and Elissa will probably be here tonight."

Jonathan took care of Naam, and father helped me. Jonathan was out side playing with Naam when Magon came by to inform us that he and Elissa would be here for dinner. Magon said, "I thought it would be tomorrow evening, but they arrived today."

Jonathan said, "That will be fine. We were just over at the palace, and we saw David. He mentioned that some guests had arrived from Tyre. So, we came home to get ready. It will be fine. Don't worry."

"I won't worry, and we will see you later."

"We are looking forward to having you at our table."

Jonathan came in the house to tell me that he had just spoken to Magon. He said that all was well, and they would be here at dinnertime. I said, "It's going to work out, because I am well prepared. I can't wait."

Later, Magon and Elissa arrived. Father greeted them at the door and led them into the dinning area. Magon introduced Elissa to Jonathan and me, and I was holding Naam. Elissa said, "And this is Naam."

Then she embraced both Naam and me. Elissa was a beautiful woman, about thirty-five or forty. Her dress was not fancy but just right for traveling, and it was easy to see that she was an able person.

I said, "This is an important day for us. I have wanted to talk with you in person, ever since we started writing. I wish that you could have brought Naomi with you."

The Dedication of David's Palace

"She needed to stay with her father. She will help to keep him fed. Someday, when you come to Tyre, you will be able to meet her."

Jonathan said, "How was your journey?"

"It is a long journey. We did not hurry because of the wagons, so it took us seven days. At first it was hot, but after we climbed up into your high country, it was better. The views from the mountains were beautiful. I enjoyed the trip. But, it will be nice to rest here for a few days before returning. When I say it was a long journey, I don't mean to discourage you in any way. I still want you to visit us in Tyre. It can be hot, but it is so beautiful, and the sea is so blue."

Jonathan said, "We still want to come to Tyre, but it is a good thing that we did not try to do it this year."

I said, "I want to see where you live. In our poetry we talk about the power and the beauty of the sea, but we have never seen it. Now let's sit down at the table. Jonathan, you hold Naam and father will help me in the serving."

Elissa said, "I see that your men help you, what do your friends think of that?"

"They are not certain if we are sane, but we do not have time to wait for the future to arrive. We enjoy the future in the present, and we enjoy working together."

"It is a wonderful thing to do, and Magon has usually pushed us in that direction. However, I would like to hold Naam if Jonathan does not mind."

"I don't mind."

Soon dinner was on the table, and we all sat down. There was yogurt, plenty of cucumbers, figs and raison cakes, cheese, and my best bread with honey. I said, "I hope that this will be enough to eat. We don't have any lamb, but during the next week, I'm certain we will have more than enough lamb to eat."

Magon said, "We may not have lamb, but everything is so good. Our food over at the students' house is fine, but it does not taste like this. Over there we use bread for filling; here it has such a wonderful taste. So, Jonathan, are you ready for the dedication?"

"Yes. I think we are ready. I have not participated in most of the preparations. I have worked some with the singers. They are amazing. They already know most of the stories that we used. A scribe or a minstrel can read from our list of first lines and off they go. However, some of them read from our text."

Father said, "Do you know how long it would take a person to read through the entire epic?"

"Yes. In the early fall, like now, if you started reading when the sun was directly overhead, you would have enough light to finish the epic. This means that if we break the reading or singing into seven days we will not have to spend much time each day with that part of the program."

Father replied, "That's good, because then there will be more time for eating, drinking, and dancing. By the way we need some more wine, and I'll get it."

I noticed that Naam had fallen asleep in Elissa's arms, so I took Naam to the bedroom. When I returned I said, "Elissa, we heard that you were going to bring a tablet for Magon to translate. Were you able to bring it?"

"Yes. I brought it, and Magon has already looked at it. Magon, you should tell them about it."

"I will tell you what I know, but I will need more time before I finish working on it. The tablet is written in Babylonian. This was the usual way of writing to foreign kings. This was undoubtedly a copy for the king's files. The letter begins:

> To the king of Ugarit,
> my brother, say:
> The message of the king of Tyre, your brother.

I wish that this scribe had given the Ugaritic king's name. However, most of the letters that I have seen which look like this one were written to the last king of Ugarit, King 'Ammurapi. This was about two hundred years ago. Elissa says they found this tablet along with some others in a walled-off closet during some remodeling of the palace in Tyre. Someday we will have to take a look at the others."

Jonathan said, "This is interesting. I would like to see it."

"Then come by my office tomorrow, and when the work is finished we will share it around this table."

Then Elissa said, "I want to spend some time with Keziah during the next few days. When will the dedication begin?"

Jonathan said, "It will start in three days, and you will also have the seven days of the dedication to be together."

"So, we will have at least ten days to get acquainted, and since I'm tired, I should get some rest. I'm so glad to meet all of you."

I said, "We are glad you are here. Tomorrow, you can come over here at any time. Also, just ask us if you need any help or anything."

The Dedication of David's Palace

The next day I took Elissa for a walk around Jerusalem, and we saw the new palace. Father was looking after Naam, so Jonathan went to Magon's office. It was a bit crowded in his office, because he had moved a cot in, and Elissa had slept there last night. Magon was working on the tablet. He said to Jonathan, "This is not easy. I understand most of it, but it is difficult to find the right words. The text is all about a ship that the king of Ugarit sent to Egypt. It encountered a storm near Tyre, and it was about to sink. It seems that all the ships "hands" were near death. The tablet says, 'And the Chief of Death took every "hand" from the best of health.' So all of these able-bodied seamen or deck hands were about to go down with the ship. But, this scribe had to get fancy. The 'Chief of Death' took them. What is a better way to say 'Chief of Death?' This is some kind of an officer of Mot, the god of death."

Jonathan said, "'Rab Temutah' is not that bad, but perhaps you could say 'Messenger of Death'?

"Yes, I could, but the scribe should have said messenger, if that is what he meant."

"Perhaps. In any case finish your work and read it for the rest of us tonight. You know that Keziah is expecting you and Elissa."

"We will be there, and I will bring the translation."

After dinner, Magon read his translation, with many qualifications like, "I may change this, or I am not sure of this." Here is the translation:

> To the king of Ugarit,
> my brother, say:
> The message of the king of Tyre, your brother.
>
> ---
>
> Let there be *Shalom* for you. May the gods
> guard you and grant you *Shalom*.
> Here with us
> there is *Shalom*. There
> with you, whatever is *Shalom*
> inform us.
>
> ---
>
> Your ship, that
> you sent to Egypt,
> she was near Tyre.
> She "died" in

The Jerusalem Academy

> a mighty rainstorm,
> which occurred. And
> the Master of Death
> took every "hand"
> from the best of h[eal]th. And I,
> al[l] of their "hands,"
> [eve]ry [per]son,
> and [a]ll of them, from the grip of
> the Master of Death, I took,
> and I rescued them.
> And your ship is anchored
> at Acco; she is empty.
> And may my brother
> not put worry in his heart.
> (For the text see Virolleaud, *Le Palais Royal D'Ugarit*, V, RS 18.31, p. 81)

Jonathan said, "I see that you have changed several things since I saw you earlier today."

"Yes, and I must say that it is an interesting letter. This text shows you the great changes that have taken place. Ugarit used to be an important port. They did a great deal of shipping. Now that role has fallen to Tyre. The king of Tyre saved all the sailors or 'hands.' I assume that the ship was unloaded at Acco and then tied up there. Acco is just south of Tyre."

I said, "How far south?"

"The distance is about the same as the distance from Shechem to Jerusalem."

Elissa said, "When we were children, we went to Acco on several occasions. It is a beautiful trip along the coast."

Then Magon said, "In the letter it says, 'And the Master of death took every "hand" from the best of health.' In other words, these young able-bodied seamen were all facing death. For those of us here tonight, it should be noted that I translated the Babylonian *balatu* with 'Naam' ('health'). Here we have Naam and Naomi. This word means 'good' or even a 'good singer,' but it is also used to indicate 'good health.'"

Father said, "Who is this 'Master of Death'? He is interesting to me."

Magon said, "I do not know who he is. I suppose that he is either Mot's chief officer or perhaps Mot himself. Of course, Mot is the god of death. I guess that I cannot really answer the question. I have not met the

The Dedication of David's Palace

'Master of Death' in any text before, and I am not interested in meeting him in person."

Jonathan said, "I don't know anything about the Master of Death, but he is interesting to me. In the story of the ancient Job, which I have recently discussed with you, Job is complaining about his plight, and then he says, '. . . But I know that you will rescue me [from] Mot'" (Job 30:23a).

Father laughed and said, "I don't have the confidence of old Job, but I'm sure that I will know the answer to my question before anyone else in this room, but I hope that I don't meet him too soon."

Jonathan said, "Such letters do not say much, and they fill our minds with questions. I would like to know how the king of Tyre saved these sailors and what they did with the cargo. However, even a little letter informs us about so many things that are not even in the text. In other words, two hundred years ago there was shipping between Ugarit and Egypt, and there must have been much more of this going on than most of us have dared to think. Also, it appears that these two kings exchanged letters on other topics as well as crisis situations."

Elissa asked, "Were the two kings really brothers?"

Magon said, "No. This was just polite speech, which as you know we continue until now."

Elissa said, "We had another good meal and the conversation was good. Now we should be getting back to Magon's quarters."

I said, "Thanks for coming, and the translation was for me a wonderful window looking back to the past. We will see you tomorrow."

The next two days came and were gone in record time, so it seemed. Elissa and I spent a lot of time together during those two days, and now it was the first day of the dedication. This meant that we had seven more days to enjoy. Jonathan had gone to his office quite early. He gathered up his copy of the epic, because he wanted Elishama and Elimelech to sit in back of the portico and follow the text as the singers performed. It was going to be interesting to see if they followed the text or used other forms of some of the stories. After getting his text, he stopped by Sheva's office. Ahban was there, and Jonathan was glad to see him.

Sheva said, "Well Jonathan this is the day. I'm hoping all goes well."

Ahban added, "It will be a great celebration. David seems a little disappointed that some of the invited guests will not be here, but I told him that Jerusalem is full of guests, and after all, this is just the beginning of your reign."

The Jerusalem Academy

Jonathan asked, "Are any other kings here?"

Ahban said, "Yes. Hiram of Tyre, Talmai of Geshur, Nahash of Rabbah, and Toi of Hamath are all here. Then there are delegations from places like Megiddo and Hazor. Of course most of the people will be from our own towns. Shechem and Hebron will be well represented, and they are eager for these great days."

Sheva said, "We should go on over to the palace. Everything is ready, but one never knows. The priests will start out with prayers, sacrifices, and blessings, and then Heman has organized all the singers and choirs. Heman has really worked hard on this. We really didn't have much to do with the dedication after you finished the epic."

Jonathan said, "I will probably see you there. I must run along. I need to take this text to Elishama, and then I'll join Keziah, Magon, and his sister, Elissa."

When Jonathan left Sheva's office he ran into Elishama, and he said, "Here is the text so that you can follow the singers. I can also help with this on the subsequent days. It will be interesting to see how it goes."

"I'll take the text and Elimelech is going to meet me there."

Jonathan came to the house, and the rest of us were waiting for him. We left at once for the palace. Father and Naam also joined the group. When we arrived at the palace, there was already a large crowd in the courtyard. The priests were praying and offering *shelamim* sacrifices. These sacrifices were for such royal occasions; they represented a gift to God, but the people were able to eat from these sacrifices (but not the choice or fatty portions). Almost everyone had a piece of lamb. It seemed clear that the people were here for good food and for *The Royal Epic*, which would soon follow. The singers and musicians were gathered on the portico or stage, and all of the dignitaries were already seated in the front row. When the priests were finished, Ahban walked up the steps, and as he turned to face the audience, the people became quiet. Ahban spoke in a clear manner.

"This is the beginning of a seven day ritual and story. We are here to dedicate this palace, which was built for our King David by King Hiram of Tyre and his master builders. Earlier today, around King David's table, King David personally thanked our friends from Tyre for their fine work. This then is the palace of our king. But, how did we get to this point? During these seven days of celebration, our minstrels will sing of our beginnings; they will sing of the ordering of our world and of the ancestors of this united Israel. From those ancestors came King David who became king at their tombs. He was blessed by them and now exercises his legiti-

The Dedication of David's Palace

mate rule over this land and its people. The Jerusalem Academy has put together this epic, and the scribes, who were responsible for it, hope that everyone will enjoy this performance of *The Royal Epic*. It is your story."

As Ahban returned to his seat, Heman stepped forward, and he said, "The singers and the musicians have worked for many days to prepare for this great occasion. We have divided this epic into seven parts; we will perform one part on each day of this celebration. It is fitting that we begin with an old seven-day ritual text concerning the ordering of our world. Then, he began to sing:

> When Elohim first began to form the heavens and the earth,
> The earth was devastation and desolation,
> Darkness was over [the] deep,
> The wind of Elohim was storming over the waters,
> Elohim said:
> "Let there be light."
> There was light.
> Elohim saw that the light was good.
> Elohim divided between the light and between the darkness.
> Elohim called the light day.
> The darkness he called night.
> There was evening.
> There was morning:
> Day one. (Genesis 1:1–5)

Elissa was deeply moved by Heman's singing. She whispered to me, "This man is marvelous."

I thought, "Heman has never been so dynamic, and he has many more musicians to back him up than he had for the coronations."

The first four lines were on the border between speech and song, but there was great power and emphasis, with the use of high notes, when he came to the phrases: 'Elohim said,' 'Elohim saw,' 'Elohim divided,' and 'Elohim called.' As Heman continued through the seven ritual days of this first creation story, there was a gradual crescendo and the music went from moderato to allegro di molto. The audience was becoming tense. Then there was a pause, and the cymbals clashed. Then he sang slowly and distinctly:

> Elohim formed the human beings in his image;
> in the image of Elohim he formed them;
> male and female he formed them. (Genesis 1:27)

The Jerusalem Academy

The audience cheered, and Heman finished this section:

> Elohim saw all that he had made,
> and behold, it was very good.
> There was evening.
> There was morning;
> [A seventh] day.
>
> The heavens and the earth were finished
> and all their entourage.
> Elohim finished on the seventh day his work
> that he had been doing. (Geneis 1:31—2:2a)

Jonathan thought, "Well at least old Abiathar did not get to change the story to six days, as he wanted, but he may still do it."

Just then the musicians played an introduction for the next part. In this group there were lyres, lutes, woodwinds, and pipes/flutes. Everyone liked this music. During this introduction, four more singers joined Heman. Heman would do the narration, but the other three men and one woman sang the parts for God, the human, the serpent, and the wife. Heman began:

> *These are the stories of the heavens and the earth since their formation.*
> On another day, when Yahweh-Elohim was about to make earth and heavens,
> there was as yet no wild shrub on the earth,
> as yet no wild grass had sprouted,
> because Yahweh-Elohim had not sent rain upon the earth,
> and there was no human ('adam) to till the ground ('adamah),
> but a flood began flowing from the netherworld,
> and watered the entire surface of the ground,
> Yahweh-Elohim formed the human [from] the clay of the ground;
> he blew into his nostrils the breath of life;
> the human became a living being. (Genesis 2:4–7)

I noticed that the audience enjoyed it. Once again they cheered when the human became a living being. Obviously, they did not care that this was the second time around for the forming of the human. It was like a chorus with some different words. The people continued to enjoy the search for "a helper just like" the human. They seemed disappointed when Yahweh-Elohim could not form such a one from the ground, but when

The Dedication of David's Palace

Yahweh-Elohim took some human substance to work with and was successful, the crowd was once again applauding. So much so that one could hardly hear the singer who sang for the human:

> "This one, at last, is bone of my bones
> And flesh of my flesh.
> This one shall be called woman (*'ishshah*),
> For from man (*'ish*) this one was taken." (Genesis 2:23)

For Jonathan it had always been important that since these two were of the same substance, they could become "one flesh," but this point went by with little notice. As the singers moved on to the part about eating from the tree of the knowledge of good and evil, it was clear that the audience was all for eating and gaining all knowledge. They were for knowledge. They said, "Eat! Eat!" After all, who wants to live and work forever? So, there will be death. So, what's new? The audience already knew that they would not live forever, but they needed knowledge. But this story had to spell it out. Humans cannot become gods. If the humans were immortal and had all knowledge, they would be gods. The humans must give up something, and this is why Yahweh-Elohim says:

> "Yes, the human has become like one of us,
> Knowing good and evil, so now,
> He must not reach out his hand,
> Taking also from the tree of life,
> He would eat and live forever!" (Genesis 3:22)

The next section was about Cain and Abel was important to everyone. Again they used several singers; they needed a narrator, some one for Yahweh, and some one for Cain. The audience did not cheer the introduction of murder, but they did like the part about building cities and the development of trades. When the narrator sang concerning Jubal: "He was the 'father' of all who are skilled with lyre and pipe" (Genesis 4:21b), all of the musicians gave a long cheer.

The next part, that is, the listing of the ten pre-flood sages did not seem to be as interesting for the people. Knowing that this might be the case the musicians and singers worked hard to make the music extra special.

The last section for the day was one that the people really liked:

The Jerusalem Academy

> When the human beings began to multiply,
> upon the face of the ground,
> and daughters were born to them,
> the sons of the gods saw that the daughters
> of the human beings were beautiful,
> they took for themselves wives from any of those they chose.
> Yahweh said:
>> "My spirit can not be bottled up in human beings forever,
>> In as much as, they are flesh.
>> Their days will be a hundred and twenty years."
>
> The Nephilim were on earth in those days, and afterwards,
> for the sons of the gods did mate with the daughters of the human beings;
> they bore [children] to them—
> they were the heroes of old,
> the men of renown. (Genesis 6:1–4)

After the closing words, there was a lot of cheering, and one old fellow, who had had his share of wine, got up on the steps to lead the crowd in a song:

> Heroes, heroes part divine,
> Made them famous every time.
> But they are mortals like us,
> Made of clay, they turn to dust.

After this many people were going for more lamb, but the crowd did begin to thin out. On our way back to the house Elissa and I began to sing, "Heroes, heroes part divine." Soon we were all laughing and singing. As we entered the school courtyard, we met Sheva, Sarah, and Naomi. I introduced Elissa to them, and said, "Please join us for some bread, fruit, cheese, and wine."

They agreed, and the party increased to eight. Later Elishama, Deborah, and Rachel dropped by. Elishama wanted to talk with Jonathan and Magon about the reception of the epic. Jonathan asked, "Where is Elimelech? He should be here."

"The last I saw of him was at the palace. He was leaving the courtyard with some lamb, wine, and a beautiful girl. I don't think you will see him soon."

"He needed a vacation, but I hope he will help you tomorrow. So, as you were following the text, did you find any places that they left some out?"

"They left it as we wrote it. It all went well. But, we were sitting behind the musicians. How did the people like it?"

Sheva said, "The people loved it."

Magon said, "Yes. They did love it, and in fact, they participated in it. I was fascinated by the way the audience encouraged the humans to eat from the tree of knowledge. The Babylonian story of Adapa ('human') ends in the same way as your story of *ha'adam* ('the human'); in both stories the humans end up with knowledge but not life. They are mortal. But the two stories do not begin in the same way. In the beginning, Adapa is given knowledge by the god Ea, but in the beginning your human is given life. The gods decide to give Adapa life, since he had all knowledge, and then he could become one of the gods. But, acting on bad advice from Ea, he refuses the bread and water of life. But today we saw humans who did not care about life but wanted knowledge. They took knowledge and became mortal, and the people approved of that move."

Jonathan said, "I was interested in the same thing. The people see the need for knowledge, and they know, at least from where they stand, that everyone dies."

Magon said, "That's right, and in a happy setting like today, it may be easy to say, 'eat, eat,' but the other side of this issue is that many people are, at the same time, dominated by death and the swiftness of life. For this reason many Egyptians deny death."

I said, "I don't want to stop the conversation, but the food is ready. Get something to eat and then talk."

Rachel and Naam were on a blanket on the floor crawling around and having a good time. Sheva and father were talking about something, and Sarah and Jonathan were helping me. Elishama, Magon, Elissa, Deborah, and Naomi were in a group about the table. The food was good and after a little more wine, the conversation went on undisturbed. Around the table, most of the folks questioned Elissa about her life in Tyre. It was obvious to all that she had a detailed knowledge of her home state.

As they were leaving, I said, "I expect you to be here tomorrow after the celebration, and we will do this again."

And as they began to walk away, Magon said to Naomi, "I want to apologize for bringing up the subject of death in the conversations. I know

The Jerusalem Academy

that you have just experienced a real lost, and I should have been more sensitive on that point."

Naomi said, "I have to work through these things in the real world. It does not help to avoid such subjects, but I thank you for your kind words."

The second day of the dedication was very much like day one. The first thing that Jonathan noticed was that the singers left out the general introduction to the flood story and started with:

> *These are the stories of Noah*
> Noah was a righteous man;
> He was perfect in his generation.
> With the gods, Noah walked.
> Noah fathered three sons:
> Shem, Ham, and Japheth.
>
> The earth was found corrupt before the gods;
> The earth was full of violence.
> Elohim saw the earth;
> Yes, it was corrupt,
> For all flesh had corrupted their ways upon earth. (Genesis 6:9–12)

Jonathan thought, "They may have just turned to this title and accidentally left out the introduction, but I doubt it. They probably figured they didn't need it. It is not a great loss, and the section they have sung is the most important. Heman was clever to have some singers sitting as the judges/gods in a court to hear this case against the earth."

Today the crowd was more subdued. The destruction of the world by the great flood or a return to chaos was not really designed to enliven such a crowd. In fact, there were a few tears, when the singers sang together:

> All flesh perished, the ones who move upon the earth:
> the birds, the domestic animals, the [wild] animals,
> the swarmers, the ones who swarm upon earth,
> and all the humans. (Genesis 7:21)

But later, when once again the earth was dry, and Noah had offered burnt offerings to Yahweh, the mood changed. This was because of Yahweh's response:

The Dedication of David's Palace

Throughout all the days of the earth,
Sowing and reaping,
Cold and heat,
Summer and winter,
Day and night,
They shall not cease. (Genesis 8:22)

When I heard this, I took Jonathan's hand, and said to Elissa and Naomi, "That is my favorite part." Others must have shared my view, because once again the audience was happy. When the singers sang about Noah planting a vineyard and drinking wine from his vines, the people entered into the drama of it. Many of them chanted, "Thank God for Noah! Thank God for Noah!"

Heman introduced the last section of the day by saying, "We gave you ten generations from the first human to Noah, and now we give you the ten generations from Shem to Abraham. These words were helpful.

Later, in the evening, everyone had a good time around the table. Perhaps Magon made the most helpful comment. He said, "There are two great things about your flood story if we compare it to other flood stories: 1) You have given a reason for the flood (the court decision on corruption), and 2) you have managed to keep your flood hero as a human. He does not become a god. This is important."

And Jonathan said, "That statement is important to us, because it came from you."

Sheva said, "Sarah and I want you all to come to our house tomorrow evening."

Jonathan said, "We'll be there."

Elissa and Magon stayed a little longer, and Elissa helped me get things cleaned up. Elissa said, "I'm having a wonderful time, and it is going to be difficult to leave when the dedication is finished. You should know, and I'm sure that you do know, how special you and your household are. In Jerusalem or in Tyre most women would not be invited to participate in discussions like you have in your home. Also you seem so free."

"I'm free. Both Jonathan and father have helped to make this possible; it would be difficult if this were not the case but not impossible. I'm determined to allow my curiosity all the freedom it needs. We do have some great times here, and I am thankful for those times. In the future, we will just have to write more often, and I know that someday we will get to Tyre."

The number of people increased on the third day of the dedication. Apparently word was getting around that there was plenty to eat and that the singing and the music were good. The minstrels began *These are the stories of Terah* (Genesis 11:27a). This section contained the Abraham materials. The minstrels planned to do about half of this on the third day and the other half on day four. There were some important matters to deal with, but the people seemed more interested in the places where Abraham traveled. After Abraham buried his father Terah and was blessed by Yahweh, he, Sarai, and Lot departed for Canaan. They reached Canaan, and "Abram passed through the land as far as the sanctuary of Shechem, . . ." (Genesis 12:6a). Of course when the people from Shechem heard that there was great applause. This does not mean that the people were uninterested in the trip to Egypt. In fact, they seemed appalled when Pharaoh took Sarai for his wife. After they returned from Egypt and Lot went his own way, Abram "settled at the oaks of Mamre that are in Hebron" (Genesis 13:18). Again there was great applause, this time from the people of Hebron.

When the singers came to the part where Abram rescues Lot from King Cherdorlaomer and the three other kings, most of the people looked puzzled, because they were not familiar with this story. But when Melchizedek, king of Salem, blessed the victorious Abram (Genesis 14:18–20), it was the people of Jerusalem's time to cheer. This program had something for everybody.

That evening at Sheva and Sarah's, Elissa was saying that she thought the final part of the day's program was good. She said, "I loved the old withered lady who sang for Sarah:

> After I was withered,
> And my husband was old,
> Passion was mine. (Genesis 18:12)

She was a great choice on the part of somebody. Then at the end of that section, Abraham's pleading with God to not destroy Sodom was entertaining, and he finally managed to get God to say he would not destroy Sodom if ten righteous people could be found" (Genesis 18:32b).

I said, "I liked those parts as well, but I am beginning to wonder if Sarah will ever have a child. I can understand Sarah's doubts and so can every person in the audience. This is a good story."

On day four, the singers had to finish the Abraham material. They started with the story of Lot and the destruction of Sodom and Gomorrah. First the two messengers of Yahweh came to Sodom, and Lot offered them hospitality in his home. The story continued:

> Before they lay down, the people of the city
> (the people of Sodom) closed in upon the house—
> from young to old, the entire population.
> They called to Lot; they said to him:
> > "Where are the men who came to you tonight?
> > Bring them out to us, that we may know them."
> Lot went out to them, to the entrance; he shut the door behind him.
> He said:
> > "Please, my friends, do no evil.
> > Remember, I have two daughters who have not known a man.
> > Allow me to bring them out to you;
> > you do to them what is good in your eyes.
> > But to these men, do nothing,
> > because they have come under the shelter of my roof."
> (Genesis 19:4–8)

I said to Jonathan, "This is horrible. Obviously, Lot is more interested in the messengers and the rules of hospitality than his daughters."

Jonathan said, "We'll talk about this tonight."

It was clear that both Elissa and I were upset with Mr. Lot. However, most of the people seemed to like this part. Or, perhaps they knew that things were about to get exciting. Next the people of Sodom pushed against Lot and tried to break down the door. Then the two messengers pulled Lot into the house and shut the door, and they struck the crowd with a blinding light. The messengers warned Lot that they were going to destroy the city. The singers continued:

> As dawn broke, the messengers hurried Lot saying:
> > "Get up! Take your wife and your two daughters, who are
> > here or you shall be annihilated in the punishment of the city."
> He hesitated. The men grabbed his hand, the hand of his wife,

and the hands of his two daughters—
the compassion of Yahweh was upon him.
They brought him out; they let him rest outside the city.
When they had brought them outside, he said:
> "Flee for your life!
> Do not look behind you.
> Do not stop anywhere in the plain.
> Flee to the hills,
> Or you shall be annihilated."

Lot said to them:
> "Oh no, my lords!
> Obviously, your servant has found favor in your eyes;
> you have multiplied your kindness
> that you did to me in saving my life,
> but I am not able to flee to the hills
> or the evil would possess me; I would die.
> Here is this town; it is near enough to escape there;
> it is little! Let me flee there. Isn't it little?
> My life will be saved."

He said to him:
> "Let it be known, I have given in to you even in this matter;
> there will be no devastation of the city of which you have spoken.
> Hurry, flee there,
> for I am not able to do anything until your arrival there."

Hence the name of the city was called Zoar.
The sun rose upon the earth as Lot entered Zoar.

Yahweh rained upon Sodom and Gomorrah burning rock
and fire from Yahweh out of the heavens.
He devastated those cities and the entire plain
with all the inhabitants of the cities and the produce of the ground.
[Lot's] wife looked back; she became a pillar of salt. (Genesis 19:15–26)

The people did like this story, and they began to shout:

> Mrs. Lot! Oh, Mrs. Lot!
> Just what did you really lack?
> Why did you have to look back?

The Dedication of David's Palace

This was a lot of fun for the audience, but they also liked the last part of the Lot story:

> Lot went up from Zoar; he settled in the hills with his two daughters,
> because he was afraid to live in Zoar.
> He and his two daughters lived in a certain cave.
> The firstborn said to the younger:
> > "Our father is old. There is not a man on earth
> > to come in to us as is the way of all the earth.
> > Come; let us make our father drink wine,
> > and we will lie with him.
> > We will keep alive descendants from our father."
> That night they made their father drink wine.
> The firstborn went in; she lay with her father.
> He did not know of her lying down or of her getting up.
> The next day the firstborn said to the younger:
> > "Yes! Last night I slept with my father.
> > Let us make him drink wine again tonight.
> > Go in! Lie with him!
> > We will keep alive descendants from our father."
> That night also they made their father drink wine.
> The younger was ready; she lay with him.
> He did not know of her lying down or of her getting up.
> The two daughters of Lot were pregnant by their father.
> The firstborn gave birth to a son.
> She called forth his name, "Moab."
> He is the father of the Moabites of today.
> The younger also gave birth to a son.
> She called forth his name, "Ben-Ammi."
> He is the father of the Bene-Ammon of today. (Genesis 19:30–38)

The singers were correct; the people did like these stories about Lot. But, even the true Lot fans were thinking about Sarah. Will she have a child? The singers could not delay any longer. Heman stepped forward for these important lines:

> Yahweh visited Sarah as he had said;
> Yahweh did to Sarah as he had spoken.
>
> Sarah became pregnant.
> She bore a son to Abraham for his old age

> (at the appointed time of which Elohim had promised him).
> Abraham called forth the name of his son
> (the one born to him, that is whom Sarah had borne to him), "Isaac."
> (Genesis 21:1–3)

This was a happy moment for the singers and the audience. Abraham and Sarah had an heir, and Isaac was his name. However as the story continued there were still many things that could endanger Isaac's status and his life.

The people in the audience seemed to agree with Sarah that Hagar, the surrogate, and Ishmael, her son by Abraham, had to leave. Sarah said:

> Drive out this servant girl and her son,
> because the son of this servant girl
> shall not inherit along with my son, with Isaac. (Genesis 21:10)

Next came the great test or the binding of Isaac (the Akedah). Here Abraham was told the unthinkable. He was to offer up his only son as a sacrifice. This text was used in the second coronation and the audience at that time was terrified. But now their reaction was even more extreme. Here the test was in context. After such a long period of waiting for Isaac, the audience was not willing to give him up. When the messenger of Yahweh stopped the test and provided a substitute ram there was a huge sigh of relief. This was the actual conclusion to the Abraham story.

Now the singers had to perform the traditional ending which was present in each of the major cycles of stories. This means three things must be presented: 1) Sarah's death and burial, 2) an extra word concerning the heirs (in this case the marriage of Isaac and Rebekah), and 3) the death and burial of Abraham.

The audience had a good time with the narrative concerning Abraham's purchase of the tomb, which was in the cave of the Machpelah in Hebron. Also, they liked the long story of Isaac's marriage, but day four was so full that the people were getting a bit restless. When they reached the death and burial of Abraham everyone was tired. It was interesting that both Isaac and Ishmael buried Abraham, and Isaac was blessed.

Sheva and Sarah had to go to some function and dinner that David was having for his guests at the palace, so once again everyone met at our house for food, drink and discussion.

Elishama was the first to speak concerning the program. "I have been following our text each day, and these singers are doing a good job.

The Dedication of David's Palace

They have not changed much. Tomorrow they will start with *These are the Stories of Isaac*, and we can see if they follow our plan and start with Isaac and Rebekah in Gerar."

I said, "Today was a full day. I was glad that Isaac was born and that Abraham did not sacrifice him. Isaac was even married. So, it all turned out very well, but that first story about Lot was awful. Why did you put that in the epic?"

Jonathan said, "We put it in, because we could not leave it out. We were told by the singers that this was one story that most of the people liked, and don't forget that our purpose was to entertain and unite the people in this new Israel."

Deborah, who seldom voiced her opinion, said, "I agree with Keziah that it was a bad story. I could never even imagine Elishama offering our Rachel to such a crowd in order to protect some guests, be they human or divine."

It was clear that Elissa and Naomi also agreed with Deborah and me.

Jonathan said, "Most of you know that I do not agree with the view points of many of these stories, but right now around some one's table old Lot is being praised for upholding the laws of hospitality. According to those laws, you must protect the well being of any guest under your roof regardless of the cost. We don't have to like it, but that is what it's all about."

Father said, "There is another story that is almost like this one from our earlier times, before we had a king. It concerns a Levite and his concubine. They were traveling from Bethlehem to the hill country of Ephraim. They stopped in Gibeah, and there an old man took them into his house. The men of the town gathered around the house, and they demanded that the old man bring out the Levite so that they could rape him. This time the old man offered the men his virgin daughter and the Levite's concubine. They took the concubine and raped and abused her all night. The next morning she was found dead at the threshold of the old man's house (Judges 19). The laws of hospitality must be obeyed."

I said, "That story is even worse than the story about Lot. Father, do you obey the laws of hospitality?"

"I would try to protect my guests, but I would never offer up my daughter to satisfy the desires of such men."

Magon said, "This is an interesting situation. There are people who will use some law as an excuse to do more for others than for their own family. Why? Because they will be praised or perhaps paid by others even though their own family may have to suffer. It is important to care for the 'widow and the orphan' but we cannot endanger our children in caring for others. This is difficult."

Naomi said, "I thought that it was in bad taste for the people to shout:

> Mrs. Lot! Oh Mrs. Lot!
> Just what did you really lack?
> Why did you have to look back?

From the story, it was clear that Mrs. Lot had other daughters whose husbands would not listen to the warnings. Yes, Mrs. Lot did not obey, but she cared about her children, and she had to look back."

Magon said, "This part of the story may just be a lighthearted attempt to tell children why there are salt pillars near the Salt Sea that look like humans. However, in the context of this story the crowd was insensitive to the needs of Mrs. Lot."

Elishama said, "It is safe to say that the women around this table did not like the story of Lot. None of us liked it; for one thing it was too long. As Jonathan said, 'We were pushed into using it by the singers.' But it was our decision. Also our reasons for not wanting to use it were different than those expressed here tonight. We may have to think about this for our second edition."

Jonathan said, "The priests may prepare a second edition but not me. Also, the women are correct with their objections. The epic does bring our people together, but I certainly do not want to defend what goes on in some of these stories. As Keziah and I have discussed many times, we must move towards the future with more thought than we see in many of the traditions from our past."

I said, "You all should have given 'more thought' to your decision on this. You didn't think it through, and you let the singers push you around."

All the women cheered me on.

Jonathan said, "I agree. We did not think this one through."

Father said, "Our women are sharp tonight, but even so, I would like to comment on the last scene of the Lot story; it is certainly not a children's story. It has to do with the birth of states, and his daughters were clever and pregnant. Again, the people seem to like that sort of thing."

Elissa said, "At the end of the first day, there was the story of the sons of the gods mating with the daughters of the humans. This accounted for the heroes of old. It seems to me that you are saying almost the same thing when Sarah gets pregnant. Is that the case?"

The Dedication of David's Palace

Jonathan said, "You are correct. God visits Sarah, and she gets pregnant. This may not be the only way to understand this text, but it is clear that great leaders in the past were thought to be part divine. This does not mean that they are gods; they are still mortal."

Father said, "We have had our problems with today's program, but I must say that the conclusion with Sarah's death, Isaac's marriage, and Abraham's death was performed in a classic manner."

I said, "Tonight I have had an excellent time, and we have even taught our men a thing or two. But we have talked so much that you have not been eating, and we have hardly touched the wine. I want to fill your cups, and let's sing: 'Mrs. Lot you're one of us!'"

This turned out to be one of the best evenings of the week. When the folks left, Magon and Elissa walked Naomi home. As they said good night to Naomi, she said to Magon, "And now you have helped a widow if not an orphan."

He said, "I should not have used that example."

She said, "Hush. I was only joking."

On day five of the dedication everyone slept late. Jonathan said to me, "We were up so late last night. This is day five of the dedication. It will be another full day, because they are doing one long section, *These are the Stories of Isaac*."

"We can handle that. I'm glad that Naam has been so good through all of this. When he gets tired, he just goes to sleep. The noise does not seem to bother him. However, today Deborah is not going to the dedication, and she will be here to stay with Naam. Naam and Rachel can play. Also, Elissa, Naomi, and I are going to the celebration a little early. We will get some lamb and meet you at the regular time and at our bench."

The three of us were picking up our lamb, and we had our hands full. Just then I saw Joab, who was walking toward us, and I warned the others to be on guard. He stepped in front of me, causing me to stop. He said, "I have not seen you for a long time. Does your scribe keep you at home all the time?"

"You get out of my way."

"Someday, I'll have you, but in the meantime these two friends of yours look pretty good. You should introduce me to them."

"Right. I'm sure that they want to meet a dog's head."

The Jerusalem Academy

Joab was just raising his hand to hit me when David walked by with his entourage. I jumped away from Joab, and said to David, "My king, this dog belongs to you. He has just threatened my friends and me. Our guests do not need this sort of thing."

David motioned Joab to move on and apologized to Elissa and Naomi. I introduced them to David and told him that Elissa was Magon's sister and was from King Hiram's delegation. He apologized again, and everyone went to their places.

I said to Elissa and Naomi, "Let's not mention our encounter with Joab just yet. I'll tell Jonathan first. I'm really sorry that this happened. Joab is the commander of the army, and he is an evil man."

When we got to Jonathan and the others, Jonathan said, "I looked down to the front a moment ago and saw you talking with David. What did he have to say?"

"Joab bothered us, so I ran over to David and complained. He sent Joab away and apologized. Jonathan, please don't do anything about this today. I want to enjoy this afternoon. We can deal with it later."

"As you wish. Actually before I see David again on this matter, I want to find out about some things that Joab has been doing with Absalom. He may be helping Absalom in his efforts to be next in line for the throne."

"Thank you so much. Here. Have some lamb and let's enjoy."

Now the music started and Heman came forward. He said, "Yesterday, we sang concerning the marriage of Isaac and Rebekah. Today we continue our story of Isaac. Isaac and Rebekah go to Gerar, and there they meet King Abimelech. Once again the barren and rightful wife is endangered."

Jonathan was happy. The singers were following the new arrangement. He said to me, "Remind me to thank Heman for following this new order."

Heman continued, "When Sarah and Abraham went to Egypt, Pharaoh actually took Sarah for his wife. In this story, Abimelech takes Rebekah, but God stops him from following through. God says, "I did not allow you to touch her" (Genesis 20:6b).

Next the singers dealt with the birth of Jacob and Esau. Rebekah was barren, but with the help of Yahweh Isaac managed to get her pregnant. She had a difficult time; she was carrying twins. Yahweh said to her:

> "Two states are [now] within your womb;
> Two peoples shall come from your body.
> One shall be stronger than the other,
> And the elder shall serve the younger." (Genesis 25:23)

The Dedication of David's Palace

The people liked the stories of Jacob and Esau, and they appreciated the fact that Jacob was clever and fit to rule his older brother. Jacob obtained both Esau's birthright and his blessing. The story about the blessing was the most interesting for the audience, because here, Jacob was at greater risk, and the stakes were high. The singers were getting better each day, and the scene for the blessing was the best yet. Heman sang Isaac's part and they had a young singer for Jacob. They actually performed a well-known blessing ritual when it was time for the blessing. This contained: 1) The Identification, 2) The Meal, 3) The Kiss, and 4) Pronouncement of Blessing:

> [Isaac] blessed him:
> 1) He said:
>> "Are you my son Esau?"
>
> He said:
>> "I am."
>
> 2) He said:
>> "My son, serve me, and I will eat game, so that
>> my very being may bless you."
>
> (He served him; he ate. He brought wine for him; he drank.)
>
> 3) Isaac, his father, said to him:
>> "Come closer, and kiss me, my son."
>
> (He came close; he kissed him; he smelled the odor of his clothes.)
>
> 4) He blessed him; he said:
>> "Yes! The odor of my son
>> Is like the smell of a field—
>> A field that Yahweh has blessed.
>> And may that God grant to you,
>> From the dew of the heavens,
>> And from the fat of the earth,
>> Abundance of grain and wine.
>> Peoples shall serve you;
>> States shall bow down to you.
>> Be the ruler of your brothers;
>> The sons of your mother shall bow down to you.
>> Cursed be those who curse you;
>> Blessed be those who bless you." (Genesis 27:23c–29)

This was becoming one of the best days of these celebrations. Everything was dramatic and full of emotion. No sooner had Isaac blessed

Jacob than Esau returned with the game. He wanted his blessing, but it had already been given to Jacob. Esau wept.

> Esau hated Jacob on account of the blessing that his father had given him. Esau spoke his mind:
> "The days of mourning for my father are drawing near;
> I will kill Jacob, my brother." (Geneis 27:41)

So both Rebekah and Isaac warn Jacob, and they send him away. Rebekah tells Jacob to flee to her brother, Laban, in Haran. Then, there is the journey, the long sojourn in Haran, Jacob's marriages, the birth of most of his children, and the exciting return. At Bethel, God spoke to Jacob:

> Elohim said to him:
> "I am El Shaddai.
> Be fruitful and multiply;
> A people, [yeah], a community of peoples,
> Shall come from you;
> Kings shall come forth from your loins.
> The land that I gave to Abraham and to Isaac,
> To you, I give it;
> To your descendants, [the ones who] follow you,
> I will give the land." (Genesis 35:11–12)

When the singers sang: "Kings shall come forth from your loins," there was an uproar, and the people chanted: "David, David, long live our king!" It seemed to Jonathan that this was probably staged but rightly so. Heman thought of everything.

At this point they dealt with the traditional ending for a cycle of such stories. First, there was the death and burial of Rachel. Then, there was the note about Reuben having intercourse with his father's concubine, Bilhah, and a list of Jacob's sons. Finally, at Hebron, they told about the death and burial of Isaac. Jacob and Esau buried their father.

On the way back to the house, Elissa said, "What a day! We started it with action, our confrontation with Joab, and the program was packed with action."

Jonathan said, "It certainly was, and this was also the longest session. I am sorry that you had to experience Joab's rudeness. He is an evil man.

The Dedication of David's Palace

Gad, Keziah and I have been trying to understand why David puts up with him, but as yet we have no answer."

When they reached the house, Sheva and Sarah announced that they needed to go on home and get some rest, but Naomi decided to stay for the discussion. Magon and Elissa said they would see that Naomi got home a bit later. I had the food ready, and I took Naam from Deborah and nursed him. Deborah had nursed both babies during the afternoon, but Naam was glad to get some more of his mother's milk. No one was interested in more lamb, but the fruit and yogurt were in demand. Jonathan kept the cups full.

Jonathan started the conversations. He said, "I want to tell you that the singers were good today, and they kept the order of these stories just as we had arranged them. The story about Isaac and Rebekah in Gerar was new to the singers in this spot, but we thought that Rebekah should be endangered, just as Sarah, before the birth of Jacob and Esau. Also, I should tell you that this story, when we found it, was about Abraham and Sarah. We changed the names to Isaac and Rebekah for two reasons. One, we already had a story like this for Abraham and Sarah when they went to Egypt. Two, another story concerning Isaac and Rebekah in Gerar, which we found, was not interesting and came after the birth of Jacob and Esau. This is one of the most extensive changes we made to our sources, and we did not expect the singers to follow our lead."

Father said, "I should add that in a few years the singers might go back to the earlier form of these stories, but for now it appears that you have improved the sequence of events. What interested me about the birth of Jacob and Esau is that it is almost identical to the story of Perez and Zerah in the story of Judah and Tamar. In both cases, 'the elder serves the younger,' but I guess we will hear about that tomorrow."

Elissa said, "I was most interested in the emotional outbursts of both Isaac and Esau when they discovered that it was Jacob who received the blessing. They trembled and cried out, and the singers stomped their feet and flailed their arms. We have this sort of reaction to bad news or even the anticipation of bad news in our literature at home."

I said, "I liked the part where Laban tricked Jacob and gave him Leah instead of Rachel. 'When morning came, there she was, Leah' (Genesis 29:25a)! When Jonathan and I were married, he lifted my veil and kissed me before he carried me over the threshold. Now I know why Jonathan's friends shouted, 'We have a new tradition.' Jacob should have known that he had someone other than Rachel long before morning."

Elishama said, "Elimelech should be here to speak to this point. When we were working on that section he came up with a bit of a poem. I don't remember the poem, but it had something to do with Jacob being 'blindly in love.'"

I said, "Even a blind man would know the sound of his beloved's voice."

Naomi said, "Obviously Leah was quiet. I liked the part where Rachel sat on the 'household gods,' hiding them from Laban. Rachel was as clever as Jacob."

Magon noted that the change in Jacob's name was for him the most important part of the day. He said, "When Jacob becomes Israel, that is, the union of Judah and Israel, he becomes the symbol of that unity. After all he is the father of Judah and Joseph, and so the two have become one; they have become Israel. Then they sang that kings shall come forth from Israel's loins. That is a nice touch."

Jonathan said, "And you noticed that the people responded to that line. Perhaps Heman coached them on that response. In any case, I agree that the change from Jacob to Israel is important. During the next two days, we will see how it is possible for Judah and Joseph to pull together for Israel.

"But, I have another question. After five days of this, are the people getting tired of it?"

Elishama said, "I have been sitting up front following the text, and I could not really answer the question."

Naomi said, "They are more interested in lamb at this point. They still like the music and the meat, but their interest in the epic is less than it was."

Jonathan said, "You are probably correct."

Elishama said, "This means that the Joseph material is just what we need for days six and seven. You may think that I only say this because I'm from Shechem, but there are some other reasons. The Joseph story will recapture their interest, because it is not a group of stories, which we used to fill out our outline for our epic cycles. Rather, it is a tightly woven story, which is not only interesting as a story but at the same time met our needs. This story draws the audience into its fast moving currents. The audience will be involved, and at the end of day six, they will have a difficult time waiting for the conclusion on day seven."

Magon said, "It is a great story."

Naomi said, "I will watch some of the people that I have been watching each day, and tomorrow evening I can report on their interest."

"Your observations are interesting and your report will be important," said Magon.

Jonathan said, "Tomorrow, we should ask Zadok and Ahban to join us. They worked hard on this new edition of the Joseph story."

Father said, "That is a great idea. I will make it my job tomorrow to find them and invite them."

After that, everybody left. I thanked Deborah for taking care of Naam. Deborah said, "I was glad to do it. Also, I want to thank you for all these evening together. I never say much, but I do enjoy them. I can now understand why Elishama gets excited about his work."

Jonathan, father, Naam, and I were all asleep in a short time. We slept until late the next morning, but the flies finally woke us. Their crawling over my face was awful. Once when I tried to swat them, I hit Jonathan on his ear. He mumbled something about the fact that I must be mad. It was going to be a warm day. Day six had arrived. When Jonathan got up he could already see the smoke from the sacrificial lambs when he looked out towards the palace. As we were eating breakfast, father noted that he was having a good time, but he added, "Seven days is too long. I'm glad that the coronations were not seven day rituals."

Jonathan said, "I agree with you concerning the coronations, but this dedication needed the seven days. Today and tomorrow will show us a great deal about our success in our unification program."

That afternoon, just before the minstrels began to sing, Jonathan said to Magon, "There are more people here today. Perhaps the people from Shechem have come in greater numbers to hear Joshua, who is from Shechem and sang at our second coronation. Also, for the Joseph story there will be other singers from Shechem."

Magon said, "This is good."

I said to the rest, "I see that father is speaking with Zadok and Ahban. He was going to invite them to our discussion. I hope they come."

Jonathan said, "Which reminds me, I'm going over to where Elishama is sitting. I'll ask him to invite Joshua for our evening discussion. I should have thought of this before now."

Soon everything was ready. Heman introduced Joshua, and he started to sing. Joshua was at his best; as he sang, you could feel the tension between Joseph and his brothers. Joseph obviously enjoyed being the darling of his father, and the brothers hated him for it. Joseph had been sent by his father to check on his brothers who were tending sheep near Shechem. When they saw him coming, they decided to kill him. First they "stripped Joseph of his robe, the royal robe that was his" (Genesis 37:23b). Then they threw him into a pit. Judah suggested that they should sell Joseph to some Ishmaelites, but before they could act on this suggestion, some Midianite traders pulled Joseph from the pit. They sold Joseph to the Ishmaelites, and the brothers did not know what happened to Joseph. So, the brothers took Joseph's robe and dipped it in the blood of a goat. At that point,

> They sent the royal robe [ahead]. They came to their father.
> They said, "We found this. Please observe. Is it the robe of your son or not?"
> He recognized it. He said, "My son's robe! An evil beast has devoured him; yes, Joseph has been torn up!"
> Jacob tore his clothes; he put sackcloth on his loins; he mourned his son many days. All his sons and all his daughters tried to comfort him; he refused to be comforted.
> He said, "In mourning, I will go down to my son in Sheol." His father wept for him. (Genesis 37:32–36)

Joshua sang this with such great emotion, and at least half of the audience was in tears. I was holding Naam and weeping for Joseph. Joshua with his hands on his forehead covered his eyes and stepped back about four steps.

Heman stepped forward and said, "Jacob wept for Joseph, and we are weeping for Jacob and for Joseph: for Jacob because of his great loss and for Joseph whose future is uncertain. What will become of Joseph? Joseph is on his way to Egypt; it will take some time to make this journey. For us, this time is an opportunity to learn something about Judah, who saved Joseph from the hands of his brothers. Judah is also a hero in this story. I will sing from the first part of *These are the Stories of Judah*."

Heman had sung this story for David's first and second coronations, but this time it was more powerful. This was in part due to the fact that the audience was already weeping, and in this story of Judah, Judah also has reasons to weep. His first two sons, Er and Onan, were killed by Yahweh, and then his wife died. And yet, this part of the story ends with the birth of the twins, Perez and Zerah (Genesis 38:27–30) leading to the line of David. Perhaps there is hope in the midst of tragedy. After this Joshua resumed the story of Joseph:

> Joseph was brought down to Egypt; an Egyptian, Potiphar, an officer of Pharaoh (the head of the stewards), purchased him from the hand of the Ishmaelites who had brought him down there.
>
> Yahweh was with Joseph; he was a successful man; he was over the household of his master, the Egyptian. His master saw that Yahweh was with him, and Yahweh made successful in his hands everything that he was doing. Joseph found favor in his eyes; he attended him. [The Egyptian] appointed him over his household; he put all of his possessions under his supervision. From the time that he appointed him over his household and over all of his possessions, Yahweh blessed the household of the Egyptian on account of Joseph; so that the blessing of Yahweh was upon all his possessions in the house and in the field. He left all his possessions under the supervision of Joseph, and he did not have common knowledge with him [about] anything except the food that he was eating. (Genesis 39:1–6a)

Now the audience was feeling good once again but not for long. Joseph was soon a successful man, but he was also good-looking. Mrs. Potiphar wanted him. She continually begged him saying, "Lie with me." Every time, Joseph refused. Then there was the day when "she caught hold of him by his garment, saying, 'Lie with me.' He left his garment in her hand; he fled; he went outside" (Genesis 39:12). It was then that she accused Joseph of trying to rape her. She had the proof, namely, his garment. Once again, Joseph was in real trouble, and his master put him in prison.

The people were caught up in this story. The happy moments were followed by sad moments, but the singers had the attention of the audience. Here was a carefully constructed narrative, which held their interest. The other cycles of the fathers were more like beads on a string. Some of the beads were beautiful, but in this story of Joseph, the people were not aware of the parts; rather they were involved with Joseph. They enjoyed his success, and they suffered with him in the midst of hardship.

Of course there were a few soldiers around who were laughing and yelling to Joseph to take Mrs. Potiphar if she was so willing. But most of the people looked at them with disgust.

In prison, Joseph became an important person. Interpreting the dreams of the cupbearer and the baker were only a couple of his accomplishments. Even so it took at least two years for Joseph to be summoned from prison to interpret Pharaoh's dream. Joseph's interpretation seemed good in the eyes of Pharaoh, and Pharaoh appointed Joseph to be in charge of the palace and the land and to prepare for the coming famine. Once again Joseph was wearing a royal robe. This time it was made of fine Egyptian linen. As Joseph drove through streets in his chariot heralds would run before him shouting in Egyptian, "*Ib re ka*," which means, "heart/mind to you" or "attention." In fact, the singers repeated the Egyptian phrase several times and the audience joined in.

Day six ended with these words: "The entire world came to Egypt to buy grain from Joseph, for the famine was severe in all the earth" (Genesis 41:57).

When we all gathered at our house after day six, we met outside. The group was getting larger each night. After conferring with Zadok, Sheva said, "We all want to thank Jonathan and Keziah for these wonderful sessions each evening, and we keep growing. Zadok and I want to invite everyone to the Old School tomorrow evening for the final discussion. We will need more room, and the students would like to listen to the discussion. So, Jonathan, does that meet with your approval?"

"It would be a good thing for us and for the students. Also, I would like to thank the three people who gave us this great Joseph story. Elishama, Zadok, and Ahban have worked hard on this material. In addition, we want to thank Joshua who did a lot of the singing today. He helped us with the second coronation, and we are glad to have him back."

Ahban said, "The three of us have helped to put the Joseph story in its final form, but this story was a good story before we ever knew anything about it. For several generations the minstrels of Shechem worked on it, and they were schooled in the ways of the Egyptian literary greats. In fact, this story is a real adventure, and it also contains a lot of Egyptian wisdom that was common in the Egyptian scribal schools. Joseph is very much like the ideal graduate of the Egyptian schools for diplomatic scribes, and he knows how to organize the country and live with the power that is his. We should probably mention this tomorrow evening when the students are with us."

The Dedication of David's Palace

Jonathan said, "I agree with all that you have said, but I still want to give the three of you credit for a great final form. I know that it would take a long time to put the stories of Abraham and Jacob into such a finished form."

Magon said, "I want to join with Jonathan in praising this work of Elishama, Zadok, and Ahban. At times, we all work with sources produced by others, but this usually means that we are faced with the chaos of multiple and conflicting traditions. Only those who are really creative can bring order out of such chaos, order that is truly beautiful. Also, since we are handing out some 'awards' this evening, Heman should receive the award for the best of 'all transitions.' The way in which he moved into the story of Judah, when Joseph was on his way to Egypt, was a masterpiece of transition."

At this point everyone cheered, and father and I began to pass around the food and drink. Because the numbers had increased, small conversational groups developed. Later in the evening, Jonathan asked Naomi to report to the group on her observations. She said, "I told you last night that I had been watching some of the people, and that they seemed to be losing interest in the epic. However today those same people were once again interested. Not only were the additional people from Shechem interested in the Joseph story, but this story revived the interest of most of the people just as Elishama predicted last night."

Elishama said, "I'm glad to hear about that. I just knew it would happen."

Father said, "This royal epic is really working. The north and the south can become one. This unity may not last forever but then nothing does."

I said, "Elissa and I have been having some interesting conversations. We are aware that the unity of Judah and Israel was a difficult thing to accomplish, so we asked ourselves the question, could the new Israel ever unite with Tyre? If this happened the royal epic would have to be enlarged. We were thinking about this, and we wrote a poem concerning the scope of such an epic. I will read it:

> Who were the heroes of old?
> Danel, Aqhat, and Keret,
> All from our northern neighbors.
> From our own stories and songs:
> Abram, Isaac, Jacob, plus

The Jerusalem Academy

Judah, Joseph, our fathers.
Each a Na'im, yea, seven,
These ancient singers were eight.

Elissa said, "We were having fun when we wrote this poem, and I must tell you all that I have enjoyed every moment of my time with you. Keziah and I know that neither in Tyre nor in Jerusalem are there any other groups who would allow women to discuss these matters. Yours is a very special group, and I thank all of you for this experience."

Jonathan said, "We have enjoyed having you here, and your brother Magon has helped us in many ways. We know that not all of our dreams will be actualized, but we are happy that part of the future is present in this group. You should know that we are not interested in the impossible. We can not change the world or even Jerusalem, but we can change ourselves."

Ahban said, "I have been working for David, but I want to say to Elissa that she is exactly right. This is a special group, and soon I hope to quit my work at the palace and return to the Jerusalem Academy. The old and the new schools are becoming one, and this is a great place to be."

Zadok said, "I'm glad that Ahban said that, and I want you all to know that I want Ahban to come back. Our students need him in the class room."

Sheva said, "That would be a wonderful thing for the Academy."

As the party was breaking up, Magon spoke with Jonathan. He said, "I want to ask you a favor."

"Anything you want, just ask."

"Next week when things get back to normal, I would like for you to invite Naomi and me to your great table for dinner. I would like to get to know her. She seems genuine, and she is a lovely person."

"It is done. You can count on it."

"Thanks, you are a real friend."

That night before we went to sleep, Jonathan told me about Magon's request. I said, "We'll do it. Elissa and I thought that Magon was beginning to like Naomi. Elissa said that she hoped that something like this would happen."

"But nothing has happened yet"

"No, but it will."

Day seven was the last day of the dedication. There were even more people. Before the minstrels continued the story of Joseph, David spoke

The Dedication of David's Palace

to the audience. He said, "This has been an important and entertaining celebration. First, I want to thank King Hiram of Tyre and his artisans for this grand palace. It is one of the finest buildings that I have ever seen. It is rare indeed when the finished work is better than the dream, but this palace surpasses all of my expectations. Second, Ahban informed you on the first day of this dedication that the Jerusalem Academy produced our Royal Epic, but I want to thank three scribes from the Academy who spent many days on this epic. These three were Elimelech, Elishama, and Jonathan. Jonathan, I would like for you to say a word concerning the creation of this epic."

Jonathan's first thought was "he could have warned me about this," but Jonathan came to the front and stood before the audience. He said, "The three of us put this epic together, but we did not work alone. Many scribes and minstrels prepared texts for us in earlier times. Some of the creation stories have been used for years. The materials on our ancestors that we used from Hebron were developed over the years by the minstrels who remembered our ancestors during tombs rituals. Likewise, the minstrels from Shechem kept alive the story of Joseph at his tomb, and Elishama, Zadok, and Ahban are the ones to thank for the final form that you heard yesterday and that will be completed today. We had more material than we could use, so we asked the minstrels, more than once, which stories were the favorite ones of the people. Also, even as King Hiram and his artisans helped with the palace, so Magon of Tyre, who teaches in the Academy, helped us. This epic is better in every way because of Magon's help. Our main concern is that this epic will become our story, that is, Israel's story. It gives us our identity, and shows why David is our legitimate king. Finally, I want to remind everyone that it is the musicians and singers who have made this story live. Their performance of our story is more than the text; it is an experience that is thrilling. They have allowed us to experience this story as participants and not just as observers."

As Jonathan walked back to his seat there was a great round of applause, and then the music started. Today's account opened with the brothers going to Egypt to buy grain. Most of the people knew the story, but even so they anxiously awaited their favorite parts.

Upon hearing this story again, Jonathan thought to himself, "This is a remarkable story. During the brother's second trip to Egypt, one expects the crowd to enjoy the description of the meal that Joseph had with his brothers and delight in the words 'They drank; they got drunk with him'

(Gen 43:34b). But this composition is more than clever and artful in appealing to the public. The author or authors allow the audience to see the foolishness of popular beliefs. When the brothers were returning from their first trip, their silver was discovered in the mouths of their sacks. The brothers were fearful and said, 'What is this that Elohim has done to us (Gen 42:28b)?' As the audience, we are privileged to know that Joseph ordered the return of the silver. Here, the audience's additional knowledge moves them beyond the popular habit of giving credit for good and evil to Elohim. The audience becomes aware that there are other explanations for the things that happen to us, and yet Joseph also participates in the same set of beliefs when he says later on, '. . . it was for a savior that Elohim sent me ahead of you' (Genesis 45:5b). Hence, the audience, once again, has the advantage; Joseph's statement should be questioned as well, because there could be other explanations. Was it really Elohim? Only in such a narrative is the audience placed or rather led to a vantage point where tradition can be properly evaluated. This is most interesting, and the story is the work of a true sage."

Jonathan's thoughts were interrupted when Magon said to him, "After Joseph makes himself known to his brothers, and they report the good news to their father, the story is finished. The audience is still interested in how everything will work out, but in the words of Jacob/Israel, 'Enough! Joseph, my son, is still alive; I must go; I will see him before I die'" (Genesis 45:28).

Jonathan said, "That is exactly the case. But of course, we had to deal with the usual conclusion to these cycles."

"The burial of Jacob was most interesting, and I could give you some parallels from Tyre."

"Interesting. After doing this, it was tempting to go back and rewrite some of the other burial scenes."

After the final day, Jonathan and I hurried home to get ready for the evening meeting at the Old School. I nursed Naam and put him to sleep. Deborah came over with Rachel and soon both babies were sleeping. Deborah wanted to stay with them. She had told me that she was not interested in going to the larger meeting at the school. As it turned out, Deborah's decision was not a bad one. The larger meeting at the school turned out to be too formal, and the students did not have many questions. In part, this was due to the fact that Sheva took too much time discussing

The Dedication of David's Palace

his views on the last day's program. When the meeting was finished at the school, Elissa, Magon, Naomi, and Elishama came back to the house with Jonathan, father, and me. After the wine was poured, Magon said, "I like this a lot better. Deborah, you did not miss a thing."

Jonathan asked, "Elishama, what does the Joseph story really mean to the people from Shechem?"

"It means that Joseph was the greatest of all the fathers, because he was the only one of the twelve able to become a great power in Egypt. As Ahban said last night, he was the perfect student. They credit Joseph with saving Israel, and they are proud to have granted Joseph his final request. His bones were brought to Shechem, and there he was buried and remembered."

Jonathan said, "Today when I heard it, I came up with some new ideas concerning what stories can do for us, and what you have just said helps me. You said that the people 'credit Joseph with saving Israel.' In part they do this because they are an understanding audience. Even though Joseph gives the credit to Elohim for saving Israel, the audience knows that Elohim should not receive credit for everything. The audience has been told that it was Joseph rather than Elohim who put the money back in the brothers' sacks. The story teaches the hearers to think."

There were many other comments, but on this night the conversations tended to be more personal.

I said, "I want to tell everyone that these have been happy days. The sad thing is that now our new friend, Elissa, has to go back to Tyre." I turned to Elissa, "We are going to miss you."

"I will miss you as well, but I can't talk about it now. I can talk through tears, but not when my throat aches."

"We will expect a long letter from you after you get home and after your eyes are dry," said father.

I ran up to Elissa, hugged her, and spoke through my own tears, "Elissa, I'll see you in the morning before you leave."

Jonathan and I talked for a long time before going to sleep. At one point I said, "Why did you ask Elishama that question about the people of Shechem?"

"Elishama said that they 'credit Joseph with saving Israel.' Elishama never mentioned God, neither Elohim nor Yahweh. This is important, because Joseph gives the credit to Elohim. So the people do not necessarily follow Joseph on this point. Why? The actors have the disadvantage of not knowing much, like all humans, but the audience knows a great deal more if the storyteller reveals it to them. Joseph ordered his men to put the silver in the sacks. The audience knows better than to always give the credit for good or evil to Elohim. When Joseph says that Elohim saved Israel, the audience has been prepared to say, 'really?' They give Joseph the credit he deserves. The narrative becomes one way that the audience is placed in a position to say 'no' to popular beliefs and to tradition. This may help us as we prepare our work."

"So the story is an indirect way of moving people towards a new way of thinking."

"Right."

Jonathan held me in his arms, and I expressed once again how much I was going to miss Elissa. Jonathan said, "Parting is never easy. What I hope is that you can begin to relate to Naomi. She will need you in the near future."

"I intend to do that. I'm looking forward to her friendship. Jonathan, make sure that I get up early. I must see Elissa before she leaves."

41

Trouble in the Royal Palace

THE NEXT MORNING BEFORE the sun was up, I met Magon and Elissa as they were leaving the compound. They were on their way to meet the others who were returning to Tyre. Elissa and I talked along the way. When the group left, Magon and I both had tears in our eyes, but Elissa turned and looked back and said, "Smile, Mrs. Lot; no more salty tears." Magon and I smiled and returned to the school.

Jonathan was up, and we ate some breakfast. He told me he was going to Bethlehem and try to find someone who might know something about Joab. "If so, I'll talk to David about what we can do to get rid of him and his threats. I may be gone for two days. I will stay tonight in Bethlehem with an old friend, Elhanan."

"I don't want you to go," I said. "You said you would help me write as soon as the dedication was finished."

"I know, but that was before Joab's latest misbehavior. He's too bold. I must find out what he and Absalom are planning in order to convince David that something has to be done. While I'm gone, I want you to stay home; I have asked Gad to stay close."

"Who is Elhanan?"

"He is a good friend, and I do not want you to mention his name or tell anyone that I'm going to Bethlehem. I'll not get a ride to Bethlehem, and I'll not walk on the roads; I know some trails."

I got up and hugged Jonathan for a long time saying, "Be careful, and don't stay away any longer than two days."

With that Jonathan was on his way. When he arrived in Bethlehem, he went at once to the home of his old friend Elhanan. Jonathan had known Elhanan for many years; they played together as kids. They had a lot of catching up to do. After eating and several cups of wine, Jonathan said, "I have complained to David concerning Joab, who has threatened my wife, Keziah, on several occasions. As you know, Joab is a good for nothing bastard, and he even threatens David. David told me Joab has said he is going to tell all Israel that David did not kill Goliath, and that you killed Goliath. That is, he will tell if David does not do what Joab wants him to do. David promised me he would stop Joab from threatening Keziah. He also said that he did not care if Joab made public the point about the killing of Goliath. However, Joab has something else on David, and David will do nothing to stop Joab. The point about Goliath does not mean a thing. I am your friend, and I have known for years that you killed Goliath."

"I did kill Goliath, but I have never said much about it to anyone. In an ugly tone of voice, Joab once told me not to speak about this, and I have not said a word. But, there were plenty of people who already knew about it. I really don't care; David can claim whatever he wants."

"I understand, but can you help me find out this: why does Joab have so much power over David? Also, I have heard that Joab spends a lot of time with Absalom. Why are they so close?"

"Jonathan, these kinds of questions will get us both into a lot of trouble."

"I know it, but I must ask. I will figure out how to use what I learn in such a way that no one will get hurt. After all, David must be aware that I know a great deal from living here for so many years. Also, you must remember that I spent days with David keeping sheep."

"I remember that you both had some tall tales about those days, and I guess for that reason, I thought that you would know the answer to at least one of your questions. However, you were really quite young at the time. You must have been about six when you began to help David. He was probably about sixteen. Where should I start? A few years ago, I lived with Zeruiah, for about a year. She is getting older now, but she is still a great woman in the bed. Plus, she is still beautiful. As you remember, she and her sister Abigail were David's half-sisters. Abigail married and gave birth to Amasa, but Zeruiah never married. Yes, she gave birth to Abishai, Joab and Asahel, but she never married. She was always beautiful, and every man who saw her wanted her. I swore that I would never succumb to her charms, but I did. In any case, during the time that I was with her, she told me that she used to come out to see David when he was tending the flocks. He would send you off to stay with the sheep, and she and David would re-

Trouble in the Royal Palace

ally have a romp. Zeruiah claims that she taught David everything he ever knew about sex and pleasing women. They were good-looking, strong, and well equipped for such things. In any case, Zeruiah got pregnant, and she told me that even though she had been with many men, she knows that David is the father of Joab. She was having so much fun with David that she was not with another man during that time. What does Joab have on David? Many things, I'm sure, but the main thing is that David does not want it known that he had some wild times with Zeruiah, and that Joab is his son. Also, David has never punished any of his children, and Joab knows this. Joab is mean and bold, and he knows David will do nothing. I hope you know that if Joab knew I was telling you this, he would kill me. If Joab couldn't do it, Zeruiah would."

"I understand, but I feel dumb. I should have guessed. Perhaps I was too young to know what was going on, but Zeruiah must have been a good teacher. When I was a bit older, David often had other girls with whom he would spend the night."

"There is no doubt that Zeruiah was a good teacher. Now what was your second question?"

"What about Joab and Absalom? They are so close. They are seen together a lot, and it seems that it is more than the mere fact that their land grants are side by side. I now understand at least one of the reasons why Joab received a grant."

"Joab has been seen with Absalom in Hebron at the tombs, but I don't know much about it. However, I have a friend who is a minstrel, and he could tell you more than I can."

"Where is he?"

"He is usually in Hebron, but just now he is here in Bethlehem visiting his mother. You stay here, and I will go get him. It will not take long. By the way, you should not be seen here, and you should leave before daylight."

"I understand, and I will leave long before daylight."

Elhanan was soon back with Hanani, one of Heman's sons. Jonathan said, "I know you. You sang in our second coronation. Do you know what has been going on between Absalom and Joab?"

"I know some things, but I don't know if I should talk about them. I might either lose my job or my life. Correction. I could lose both."

"I know your father; he has helped me in many ways. No one will ever know that I have talked with you."

"My father has talked about you, and I heard you say some fine things about my father and the singers at the dedication of David's palace. But, I do not want you to tell anyone about this meeting, not even my father."

"I agree."

Then Hanani said, "Absalom comes to the tombs to seek a blessing from the fathers. When he calls forth the name of one of the fathers, I have on several occasions sung of that father. One day, after Absalom had been to the tombs, I was sitting under a tree eating some bread and cheese. Not far from me under the shade of another tree, Joab and Absalom were speaking, sometimes in angry tones. I did not understand everything they said, but it seems that Absalom, with some input from Joab, planned the so-called rape of Tamar by Amnon. Absalom talked his sister into seducing Amnon and then crying rape."

"My father-in-law, Gad, suggested to me that Absalom could have staged the rape. This is interesting. Do you know why they were angry?"

"Joab thought that Absalom should have killed Amnon for the rape of Tamar before now. But, Absalom wanted to wait longer. Joab said David never did anything to Amnon for his rape of Tamar, and David would not do anything if Absalom killed Amnon. David never corrects his sons. Joab urged Absalom to get on with it, and said he would help if there were any problems. They both wanted to get rid of Amnon, who is next in line for the throne."

"Is that all you heard?"

"Yes. After that they walked away. They were still talking, but I could not hear. However, I have seen them together since that time.

"I want to thank you for this information. I may never use any of it in any direct way, but at least, I'm now aware of some of the problems. You have been very helpful. If anyone ever asks you about speaking with me, you can tell them that I was collecting material for the stories of Obed and those of Jesse. In fact, I will talk to you some day about such a project. Since I am the son of Obed's old age, I should know all about the family traditions, but I don't. Thanks again."

With that, Hanani left. Elhanan and Jonathan continued their conversation for some time. Elhanan said, "Joab really is a bastard. Joab says that he will help Absalom, but even if he does help, Absalom had better be on his guard at all times. Joab is in a position of great power. He could help Absalom become the next king, or depending on the situation at the time, he could turn against him and make points with David."

"That is exactly the situation. Now, I must rest for a short time, and then I will leave. You have helped me more than I can say."

"I hate Joab, and I wanted to help you. I will do a few things around here, and then I will get you up and on your way."

Jonathan followed the road to Jerusalem while it was still dark. When the sun was about to rise, he got off the road and followed some trails all the way to Jerusalem. These trails were difficult, because they were steep and rough. When he got close to the city, he climbed the hills to the east and entered the city from the north. Some of his friends saw him enter from the north. He got home before lunch. I was so glad to see him. I ran and threw my arms around him. "I was so worried. I knew you would be late. You are early, and I can't believe it. Did you find out anything?"

"Yes, but I will not use the information unless I am forced to."

Just then father joined us and asked the same question. Jonathan said, "I found out some things that may turn out to be important, but I can't tell anyone anything about my sources. I don't even want anyone to know I went to Bethlehem. If anyone asks why I went to Bethlehem, this is our story: I went to gather some stories about Obed and Jesse. One of the first things that Sheva asked me to do when I first arrived in Hebron was to collect these stories."

I said, "You should write down a few." I covered my eyes with my hands and said, "I wish we could just forget it. Will you see David?"

"Yes, probably soon, but I will not tell him what I know at this point. The things I have learned just help me to know how to approach David. For example, and this may shock you, Joab is David's son."

Father said, "I am shocked, but it makes sense. Military commanders sometimes receive royal land grants from kings, but this explains why Joab received that beautiful grant next to Absalom's."

Jonathan said, "Also it explains why Joab gets away with almost everything. David won't even punish Amnon for the rape of Tamar, and this brings up another subject. Gad, when you told us about the rape of Tamar, you said perhaps Amnon is like Joab and just takes what he wants. Then you asked the question, 'Or did Absalom and Tamar set a trap for Amnon?' Your question was close to the truth of the matter. Absalom staged the whole thing. Tamar seduced Amnon, who was not an unwilling subject, and then cried rape."

I said, "I wonder if Absalom forced Tamar to play the part?"

"Probably, and he may only pretend to love his sister. But now since Absalom has a good excuse to punish Amnon, he will do it, probably sooner than later."

I said, "But I am not sure that any of this helps us."

"You may be correct, but we don't know yet."

Father said, "Any information is of value in a situation like this. Of course what you really need is some information that would connect Joab to Absalom's attempts to be next in line for David's throne."

"Jonathan, you told me earlier that Joab and Absalom might be plotting something, can you say anything about that?"

"Both of you are just too sharp and your memories are too good. Yes, Joab is involved, but I do not have the proof I need."

Father said, "Perhaps not at this time, but you will before this story is finished."

"I hope so."

I said, "We have to be careful. You should not see David now. We should wait and see what happens next."

"You are probably correct again. Also, I would like to have a better plan in mind or better yet several plans for the different situations that might develop. I will not see David now."

During lunch, Jonathan did a lot of eating, and he also played with Naam. He said, "This boy is growing so fast. He will soon be walking."

I said, "After your long walk and little sleep, you should take a nap. Magon and Naomi will come for dinner in two days, so you can sleep until then."

Jonathan was tired and he slept all afternoon. The next two days, Jonathan spent in his office. He gathered up all sorts of notes for *The Minority Report* that he had made before I had started to keep a list for our book. I wanted more help in writing it up. He came home early, because he wanted to help me with the dinner for Magon and Naomi.

I was excited. I knew that Naomi and Magon were the perfect couple. I said to Jonathan, "I know that Naomi loved her husband, but I also know that she did not like to live in Ziklag. She also told me that the life of a soldier's wife could be rather dull. Such a life is full of worry and little thought."

"They didn't have children did they?"

"No, but they were not married long."

"I wonder how Sarah and Sheva will like Magon for a son-in-law if this courtship bears fruit?"

"I'm not sure. Sarah never says much about her opinions, and Sheva always seems too busy to consider new things. Of course, I may be wrong."

"Keziah, you are seldom wrong."

"So, let's have fun tonight. Later on father will put Naam to bed in his room. We will have plenty of time to talk."

Magon and Naomi arrived and the dinner was splendid. The conversation was lively. However, my plans for a long evening with Magon and Naomi did not work out. Shortly, after dinner Magon thanked Jonathan and me, and then he said, "Naomi and I want to take a walk tonight. There will be a full moon, and Jerusalem will look nice from the hills just east of here."

I said, "You will have a great view. We will say good night, but we want you to come again as soon as possible."

After they left, Jonathan said to me, "You know what you have been talking about. They're in love, and they want to be alone."

Spring arrived. Jerusalem was a happy city. It had been a cold winter, and everyone was glad to be warm again. Jonathan and I were getting ready for Naam's first birthday. He could walk now, and he had lots of fun playing with Rachel.

Magon and Naomi were married. Elissa wrote several letters to me, and she said that she was happy for her brother.

On this next part of my story, I must trust my memory concerning some conversations that we had with Ahban.

David and his troops found it necessary to re-take some border areas. However, David remained in Jerusalem while his military forces besieged Rabbah. One day, while walking on the roof of his royal palace, David looked down and saw in the courtyard of another building a beautiful woman, who was bathing. As he looked he said, "This woman's beauty is beyond words. I must have her."

Immediately, David sent someone to find out who she was. The report came back that she was Bathsheba, daughter of Eliam and wife of Uriah the Hittite (2 Samuel 11:3). David did not let this calm his lust in any way. He had her brought to him, and he enjoyed her passive body until late that night. He probably did not know that she had just purified herself after her period. In other words, the time was just right for her to conceive, and she did. David knew exactly what to do. He sent the following word to Joab: "Send Uriah the Hittite to me."

When Uriah arrived, David asked him about the war and about Joab and the troops. Then David told him to go down to his house and bathe his feet. But Uriah did not do that. Instead, he slept at the gate of the palace with other servants of David. David was informed of this, and he said to Uriah, "You have just returned; it was a hard journey. Why didn't you go down to your house?"

Uriah said, "Your troops are camped in the open fields. I cannot go down to my house, eat and drink, and lie with my wife" (2 Samuel 11:11).

David said, "Stay here today, and tomorrow I will send you back."

That night David had dinner with Uriah, and David got Uriah drunk. Even so, Uriah slept once again at the gate, and he did not go down to his house. In the morning, David had to shift from plan A to plan B. David wrote a letter to Joab saying that he should place Uriah in the front lines so that he would be killed. Uriah carried his own death sentence and placed it in the hand of Joab. Uriah was killed as planned, and David was informed. Bathsheba's father, Eliam, who was also at Rabbah during the fighting, recovered Uriah's body, and he buried him near Rabbah. Then he said to Joab, "I must go back to Jerusalem during the period of my daughter's mourning."

When Eliam arrived in Jerusalem, he did not go directly to see Bathsheba. Instead he went to Ahban's office. He said to Ahban, "Father, I came back to be with Bathsheba during this time of mourning, but I need to talk with you before I see her."

"Fine. I am glad that you are here. I have seen Bathsheba, and she is having a hard time. Are you well?"

"I'm well but disturbed. At the time I recovered Uriah's body for burial, I wondered why he had been in such a dangerous position. I asked one of Joab's aids, who was helping me, about this. He said that it was strange, and that it was not according to the original plan. Then the aid continued, 'When Uriah returned from Jerusalem, he handed Joab a message from David. As Joab read the message, he looked puzzled, and I heard him say to his brother, Abishai, "I don't understand this message, but David has something against Uriah. Send him and a few men to the main gate. There, they will draw the arrows of the best archers. We will attack from the other side." Abishai said, "Uriah and his men will never know tomorrow."' The aid said that he knew that he should not be telling me these things, but he considered Uriah to be a great soldier and his best friend. My question is this: do we tell Bathsheba that David probably planned the death of Uriah or do we keep this information to ourselves?"

"We keep it to ourselves for two reasons. One, we do not understand everything about this, and two, Bathsheba does not need such additional news at this time."

"That's fine. I just wanted to talk about this with you. Now, I will go to see Bathsheba."

"I'll go with you."

Along with her father and Ahban, Bathsheba mourned the death of her husband. After the period of mourning, David sent for Bathsheba and brought her to his palace; she became his wife. David had harvested forbidden fruit. Both Eliam and Ahban were angry, because it was now becoming clear why Uriah's death was convenient for David. Also, Bathsheba had mixed feelings about going to the palace at this time. She did not tell Eliam or Ahban that she was pregnant, and as yet Eliam and Ahban had not told her about David's possible involvement in Uriah's death. They felt that it would not help in her present situation, but they both agreed that David was just like Joab. He took what he wanted regardless of how he had to do it.

After Eliam returned to Rabbah, Ahban thought to himself, "I cannot function anymore as David's counselor. I want out. I have wanted to go back to the Academy and now is the time to do it. I doubt if David really wants Bathsheba's grandfather around anyway."

Ahban went to see David, and David said, "What's on your mind?"

"I note that Hushai is helping you with some of the matters that I used to do for you. I would really like to go back to the Academy and do some teaching and writing. I would like your permission to move back."

"That's fine with me. I do have extra help, but I may call on you from time to time for some help."

That evening, Ahban informed Zadok and Sheva that he would be coming back. He said that he did not want to work for David any longer, but that is all he said about David. He stressed that he did not want any leadership role in the schools. He only wanted to teach and write. They both welcomed him back with great enthusiasm. After his conversations with Zadok and Sheva, he came to see Jonathan, father, and me.

The Jerusalem Academy

We were still at the table. Father poured a cup of wine for Ahban, and then Ahban told us he was back for good. Jonathan asked him if this had anything to do with the death of Uriah or with Bathsheba becoming one of David's wives.

He said, "As you know, I had been thinking of coming back to the school but not this soon. But, after the death of Uriah and after Bathsheba went to the palace, I could not stay on. Eliam and I have good reason to suspect that David ordered Joab to put Uriah in a position where he would be killed."

Father said, "This is terrible."

I said, "Does Bathsheba know about this?"

"No. Eliam and I both thought that we should not tell her until we knew more about the entire situation. We did not know what to do. I'm certain none of you will talk to anyone about this."

Jonathan said, "We will not say a word. My first concern is for Bathsheba, Eliam. and you. In addition, I am concerned that this will give Joab more power over David. If David gave such an order and Joab carried it out, then Joab has one more thing to hold over David. It also means that David is just like Joab. He takes what he wants."

Jonathan continued, "We also have some secrets. Joab has threatened Keziah on several occasions, and we are trying to find some way of stopping this. Joab is helping Absalom to eliminate Amnon as an heir to the throne. Absalom and Tamar staged the rape of Tamar by Amnon, thus giving Absalom a reason to do away with Amnon. But, we are like you; we do not have all the answers to our many questions. One thing we do know is that Joab is the son of David by Zeruiah. Have you heard about that?"

"No. I have not heard, but some how it does not surprise me. This additional information does not help me much with my problems, but it does show that powerful men seem to be corrupt and unable to control their lust."

Father said, "We should all be cautious, and we do need to stay in touch with each other concerning these matters. However, we need to fill our lives with important relationships and projects which will overshadow our worries."

Ahban said, "And that is exactly why I am coming back to the Academy. At this time my hatred for David is getting in my way more than my worries, but I will be able to handle that."

I said, "At least, you will not have to see him every day if you live here."

Jonathan said, "Tomorrow, I will help you bring your things back to your room at the Old School. I am glad you are back. I did not want you to leave in the first place. However, you cannot expect to come back here and give all of your time to your students and to your writing. I will be calling on you for help, and we will covet every moment you can spare to sit with us around this table."

Father walked with Ahban to Zadok's room at the Old School where Ahban was spending the night.

Jonathan and I went to bed, and Jonathan said, "It is spring. I think I need to spend some more time in my garden."

I said, "That's fine, but beware! Your garden is fertile.

42

Rebellion

THE NEXT FEW YEARS were good years for us. We were busy with the children and with our work, and we distanced ourselves from David, as did Ahban. Naam and Rachel were growing up, and they were looking after the younger children. These two were now twelve years old, and they were helpful. They would care for the children each afternoon so that Deborah and I could do our work. My two young children were eight and five, and Deborah also had two younger ones, ages nine and seven. These six had some good times together, and several times each week Magon and Naomi's two children would also play with them. All of the children started their schooling when they were seven. Their school was at the Academy, and they met in the mornings. Naam and Rachel were already five years into their studies. There were some scribes at the school who did not approve of education for the girls, but Jonathan, Elishama, and Magon would smile and say, "It is true that some of our scribes could not teach our girls; these girls are so fast and so smart. The teacher should really know more than the students."

Jonathan was still busy with his many projects. I had not made much progress on *The Minority Report*; it was a never-ending work. Also, I had started a journal (*devrey hayyamim*, "words/acts of the days") that I worked on one morning each week. The other mornings were for my other writing projects. Today I was looking back through this journal. My first entry was as follows:

"At the turn of the year (that is, the spring) after the dedication of David's palace, several important events took place. Uriah was killed in battle; Eliam and Ahban found out that David ordered Joab to put Uriah in the front lines to be killed; David took Bathsheba for a wife; and Ahban returned to the Academy."

Rebellion

I thought, "Ahban's return to the Academy has been good for all of us, and it has been good for him. The next year was not an easy one for Ahban, and it was extremely difficult for David, but he had it coming."

The next entry relating to all of this reads:

"About forty days after David took Bathsheba into the palace, Absalom was shearing his flocks at Baal-hazor. He invited all of David's sons to a shearing party. After Amnon was drunk with wine, Absalom ordered his attendants to kill him for the rape of Tamar. Absalom had waited for two years to punish Amnon and to clear the way to the throne. Absalom fled to his grandfather, Talmai, king of Geshur."

Each time I read one of my entries I would stop to think about it. I thought, "Some day this will all fit together, and we will be able to prove that Joab was a traitor."

The next entry to catch my eye was:

"About thirty days past the first anniversary of the dedication of David's palace, David lost another son. Bathsheba had a baby boy, and he died after seven days. Some time passed before Ahban could see Bathsheba. It was then that he told her about David's role in the death of Uriah. She said to her grandfather, 'Then Nathan was right. Yahweh did kill my baby for David's sin.' But, Ahban told her that Nathan might have known a lot about what David had done to Uriah, but he was not right about the baby's death; he was only repeating an old popular belief. Ahban also said to her that he did not like David, but no one will ever know why the baby died. But, we do know that David's sin killed Uriah. That we know. Then Bathsheba told Ahban that it was not a good situation, but she would just have to make the best of it. She told him that she was already pregnant again."

I remembered that when Ahban told us about this he said, "If the baby was conceived after Uriah's death, then it was premature, but if it was conceived before Uriah's death, then we have no idea why it died."

Father was with us during this conversation, and Ahban said to him, "Gad, Nathan is the kind of a prophet that I cannot tolerate."

There was another entry concerning Bathsheba's next child. They called him Solomon, but I did not read the rest of that one.

The next item that I read brought back some great memories:

"On the second anniversary of the dedication of David's palace, Naam was two and one half years old. We finally went to Tyre. This was a good trip. We went with Magon and Naomi plus some others who were returning to Tyre. Magon and Jonathan saw some more tablets like the one that Elissa had brought to Jerusalem, and all of us enjoyed the beaches and the sea. The sea does change one's view on many things. It is powerful and thrilling. To be with Elissa again was wonderful, and we met the rest of Magon's family and friends. We stayed in Tyre for ten days."

After this reading, I had tears in my eyes. I thought, "That was ten years ago. I want to go back again. Elissa has been here once to see Magon and Naomi's children, but we must go to Tyre again. The children need to experience the sea."

I was not reading all of my entries in the journal, but the following one was important:

"During the spring after our trip to Tyre, Absalom returned from Geshur. He had been there for three years. It is clear that Joab finally talked David into allowing Absalom to come back. However, Jonathan wonders what Joab and Absalom will plan now that they are back together again."

I skipped some more things, not that they were not interesting, but I was trying to focus on the events, which dealt with Joab and Absalom. Here is one:

"Two years after Absalom returned from Geshur, David finally allowed Absalom an audience at the request of Joab. After meeting with David, Absalom began to participate in the life of the city. It is clear that Absalom, who is now next in line for the throne of David, is trying to do everything that he can to win the trust of the people. He seems to suggest that if he were king the people would have a much better life, and they would experience real justice."

I thought, "Joab certainly wants to help Absalom. Obviously, Joab wants to continue his job if and when Absalom becomes king. However, Absalom must have decided not to include Joab among his friends. Joab had too much power. He even pushed David around. I wonder if Ahban warned Absalom about Joab?"

Another entry:

"After about four years of wooing the people of Israel, Absalom decided that he was strong and could lead a rebellion. He must have thought that he would have to wait too long for David to die. When Absalom picked Amasa to be the commander of his army, he was in a position of strength in Judah. After all, Amasa was Joab's cousin, and David's nephew. He really gained points with the Judeans when he made Ahban his counselor. The scribes at the Academy were shocked to hear that Ahban had joined with Absalom. Jonathan and I were not shocked, and father said he had expected something like this. Since the death of Uriah, Ahban had no use for David. So, Absalom was declared king in Hebron at the tombs. He knew that he must be at Hebron to receive the blessings of the fathers. Then he marched to Jerusalem. David left the city in a big hurry. Everyone at the Academy just stayed in their houses. The rebellion of Absalom did not last long. Joab defeated his army, and Joab, going against the wishes of David, killed Absalom. David mourned the death of Absalom; this made Joab angry. He threatened David with desertion if he did not thank his men. Then David did a strange thing, he appointed Amasa as commander of his army, but Joab killed Amasa. Things were out of control."

I wondered if things would ever get back to normal. Things were much better, and there was another rebellion. This time it was Sheba, a Benjaminite. He felt ready to lead the north or the followers of Saul away from David. He had received blessings, so he thought, during rituals at the tombs of Saul and Jonathan. Father had predicted this, but David just had to re-bury Saul and Jonathan, which gave encouragement to those who wanted to keep Saul's line alive and well.

That evening I told Jonathan and father that I had re-read my journal notes on Joab and Absalom. I said, "I once believed that Absalom rejected Joab or was warned that he should dump the one who had helped him so much, but now after my reading today, I think Joab helped and encouraged Absalom to rebel. However, Joab deserted Absalom at the last moment, because now he would have a chance to kill Absalom. It is clear; Joab wants to be king, and heaven help us if that happens. Joab had encouraged the murder of Amnon, and he was able to kill Absalom for his act of rebellion. This is why Joab got so angry with David. David had ordered him not to kill Absalom, and Joab had worked for years so that he could legally kill Absalom. So, he did it."

Jonathan said, "You just may be correct. This would mean that if I encouraged David to get rid of Joab, I could stress that it is Joab who wants to be king, and he will kill anyone who gets in his way. He would even kill David."

Father said, "And he would also kill you if he ever found out that you had told David these things."

"Gad do you know what has happened to Ahban after these rebellions?"

"Yes. He has gone home to Giloh, and I wonder what David will do about him?"

"I do not know. David made Amasa head of the army, so I guess that he could take Ahban back as a counselor or let him come back here. I wish that Ahban had stayed out of this. It was so great to have him back at the Academy."

43

The Death and Burial of Ahban and Gad

What would David do about Ahban? Jonathan's suggestions were much too optimistic. David told Joab, who was back in control of the army, to go to Giloh and arrest Ahban. David said, "I want to question him."

Joab and a few trusted men went to Giloh, but they came back in a short time without Ahban. Joab told David, "The traitor was dead when we arrived; he hanged himself; we left him swinging on his rope."

David said, "This is difficult to understand. He was a wise man, but he did join the rebellion."

David issued an order to Sheva and Zadok. It read as follows:

"The traitor, Ahban, has killed himself. You are to search and find all documents by Ahban or stories about him. All such texts shall either be destroyed or rewritten. From this day, he shall never be called Ahban, but rather he shall be called Ahithophel. He was not a 'brother of intelligence;' he was a 'brother of reproach,' a 'brother of stinking spit' like the spit of a camel."

Zadok stormed into Sheva's office, "I will not participate in this crime, and I hope you will not comply with David's order."

Sheva said, "We have to follow it."

"But it is based on a false report by Joab. I was on my way to Giloh. Joab and his men passed me, but they did not recognize me. I continued on my way, but I was too late. However, others witnessed the murder of Ahban. Joab hanged Ahban. There were witnesses!"

"I still do not know what we can do. If David cannot control Joab, I surely can't. We will have to follow the order."

"I will not."

Zadok told Jonathan and Magon the bad news and about his argument with Sheva. Jonathan said, "Let's meet at my house after dinner. Then some of us will head out for Giloh. We must give him a proper burial."

They each went home to get ready. Father and I were preparing dinner when Jonathan arrived out of breath. He told father and me about the entire situation. We were all in tears. Father said, "Ahban had so much to contribute. It is easy to say he should have stayed here, and he should not have joined with Absalom. However, he also thought that David was as bad as Joab, and that both of them should be defeated. Yet, he never tried to win converts to his cause. For me it is Joab who is the 'Ahithophel.'"

"How dangerous is it going to be for the friends of Ahban?" I asked.

Jonathan said, "I don't expect that there will be much trouble because of that. We have to bury Ahban. Even David has buried his enemies. Then we will have to consider what if anything we can do about David's order. Sheva may be a lonely person now, but perhaps not. A lot of scribes will go along with him. I could not. Ahban was a 'brother of intelligence.' On the other hand, I do want the school to continue. We have a lot of work to complete."

I said, "If the three of us go for the burial, the children need to go to Elishama and Deborah's. We should leave tonight."

Father said, "That's right. I will take them over there. When I get back, we will need to eat and also pack some food and wine."

As we were eating Zadok and Magon arrived. "Naomi wanted to come," said Magon, "but she did not want to take the children to her folks. She says she will never speak to Sheva again."

I said, "So this has already caused a lot of trouble."

"Yes," said Magon, "and it will be more difficult for Zadok than for Jonathan and me. Having said that, I am about to take it back. Jonathan and I are not faced with any immediate decisions, but we can not bury ourselves in our work forever."

"I'll manage," said Zadok.

Father said, "This is going to take you three days, two days traveling and one day there. On the way back to the house, I decided that I should not go. I want to go, but at eighty-two I could not keep up the pace. However, I did borrow a donkey from one of the students. You will need it for your supplies. If you go part way tonight, it will be much easier tomorrow."

"I wish that you were going to be with us, father, but you know what you can do. If you remain here, you should probably pick up the children tomorrow."

The Death and Burial of Ahban and Gad

Magon added, "If you need any help get Naomi."

Soon we were on our way. It was a hard trip because we had to hurry. When we arrived some of the people of Giloh had already taken the body down and prepared it for burial. They were getting ready to bury Ahban in his city, granted to him by David. But Jonathan told the people that David would probably take Giloh and give it to some one who was now serving him. Then he said, "We should go to the next village and bury him in the tomb of his father. There he will not be thrown out for the birds."

The people agreed, and they all went to the tomb of Ahban's father. During the burial Zadok did most of the ritual. He was like Ahban's son, and of course Ahban's son, Eliam and Bathsheba were not present for the burial.

At one point in the ritual, Zadok said:

"I call forth your name, 'Ahban.'
You were always my father,
My teacher, my friend, and yes,
Ahban, you were my brother.
So, we will call forth your name.
Ahban, we seek your blessing;
We desire your great wisdom.

Now, for those who murdered you,
And who seek to change your name,
May their bones all be scattered,
Picked clean by the birds of prey.
May they never have a tomb;
May no one ever call forth,
Call forth their names at the grave."

After the burial, Magon, Zadok, Jonathan, and I spent time with the people of Giloh. There was plenty to eat and much wine. In the evening we slept for a time, but we got an early start the next morning. On the way home, Zadok told us he could not stay at the Academy, and he talked with Magon about moving to Tyre. Magon said he could help him get settled in Tyre. He also told Zadok he should wait for the next group going to Tyre.

When we got back to Jerusalem, we were all tired. Jonathan and I were glad to be home, and the children were happy to see us. Father got us something to eat, and we told him all about the trip and the burial. I said it was a great moment when Zadok called forth the name of Ahban and when he pronounced a curse on Ahban's murderers. Then I said, "We need to talk about what we are going to do concerning this series of events."

Jonathan said, "I still feel that I would like to work here in this school, but I do not intend to obey David's order. Also, I will not have anything to do with Sheva, unless he wants to change his mind. If all of this means that I cannot continue here, then we will find some other place to work. However, we should try to keep going, at least for a while. Magon made an interesting point on the return trip. He said some wise scribes have some times out-lasted several kings. If we can still do our work and maintain our standards, it may work itself out. So I want to try."

Father said, "It is worth trying."

I said, "You are both making good sense, but I have had moments when I would like to do as Zadok; I would like to head for Tyre."

When Sheva started removing Ahban's name from all texts at the Academy, he had the good sense to get help from new students who did not know Ahban and from some older teachers who did not like him. Those teachers claimed that Ahban's sins brought on all of his suffering and his death. Noah, Danel, Elimelech, Elishama, Magon, and Jonathan were among those who were never asked to work on that project. This was clever on Sheva's part. At least it allowed the Academy to function in silence. Sheva now was in charge of the Academy, both the Old School and the New School, since the departure of Zadok.

Jonathan had been getting a lot of work done, because he no longer received extra assignments from Sheva or David. One week he took a short trip to Shechem with Elishama. They stayed with Elishama's folks. Elishama was copying some texts, and Jonathan went around to some of the singers to ask what they knew about the old story of Job. They had a good time, but things did not go well at home.

Joab found out that Jonathan was gone, and he decided to make his move. The children were at school, and I was working on my writing. Somehow, Joab knew my work pattern. When he appeared at the door, he said, "I've waited for this for a long time." I was so frightened I couldn't breath. I started to run, but he caught me by my hair and pulled me close to his stinking body. I struggled, and he knocked me down. I tried to scream, but he put his hand over my mouth and ripped off my dress. He grabbed my breasts and was about to rape me, when I managed to scream.

The Death and Burial of Ahban and Gad

Father was on his way to the house and heard the scream. He ran in the door and jumped on Joab's back. Joab threw him against the wall, and then put a knife into father's side. I ran to the kitchen to get a knife, screaming all the way. As I ran back to defend father, several students arrived to help, and Joab ran away.

I pulled a blanket around me and ran to father to check his wound. I said, "It could be worse. In all the confusion, Joab for the first time missed his mark."

I tried to stop the bleeding, and the students helped me carry father to his room. Then they put him on his bed. I thanked the students and asked them to send Naomi over to help me.

Naomi and I soon had things picked up and father was not hurting as much as he was at first. Soon after this, Jonathan returned home. After hearing the entire story he said, "This is the last time. I told David what I would do if anything like this ever happened."

I said, "Please do not go after him now. He will be expecting you. I want you to help me with father. We must see how he does; then you can deal with Joab."

Jonathan was not certain this was the way to do it, but he said, "You were all in great danger. Gad needs me, and you need me. I will wait."

Father's wound did not heal as it should, and he was weak. We worked with him day and night, but after about ten days father died. Shortly before he died, father said, "I lost my wife, and I thought I would never recover. I want to thank both of you for giving me some of the best years of my life. I have lived to see my grand-children; for what more could I ask?"

Jonathan, the children, and I wept through the night. I kept saying, "I had to lose my mother in that awful fire. She saved me, but I could not save her. Now, father saved me, but I could not save him. Jonathan, you are so right; there is no justice. There is only this world and the love we have for each other."

In the morning, Jonathan said to me, "We should bury Gad in Bethlehem. I have a tomb there. We could bury him with your mother in Ziklag, but things are uncertain there."

I said, "Bethlehem is fine."

"So, I am going to the palace. I will have David send a wagon to carry us and Gad to Bethlehem."

I kissed him and said, "Be careful."

The Jerusalem Academy

It did not take long for Jonathan to reach the palace. As he walked up the steps, it seemed that things were busy. However as he walked through the main entrance and on toward David's offices, there were only a few people. When he planned this event, he thought that it might not work the first time, but today he was in luck. He saw Joab was in an argument with some underling, and Jonathan just walked up quietly behind him. Jonathan carried only a small stick in his right hand (about a cubit in length), and he held the stick in a slightly vertical position and thrust it between Joab's legs from behind. Immediately, he turned the stick to a horizontal position in front of Joab's legs, and at the same time grabbed the back of Joab's neck, lifted just a bit on the stick and ran forward toward the wall. Joab uttered a curse as his head hit the wall. Jonathan grabbed Joab's knife from his belt. Joab was unconscious, and Jonathan slit his clothing. He grabbed Joab's scrotum, and quickly cut off the lower half of it. Then he cut off each testicle and threw them one at a time against the wall directly behind him. There they stuck, and then he threw Joab's knife, which stuck in the wall beside his balls.

Jonathan wiped his hands and went into David's quarters. David was there and said, "What's going on? I heard a lot of strange noises."

"Nothing is going on now, but Joab just lost his balls. David, I told you that some day I would take care of Joab. You should have done something about this years ago, but then you have a difficult time with your sons."

"You know?"

"Yes. I know, and what you do not seem to know is that Joab wants to take your throne. He is the traitor in this palace. He planned the death of Amnon; he killed Absalom, as you know. He killed Amasa, and did you know that he killed Ahban? Now, he has tried to rape Keziah, and he killed Gad who was defending his daughter. When will this stop? Who of your remaining sons will be next? Will it be Adonijah, or will it be you? I could have killed Joab, but I didn't. That would be too Joabian. I did not kill him, but I did disqualify him from being in the presence of Yahweh and from sitting on your throne. You had better keep Benaiah and your Cherethites and Pelethites close at hand."

"Jonathan you have a way with words; you get right to the point. So, now what do you want?"

"I want my family to be able to live without the fear of Joab. If he ever comes near our home again, I will send him to Sheol. Also, I want a wagon to transport Gad's body to Bethlehem for burial, and I want it before noon today."

"You'll have it."

As Jonathan left the room he turned and said, "When Joab wakes up, you can tell him that he will need a ladder to retrieve his balls and knife from the wall."

Jonathan hurried home. He told me what he had done to Joab. I hugged him, and my tears were sad tears for father and happy tears for Jonathan. Jonathan was safe.

"Will David try to do anything to you for what you did to Joab?"

"I don't think so. He knows that he should have stopped Joab before all of this, and Joab even pushed David around. Now we must get ready. We will be leaving at noon for Bethlehem."

Both Naomi and Deborah were there, and they helped Jonathan and me get ready. Jonathan sent one of his students to Bethlehem ahead of us, and he gave the student these instructions:

"Go to the Beth Marzeah ('house of mourning') in Bethlehem; there is only one such funeral association there. I am a member and ask them to prepare for a burial in my tomb for Gad, my father-in-law. They should also have plenty of food and wine. There will be some of my relatives and friends from Bethlehem and some friends from the Academy. Tell them that I will replace all the food and wine that we use."

Magon and Elishama were taking care of their children, but they came over just before Jonathan, the children, and I left. Jonathan said to them, "This morning I was lucky. I went to see David, and I ran into Joab. I'm not proud of what I had to do, but I castrated him. He will not be bothering anyone for some time. Also, David will not bother us any more. In fact, I asked him for this wagon, and he sent it. Two days from now we will bury Gad. If it is possible for you to be there, just come to the Beth Marzeah about noon."

Elishama and Magon both said they would be there.

I said to Naomi and Deborah, "Thanks for all your help. Both of you have been my loving sisters."

When we arrived in Bethlehem, the men of the Marzeah were prepared for us. Actually, the next day was interesting for me in spite of my tears. I was able to meet many of Jonathan's relatives and friends. The children were sad, because they had been close to their grandfather. However,

The Jerusalem Academy

they were at the same time interested in all the new sights and sounds. Jonathan and I spent some time in the afternoon getting ready for the funeral. Even Naam was planning to read something.

We got up early on the day of the funeral, and by noon we were ready. About that time some of the people from Jerusalem arrived. Magon asked Jonathan if he could say something during the ritual about Gad, and Jonathan said, "That would be most welcomed."

Before going to the tombs, we went to the Beth Marzeah and had something to eat and drink. After the ritual at the tombs, we would return for more food and drink. At the tomb, Jonathan began the proceedings:

"We know very little concerning Gad's immediate ancestors, but as usual we will call forth the names: Abraham, Isaac, and Jacob/Israel. We summon these fathers that they may grant us their blessings. We also summon Gad our recently departed father, grandfather, and friend."

The children came forward and said:

"We call forth the name 'Gad,' our grandfather. We ask for your blessing."

Jonathan continued:

"Now it is time to remember Gad. Several of you have indicated that you would like to remember him in your own words."

Magon said, "I will always remember what Ahban said concerning Gad. He said, 'I have never liked prophets, but I have always liked you.' Ahban could say this, because Gad was a real human first and a professional second. He cared about the truth, which had to correspond with the reality. Finally, he was always on the move. The last line of the poem that he read on his seventieth birthday was: 'Live in the future today.' Gad has made a great contribution to my thinking and to the lives of his family."

Naam said, "My grandfather was a kind man. He was willing to give small children his time, and he was actually interested in their questions. He loved my mother more than he could tell, and the memory of my grandmother brought tears to his eyes. I could say much more about him, but I cannot say it now. My tears are washing away my words."

Elishama said, "I want to say that Gad helped those of us who were involved in the editing of *The Royal Epic*. When he was at our meetings he always made an important contribution."

Then Jonathan and I stepped forward. I said, "I can not speak at this time for the same reason that Naam ceased to speak, but Jonathan will say something for both of us."

The Death and Burial of Ahban and Gad

"I have never met a man like Gad. He was not an expert in all areas of life. He did not claim to know all things, but in any conversation he knew exactly what to ask in order to get to the heart of the matter. Also, he knew how to make his table a happy place. Some of the best moments of my life happened at Gad's table, and that is where we will miss him the most. Therefore, when we return to the Beth Marzeah, I am asking you to remember that we are sitting at his table. He will in some way put a smile on your face of tears. There will be a chair for him, but it will be empty only because he will be busy keeping the food before you and your cups full to the brim. Gad says to us:

> '*Shalom*!
> *Shalom* to Jael!
> *Shalom* to Keziah and Jonathan!
> *Shalom* to my grandchildren!
> *Shalom* to the Academy!
> *Shalom* to her sages!
> *Shalom*!'

Now, we will return to the Beth Marzeah."

The feasting and drinking went on until late that night. None of the Jerusalem guests returned until the next day. At that time, we all returned together. During the journey, Jonathan was able to explain to Elishama and Magon what he had done to Joab, and why he thought that David might be able to control Joab. Jonathan said, "Joab can still be dangerous, but he would be embarrassed to let people know that he was mutilated by a mere scribe. Also, he will have less ambition, because he is unfit to stand before Yahweh or to rule Israel, as are some other leaders who have balls, but you would never know it. We can now turn our thoughts to our families and our work."

Elishama said, "But can we work with Sheva?"

Jonathan said, "That is a difficult question, because it depends a lot on him. Perhaps we can work around him, and he will not be in his present position forever. I know that is not a good answer."

Magon said, "We should try to move in new directions. New directions might tend to unite us instead of keeping us close to our old positions. For example, we could try to get another teacher, some one who knows Egyptian. Sheva might work with us if we could convince David that it was important."

The Jerusalem Academy

Jonathan said, "That could help, but we would still have to work with David."

"And he is no gem considering his orders to sacrifice Uriah and change Ahban's name," replied Elishama.

Magon said, "He is no gem, but he would like to have a great school. Also, if Jonathan can get a wagon after castrating Joab, he might be able to get a new teacher. There is no excuse for some of David's decisions, like the Uriah affair, but in other cases he had bad information. In either case, we can find a way to resist. When he has bad information, we should try to correct the information."

The next day was a day of rest. Everyone had to catch up. Jonathan and I were still having problems; we were lonely without father. When Jonathan got back to work, he took some time to check out what had happened to *The Royal Epic, Part I*, during the last ten years. There was a new priestly edition of the epic that did make some changes. Jonathan had predicted most of them a long time ago. After looking at it for just a moment, he called Elishama in to see what had happened to the epic. Jonathan said, "The first account of world ordering has been changed. Look at this."

> First Edition:
> Elohim saw all that he had made,
> And behold, it was very good.
> There was evening.
> There was morning;
> [A seventh] day.
>
> The heavens and the earth were finished
> And all their entourage.
> Elohim finished on the seventh day his work
> That he had been doing.
>   (Genesis 1:31—2:2a)
> Second Edition:
> Elohim saw all that he had made,
> And behold, it was very good.
> There was evening.
> There was morning:
> The sixth day.

The Death and Burial of Ahban and Gad

> The heavens and the earth were finished
> And all their entourage.
> Elohim finished on the seventh day his work
> That he had been doing.
> He rested on the seventh day
> From all his work that he had done.
> Elohim blessed the seventh day;
> He hallowed it,
> Because on it he rested from all his work
> That as Elohim, the maker, he had formed.
> (Genesis 1:31—2:3)

Jonathan said, "Abiathar got his way on this change. He eliminated 'a seventh day' from the final time clause and inserted 'the sixth day.' Of course he did this after he deleted our time clause for day six. That is what he always wanted to do. But his addition causes a lot of confusion, because three lines after his 'the sixth day,' he keeps the statement that 'Elohim finished on the seventh day!' It does not make sense. His additional six lines at the end show his interest in the Sabbath, and they are also confusing. Is Elohim working or resting?"

Elishama said, "If you want to change things, you should do it and not create this kind of confusion. Whoever did this was not thinking. Are there other changes?"

"Yes. You will remember that in the Abraham/Melchizedek story that Abraham swears to the god El-Elyon. Elimelech said that if we didn't change El-Elyon to Yahweh some priest would change it. Elimelech was about right. Yahweh was added. Also you will remember that we had a story of Abraham and Sarah in Gerar. We changed the names in this story to Isaac and Rebekah, and we called it story A. We put it before the birth of Jacob and Esau. Well, this edition gives the story back to Abraham and Sarah. They rescue story B that dealt with Isaac and Rebekah in Gerar but put it after the birth of Jacob and Esau. This is confusing and it does not follow the literary pattern. So, I'm not happy about this, but I do not intend to worry too much about it. What are you going to be doing in your extra time now?"

Elishama said, "I will start some work on *The Royal Epic, Part II*. We will have to do it at some point, and I would like to have a head start."

The Jerusalem Academy

"That is a good idea. I'll try to finish my Job poem, and I'm helping Keziah some on *The Minority Report*. I'll also try to do some project with Magon. The Job poem should have been finished long ago, but now I have had the kind of experience that will help me do just that."

"What is this *Minority Report* that you have mentioned on several occasions?"

"It started out as a long poem on some of my opinions that seem to be so different from those of many other scribes. Then I met Keziah, and we had so many discussions concerning poetry, our dislike of many traditions, our desire to live in the future now, and many other things. Keziah started keeping a list of things, so it is no longer a poem but a long work on many subjects. It will contain poetry, stories, and even notes on our daily lives. We may never finish it, but it is a lot of fun to think about such things."

Elishama said that he had to leave. Jonathan agreed that it was time to get home. As they were leaving, Abiathar passed them on his way to see Sheva. Jonathan said, "We have just looked at your new edition of *The Royal Epic*. I must tell you that some of your changes were careless. I want you to know that I will try to keep your edition from becoming any kind of an official text."

Abiathar said, 'I would expect that from you and your kind. People like you and Ahithophel—"

"Like who? His name is Ahban!"

"Not to me. Someday you may get the point that people like you, Gad, and Ahithophel bring great suffering upon your families because of your sins. When was the last time you prayed?"

"That is none of your business, but I will ask you, when is the last time that your prayers were answered? Or better yet who has ever heard the cries of the poor in this city?"

With that Jonathan turned toward home, and Elishama went his way.

Jonathan got home, and we had a good meal around father's table. Naam said, "I still feel lonely even when we are all together."

I said, "I know, and it was a long time before I felt any better about the passing of my mother. In fact it was not until I met your father that I began to laugh again. It was the same for your grandfather. So, we will meet new people, do interesting things, learn to laugh again, but we will never forget our loved ones."

The Death and Burial of Ahban and Gad

After the children had gone to bed, Jonathan told me about his conversation with Abiathar. Jonathan said, "We really need a long section in *The Minority Report* on prayer. I know I have said these things before, but these priests and prophets are so self-centered. They can only see suffering as a result of sin, which means they are completely blind. We know about powerful men who decide the fates of rich and poor. Abiathar tells us to pray. Such people are full of false humility when they ask the creator to beckon to their call. They only pray to impress and oppress. They do not believe one word that they say. Perhaps they believe in their God if the pain is sharp enough, and it occurs in the middle of the night."

"Abiathar really set you off."

"Yes, and partly because I had just read his changes in the text of *The Royal Epic*. On second thought, those were not too important. But, he referred to Ahithophel, and he gave the rest of us the same name. We can live without priests and their prayers or selfish babbling from the rumen; we can live without justice, because there is no justice; but we cannot live without love.

After Jonathan went to sleep, I wrote these words:

> In our world, there's no justice,
> Amazement, yes! Justice, no!
> The thrill of music we have;
> The might of the sea we know.
> What gives amazement meaning?
> Sharing it with our loved ones.

Afterword

HISTORIANS NEED TO RECOGNIZE that they are tellers of tales. History is not what historians produce. History is the past; it is what historians write about. Historians, who try to be objective, attempt to limit themselves to observable facts. But when they do this, they produce dull lists of events, and the reader learns little about the past. Or to put it another way, detectives need more than fingerprints to tell their stories. The facts are essential. Personal notes, writings, and diaries are of the greatest help. But in the end, detectives must use an informed imagination in order to put together what happened. Only then can they tell their stories. Historians' stories are sometimes correct and sometimes incorrect, because we never have enough information. (It is fortunate that they are usually told to a "jury," and it is the "jury" that has the last word).

I have used the words "story" and "tale" with care. Larry McMurtry in his little book, *Walter Benjamin at the Dairy Queen*, (Simon & Schuster, 1999) says that Walter Benjamin does not want anyone to "confuse a novelist with a storyteller." Benjamin says, "What distinguishes the novel from all other forms of prose literature is that it neither comes from oral tradition nor goes into it. The birthplace of the novel is the solitary individual . . ." (p. 34). This is not just the way I would put it, but in any case, it helps to argue that historians are storytellers. Historians move in the direction of the historical novel if their concern is history, and their intent is the construction of a story (here history needs to be more than a stage). Today there are several novels related to the Hebrew bible. Perhaps the best is the one by Stefan Heym, *The King David Report* (G. P. Putnam's Sons, 1973).

I like what Charles Mee did in his book *Meeting at Potsdam*. For an excellent discussion of this book, see Liane Norman's "Explanations of History" (*The Center Magazine*, Sept/Oct 1975). Norman says, "I want . . . to consider the implications of Mee's concept of himself as historical storyteller. Any story requires a hearer . . . The hearer (or reader) is thus, an active element of the story. Mee's active reader, by virtue of Mee's

Afterword

subject [i.e. power and how it corrodes the sensibilities of its wielders], is charged to consider his citizenship in the world of great-power politics" (p. 26). Most professional historians did not like Mee's book. They thought that his thesis should be discussed among historians and not be narrated in a popular manner. Norman adds, "By speaking directly to the reader, by offering him a serious hypothesis to consider, Mee implies the reader's competence . . ." (p. 33). It is too bad that many historians think that the past is none of the ordinary citizens business.

This story of the production of royal literature by the Jerusalem Academy, which I have set in the time of David, may have happened later (say in the time of Solomon or Hezekiah), but it did happen. Also this literature is not pure fiction from the Persian or Hellenistic age as some are saying today (see my *Genesis, A Royal Epic*). I have opted for David's time, because it was possible at that time to produce such literature. David's time (about 1000 BCE) is late in Mediterranean history, and there are examples of royal literature produced and used by scribes long before this. Also it is important to know that by 1400 BCE, in the Mediterranean World, there was a fusion of cultures due to shipping by sea, overland trading, and diplomatic relations between all the major centers of the Babylonians, Assyrians, Hittites, Hurrians, Egyptians, Aegeans, Ugaritians, and Canaanites. The scribal schools of the major cities were cosmopolitan; the scribes really got around. At Ugarit, on the coast of modern Syria, they even made four language dictionaries. Babylonian or Akkadian texts have been discovered in most of the major centers, and a remarkable find was the discovery of an Akkadian text of Adapa in Tell el-Amarna, Egypt (fourteenth century BCE) along with many letters of which some were from the ruler of Jerusalem to the king of Egypt.

Jonathan's wife, Keziah, narrates *The Jerusalem Academy*. This story is obviously fiction, but in my opinion there was a scribal school in Jerusalem. Also, I think this school did create Genesis from the stories they collected, and they could have done it in the manner I have suggested.

1 April 2002
Loren R. Fisher
Willits, CA

www.ingramcontent.com/pod-product-compliance
Lightning Source LLC
Chambersburg PA
CBHW061421300426
44114CB00015B/2020